A Mad World, My Masters

JOHN SIMPSON is the BBC's World Affairs Editor. Born in 1944, he was educated at St Paul's School and Magdalene College, Cambridge, of which he is an honorary fellow. He has worked for the BBC since 1966, filling many of its main news positions, from foreign correspondent to Political Editor. From 1990 to 1996 he was Associate Editor of the *Spectator*, and is now a columnist with the *Sunday Telegraph*. He is one of only two people to have twice been the Royal Television Society's Journalist of the Year, first in 1991 for his coverage of the Gulf War from Baghdad, and again in 2000 for his reporting from Belgrade during the NATO bombing campaign. He has also won three BAFTAs, including the Richard Dimbleby award in 1991 and the News and Current Affairs award in 2000 for his coverage, with the BBC News team, of the Kosovo conflict.

He has written several books, including his first autobiographical volume, *Strange Places, Questionable People*.

Also by John Simpson

Strange Places, Questionable People

JOHN SIMPSON

A Mad World, My Masters

TALES FROM A TRAVELLER'S LIFE

PAN BOOKS

First published 2000 by Macmillan

This updated edition published 2001 by Pan Books
an imprint of Pan Macmillan Ltd
Pan Macmillan, 20 New Wharf Road, London N1 9RR
Basingstoke and Oxford
Associated companies throughout the world
www.panmacmillan.com

ISBN 0 330 35567 8

1 3 5 7 9 8 6 4 2

A CIP catalogue record for this book is available from
the British Library.

Typeset by SetSystems Ltd, Saffron Walden, Essex
Printed and bound in Great Britain by
Mackays of Chatham plc, Chatham, Kent

To Dee, in love and gratitude for sharing my world;

to my granddaughter Rachel, in welcome;

and in affectionate memory of Arthur Sale

Acknowledgements

Extracts from *Scoop* by Evelyn Waugh (copyright © Evelyn Waugh 1938) reprinted by permission of PFD on behalf of the Estate of Evelyn Waugh.

Extracts from *Our Man in Havana* by Graham Greene reprinted by permission of David Higham Associates.

Extract from *Who are the War Criminals?* by George Orwell (copyright © George Orwell 1944) reproduced by permission of A. M. Heath & Co. Ltd. on behalf of Bill Hamilton as the Literary Executor of the Estate of the late Sonia Brownell Orwell and Martin Secker & Warburg Ltd.

Extract from 'Leap Before You Look' by W. H. Auden in *W. H. Auden: Collected Poems* reproduced by permission of Faber & Faber Ltd. as the publishers.

Extract from 'When Franco Died' by Martha Gellhorn in *The View from the Ground* reproduced by permission of Dr Alexander Matthews as the Literary Executor of the Martha Gellhorn Estate.

Extract from *Invasion 1940* by SS General Walter Schellenberg reprinted by permission of Little, Brown and Company.

each playboy in the world whips the same top
on a different axis

Contents

List of Illustrations

Photos not credited are from John Simpson's own collection.

SECTION ONE

Real travelling. *(Peter Jouvenal © BBC)*
Document check. *(Peter Jouvenal © BBC)*
Escorted by soldiers. *(Steve Morris © BBC)*
The drug dealers come to market. *(Steve Morris © BBC)*
Father Leonel Navaez. *(Steve Morris © BBC)*
The cocaine business. *(Steve Morris © BBC)*
The Serbian warlord Arkan. *(© BBC)*
Osama bin Laden. *(© EPA/PA Photos)*
Maurice Rossel. *(ICRC © BBC)*
Colonel Gadhafi contemplative. *(Bob Prabhu © BBC)*
Colonel Gadhafi declaiming. *(Bob Prabhu © BBC)*
Colonel Gadhafi discreetly breaking wind. *(Bob Prabhu © BBC)*
Fidel Castro. *(Nigel Bateson © BBC)*
The Emperor Bokassa. *(Dougie Dalgleish © BBC)*
The imperial ring. *(Dougie Dalgleish © BBC)*
Somali bodyguards. *(Jonathan Cavender © BBC)*
Hussein Aideed. *(Jonathan Cavender)*
Reading Hitler's diary. *(Chris Marlow © BBC)*
A trial in St Petersburg. *(Ron Hooper © BBC)*

SECTION TWO

Martha Gellhorn and Dee.
Luis Zambrano. *(Steve Morris © BBC)*

Preface

Every part of the world shoots up daily into more subtlety.
The very spider weaves her cauls with more art and cunning to
    entrap the fly.
The shallow ploughman can distinguish now
'Twixt simple truth and a dissembling brow . . .
How does't behoove us then that live by sleight,
To have our wits wound up to their stretched height!

       Thomas Middleton, *A Mad World, My Masters*, c. 1605

I decided to lift the title of this book from the Jacobean playwright
Thomas Middleton because I felt it expressed the sense that many
people have now, and clearly had four hundred years ago too, that
things around them have gone mildly crazy. Of course, today's
craziness is invariably transformed into tomorrow's rational order,
which becomes disrupted once again at some future point and then
becomes a new and perfectly workable basis for society; and so on.
Maybe these things are particularly noticeable at the turn of our new
century, just as they were for Middleton. Nevertheless at the age of
fifty-six I have seen the system in which I grew up turned inside out,
and although I am glad to see most of it go and find plenty of things
to approve of in the strange new world order, I feel some of the
changes are worth cataloguing. Some of these changes that have
taken place in the world are encouraging and deeply attractive; others
less so. This book, which is largely autobiographical, grumbles long
and loud about the sameness which is starting to afflict our lives,
while celebrating where possible the welcome areas of difference and
complexity.

    Nowadays I no longer live in Britain, and come back to it almost as a foreign country. I have become the modern equivalent of one of those old colonial types who 'works for England, fights for England, would die for England, but doesn't actually want to live in England'. (The source of the quotation has so far evaded me, but I hope I have rendered it accurately.) I am extremely fond of the place, but tend to find it better in the memory than in actuality. No doubt I will come back to lay my ancient bones in it one day, but while the bones are still in reasonable working order I prefer to exercise them elsewhere. And so my most extensive experience of Britain tends to come nowadays when I have just published a new book, and I travel round the country trying to encourage people to buy it. My friend Martin Bell (at least I hope he is my friend, though for some reason we have traded some tetchy words about each other since he became a Member of Parliament) wrote recently that it was the foreign correspondent's golden rule to get out of the capital. He is absolutely right. You can only understand what a country is really about if you get away from the ultra-sophisticates and the clever dicks, and see its heartland.

During my travels around Britain and Ireland I have come across all sorts of people, from every different class and background, whose only common denominator seemed to be an interest in books and in current affairs. I found them as fascinating and extraordinary as if I had come across some long-lost relatives of mine. We shared the same jokes, and had the same general vocabulary in common. When you live in Britain you tend to see the complexity of the country, and regard people from the South as being radically different from the North, Scots from Londoners, the North Walians from the people of South Wales, and so on. But when you come to them as an outsider, they appear altogether different: as a general type, and rather an attractive one too. As Dr Johnson said, if you meet someone else from your village in the nearby town, you greet them with far more enthusiasm than you would if you were both in your native high street; if you are visiting the Continent you will find pleasure in the company of anyone else of the same nationality; in the African jungle you will greet another European with delight; and on the Moon you would be overjoyed to meet another human being, no matter where they came from.

I was perhaps less than enthusiastic about the elderly character in tweeds at the back of the tent at one literary festival I went to, who called out 'Shame on you!' because of an answer I gave to the question, 'Has anyone from a dictatorship ever lied to you?' (I said, 'Do you mean apart from the Thatcher administration?') But at least he didn't walk out. I met people who had done extraordinary things during the Second World War, or had just slipped away from their nursing duties at the local hospital where they saw things on a daily basis which were worse than anything I had witnessed in thirty-one wars and revolutions, or were soon going to leave university and couldn't decide whether to travel round China alone or teach in the depths of Borneo or give up everything and settle in Central America. I met a young assistant in a bookshop who was about to become a multi-millionaire through a book he had written for young children. I met an engineer, recently widowed, who was going off to spend the next three years helping the victims of a major disaster in India. Interesting people; people with a surprisingly open sense of themselves and their lives; people felt I understood and could relate to, because we had the same basic codes and references in common. By speaking to them, I felt I had come home.

Home is a commodity which I confess I am a little short of. As I explained in the first volume of my autobiography, *Strange Places, Questionable People*, I come of restless stock. My father ran away to sea when he was fifteen, and spent much of the 1930s travelling the globe as a steward on board P&O liners. Half a century earlier my mother's grandmother abandoned her English husband and eloped with a Texan cowboy called Colonel Samuel Franklin Cody, who became a Wild West showman and then a pioneer of the air and in 1908 made the first powered flight in Britain. Soon afterwards my great-grandmother became the first woman in the entire English-speaking world to fly. If there is a gene for heading off into the blue, I have inherited it.

There was a time when I had a home, like everyone else. I used to know whether I would be free for dinner next Friday, and how much leave I could take this year, and where I would be spending Christmas. That was thirty-one years ago, before I became a BBC reporter. Since then travelling at short notice, often to difficult places, has become an all-consuming way of life. I miss everyone's birthdays, especially my own; I walk out of family reunions to catch a plane;

I cancel long-advertised public appearances at an hour's notice. My two daughters, Julia and Eleanor, grew up seeing relatively little of me. In short, I have become a wanderer on the face of the earth.

Since I left London for good four years ago, I have at the time of writing made 256 international journeys: an average, that is, of one plane trip every 5.56 days. During that time the place where I have stayed the longest is the Hyatt Hotel, Belgrade, during the NATO bombing in 1999. I doubt if this sounds glamorous. On the contrary, it probably sounds quite sad; the Flying Dutchman meets the Wandering Jew.

I do of course have somewhere more permanent than my green canvas hold-all and a hotel room to live in. My main place is in Dublin, looking out onto the Irish Sea, and I also have a small flat in Paris, in the shadow of the Eiffel Tower. Life could, in other words, be worse; yet when I travel I do sometimes find myself troubled by the notion of home, and have had to create substitutes for it: a virtual reality home.

These substitutes come in various forms. Home, for instance, is the place where you are a known quantity and your face is familiar. I have constructed a television programme for myself called *Simpson's World*, a political travel show which is broadcast on BBC News 24 to a smallish yet surprisingly appreciative number of viewers, and on BBC World to an audience which is, quite simply, staggering; one estimate puts it at 130 million people around the globe. This means that there is almost nowhere I can travel where people do not come up to me to talk about *Simpson's World*. I belong to that tired-sounding yet increasingly real construct, the global village; and in the streets of this village I am not entirely anonymous.

But for me there is something infinitely more important about *Simpson's World* than being accosted by viewers: my wife Dee is its producer. It is a family business, which between ourselves we call 'The Simpsons'. The BBC, which knows everyone's price to the last decimal point, pays her £450 to produce, direct, edit and satellite each programme: so little that in Britain she would qualify for income support. But since the BBC also pays the costs of her travels with me, it outdoes any other type of television work she could get.

And so, when I arrive in my hotel and start unpacking, I am not alone; Dee is there too, and our room becomes our home. We set things up in the same fashion (sameness creates a sense of familiarity, and therefore of comfort) and our routines become almost domestic. There are places – New York, or Cape Town, or Rio – where it feels like that magical pre-war Hollywood world when people lived their lives in hotels and rang room service every time they wanted a hamburger, or a bottle of champagne: the ethic of the Myrna Loy – William Powell comedy-thriller.

Yet our lives aren't always as civilized as that. Dee and I worked together in Belgrade, when NATO bombs and rockets were hitting the city day and night. We have travelled to the kind of places most sane people avoid: Iran, Libya, Nigeria, Colombia, the West Bank. As a South African she too is a wanderer, who has left her home, her family and her close-knit, liberal Afrikaans culture behind. Between us we have forged a coalition against foreignness and unfamiliarity by creating our own sense of ourselves and our home, wherever we chance to find ourselves.

Far from having no home at all, then, we have many: first and foremost, of course, the pleasures of Dublin, with its bars and restaurants and bookshops. But just as T. S. Eliot used sometimes to sign himself 'Metoikos', 'resident alien', I feel myself at ease in cities from Rome to Buenos Aires, from Tehran to Beijing, from Moscow to Johannesburg. I believe, rightly or wrongly, there is nowhere on earth that Dee and I could not parachute into in the morning, and provide a respectable account of by that evening's *Ten O'Clock News*. That is what we do for a living – assuming, of course, that you call this living.

But you cannot survive on cosmopolitanism alone; you must carry with you a sense of who you are and where, ideally, you belong in the scheme of things. I have built up a mental portfolio about myself which is, like all our views of ourselves, partly romanticized and partly genuine: mine involves coming from Suffolk stock (like three-quarters of all East Anglians, my blood-group is not O like the majority of English people, but A+), and hanging particular land-scapes on the walls of my living room of the mind: the coast at Dunwich, Newmarket Heath, Stoke-by-Nayland, King's College chapel from the Backs. I have of course airbrushed out the power-lines, the little, the hideous housing developments – the reality of so much of England. Now that I scarcely see it, Britain has become a rational, calm place for me, where the trains arrive on time, the streets are tidy, and the crowds are invariably polite and unintrusive, and crime scarcely exists.

And of course there are particular, individual pleasures. In Dublin, a whisky sour at the bar at the Shelbourne, or a glass of Jameson's in Finnegan's, in our own village; in Paris, dinner at the restaurant downstairs or a stroll across the Champ de Mars. On the few occasions we visit Britain we sometimes spend the night in Cambridge amid the mediaeval architecture and Pepysian furnishings of the fellows' guestroom at my old college, Magdalene, after some particularly convivial evening; or we slump in horsehair armchairs at the London Library, reading; or we booze the evening away with friends in the noise and warmth of the Chelsea Arts Club. These things constitute our home just as much as the places where we actually live.

Everyone has to create such places, these imaginary landscapes, these oases of enjoyment, because we are all exiles and wanderers. It is the human condition, and the most rooted person on earth feels the need to make the internal journey somewhere which is uniquely theirs. Michel de Montaigne, who did some travelling himself yet lived much of his life in the tower on his estate outside Bordeaux, wrote: 'You have to create some small back-room [*arrière-boutique*] of the mind, where you can fully be yourself.'

The *arrière-boutique* my wife and I have made ourselves is, for all its insubstantial nature, a comfortable one. It is recreated everywhere we set down our cases, every time we take our seats on another aircraft, each new hotel room we occupy. It may seem an odd, unconventional kind of life, but it suits us.

In writing it, I had great help from my assistant at the BBC, Jo Mathys, who always greeted each request for help with the same gentle enthusiasm. Any number of other people have helped me with information, among them Bob Prabhu, Tony Fallshaw, Nigel Bateson and Ken Oxley.

Lists of thank yous are always dangerous, since the risk of leaving out someone important is a very real one. In my last book, *Strange Places, Questionable People*, I entered an area of high mental interference and forgot completely how much I owed in the way of thanks to Mike Weaver, who encouraged me greatly at St Paul's School and at Cambridge, and helped to ensure that I became editor of the magazine *Granta*. Humble, not to say grovelling, apologies to someone who has been a very good friend.

Especial thanks to Gavin Millar, QC, who defended the excellent iconoclastic and much-missed magazine *LM* in the libel case brought against it by ITN. ITN's editor maintained that they sued *LM* in the interest of free speech, and Mr Millar generously checked my references to the case in this book to ensure that I too would not fall victim to ITN's noble campaign for freedom of expression.

Since I am nowadays a much edited man, I should thank all my various editors, Richard Sambrook, Adrian van Klaveren and Bill Taylor at the BBC, Dominic Lawson and Robin Gedye at the *Sunday Telegraph*, and Mark Jones at *High Life*, for giving me the kind of freedom which enabled me to write this book and to experience the things which have gone into it; my editor at Macmillan, Catherine Whitaker, for being so relaxed about it, and so kind and encouraging; my literary agent, Julian Alexander, for thinking up the idea in the first place (as well as other ideas for the future), and Philippa McEwan, also at Macmillan, for being so unfailingly supportive.

But most of all I must thank my wife Dee, who as the producer of our programme *Simpson's World* shares my travels, good, bad and occasionally downright difficult, and has brought such happiness and beauty into my life.

Co. Dublin, March 2001

Introduction

We that acquaint our selves with every Zoane,
And pass both Tropikes and behold the Poles;
When we come home, are to our selves unknowne,
And unacquainted still with our owne Soules.

Sir John Davies,
Nosce Teipsum, 1599

Once we had a planet. Now, at the start of the third Christian millennium, we're left with a suburb.

In our world, you can fly from any big city to any other in twenty-four hours or less. A few rogue places exist to which you can scarcely fly at all, but their number is going down all the time; as I write they include North Korea, Chechnya, Afghanistan and Somalia. Libya was taken off the list in 1999, and a dozen big international airlines immediately started flying to Tripoli again.

When, following the collapse of Communism, an American academic made himself famous by announcing the death of history, most of his colleagues disagreed. A decade later there are scarcely twenty countries which haven't adopted the politics and economics of liberal democracy. If it isn't quite dead yet, history, in the sense of a clash between different political concepts, does indeed seem to be withering on the vine.

Our world has been mapped with complete accuracy, and there can be scarcely any peoples or species left whom we have not catalogued. In 1999 a surprisingly large new species of tree rat was discovered in Peru. The previous year two separate bands of unknown wandering tribesmen were discovered in Papua-New Guinea. They possessed no spoken language, and conversed solely in signs. In the dense forest in the far west of Brazil I came across a man who had found the arrows of various different groups of indians unknown to ethnography. There are undoubtedly groups in the Congolese jungle or the Kalahari Desert who have not made any contact with the outside world. But that is just about all. There are more people alive now than in the whole of mankind's past, which creates problems for those who believe in reincarnation. Yet for the first time we all know one another.

Worse, the differences between us are disappearing as fast as the animal, bird and insect species we share our planet with. In the 1960s you could still work out where you were when you drove across the United States by the accents and the food; not any longer. In the 1970s French was still an important second language in countries as divergent as Iran, Yugoslavia and Romania; alas, for those of us who have laboured to improve it over the years, not any more.

An inalienable sameness has settled over the globe. The spirit of place, the specificity which the mediaeval philosopher Duns Scotus called *haecietas*, thisness, is evaporating fast. So is the quality which Gerard Manley Hopkins gave thanks for:

> All things counter, original, spare, strange.

We are losing our distinctiveness, our human biodiversity, with appalling speed. As Gertrude Stein wrote of Oakland, California, 'There's no there there.' We tend to think of the process as being American-inspired, but it is merely American-led; the United States has gone farther and faster down this particular road than the rest of us, that's all.

Europe is doing its utmost to catch up. The powerful sense of regional identity which used to exist throughout Europe has faded very quickly. The first time I stayed in Venice in the early seventies I remarked to the old lady who was showing me to my room in the Pensione Seguso that there were a lot of tourists about.

'Ah well, you see, it's Easter in Venice.'

It was as if this were something special to the city, which those of us who lived elsewhere wouldn't necessarily appreciate.

Not long afterwards I spent a weekend on the charming Ile St Louis in Paris, and needed to buy a bottle of ink to write some letters.

'I'm sorry, M'sieu,' said the elderly lady in the general store on the corner, 'we don't sell ink. I doubt if you'll get it anywhere on the island.'

The Ile St Louis is about fifty yards equidistant from the Left and Right Banks of the Seine. Nowadays it is full of twee shops selling crêpes and glove puppets and paintings by Bernard Buffet, and English buskers queue up on the bridge, waiting for their half-hour turn in front of the tourists. Then it was a separate place with its own clearly established sense of identity.

'It is,' said General de Gaulle in the late 1950s, 'impossible to hold together a country which has 265 specialities of cheese.'

All but two or three of those specialities can still be found in France, though European Union regulations make it illegal to sell even Brie and Camembert if it is produced in the strictly traditional method. France, once the most idiosyncratic, regionally diverse and uncontrollable country in Europe, is settling into the same uniformity as the rest of us. There are Body Shops and Holiday Inns in large numbers there too, and more McDonald's in Paris than in London. Obesity, the defining disease of Western man and woman, distinctly hamburger- and Coke-related, is beginning to affect France as it has long affected Britain. As for America, airlines are beginning to introduce wider seats to accommodate the growth in American arse-sizes, and lavatories are being manufactured two inches wider.

In other ways the choices are lessening. Until about 1980 furniture shops in Wales sold what was known as 'the Welsh bed', wider and shorter than the types available in the rest of the United Kingdom. Officially, we are all the same size now. And we are all equal in the face of technology. There was a time when, travelling abroad, I could go for days without contacting my office. Now I am fortunate if more than a couple of hours pass without a call from London; even during the night, if they forget about time difference – the one major element of distinction between one place and another which no one has yet suggested ironing out.

When the local telecommunications system doesn't run to the use of mobile telephones – and I have used one to call my office from the Khyber Pass, the Great Wall of China and the flat of a drugs baron in Medellín – then I can always take a satellite phone the size of a small briefcase with me. In the 1970s my foreign desk used to communicate with me by telex. The technology was untrustworthy and the language strange:

'All well w u? ga'

'Yeah, tho cash a prob, ga'

'So what new, eh? ga'

This 'ga' stood for 'go ahead'.

By the late 1980s the office sent me faxes, though they were on shiny paper which curled up, and the words faded fast. If you went into the hotel business-centre, another 80s concept, and asked to use a desk-top computer, you would never know which of a dozen or so types of software it might use. Now, from Damascus to Lahore to Xian, everyone uses Microsoft. Sometimes you have to work out how to get out of Chinese or Arabic characters and into Roman ones, but that's all. It probably won't be long before that little nuisance to the manufacturers is ironed out too, and everyone will speak and write a kind of English.

Convenience has driven out variety; and not merely in the hotel business-centre. Which American mall doesn't have its J.C. Penney, its Radio Shack, its Häagen-Dazs? Which British high street doesn't have its Marks and Spencer, its Boots, its W.H. Smith, its Principles? And when you come across these shops abroad, your first response is not a pleasant flash of recognition but a dull sense that you haven't really reached anywhere different after all.

In the Yemeni capital, Sana'a, there are almost as many mobile phones per capita as in New York City. In Bokhara and Samarkand you can buy hamburgers and hot dogs on the street corner. In the remotest reaches of the Amazon the children who play in the dust wear T-shirts with the Nike or Coca-Cola logo. In Iran, I have seen posters advertising a Sylvester Stallone film on the walls of the holy city of Qom.

The feeling is growing, especially in the United States, that there is no need to travel abroad, since abroad is travelling to you. In Washington DC I have been driven by a taxi-driver who had been the leader of an Afghan mujaheddin group, and in Paris by another who had been an Iranian air force general. In Denver I once found a taxi was driven by a North Korean who spoke not a single recognizable word of English, and in New York City a taxi-driver from, I think, Equatorial Guinea who had no idea where or what Wall Street was.

Players from more than twenty nationalities play professional football in Germany, including Algerians, Peruvians and Russians. Chelsea sometimes fields seven non-British players for its Premiership matches. In the United States or Britain you are as likely to be operated on for a serious heart complaint by an Indian or an Egyptian as by someone of your own nationality, and Palestinians are among the best surgeons on four continents. The lists of students and academic staff at Cambridge University shows that they are drawn from at least seventy different countries; Oxford, Harvard and Yale could probably match that.

In London there are colonies tens of thousands strong of Colombians, Thais and Ethiopians – people without the remotest colonial links to Britain. There are Japanese restaurants in Kinshasa, Beijing and Geneva, and Italian restaurants in Amman, Minsk and Pretoria. You find the best Thai food in the world in Australia, the best Balti in northern England, and the best Persian *fesanjun* in Los Angeles. Tandoori has become the quintessential British dish, while curry has supplanted fish and chips as the most popular takeaway food. Hamburgers are more popular among the thirteen to eighteen age group in France than *steak-frites* or *magret de canard*.

'I recognized him because he was dressed like a foreigner,' says a character in a pre-war Graham Greene novel, and as late as the 1970s you could still recognize Frenchmen by the cut of their jackets, Englishmen by their checks and brogues, Italians by the narrowness of their trousers, Americans by the shortness of theirs and the thickness of the welts on their shoes. Nowadays large parts of the entire world's population, from Kuwait to Sydney and from Galway to Dalian, buy their clothes at Gap: an organization utterly devoid of anything which in previous centuries, or even decades, would have been regarded as style. These clothes are, of course, usually made in Indonesia or Guatemala.

Once, caught by a wardrobe emergency in St Petersburg, I had to kit myself out at short notice from head to toe from the local Hugo Boss shop (the original Hugo Boss prospered in the 1930s and 40s as tailor to Himmler's SS). I then found that half the members of my audience of Russian literati and local politicians were also wearing Hugo Boss clothes.

'Fundamentally,' intones the complacent voiceover on a television advertisement for an international hotel group which claims to be deeply sensitive to cultural differences, 'we are all the same.'

That's good for business, of course; biodiversity costs money, but sameness encourages economies of scale. Fortunately for the big corporations, everyone everywhere now seems to want exactly the same things: Sony Watchmen, Adidas trainers, Toyotas, Swatches, caps with the peaks worn at the back. (When I was on the *Spectator* we ran a cartoon which showed a teenager asking a salesman, 'Have you got any of these with the peak at the front?')

There are only a handful of places left on earth where you can escape all this; as I write there is no McDonald's in Cuba, no Coca-Cola in Libya, and no television in Afghanistan. But in order to find real difference you have to travel well outside the political pale. If you want to get away from the English football results and *USA Today* and advertisements with Cindy Crawford or Sir Anthony Hopkins in them, you must take your courage in both hands and go to the few really difficult, independent, unpredictable places which are left.

Sooner or later even these last sandcastles of independence will be washed over. The Havana Libre Hotel will turn back into the Hilton, Tripoli will have Häagen-Dazs ice-cream parlours, Afghanistan will tune in to *Friends*, restaurants in Iraq will accept payment in Euros, and earnest tour guides will lead you in total safety across the dividing line between north and south Mogadishu to a Holiday Inn or a Sheraton. How wonderful. I can't wait.

The stories in this book are mostly set in the wilder, less conformist places of the earth. Unlike *Strange Places, Questionable People*, which I published in 1998, it is not a personal history. It is intended to be something rather different: a collection (inevitably random) of experiences and anecdotes. I conceived it as something along the lines of an after-dinner conversation in some distant hotel where a group of journalists and cameramen has gathered at the end of a difficult day's work; the modern equivalent, perhaps, of the atmosphere in the smoking-room of a steamship, where characters like those from a Joseph Conrad or Somerset Maugham story yarned about their experiences. Above all, I want it to be a celebration of a world which is disappearing in front of our eyes – the old, complex world of difference and danger and hard travelling.

And so I have included stories about a television camera that killed people, about how Idi Amin exposed his testicle to the world, Colonel Gadhafi farted his way through an interview and I mooned the Queen, about looking in the deep-freeze of a cannibal Emperor, lunching with MI6 and visiting the KGB's private museum, about what it is like to watch a thief's hand being cut off, about throwing rocks at sharks to keep them away or lying immobile in a hospital bed being bombed, about falling under the spell of Diana, Princess of Wales or being married to Ernest Hemingway.

The great majority of these stories are mine, but not all. I can vouch for each of them, but I have rubbed a little fiction lightly over some of the details in order to avoid unnecessary difficulties for anyone I have written about. If anyone recognizes his or her experiences in an unexpected light in these pages, I apologize sincerely: it was because the story was too good to keep to myself.

1

WANDERING

After a long and toilsome march, weary of the way, [the wanderer] drops into the nearest place of rest to become the most domestic of men ... But soon the passive fit has passed away; again a paroxysm of ennui coming on by slow degrees, Viator loses appetite, he walks about his room all night, he yawns at conversations, and a book acts upon him as a narcotic. The man wants to wander, and he must do so, or he shall die.

Sir Richard Burton, *Personal Narrative of a Pilgrimage to El-Medinah and Meccah*, 1855

Overhead the clouds were as dark and bunched as a boxer's fist, and just as threatening. There was a rich, hot dampness in the atmosphere. Drops of darkish water hung on the lush bushes from the last downpour. I had to watch where I walked: the road surface was crumbling away, and some of the puddles were deep. The hair hung limply over my forehead, and I could feel the drops of sweat working their way down my back.

I was covering the war in Angola from the side of the Marxist MPLA in Luanda, and having a difficult time of it. Most military regimes impose tight controls on the movement of journalists, and with so many advisers from East Germany, Cuba and the Soviet Union the MPLA had become particularly good at it. Slipping out of Luanda at a time of siege took careful planning and a certain amount of luck, therefore, since they thought we were all spies. Not long before I arrived an American journalist had been thrown out for sending a message to his office:

Everything short here. Send bottled water, as shaving in Coca-Cola difficult.

The head of the government information service, an intelligent but rather sinister man called Luis de Almeida, decided that this could only be a coded message to the CIA.

I managed to get a lift to the outskirts of Luanda. The word was that the Cuban troops who were in Angola – this was in 1976 – had a base out here somewhere, just a mile or so from the edge of Luanda. It would, I thought, make an interesting story. I was always getting ideas like that.

The soldiers who were guarding the bridge ahead of me were relaxed. They grinned at me. Their uniforms were tattered, and their boots, unlaced as ever, were too big for their skinny ankles. One of them held out a beer bottle to me, and gestured with his other arm that I come and join them. I grinned back, without accepting; you never knew what these Angolan soldiers put in beer bottles.

In Africa, soldiers usually treat you pleasantly and do what you ask them. It may cost a cigarette or two, but that's all. There is a natural politeness and deference to the foreigner. When things go wrong, it's another matter.

A big sergeant stood on the bridge, his olive-green MPLA fatigues black with sweat under the arms and across the chest. There was nothing remotely polite or deferential about him. He shifted a bottle from hand to hand and watched me, red-eyed, as I toiled up the slight incline towards him.

Below the bridge a river swirled slickly along, gathering branches and leaves and bits of detritus as it went. The waters were a paler version of the red earth all around us.

'*Bom dia.*' This exhausted most of my stock of Portuguese.

The sergeant merely grunted. I looked round: taking their cue from him, the soldiers looked less friendly now. They gathered to listen.

The sergeant asked me for something I couldn't understand. Money? A cigarette? Since I had no cigarettes and little money, all of which I wanted to keep, I played for time. I reached for my accreditation, an oblong of plastic with an unconvincing photograph of me on it, and Luis de Almeida's illegible signature underneath. The sergeant scarcely looked at it. He gestured for more. This was when I made my big mistake. I gave him my passport.

There was something about it that the sergeant didn't like. Maybe it was the royal coat of arms on the front, maybe it was the little paper windows for my name and the passport number. He opened it contemptuously and flicked through it. Sometimes he held it upside down: not a good sign. Then he jammed my Angolan press accreditation inside it, and flicked it deftly over his shoulder.

'But . . .'

I watched the little dark blue book spin up into the damp air, opening as it went and releasing the accreditation. Then they both fell together and hit the reddish-brown water of the river a few inches apart. There was scarcely a splash. They tumbled over and over one another, and disappeared behind a rock.

'*Molt' obrigado.*' That represented virtually the last of my Portuguese, and I put as much irony into it as I could.

The sergeant ignored me. His men laughed loudly and obsequiously, as though he had done something particularly witty. By his standards, perhaps he had. I made a play of writing it all down in my notebook, as though I were getting together the material for an official complaint, but it was wasted on them. So was the shouting I did; they just laughed even louder.

I was devastated. At that stage in my life I still believed that there was powerful magic in a passport – that it somehow represented my identity, my selfhood. Maybe I also believed that pompous little coda on the inside front cover about Requesting and Requiring in the Name of Her Majesty. I probably even thought that if I got into trouble abroad the British Embassy would try to do something about it. I was inexperienced in those days.

There really is nothing very significant about a passport. When the old, hard-backed dark-blue version began to be phased out during the 1980s in favour of the smaller, softer red European one, many British people were outraged. They felt their national as well as their personal identity had been weakened and somehow compromised.

This merely showed how much we have forgotten about our own national past. From the end of the Napoleonic Wars in 1815 to the outbreak of the First World War a century later, it was the chief distinguishing mark of British citizens abroad that they didn't carry a passport. They went where they wanted, merely announcing themselves at border crossings and being allowed through because they were British.

In 1875 Frederick Gustavus Burnaby, the biggest and strongest soldier in the British army, travelled across Russia to the forbidden Central Asian city of Khiva, carrying an out-of-date *laissez-passer* from the Russian Embassy in London, but no passport. He started his journey at Victoria station, and when his train reached the German-Russian border he and the others in his compartment, who included a Russian diplomatic secretary, had to get out.

> A few minutes later I found myself, with the rest of the passengers, in a large high hall, set aside for the examination of luggage and inspection of passports.
>
> It was not a pleasant thing to be kept waiting in a cold room for at least three-quarters of an hour, whilst some spectacled officials suspiciously conned each passport. The Russian secretary himself was not at all impressed with the wisdom of his Government in still adhering to this system, which is so especially invented to annoy travellers. 'What nonsense it is,' he remarked; 'the greater scoundrel a man is the greater certainty of his passport being in the most perfect order. Whenever I go to France, and am asked for my passport, I avoid the difficulty by saying, "*Je suis anglais*; no passport;" and the officials, taking me for an Englishman, do not bother me, or make me show it.'

So the way you demonstrated that you were British was by not being able to prove it. As Thomas Paine said about the wearing of clothes, the carrying of a passport is simply a sign of our fall from grace; and in the case of British people it is a very real come-down: a sign of Britain's fall in the world, rather than something to boast about.

That most British of twentieth-century statesmen, Ernie Bevin, understood this perfectly well. Shortly before his death in 1951 the *Spectator* asked him about his foreign policy. He answered, 'My policy is to be able to take a ticket at Victoria Station and go anywhere I damn well please.' In other words, just like Frederick Gustavus Burnaby three-quarters of a century earlier, Bevin meant he wanted a world without the paraphernalia of modern controls:

this at a time when Central and Eastern Europe was closed to Westerners, and China had turned Communist (and had been recognized reluctantly by Bevin himself, who famously said afterwards, 'I didn't ought never to have done it'). Passports, visas, the compulsory possession of a return ticket and so on are simply the ways by which international bureaucracy stops us going anywhere we damn well please.

It was in Africa that I first began to understand these things.

When I got back in Luanda after the loss of my passport, Luis de Almeida shrugged his shoulders, and ticked me off for going out alone.

'At least they didn't take your tape recorder.'

I wished they had; I could cross borders without a tape recorder.

At the British Embassy there was a big chain and padlock on the embassy gates when I went round there, and a sign advising British citizens to seek help from the Swiss Embassy. There was a chain and padlock on the Swiss Embassy too, but no sign. Back at the Angolan foreign ministry the officials were pleasant, but scarcely helpful. If they gave me a piece of paper to travel with, one of them reasoned, it would be tantamount to accepting that something had happened to my passport.

'But it has.'

Again the smile, the shrugged shoulders, the expressive hands held out, palms upwards. I began to think I might have to stay in Angola for a very long time.

That evening one of the other correspondents, hearing of my problem, told me that somewhere in Luanda there was still a solitary Western honorary consul: a Dutchman, he thought. I looked up the name in a pre-war phone book, and drove out to meet him. He was indeed the honorary Dutch consul, and he turned out to be in his mid-fifties, stout, inclined to sweat heavily, and very jolly. He had stayed behind when all the other Westerners left, he said, because he liked the place: no other reason. Oh, yes, and he could still make money. An attractive young *mestis* woman in a T-shirt and shorts brought in a tray with tiny cups of excellent Angolan coffee. He winked.

'Maybe there are some other reasons too.' He pronounced it 'udder'.

Reaching into an untidy drawer he pulled out a sheet of official note paper.

'We make dis look good.'

He put it into an old-fashioned typewriter. Sweat made splashes on the desk as he hammered at the keys, sometimes pausing and going back over what he had already written. In the end he did that satisfying trick, now obsolete in the days of word processors and printers, and pulled the paper out of the carriage with a ripping sound and the sense of something achieved.

'Dere you are.'

It wasn't merely good, it was magnificent. Her Majesty the Queen of the Netherlands greeted whomever might read this document and assured them that Mr John Cody Fidler-Simpson, a representative of the British Broadcasting Corporation (spelled 'Boradcasting', as though my job was to sprinkle powder around) was a citizen of the United Kingdom, being a member of the European Economic Community, and should be accorded any help he might request; by the power vested in the Hon. Consul as Her Majesty's Representative in Angola, etc., etc.

There was no photograph to be countersigned by a justice of the peace, no date of birth, no place to write in my next of kin, and no rules about who, precisely, could be a British citizen and why people who had always thought they were could no longer claim the full package. It was just a piece of paper.

'Do you think I'll really be able to travel with this?' It sounded ungrateful.

'I don't see why not.'

He was right. I travelled across Africa and Europe for more than a month after that, producing my increasingly tattered and furry piece of paper at each border crossing and having it accepted without question everywhere I went. Eventually one of the eight segments into which it was folded separated from the rest and I lost it. That meant that part of the honorary consul's signature was gone, and at least a quarter of his official stamp. It still didn't matter: I was allowed out of Germany and back into Britain on the basis of the remaining seven-eighths.

The immigration officer at Heathrow peered at a couple of the stamps.

'You seem to have been travelling round quite a lot.'

I half expected him to call for help, or put me on a plane to somewhere else. Instead he folded the paper carefully, and handed it to me with a wry look.

'It might be easier to get the real thing.'

It was, of course. I wrote a long letter to the Passport Office explaining everything, and put my dog-eared *laissez-passer* away in a drawer somewhere. It might have been falling apart, but it was still valid; the Dutch consul in Luanda had forgotten to put an expiry date on it.

There are three bad times: the night before you leave for somewhere difficult, and you sit with your lover or your family trying to behave entirely normally in order to show how safe everything is going to be; the following morning, when the car comes to take you to the airport; and the moment when the plane touches down at your destination. Of all these moments, the last is by far the worst. It is also more unpleasant than anything you are likely to experience later.

Even if you find yourself under long, intensive shelling, which is the nastiest thing I know, or are attacked by an angry crowd, which is the second nastiest, it never quite matches that dreadful sense of foreboding when the plane jolts, the tyres scream, and the trip begins to unfold: the separation from the comfortable, safe, familiar world of an aircraft, the cold air, the uncertainty of standing in line at the immigration desk, defenceless against all the fears you have been suppressing. And of course if shelling, arrest, or angry crowds materialize – and they usually don't – you are much too busy to worry about the outcome.

All of this is a kind of comfort in itself. Knowing that your arrival is likely to be the worst thing that happens makes everything easier. You become phlegmatic, relaxed, undisturbed.

'Aren't you excited about going?' my wife Dee – the Memsahib, as I call her – asks me; or alternatively, 'Aren't you worried?'

She has worked alongside me for newspapers and television in all sorts of difficult places, from Bosnia to Nigeria, and before she met me she covered the South African townships for the BBC, and they can be more dangerous than almost anywhere else on earth.

Nowadays she is the producer on my programme for BBC News 24 and BBC World, called, embarrassingly enough, *Simpson's World*, and therefore she goes with me almost everywhere, whether pleasant or dangerous. (Not long ago I had an angry letter from a mullah in Egypt, who wrote: 'Always you are calling this world your world. You must know the world belong only to GOD. To say Simpson World is dishonour to GOD.') Travelling with Dee has brought an entirely new dimension of enjoyment to my job. But she still asks me if I am excited or worried.

The answer is that I am not, because things so rarely turn out as you expect. I have arrived in Baghdad, expecting to be taken hostage or even executed, and have found myself treated with the greatest courtesy. I have been on a routine trip to China, looking forward to an interesting few days of diplomatic reporting, and found myself still there a month later, lying in a gutter with bullets cracking a foot or two above my head.

The trouble with real life, as you may have noticed, is that it isn't like the movies. Happy endings usually turn out to be neither happy, nor proper endings. This is one of the reasons why, like the movies, tabloid journalism bears no relationship to life as we know it; it is too extreme, too lacking in complexity. There are too few categories of existence. The people the tabloids write about are either two-dimensionally glamorous or successful, or they are victims, or they are 'evil'; and the characters in the heart-warming stories which the tabloids love have to live happily ever after.

None of us ever looks as good or acts as well as we would like. And when we find ourselves in danger, there is no low, disturbing minor-key music on the sound track to warn us that something is just about to happen. We are just as likely to get into trouble on a bright spring morning as on a dark night, and the people we meet along the way will probably smile at us and wave. Until, that is, the trouble starts.

So if the only thing you know is that you cannot know anything about what will happen, it has a remarkably calming effect. You become like some grizzled sergeant-major, an old campaigner who prepares for the worst and actively relishes every quiet, pleasurable moment which comes his way. As Mr Salter tells William Boot in *Scoop*:

There are two invaluable rules for a special correspondent – Travel Light and Be Prepared. Have nothing which in an emergency you cannot carry in your own hands. But remember that the unexpected always happens.

The unexpected happened to a famous BBC correspondent of the 1960s and 70s and his wife, who was also a journalist, when they were invited to visit President Mobutu in what was then called Zaire. To ease his path through the system – if any such thing exists in that country – he had letters from the foreign minister and from the president's office. The pair of them arrived at night, which on the outskirts of Kinshasa is a dangerous time.

The first couple of road blocks were no problem: a few cigarettes sorted out the bored, greedy soldiers there. The third was much more difficult. The soldiers who manned it were more drunk and much nastier than the ones who stopped me in Angola, and they forced the BBC man and his wife out of their car at gunpoint.

'*Vos papiers,*' the soldier in charge shouted.

The correspondent produced his letter from the foreign minister. The soldier in charge scarcely glanced at it, and ripped it up. Meanwhile the other soldiers were getting ready to rape the correspondent's wife.

'*Vos papiers.*'

The letter from the presidential palace went the same way as the earlier one. The British passport he produced was thrown into the bushes. By now the correspondent's wife was on the ground, and they were starting to tear her clothes. Rape was imminent. The correspondent was desperate. Reaching wildly into his pockets he came up with a credit card and handed it to the soldier in charge. God knows what he thought he was doing.

The man held it up, and ran his finger over the raised lettering, where it said 'Cardholder's Name'. He grunted.

'*Oui, ça c'est bon. Tu peux t'en aller.*'

The correspondent's wife, a woman of considerable pluck, stood up and brushed herself down with dignity. The soldiers opened the car doors for them, and saluted drunkenly as they drove off.

That, at any rate, is the story the correspondent told me. If he hadn't worked for the BBC, which forbids its employees from taking part in commercial advertising, he could have made a lot of money from it. But then no one works for the BBC in order to make money. And if I hadn't had all sorts of unnecessary bureaucratic problems with the company that operates the card in question, I would have revealed its name here.

The dull sameness which afflicts the shopping malls of the world has not yet started to seep into airports. Not, at any rate, too much. Heathrow is haphazard and utterly unplanned, yet manages at times to be surprisingly stylish. Charles de Gaulle is built around a single concept, which sometimes makes life easier and sometimes not, and it is the only major airport I know to have a fully stocked antiques shop. Miami has three times as many stalls selling ice cream as bookshops, there are no baggage trolleys because the porters won't permit them, and it is horribly difficult to make an international phone call. At JFK I have had to carry two heavy suitcases half a mile between terminals in the summer's heat because the porters refused to do it and I couldn't find a taxi-driver who was prepared to take me. Smaller American airports – Minneapolis, for instance, or Dallas-Fort Worth – are usually charming.

At Rio de Janeiro you can doze for hours in comfortable seats (even if you can't talk your way into one of the airline lounges). You can have a shave and a haircut for almost nothing, borrow books to while away the time from the excellent bookshop, and sip *caipirinhas*, those wonderful Brazilian cocktails whose name means 'little country girls', and smoke the strange, sometimes wayward Brazilian cigars. I would rather spend a day in Rio de Janeiro airport than any other airport on earth. For that matter I would rather spend a day in Rio than anywhere else.

There are dreadful airports like Delhi and Beijing, neat and agreeable ones like Helsinki and Amsterdam, graceless ones like Frankfurt, and ludicrously planned ones like Munich. One or two, in the words of the Michelin guide, *vaut le voyage* – they are worth a journey in themselves: Singapore, Barcelona and Kansai in Japan for instance. A pleasant and interesting airport like Buenos Aires or Bogota is a pleasure to pass through. They're not particularly fast or well-organized, but the shops are interesting, the food is edible, and the system works in an easy-going kind of way.

The most exciting airport in the world used to be Kai Tak at Hong Kong. Even though I dislike being trapped in an inside seat on a long journey, I always used to ask for 'window' rather than 'aisle' on a Hong Kong flight. Arriving there was the great flying experience. As the plane came in over the crowded suburb of Mon Kok the high-rise buildings crowded in on either side until you were actually looking up at the inhabitants on their minuscule balconies, watching them hanging out the washing. The noise in that narrow canyon was mind-numbing.

'How can you bear to live here?' I asked a man in Mon Kok shortly before Kai Tak airport was closed down for ever. He was a cook, and wore a white coat with orange and brown stains down the front. His English was scarcely comprehensible, but he was the only person in the whole street who seemed able to speak it.

I had to repeat the question, because another plane went overhead so close I felt I could read the small print on the wings or recognize the passengers' faces at the windows, strained or excited like riders on a fairground ride.

'It is very comfortable,' said the cook. 'We know every plane. When they are not flying, it feels different – not so good. If you live here, you live with aeroplanes.'

For the pilots, Kai Tak was the last really interesting place in the world to land. The captain traditionally took control as soon as Hong Kong appeared in front of them, and he would know exactly when to heel over and raise one wing high, allowing for the difficult crosswinds.

Of course it couldn't last. Nothing in Hong Kong does – not even the skyline, not even the view from the Peninsula Hotel, not even British rule. The terminal building at Kai Tak, an excellent example of 1950s airport architecture, was eventually closed. Nowadays the new airport at Chek Lap Kok, on Lantau Island, is a larger version of Stansted Airport, rational and quiet and pleasant, a kind of genetically modified airport created with the help of focus groups and in-depth passenger surveys. The taxi journey, across some of the world's most exciting bridges, is extraordinary; so is the price. Chek

Lap Kok is closed much more often than Kai Tak ever was, thanks to the winds, and landing there can be just as alarming but lacks the charm.

The very worst airport I have ever been to, bad enough to give anyone nightmares, was at Baku in the former Soviet republic of Azerbaijan. They're building another one now, and maybe they've finished it. I don't know: I certainly don't want to try it out. My colleagues and I arrived with a good deal of television equipment after the usual dreadful journey from Moscow: crammed into seats suitable only for children, our knees pressed against the seat-back in front which never seemed to be properly anchored and invariably fell back when the plane took off. The flight was a long one, but all we had been given was a white bread sandwich with a filling of oily cheese and a bottle of salty water.

The lavatories were blocked and disgusting, and when the plane finally landed we all had to sit meekly in our seats and wait until the pilot and his crew left the cockpit and processed down the aisle. In Aeroflot, pilots were more important than passengers. (The camera-man I was with, Ron Hooper, became more and more enraged with all this as our trip round the former Soviet Union progressed, and he would work out ways of tripping them up or maiming them as they passed.)

There was no luggage carousel in the smallish, dirty room which served as a baggage hall. Instead, the cases were tipped carelessly off the back of a commandeered army vehicle through an open hatch, and we had to pick them out of the heap. Nor, of course, were there any baggage trolleys. The four of us were travelling heavy – it was a long trip – and our personal suitcases and the camera gear amounted to fifteen cases altogether, most of them back-breakers.

At the far end of the baggage hall was a sliding door, which someone had jammed so that the opening was only about eighteen inches wide: so narrow, that is, that an adult was forced to squeeze through it sideways. We would ease one case through the gap first, get our bodies through, then pull the second case after us.

It would have been unpleasant enough in an empty airport. Baku Airport wasn't empty. It was packed with shouting, gesticulating, imploring people, gathered around this single narrow entry. As a result, we had to put one case out blindly into a forest of hands, all trying to grab it and make off with it. Their faces, when I finally pulled my body through the gap and looked around aghast, all seemed to me to be scarred and hideously distorted. I was met with a wall of garlic breath as I tried to hold on to the first case, fending everyone off with its sharp metal corners, and manoeuvred the second one through after me.

The porters who could have helped us were standing on the far side of the beseeching, smelly crowd, gathered round one of their number. As I came closer I saw that he was a tiny hunchback, with the arms and shoulders of a grown man. He had the only luggage trolley in the airport. The other porters were poking him with their fingers and slapping him, laughing.

'What are they saying?' I asked our translator.

'Say, "Your wife at home being screwed by animal." '

The translator thought this was really witty, and he didn't stop laughing for a long time afterwards.

The poor man eventually broke away from the taunting crowd, weeping, and ran into a side office where he locked himself in. He took with him the only luggage trolley in the airport, so we had to carry everything out of the airport ourselves, fighting off the grabbing hands. The other porters were too busy sniggering at the hunchback to help us. Nothing in Baku afterwards, not even the unending line of tiny colourless ants which patrolled the wall of my hotel room beside the bed and bit me all night long, was quite as bad as that nightmarish scene at the airport.

Things happen at airports. At the one in Kinshasa, another terrible place, I hid in the disgusting lavatories from the white mercenaries who were hunting for me. At Frankfurt Airport I encountered a Soviet agent who – to my surprise – told me his whole story on camera. At Brussels Airport, deserted and late at night, I realized I had left my passport behind and was only able to catch the last plane by crawling on my hands and knees below the eyeline of the immigration officer, who was reading a sex magazine. At Blantyre Airport in Malawi the soldier searching me found I had 2,000 times the amount of money I was permitted to take out of the country, but he let me keep it because I worked for the BBC. At Lima Airport we were warned privately by the Peruvian vice-president that a government agent was going to plant cocaine on us as we left, but we made such a public fuss about the possibility that nothing happened.

In 1989 I spent six weeks in Afghanistan, living rough and travelling across mountainous country to reach Kabul, where the cameraman Peter Jouvenal and I stayed for three days before escaping shortly before the security police could capture us. On our way back through the mountains a mujaheddin leader, in tribute to our escape, gave me a Russian bayonet as a keepsake. I tucked it into my kitbag and forgot about it.

We had a harrowing drive through the snow-covered mountains along the border with Pakistan, and I thought I was a dead man several times before we finally made it to the Khyber Pass and safety. At Peter's house in Peshawar I stripped off my stinking clothes and prepared to wash in hot water for the first time in a month and a half. It was a pleasure simply watching the steam rising from the shower. I introduced my right foot into the hot water.

Then the phone rang.

'It's your office in London,' Peter shouted. 'They say they want you back there as quick as possible.'

Struggling with a towel, I took the phone. There was a stream of instructions from the other end: times of planes, road distances, estimates of possible arrival. The only things I grasped properly were that the plane was full except in first-class, and that I would have to leave right away. I turned the shower off without getting into it, and put my filthy clothes back on. They, and I, still hadn't been washed for six weeks.

The taxi journey to Islamabad Airport lasted an hour and a half, and was a nightmare. The Grand Trunk Road, straight and tree-lined, is a splendid route for a lover of Kipling, but by night it can be terribly dangerous, with unlit cars, trucks and cyclists suddenly rearing up in the headlights. I had borrowed a very large banknote from someone, and every time the driver slackened his pace I would fold it up in a marked kind of way, put it in my pocket, and say, 'What a pity you aren't going to earn this now.' But he did earn it. He got me there thirty-five minutes before the Swissair flight was supposed to leave.

Running through the airport with my heavy kitbag took time,

and made me sweatier and if anything smellier than ever. I threw it onto the X-ray machine, went through the metal-detector and stood waiting for it.

Someone shouted something in Urdu. Someone else translated.

'You have some kind of large knife. This is a dangerous weapon. We must report it.'

I explained, still out of breath: Russian bayonet – given me by mujaheddin leader – no problem – pacifist myself – desperate to get to London for BBC – couldn't they just overlook it?

Dubiously, they agreed that they could overlook it as long as I promised not to get it out of my kitbag during the flight. God bless the British Raj, I thought, and promised with enormous sincerity.

'Sir, you'll have to run now. You might just be able to get on board.'

I picked up the kitbag, which seemed heavier than ever, and stumbled out across the tarmac. Ahead of me, they were just starting to wheel the steps away from the aircraft.

'Hey! Stop! I'm coming! I have to catch the flight! Please!'

Maybe the sight of this wild creature, clothes fluttering, carrying a kitbag the size and weight of a dead body in his arms and smelling like a detachment of mujaheddin affected them with pity: I had clearly been touched by Allah. They pushed the steps back up. I stamped my way heavily up them, completely done, and reached the top. A Swissair stewardess stood there. She looked as though everything she had ever worn had been ironed three times before she put it on, and she didn't like the look of me.

'We are closing this flight,' she said disapprovingly.

'First class,' I said, and I didn't mean it as a term of approval.

The stewardess reacted as though I had confided to her that I owned Blenheim Palace. But I was still gripping the wonderful red boarding-pass, and she could see that.

'Well, I suppose—'

She let me on board.

Heads still turned to look at me. Having stuffed the kitbag into a cupboard, I stretched out at full length in my seat. I was breathing pretty heavily, and such sweating as I had done before was a mild trickle to what I did now. The Swiss businessman beside me looked as though a dog had fouled the seat.

'Hot, isn't it?' I said with an engaging smile.

Actually, since it was February, there was snow on the runway. He looked away with a shudder, and moved as far away as a first-class seat will allow; a lot further, that is, than a tourist-class seat, but still within smelling range. I grabbed the glass of champagne which the stewardess brought me, and drank it down in one gulp.

'First drink in six weeks,' I confided to the cabin at large, and laughed from pure relief. Even to my own ears I sounded a bit loud.

The Swiss businessman reached up and pressed the call button.

'I would like another seat,' he said.

I was returning from a difficult tour of duty in Beirut, and was going to take a week's break in Rome. My roundabout route took me to Milan, where I boarded a very full Alitalia flight. It was 7 o'clock on a wintry evening, and already dark.

My seat was near the back, next to an uncommunicative German of about my age: early forties. He grunted. I stole a glance at what he was reading: Günther Grass. I pulled out T.S. Eliot's *Essays*. His eyes strayed across to my book, as mine had to his.

There was a pleasant buzz of conversation on the plane. Italians are sociable, convivial souls, and like to give advice and encouragement to complete strangers.

The food will be very good, you know. It's only a short flight, you'll enjoy it. Can I get you a pillow? You look tired. Such a pretty jacket.

The German and I said nothing, but sat in uncompanionable Northern European silence while people got up around us and wandered around, regardless of what the stewardess or the warning lights said. When the plane was in the air, but long before the seat-belt sign was switched off, they were queuing for the lavatory, laughing and smoking. (In 1985 you could still smoke on planes, but not when you were standing up. They were all standing up.)

The meal came round, and it was as pleasant as the passenger across the aisle from me had promised. There was a particularly good bottle of Barolo, and the veal was memorable. Then the trays were cleared, and Grass and Eliot came out again. My neighbour and I had still not spoken. Outside in the clear winter's night the lights of little Italian towns glittered and twinkled pleasantly below us.

We must have been about eighty miles from Rome when we hit the rain. It came down as hard as metal rods, lashing straight across the windows. The plane heaved under the shock, and the passengers woke up. A little ripple of concern went around.

That seemed rather strong. I'm not a good flier, myself, I hope it won't get any worse. Don't worry, the pilot knows what he's doing.

The first bolt of lightning came a few seconds later. It didn't hit the plane, but it was so close that we were thrown off course. The screaming had scarcely stopped before another bolt, as blue as a gas flame, struck the left wing and ran all along it, front and back.

Italians are wonderful people, but it is better not to be among them when unpleasant things are happening.

My God, we're going to die! We're all going to die! God in heaven forgive me for everything I have done wrong. This is the last hour. Nothing worse can happen. O my mother!

Another bolt of lightning hit the left wing, and seemed to run along the fuselage. Then another hit us on the right wing, and almost steadied us for a moment before we pitched downwards.

'This is your captain. We are suffering some turbulence and some electrical discharges, but I assure you there is no danger. This plane is very strong.'

His voice was drowned by the screaming. One elderly man half-rose from his seat and pulled open his seat-belt, then ran, lurching, down the plane towards the back.

Death! Death! Father, I repent of my sins and seek forgiveness. Ah, Giulietta, shall I ever see your beautiful face again? Why did I come on this terrible flight, when Mario could have driven me?

My neighbour and I sat side by side, locked in an Anglo-German staying-cool-in-a-tight-corner competition. He read his book, I read mine. Neither of us turned a page, and I don't suppose his eyes moved along the lines any more than mine did. I gritted my teeth and wished I could run around and scream like the others.

Another bolt of lightning. Could the plane survive that, and the combined terror of two hundred Italians? I gripped my briefcase tighter. After going through all that in Beirut, I thought, I've let myself in for this.

*Jesus, Mary, Joseph and all the saints! Just let me live through
this and I will do anything. Ah, my mother, look what has happened
to your son! Forgive him all his unkindness to you.*

And then we were through it. The rain eased up, and the
turbulence faded. The man who was kneeling down and clinging
to the back of the seat near the lavatory stood up unsteadily and
brushed the knees of his trousers. Someone laughed, and a couple of
younger men shook hands. Everyone was smiling now.

'So you see, ladies and gentlemen, this aircraft is very strong.
There really was no reason for anxiety. Now we will be landing in
fifteen minutes, so if you will observe the no-smoking sign—'

But that was unreasonable. Everyone seemed to be puffing away
in the happy atmosphere.

*Now we have been through this terrible experience together,
we must see more of one another. I was never worried for myself,
of course, but I thought you must be feeling so ill. I'm starting to
feel hungry; funny how soon an upset stomach can settle again.
Cigarette?*

Beside me, the German turned a page. I turned a page too, to
show I really had been reading all along.

We landed soon afterwards. There was a storm of applause,
as though Pavarotti had just sung '*Nessun dorma*'. Then we all
stood up and reached for our coats and bags. The Italians were
all chattering and laughing, as they do in an opera-house after the
performance. I stole a look at the German, just as he started to steal
a look at me. I thought of saying, 'It was a no-score draw, then,' but
changed my mind. I grinned at him instead, and he grinned back.
But we didn't say anything. We were the only ones on the entire
plane who weren't talking.

I have, of course, had plenty of other bad flights in my time. Once,
setting off for a trip in a small plane in Mexico, my colleagues and I
solemnly shook hands with one another in case we didn't get the
chance again, and to show that there were no hard feelings. We were
going to fly over difficult territory with a pilot who was a lapsed
alcoholic.

In Brazil I flew in a single-engined plane over the jungle with the sole survivor of a team of seven pilots. Each time one of them had crashed, he said, he had replaced parts of his own plane from the wreckage.

'So you're a mechanic?'

'No, not at all,' he answered, and hooted with laughter.

At such a time, looking out at the forest canopy as it reaches unbroken for hundreds of miles in every direction like the surface of the ocean, you find yourself listening very carefully to the note of the engine.

During the Iran-Iraq War I flew over the Mesopotamian desert in a helicopter belonging to the Iranian air force. Before we left the pilot had tried to keep down the payload by turning people away, but they merely dodged round to the other side and climbed on there; so he eventually shrugged and ignored the problem. Most of us were Western journalists who had to get back to file our material, though there were also at least a dozen injured soldiers who needed urgent medical care.

The helicopter was an ancient American one, for which the Iranians had received no spares for a long time. It shook and shuddered as it took off, and ran much farther down the improvised runway than usual. At the end was a grove of palm trees, and we flew so low over them that I could see the individual dates clustered under the fronds.

It was late afternoon, but still appallingly hot. We were all crushed in together, and my left foot was twisted painfully underneath my right leg. The only good thing was that I could see out of the window.

'If I ever get out of this alive, I'll sink a couple of really cold beers,' said the Australian cameraman jammed in beside me.

'Islamic beers,' I answered sourly.

Islamic beer is the disgusting non-alcoholic malt drink you get in Iran. Alcohol is forbidden.

'I forgot,' he said.

The helicopter ground along for another three-quarters of an hour. We were safe by now from Iraqi anti-aircraft guns, and were flying too low to be in danger from fighters. I could see the ridges of sand rippling away to the horizon, an angry yellow-red in the dying sunshine.

'Only about another fifteen minutes,' said the cameraman who wanted a cold beer.

'Thank God,' said someone; probably me.

I was still looking down. The ridges of sand seemed somehow less precise now. I stared at them, trying to work out what it was. Maybe my eyesight was blurring? Or had the window become smeared?

'Christ, quite a sandstorm starting up down there,' said the cameraman.

It seemed to mount towards us as we flew on, a body of thick reddish cloud which wrapped around us like a sheet and penetrated the helicopter so that our eyes became sore and the grains of sand grated between our teeth.

On the flight-deck, which was open, the three crew members were starting to shout at each other. By twisting my head and easing one leg round I could watch them.

'Bloody pilots falling out among themselves,' said the cameraman. 'All we need.'

My limited Farsi indicated that they were blaming each for allowing so many of us to climb aboard. Then the argument became fiercer. It seemed as though they were trying to decide whether to put down in the desert at once, or attempt to make the final thirty miles or so to the air force base. One of them shouted into the radio, then pushed his mike aside in disgust: we had lost radio contact. If we crashed now, no one would even know where we were.

The note of the rotor-blades suddenly seemed to be different. The sand was obviously clogging the engine. More angry discussion between the crew. Then two of them raised their hands: they were voting, and the navigator, who wanted to put down here in the desert, lost. He buried his head in his hands.

'*Allah akbar!*' shouted the pilot.

It didn't instil confidence.

We limped on heavily, losing height. We all thought now that we would crash before we got anywhere near the base.

Strangely, there is a kind of comfort in being up against it to this extent. There is, after all, nothing you can do. I couldn't even find the room to move, let alone to wrest the controls out of the pilot's hands. There was no point in wracking my brain for some kind of solution, because there was no solution. Either we got there, or we didn't: the next ten minutes would tell.

I thought idly about the arrangements I had always planned to make about my funeral, and had never got round to: where it was to take place, the guests for dinner afterwards, the instruction to everyone to enjoy themselves and remember the good times. I was just starting to imagine how the different mourners would behave when the pilot shouted out again.

'*Allah akbar!*'

This time it sounded different. He was pointing through the windscreen at something. It could only be the base.

'Looks as though we're nearly there,' I said to the cameraman.

He looked as emotionless and flat as I felt.

'Oh, great.'

'You still won't be able to get a beer.'

'That's what I was thinking.'

Tblisi, the capital of Georgia, is large and, for the most part, featureless, and seventy years of belonging to the Soviet Union did it no good whatever in terms of architecture. Georgian food and wine are justly famous, and there is one particular restaurant on a hilltop overlooking a major road out of Tblisi which, though full of flies in summer and freezing cold in winter, serves an unforgettably good bean soup.

There is only one decent modern hotel in the city, and staying in it feels like being under siege in the Middle Ages. The architecture encourages this feeling, since the hotel was built in the atrium style and is like a mediaeval castle, with a keep which is open inside and has galleries as high as the eye can see. Flags of the nations whose embassies have huddled inside for shelter add to the heraldic sensation. The diplomats sit in the lounge drinking coffee and talking CNN English or Spanish or Hebrew with each other and with foreign businessmen and local crooks, and scarcely ever set foot out of the door. Inside the hotel, you could just imagine yourself to be in what most Westerners regard as the real world. Outside it's crazy and dreary, sometimes by turns and sometimes at the same time.

In 1991 a local mafia gang threatened to murder the Austrian manager, and he didn't leave the hotel for the next couple of years. By chance I was on the heavily guarded bus which took him to the airport at the end of his term of duty, and he was not a happy man: until, that is, the plane took off and he could turn his attention to getting very seriously drunk.

The Metechi Palace isn't my kind of hotel. It was built at the time of the break-up of the old Soviet Union, and the inspiration is distinctly 1980s: not a good decade for architecture. But the only alternatives in Tblisi are far, far worse.

And at least the place is more or less gun-free. A sign at the entrance shows a pistol with a red line through it. Bulky characters in black leather jackets have been hired by the management to lounge around there, sizing up the people that come through and occasionally pointing to the sign. These obediently fish an automatic or two out of their pockets, and pass through a metal detector. The detector pings anyway; the anti-gun sign is, as an Iranian friend once said to me about traffic lights in Tehran, purely advisory.

Once when I was staying in the Metechi Palace, lying on my bed reading and waiting for a phone call to tell me to come and interview President Eduard Shevardnadze, I felt my nose and eyes prickle in a way that seemed somehow familiar. Then I heard shouting and screaming. Casually, as one might flick through the programmes on television in search of something at least passably entertaining, I wandered out and looked over the balcony to the lounge, thirty feet below. A group of black leather jackets had gathered round a man lying on the floor. From time to time one of them would kick him. Then, having decided what they should do next, they pulled him by the feet and lugged him towards the door. His head bumped nastily on the steps, and left a smear of blood. He looked very dead.

By now, though, I could scarcely see for tears. I wasn't shedding them for him; I had remembered what the sensation in my nose and eyes was: tear gas. The man, we were told later, had wandered into the coffee shop carrying a bottle of Georgian red wine, the kind that is so thick and strong you virtually have to hit the heel of the bottle when you pour it out, like tomato ketchup. A waiter had told him politely that he couldn't bring his own wine into the hotel, and the man had replied by firing a tear-gas pistol into the waiter's face.

In the lobby the diplomats and crooks and foreign businessmen turned round briefly to see where the screams were coming from, and to look at the head bumping down the steps, and then they went back to their discussions. The outside world had infiltrated the hotel briefly, but like the smell of tear gas it would soon evaporate.

All the same I like the atmosphere of a big hotel: the neat young women at the reception desk, the older porters who walk on the sides of their shoes, the watchful managers, the discreet chambermaids, the room-service waiters who pretend to be surprised when you tip them. Except for the very worst and the very smallest there is a basic similarity between hotels, regardless of size and cost. The people who work in them tend to believe in what they are doing (this can include even the ghastly old Soviet-era hotels of provincial Russia) and when times are hard they can show a remarkable devotion to the ideal of service.

At the Holiday Inn in Sarajevo in the dreadful winter of 1992 the waiters wore dinner jackets and white shirts with bow-ties even though there was no water, no soap and no way of drying anything; and they made their way to and from work to the accompaniment of the sniper's rifle and the mortar-bomb. At the Commodore in Beirut in 1982 the housekeeper made sure every guest had clean laundry every morning, despite the constant artillery barrage. At the Europa in Belfast, the most bombed hotel in the world, they kept the nightclub going throughout the 1970s as though they were in the South of France, and the kitchen provided an excellent room-service steak only twenty minutes after each new bomb scare.

The telephonists at the Laleh Hotel in Tehran would stay up all the night trying to get international calls for the guests. At the Mandarin Hotel in Jakarta, during the disturbances of 1998, Chinese members of staff continued to arrive for work and were unfailingly polite and cheerful to the hotel guests, even though a few hundred yards away the mobs were burning Chinese people to death in the streets. At the Carrera in Santiago in the 1980s the waiters pretended not to notice when you staggered in after an anti-Pinochet rally, stinking of tear gas and dripping with water heavily laced with sewage, and demanded a stiff gin and tonic. You can forgive an hotel the odd over-billing or the occasional lost sock if it rises to the occasion like this.

Sometimes, though, you feel the staff are not on your side. In the summer of 1992 I arrived at the Tequendama Hotel, close to the dangerous old centre of the Colombian capital Bogota, and was kept awake for some time during the night by the sound of automatic fire and the occasional crump of a mortar. In the morning I went down to breakfast, and met the stony-faced assistant manager in the lobby.

'Bit of noise last night, eh?'

'*Señor?*'

'You know, rat-a-tat-tat. Guns. Bombs.'

'*No, Señor.*'

'But there were. I heard them. I saw the flashes.'

'*No es posible, Señor.*'

The reception desk at the InterContinental in Lusaka, the capital of Zambia, used to be known as The Wailing Wall because, no matter what documentary proof you might have of your reservation, the staff behind the counter would always deny its existence. Once when I was there a middle-aged German businessman, stout and hairy, was told that there was no record of his having booked a room there, even though he was holding their telex confirmation of his booking in his hand.

'Very well,' he shouted, 'I shall spend the night here in the lobby. I shall undress here, and sleep on that couch.'

A group of us gathered round sympathetically. He took off his jacket, his tie, his shirt, his shoes, and finally his trousers. It wasn't a particularly pretty sight, but it was only when he hooked his thumbs in the elastic of his underpants, encouraged by us, that the manager came running out. They had found him a room.

There are hotels which routinely tell the security police who you have seen and the calls you have made. On the whole, though, I like to think that the people who work in hotels prefer not to do that kind of thing. At the Al-Rashid in Baghdad, in the run-up to the Gulf War, I tried to persuade the staff at the reception desk to let me have a particular room because of its view and its closeness to my colleagues. Although I knew this room was available, the woman behind the counter refused to let me have it. In the end I had to make do with something I felt was distinctly inferior. It turned out later that the room I had been demanding had a little camera fitted into its television set, so the security people could watch what the occupants did. The receptionist had wanted to protect me from their attentions.

In a war, a revolution or a crisis, there is usually one hotel which the journalists settle into with the swarming instinct of bees. This place then takes on a completely different life of its own. The lobby is perpetually crowded with camera crews carrying their battle-equipment in or out: flak jackets, metal boxes full of equipment, aluminium stepladders for crowd work. The business centre will be taken over by newspaper journalists, plugging in their computers and sending faxes. The roof will be occupied by satellite dishes and tents where the engineers sit and talk all day, no matter how fierce the weather.

Local politicians will come in to be interviewed at the roof-top camera positions, and will give impromptu press conferences in the coffee shop or on the front steps of the hotel. The stairs from the uppermost floor to the roof, dingy and undecorated and normally used only by the hotel's maintenance staff, will now be the main thoroughfare for sharply dressed television journalists combing their hair, adjusting their ties, and running through the points they will shortly be asked about, live on air. Downstairs, meanwhile, the bars and restaurants will be full at all hours, and the staff will have to find extra supplies of food and alcohol where they can.

The more dangerous the situation in the streets, the rowdier the journalists' parties in their chosen hotel. In the run-up to the Gulf War the team from TV-am, which supplied breakfast news to commercial television in Britain until it undeservedly lost its franchise, held a famous party one Saturday night on the eleventh floor of the Al-Rashid Hotel. The hotel had been built during the Iran-Iraq war and was designed to protect its guests from missiles: concrete baffles sheltered the windows on every floor. During the course of the party an Australian cameraman, out of his skull with drink, weaved slowly across the room, went to the open window, climbed onto the sill and jumped out.

In the horrified silence, everyone rushed over to look. He was hanging by his arms from the concrete baffle immediately below, swinging gently like an orang-utan. And after a while, because he was a strong little man, he hoisted himself up and climbed back inside. The relief was intense, and when he did exactly the same thing a few minutes later (perhaps having forgotten) scarcely anyone bothered to look out; though his correspondent, a tough lady from South Africa, was sufficiently annoyed to pour a glass of wine over his head as he hung there in the Baghdad night.

People who do a dangerous or stressful job are liable to let off steam noisily. It is unpleasant for other guests – though at times of crisis the businessmen and tourists all disappear anyway – and can be annoying for the staff. On the other hand when the caravan moves on, and a new crisis somewhere else takes over from the old one, the people at the hotel miss the excitement badly. For long afterwards they will recall the time when they were at the centre of the world's attention, and yearly on the vigil the names of the most famous broadcasters will be familiar in their mouths as household words. Nothing will seem quite so much fun again. Sometimes the only reason a hotel survives at a time of crisis is because of all the room service and the phone calls and the bar bills that are generated by the journalists; but what the people who work there remember most is how exciting it all was.

The worst hotel I have ever stayed in was in Puerto Bermudez, a small town in the eastern Peruvian jungle. It was called the Hostal Feliz Viaje, the Happy Journey Hostel, and I was only there because the slightly better place next door, called the Hostal Triunfo, was full.

As I went up the worm-eaten stairs disbelievingly, holding my nose against the extraordinary stench, a large dark rat ran ahead of me across the floor as if to show me the way. I knew what the stench was, though I had never smelled it so strongly: bedbugs. The walls were made of wooden slats which you could peer through, and my room was quite outstandingly, memorably, throat-catchingly filthy. If I think about it hard enough I can sometimes summon up the memory of the smell, even now.

The dirt lay encrusted in ridges on the floor, and the sheets on the bed were a pale brown, darkening towards a long ochreous shape in the middle which had built up from the bodies of sleepers over the weeks or months. The shape was that of a kind of aggregate human being: like the Shroud of Turin, except not holy. I laid my sleeping bag on top of this composite figure, erected my mosquito-net around it, and slept with all my clothes on. Beside me I lit two anti-mosquito spirals, to disguise the stench. It still kept me awake.

My radio alarm went off loudly at 4 a.m., with the BBC theme-tune 'Lilliburlero' and news about Sarajevo. I could hear complaining noises through the thin wooden walls, merging with the snoring and the groans. My legs and chest were covered with bites. I pulled my clothes off in a fury, stuffed them into plastic bags, and rubbed myself all over with Friction de Foucard, the French colonial preparation I used to buy in the Boulevard St Germain. Then I squirted insect-repellent viciously into the plastic bag, in the hope of killing the bedbugs. It seemed to work.

The hotel's owner had dragged himself out of bed to charge me for this night of hell. My complaints about the filth, the rat and the insects were spoiled because I didn't know the Spanish for 'bedbug'. He shrugged.

'*Dos soles, Señor.*'

Can it really have been worth his while getting up this early to charge me two sols – less than an English penny? Even so, it was too much.

It is a relief to think instead of hotels with an especial charm: for instance, the Abbasi Hotel in the Iranian city of Esfahan. It was built in the seventeenth century as a caravanserai, and shortly before the revolution in 1979 the Shah and his wife took a personal interest in its conversion to a first-class international hotel. Afterwards the revolutionaries, like those in France during the Terror, changed every name with a royal connection, and the Shah Abbas was called something less specific: Abbasi. Visitors have been rare during the past twenty years. On three different occasions my colleagues and I were just about the only guests. Many of the suites had been closed up altogether, moths had got into the heavy red bed-curtains and the blankets, and there was a good deal of dust. It remained magnificent, all the same. The lobby had been tricked out in fantastical patterns with mosaics made of coloured glass, there was almost too much carved wood, and the public rooms, with their faded gold and white paint, were vast and echoing. The service, by contrast, was dreadful.

When I was there in 1986, for instance, a rodent-like old man with several days' growth of beard sat behind the reception desk and took absolutely no notice of me. When I put my face right in front of his and asked him in Farsi for a room, he eventually eased himself off his seat, still not looking at me, and called up reinforcements from a back office. The new man, even grubbier, shook his head dubiously when I asked for a room; even though I found later that there were only two other people staying in the hotel at the time. But he gave me a form to fill in, all the same.

'*Engilisi?*' he asked, peering at the words when I had finished.

In fact I was travelling on my Irish passport: the Irish look after you better than the British if you are arrested or kidnapped.

'That's like my asking you if you're Iraqi,' I answered. 'It says "Irish" here.'

An interested crowd was gathering.

'From Iceland?'

'He thinks Irishmen come from Iceland,' I told the crowd.

They laughed gratifyingly at that, even though most of them would probably have been hard put to say exactly where Irishmen did come from.

The suite I took had no fewer than five rooms: a bedroom, two dressing-rooms, a large and shabby bathroom with no hot water, and another smaller room which was empty and had no obvious purpose whatever. The bed was enormous and carved out of mahogany, covered by a slightly tatty mosquito net decorated with cherubs and birds, and sagged down the middle like a river-valley. The sheets were perfectly clean, but much-darned. It was like being the guest of a maharajah with a cash-flow problem.

The carved cedarwood doors opposite the bed opened onto a balcony which overlooked the enormous central courtyard, as big as a football field. Camels would once have been stabled on the ground floor (there were special high extensions at the top of the door to allow for the humps), while the guests stayed upstairs. When the caravan trade yielded to the motorcar in the 1920s the Abbasi was turned into a prison. Forty years later, when tourists began to come to Iran in an organized way, someone decided to turn it back into a hotel. The courtyard where the horses had once grazed and where the trading goods had been piled up now became a garden; and it was that, as I opened the cedarwood doors, that I looked out on.

Rose bushes, better cared for than the hotel, were laid out in a delicate pattern among ancient plane-trees and fountains. Feral cats stalked between them, trying to creep up on the singing birds which fluttered in the lower branches. Black-headed crows cocked their heads and looked down shrewdly, watching for the moment when the diners at the tables below might discard something.

It was time for afternoon tea. We sat at a table shaded by a plane tree and drank the sharp, strong tea of Iran, followed it with fresh pomegranate juice, and ate 'English cake', pale yellow and marbled with chocolate. As the evening drew on the cats prowled closer, demanding anything we would give them, and in the growing coolness the loudspeakers began to broadcast the gentle music from a *tar*, the ancient Middle Eastern stringed instrument which later metamorphosed into our guitar. Above the walls of the old caravanserai rose the marvellous sky-blue dome of the theological school built by the last Safavid king of Persia in 1710. The Abbasi is tatty and uncared for, and in terms of service it compares unfavourably with the worst motel in rural Honduras. But in terms of overall delight I'd rather be there than at the Paris Ritz.

'You're so beautiful,' Woody Allen tells Diane Keaton in *Manhattan* as they are being taken somewhere by taxi, 'I can scarcely keep my eyes on the meter.'

In a really expensive hotel, you can hear the meter ticking all the time. I have stayed in some splendid hotels over the years: the Raffles in Singapore, the Four Seasons in Hamburg, the Beverley Hills Hotel, the Regent in Hong Kong, the Copacabana Palace in Rio, the Waldorf-Astoria in New York. But if you are essentially bourgeois, as I am, you can never entirely forget that every single minute is costing you serious money, and merely opening the door of the minibar provokes a major guilt attack.

I have a weakness for old, grand places. Latin America is full of them: the Carrera in Santiago, the Victoria Plaza in Montevideo, the

Plaza and the Claridge in Buenos Aires. Architecture is more important to me than a recent coat of paint, and a friendly front desk is
better than glitzy furniture in the lobby. The Pera Palace in Istanbul,
once the stamping ground of the Duke of Windsor and Agatha
Christie, is a favourite of mine for these reasons. I used to stay at the
Nacional in Havana, another of the Duke of Windsor's watering
holes, until the package tourists drove me out and I discovered the
pleasantly restored Santa Isabel in the old part of the city. This is so
beautiful that it more than makes up for its barely post-Soviet staff.

The American Colony Hotel in the Arab part of Jerusalem is one
of the pleasantest places in the world to stay, and a dinner with good
company in the open courtyard is mandatory. George, the head
porter, combines just the right degree of deference with a sense that
he is superb at his job. Once, on Christmas Day, the kitchen staff
even cooked a Christmas pudding for me. It was surprisingly good.

I have fond memories of the Grand Hotel Terme in Brindisi, even
though I have only ever spent a single night there on my way to
Albania. It seemed so drab and gloomy when I arrived late at night
that I thought nothing of its vast ceilings and its panelling. It was
only in the morning that I discovered that this was where, from the
1870s onwards, travellers from Britain took ship for India. The hotel
is on the waterfront, and a gangplank ran from the first floor directly
onto the small, fast steamships which the P & O operated down to
the Suez Canal. (They acted, wrote Kipling, 'as though 'twere a
favour to allow you to embark'; which shows that means of transport
may change, but the cabin crews stay the same.)

For something of the same reason I like the old Imperial in Delhi
better than the expensive modern air-conditioned places; and every
time I go to Pakistan I try to arrange a trip to Peshawar so as to be
able to stay at the Pearl Continental. This, though unpretentious, is
my favourite hotel in the world: the level of service and politeness is
unrivalled. A great deal has happened to me there, from meeting spies
and drugs traffickers to walking through the lobby unconvincingly
disguised as an Afghan, in *shalwar kameez* and turban. The assistant
manager and head porter, while knowing exactly who I was, politely
pretended they had never seen me in their lives before.

In Moscow I prefer the National. Nowadays it has been thoroughly overhauled and modernized, but I always used to stay there

in the old Soviet days, when there were grand pianos and vast chandeliers in many of the rooms, and tiny single beds in an alcove. That hoary old traveller's tale about the drunken British/American/ French journalists/businessmen/diplomats who came back to their room drunk was invented about the National: they decided to search for the microphone, you remember, found it under the carpet, unscrewed it – and heard the chandelier crash to the floor in the ballroom below.

Late one night, when a friend of mine and I were searching hungrily for a meal (not necessarily an easy thing to find in Soviet days) we peered in from the street through the windows of the National's dining room and saw a few last guests finishing their meals. The main street entrance was shut, so we went into the lobby of the hotel and tried to get in that way. An old man in a hotel uniform was half asleep on a stool by the doorway.

'Let's give it a try,' said my friend, and started to push past him.

The old man scarcely moved. He simply reached out a hand and gripped my friend by the testicles.

'*Ne mozhne*,' he said. It was the watchword of Soviet officialdom: not possible.

My friend let out a strange noise, like a new-born lamb bleating. After that he didn't feel so hungry anyway.

In St Petersburg I like to stay at the Metropole, which was the press hotel during the 1917 October Revolution. In Peking I would always prefer the Beijing Hotel, which still has a stubbornly Marxist-Leninist flavour to it, and which accommodated me and many of my colleagues on the night of the Tiananmen Square massacre. When the Chinese government took the highly dubious decision to allow the great organs of state, including the People's Army and the Security Ministry, to involve themselves in capitalistic projects like hotel building (the name of this engaging policy was *qanming jingshang*, 'everybody doing business') they did not bother to recruit experienced hotel staff on the grounds, rightly, that anyone who had worked in the old Marxist-Leninist hotel system would have been ruined for life.

Instead they hired hundreds of Chinese teenagers, sent them to Hong Kong as part of a training programme, and then brought them back to work in the grand new hotels that were starting to grow up.

The idea was an excellent one, of course. Yet the most important part of going to Beijing is to share the Beijing experience; when I am there I do not want to feel that I could just as easily be in Manila or Madrid. I prefer to avoid sky-scraping hotels with piped music and lots of brass-work: hotels, that is, run by Swiss or Englishmen for American or Japanese companies, whose sole nod to the local culture is an ethnic restaurant and the costume of the doorman.

There is an expensive hotel in Warsaw like this. Once, in the days immediately after the fall of Communism, I fought my way through the crowd of hookers who filled the lobby, and reached the front desk. Upstairs, I knew from past experience, more hookers would be sitting on the seats beside the lift, waiting for foreigners to go to their rooms. After a pause of fifteen minutes or so they would knock discreetly on the doors; most disturbing.

'I'm sorry,' said the receptionist, 'we do not have a record of your reservation.'

I was tired and worried about the next day's shoot. Remembering the fat German in Lusaka, I asked the receptionist to call someone more senior. He came out of a back room, a little dried-up former Marxist-Leninist. He couldn't help either.

'Listen,' I said, 'see that picture on the wall?'

It was a photograph of a painting of a photograph, deeply kitsch, of an old man and a younger one: the founders, father and son, so wholesome you could almost hear the starch on their shirts crackle.

'Those two men are Mormons. That means they lead lives cleaner than anything you or I could imagine. They especially don't like hookers. Unless you find me a room in five minutes I am going to write to them personally and tell them how many hookers you allow into their nice clean hotel in Warsaw.'

Three minutes and forty-five seconds had passed when they announced that, by some extraordinary chance, a room had come free. I had to wait a little longer to get into it, though: the occupants had to be cleared out first, and the smell of cheap scent hung around it there for the whole of the next day. It was still worth it.

Everyone who travels for business thinks he knows what a city is. We arrive there at an airport, take a taxi through the sprawling suburbs, and stay at an hotel somewhere in the old centre. If it's night-time this centre will be largely empty; while we were coming in the inhabitants were heading in the other direction, out to the suburbs. By morning the centre will be full again, as the tide of population flows back in and floods the empty shell.

None of this makes much sense; it's just how most of us have come to expect things to be, except perhaps in Paris, which has always stayed more or less true to the old way. There, now as in the past, you never need to leave your own particular quarter. In the street where I stay there is a baker's shop opposite the front door, a butcher's and a hairdresser's within twenty yards, a launderette and fishmonger within thirty yards, and a bank, a vegetable market, a lawyer, a taxi rank, a police station and a dozen bars and restaurants within forty yards.

But for most Westerners, living in a city really means living in its suburbs; and we have come to think that this is how cities naturally are.

Not necessarily.

Managua, the capital of the Central American country of Nicaragua, strange, beautiful and seismic, possesses no city centre. The terrible earthquake which devastated it nearly thirty years ago destroyed an area as large as Hyde Park in London; only it was packed with little streets and shops and houses.

The entire world was shocked. I remember donating ten pounds which I couldn't afford to help the suffering of Managua, and around the world seventy million pounds was raised altogether: a great deal of money for the early 1970s.

The President, an old-style Latin American dictator called Anastasio Somoza, thanked the world with tears in his eyes and put the whole lot in his Swiss bank account. Not a pound, a dollar, a franc or a mark ever went to relieve the suffering of the homeless or to build a new city centre. It was one of the reasons why he was overthrown by the Sandinistas soon afterwards.

Somoza belonged to the old generation of Cold War tyrants who could always rely on American support, on the 'I know he's a bastard, but he's *our* bastard' principle. In fact it was Somoza whom President Truman was referring to when he said it. In some remote geological period a massive earthquake enclosed a large coastal inlet, and the sharks, swordfish, sea horses and other marine animals caught up in it had to adapt their physiology as this new lake gradually changed from salt water to fresh. (Something of the same thing happened to the Amazon, which once flowed from east to west; when a seismic upheaval blocked it off from the Pacific it flowed into the Atlantic instead, and the seagoing dolphins trapped in the delta also adapted to fresh water, and swim in several parts of the river today.) Anastasio Somoza's idea of a good time was to get a party of friends together, stock one of his American-supplied helicopters with plenty of beers and automatic rifles, and fly over Lake Nicaragua shooting up the freshwater sharks and dolphins. Sometimes, as an alternative diversion, he would pick up a political prisoner or two and drop them into the nearby volcano.

Somoza was the dictators' dictator: he was a stage villain, crazy and violent, yet (according to those who knew him) oddly in need of friends and drinking companions. During the revolution he would sometimes turn up at the main press hotel, the charming Camino Real, and get amazingly drunk with the foreign journalists there.

Once he shouted, 'Go on, if you all hate me so much, shoot me now,' and slammed his silver-handled revolver down on the bar in front of a friend of mine.

His bodyguards, who were a very nasty bunch indeed, stiffened. When my friend explained that he didn't go in for that kind of thing, Somoza burst into tears and staggered off into the darkness, the bodyguards backing out after him.

The Sandinistas didn't have the money to rebuild the city centre after they threw Somoza out, so it was left to run wild. When I first visited Managua in 1984 the entire area of the old city was covered with bushes as high as my waist, and families of beggars lived in the ruins. It was like the fall of the Roman Empire: the cathedral, its frontage cracked and ruined, emerged from the surrounding greenery with the suddenness of a deserted temple. Now the cathedral has been properly repaired, and the area is more under control. But Managua still doesn't have a real centre; what were once the inner suburbs constitute the city.

It also has a hallucinogenic system for finding addresses. If there are officially sanctioned street-names, they are never used. Instead people say things like 'I live two blocks up towards the mountain from the place where Somoza's mistress used to have a hat-shop, and four blocks towards the lake from the old tree that was hit by lightning.' If you don't live in Managua, you can't possibly work it out for yourself.

Strange though this system is, it is not unknown elsewhere. The black township of Soweto, outside Johannesburg, is a city which used not to exist officially, since under the insane old apartheid system it was expected to wither away as the races separated. So although it was one of the biggest cities in Africa and had one of the largest hospitals in the world, Soweto wasn't mentioned on the maps, and there were no signposts to it.

Nor were there any street signs inside Soweto itself. Even now when you go there you have to find your way by stopping people and asking for directions. I once wanted to find Nelson Mandela's house, and drove up and down the little streets with their thick brown dust and their neat four-roomed bungalows, some with superbly tended gardens, calling out to passers-by.

'Two more blocks that way, then turn left and ask again.'

It was like a relay-race: I found Mandela's house after being passed from person to person seven or eight times. It was bigger and nicer than the others around it, and the great man grinned, shook my hand and laughed to hear of my experience.

In Russia, cities have suddenly appeared on the maps after decades during which their existence was a secret; usually they were involved in the arms industry or the space race, or were large prison towns. Sometimes they were merely known by numbers. Millions of people lived there, without being able to tell the outside world where they were or what they were called. Now anyone can visit them; and yet the only thing of interest when you get there is that they were once unknown. In every other way they are exactly like every other Russian city. Their centres are occupied by old Party buildings and an Intourist hotel. Further out, charming, decaying old Tsarist wooden bungalows battle for territory with 1960s and 70s office buildings.

And beyond that? Vast, ugly suburbs full of tower blocks where the workers live. The very existence of these places might have been hidden from us, but they still echoed the pattern of our own cities, all the same.

There are cities like Brasilia or Canberra or Abuja in Nigeria, purpose-built capitals with no life whatever and no reason for existing, where no one wants to be and everyone leaves directly they can. There are cities like Lagos and Tehran and Mexico City, which are so huge and dysfunctional that most suburbanites never make the journey to the centre and few drive across it from one side to the other. Once, leaving Tehran for a tour of the country lasting a week or two, I realized I had left my passport behind at the house where I had been staying. By this stage we had gone right through the city from north to south, and had emerged onto the motorway to the holy city of Qom. Thinking it over, I thought it would be better to talk my way through any problems that might arise, rather than put the driver through the business of going all the way back and coming all the way out again – a process which could have lasted four or five hours. It was a bit of a gamble, but it turned out to be the right decision: rather like Fred Burnaby's contemporaries in 1875, I just announced that I was British (or, on occasion, Irish) and policemen, revolutionary guards, soldiers and hoteliers just accepted it. I got back to Tehran nearly two weeks later.

The most dysfunctional city in the world, as I write, is probably Kabul. It was bad enough before the Taliban took over: those strange characters in their long robes, turbans and beards, with nail polish and mascara. Now that the United Nations, under American pressure, has imposed heavy sanctions on Afghanistan, civilized life has become much harder to sustain. There is little electricity or petrol. Walking back at around nine o'clock at night from the UN Club, the only place in the city where it is possible to buy a drink, I noticed that the stars in the sky were the brightest lights in the centre of Kabul: much brighter than the feeble candles or oil-lamps which people put in their windows. And by nine-thirty, when the curfew on all movement comes into force, the loudest noise was the barking of dogs.

Cities must have been like this throughout the history of civilization, until the seventeenth century in London and Paris and the second half of the twentieth century in the case of parts of Asia, Latin America and Africa. But it is strange to stand in the silence under the brilliant stars of Central Asia and reflect that this, too, is a city.

2

JOURNEYS

> To pass from the cold and snow into such a village and
> its warm houses, on escaping from want and suffering, to
> find such plenty of good bread and fat sheep as we did,
> is an enjoyment that can be conceived only by such as
> have suffered similar hardships, or endured such heavy
> distress . . . passing from distress to ease, from suffering to
> enjoyment.
>
> Babur, founder of the Moghul Empire, on his journey from
> Chakhcharan to Yakawlang in Afghanistan, 1506–7

Real travelling, of course, is done the hard way. Planes merely get
you to the general area; to penetrate to the difficult places you have
to go by four-wheel drive or by horse or by boat. Or you can walk.

It is the expeditions which stand out most in the memory: being
driven across the North African desert by bedouin who relied on the
sky and the look of the sand dunes rather than instruments, and who
arrived at precisely the right place at precisely the time they had
promised; or heading out from Yekaterinburg, the former Sverdlovsk,
to visit Boris Yeltsin's home village of Butka, on a morning so cold
that the road was a slick ribbon of ice and the driver had to peer
through a strip of clarity two inches thick on the windscreen; or
leaving the Ugandan capital Kampala to drive into Rwanda, stopping
at the Equator to take photographs of ourselves, and shredding three
tyres along the way; or hiring a marvellously colourful bus which
drove us to the nastiest and most frightening of the Peruvian drugs
towns in relative safety because it never occurred to the drug dealers
or their allies, the military, that we would arrive in this fashion.

I have sailed on the *Queen Mary* and the *QE2* in my time, and flown on Concorde with a BBC executive in the seat beside me swearing me to eternal secrecy about it, even though it had only cost us the same as a business-class flight. I've been chauffeur-driven to the Taj Mahal, and airlifted from the South Pacific to Hawaii in a superbly fitted executive jet with a gorgeous hostess dispensing champagne and lobster. But it wasn't serious. Serious travelling is never comfortable or safe, and is very rarely accompanied by champagne; unless, that is, you have brought your own. Serious travelling is difficult, and the enjoyment is in direct proportion to the degree of difficulty. By which I mean, it only starts to be really enjoyable once it's over.

Our journey to the forest of Tai had not started well. Before we had even left the outskirts of Abidjan, the capital of Ivory Coast, a policeman in a khaki uniform with lanyards and a sergeant's stripes noticed that I wasn't wearing a seat-belt and waved us down. A long negotiation followed, and we had to pay a fine of 10,000 francs: £10. If it hadn't been for our guide, who shouted at the policeman in raucous French, we would have paid much more.

The police in Ivory Coast, once a model of enlightenment in West Africa, were starting to become noticeably more corrupt. They swaggered around at roadblocks every few miles, always on the look-out for ways of getting money off us, yet still not quite at the stage where they would demand it whether or not we provided them with any excuse.

We were travelling in moderate comfort: our *quatre/quatre*, or four-wheel drive, was well set up, and though our driver looked like any other skinny young hang-out in Abidjan in his T-shirt and jeans, he was excellent. He never did anything remotely risky, he drove at a steady 60 miles an hour, and he didn't fall asleep at the wheel. In Russia, in Iraq, in Colombia, in the former Yugoslavia I have had to keep my eyes fixed on those of the driver, ready to nudge him savagely the moment his eyelids started to droop. This time, there was no need; I could allow my own eyelids to droop instead.

We began with a motorway, decaying a little and yet clearly inspired by Western Europe. Then we turned off onto a side road, whose surface was still mostly good but was beginning to break up in places, so that the rich red-brown earth erupted through the tarmac like boils, leaving craters deep enough to send us spinning off the road if we hit one at speed. We travelled most of the width of the Ivory Coast on this road, before branching off along a reddish dirt track.

Shortly before we reached the little town of Tai, next to the forest, the rain began. I could see it coming, rushing towards us like a tidal wave down the darkened road and striking us heavily enough to check the powerful engine for an instant. The huts of clay, roofed with palm-fronds, were engulfed like rocks beside the sea, and half-naked figures, their bodies glistening in the streaming rain, hurried about and put up shutters to keep the weather out.

In some ways it was a relief to enter the forest. Threatening and black, it closed over us like a tunnel. Above, the canopy was so thick that the heavy rain scarcely seemed to penetrate it. The *quatre/quatre* ploughed on through the reddish mud, its lights picking out the troughs and pools of water on the little used track ahead. On either side of us the trees shut us in. The lights rested on fallen branches, strange root-systems, dead leaves. Small animals ran in front of us, their frightened eyes yellowish-red in the lights. Once a bat flew across the track, a few feet above the ground.

What the producer and cameraman felt, I didn't know. Our translator, an endlessly talkative African woman, had fallen silent; she had told us often enough how the forest scared her. I rather shared her feelings. Panic, or more properly panic fear, is the terror which the god Pan instils in anyone who strays into his domain, and often when I was a boy, wandering through the woods of my childhood, I would be overcome by this sense of panic and would run terrified through the undergrowth for safety.

A tree with fronds instead of branches lay across our path, and we had to stop sharply. The cameraman got out to see what could be done, and swore quietly: he had walked into a thorn-bush, and cut his face. The sight of blood in this of all places made us feel a little uneasy, as though a gap had opened up in our defences. The Ebola virus was endemic here, and we had come to film the efforts of scientists to isolate it.

By now it was nearly nine o'clock, and we had been on the road for more than eleven hours. The rain started easing off, and I had brought a bottle of single malt and some good Havanas in my knapsack to share around. There were a couple of German scientists working at the little station in the middle of the woods. Maybe they would cook something for us; anyway, they were bound to want a little new company in all this darkness and silence.

The road turned, and a parked Land-Rover outside a darkened building reflected our headlights back at us. Everybody in the vehicle stirred with anticipation: we were there. We drove a little farther, past some huts built in the heart of the forest, and then ahead of us in the darkness we could see the faint gleam of two candles shining out. We parked, slowly extricated ourselves from the positions we had been in for hours, and started pulling out our gear. We made a lot of noise.

It was at that stage that I realized we were not going to get the welcome we had anticipated. There were five of us, three men and two women; and one of the women was remarkably good looking. The two German scientists, specialists in different kinds of frogs, had been in the forest for six months, during which time their only company had been that of a French Ebola specialist and his three locally hired assistants. I was certain they would fawn on the blonde producer and then perhaps ask us to play bridge with them, and I wouldn't know how; in the jungle your mind tends to turn to the ethos of the Somerset Maugham short story.

But these two were out of a different book altogether. One, a pleasant-faced, chubby man in his early thirties, with a pair of granny spectacles on his nose, was standing over the gas stove, cooking something; the other, much darker and more saturnine, was hunched over the table doing something that even from a distance looked pretty obsessive. Around them were glass cases in which little jewel-like frogs, green and orange, climbed the sides with their suction-pads and peered out sadly, trying to work out why the air had solidified and trapped them inside.

Neither of the Germans acknowledged our arrival: one carried on stirring, the other remained hunched over the table.

'Hello,' said the producer pleasantly.

The cook made an embarrassed sound. The stirring continued. He seemed a little sane still, though the following night I watched him slip into his room in another building to get a bottle of Campari, then smuggle it over to his obsessive friend, presumably on the assumption that we would take it from them if we saw it.

The obsessive took no notice of her whatever. She went closer to see what he was doing. At first she was worried that she might find him cutting up frogs, but in fact he was chopping a pineapple into pieces the size of tiny dice, and piling them up in some meaningful pattern beside him. When he had finished doing that he began cutting up a grapefruit, extracting the pips one by one and piling them up too. He didn't speak or turn round.

Outside, the rain had let up. The trees around the camp soared up fifty feet or more into the darkness. Somewhere out there were forty-six different types of bat, two hundred and fifty types of bird, and more than three hundred different types of snake. One or other of them were likely to be carriers of Ebola, and the big black-and-white monkeys which might catch it and pass it on to humans were asleep in the trees.

The candles burned down, the frog-loud darkness closed in on the little station. And still the German scientists kept on cutting up pineapples and taking the pips out of grapefruit, drinking Campari and taking no notice of the arrivals from the outside world.

The forest had got to them.

By day it seemed rather less menacing than it had done the previous night. Still, being there was like scuba-diving: you could never forget that you were completely out of your element, and you must always think about everything you did with extreme care.

Even when the sun shone down so hard that the beams looked as solid as pillars, you could see no more than twenty or thirty feet through the trees. If you slipped away and mistook your way back, you might be lost forever here. It was, to quote *Heart of Darkness*,

> like travelling back to the earliest beginnings of the world, when vegetation rioted on the earth and the big trees were kings.

In a tropical forest, more than anywhere else, you are aware of the extraordinary diversity of life on the planet. I had seen this in the most distant parts of Brazil; here in West Africa the awareness was reinforced by the root-systems of trees, the variety of leaves and

fronds, the different types of bark, the flowers and petals, even the
thickly packed dead vegetation that made the ground spongy as we
walked on it.

'Whence is it that Nature doth nothing in vain,' asked Sir Isaac
Newton; 'and whence arises all that Order and Beauty which we see
in the World?' Perhaps, if we could only understand it, even the
Ebola virus was not in vain, and was a part of that order and beauty.

To call Ebola virulent is a pleonasm, since presumably every virus
is by its nature virulent; but of all the strange and savage diseases
which have emerged from the African forests in the last half of the
twentieth century it is the most horrifying. Not long before, in the
Democratic Republic of Congo, a man had found a dead monkey in
the forest near his home, and had cooked it carelessly before eating
it. Within a few days he had started exhibiting the disgusting symp-
toms of the disease, haemorrhaging from every orifice, and was soon
dead. Thirteen of his relatives, obliged by tribal custom to prepare his
body for burial in a particular fashion, all died of the disease as well.
It isn't particularly easy to catch Ebola unless you come into direct
contact with the body fluids of someone who is already suffering
from it; but in the Tai forest, where the monkeys had been dying of
the disease, it was strange how conscious I became of every little cut
and nick on my hands, legs or face.

No one yet knew which species of animal carried the disease and
passed it on, but the Tai forest was small enough for the scientists to
be able to track down the link. Even so, it was a huge enterprise,
involving the capture and killing of thousands of different animals
for study: a hundred examples of each of the dozens upon dozens of
different species here.

Our guides stopped under an enormous tree, a hundred or more
feet high, with ridged roots the height of a low wall above the ground
snaking out on every side. Close by was another, with roots like
rocket fins which lifted up the bole of the tree so it did not touch the
ground at any point. Long lianas hung down from the forest canopy,
ready for the swinging of a Tarzan.

Up the side of the biggest tree of all was a steep wooden ladder,
which led up to a platform twenty feet or more above the forest floor.
Here the men who had brought us set about rigging up nets to catch
the bats which flew through the forest at dusk; these were the most

likely carriers of the virus. But since there were forty-six different types of bat in Tai that meant trapping nearly five thousand individuals altogether.

Somehow, probably via their urine and faeces, the virus was being passed on to the monkeys. Hunters in the neighbouring villages would come into the forest to shoot them, since monkeys are a delicacy in the area, and sometimes they would pick up the body of a dead one in order to eat it or sell it for meat. In this way the virus had passed to humans. And although each outbreak of Ebola involves a very limited number of people, the possibility always exists that it might mutate and link up with, say, an influenza virus – perhaps something like the one which killed more than twenty million people at the end of the First World War. The consequences would be unimaginable.

Sounds travel well in the forest. We could hear a pack of black and white monkeys crashing through the trees a long way off, and hurried to film them. It was while the cameraman was trying to catch a glimpse of them, eighty or a hundred feet above in the forest canopy, that he and Lucien, the scientific assistant who was acting as our guide, smelled the unmistakable stench of death close by. They followed it, and found the body of a monkey lying on the thick, leafy forest floor. It had been there for around five days, and had so many white maggots on it that it seemed to seethe and move.

Lucien called his helpers excitedly. Each time they discovered a monkey's body there was a good chance it had died of Ebola, and that meant more evidence of the transmission of the disease. With great caution they put on white masks and thin hospital rubber gloves. Lucien knelt down and picked up part of the body. It crumbled in his hand. He dropped its tail, legs and ribcage into a specially sealable plastic bag, and then, like a trophy-collector, held up the monkey's head. The surrounding matter came away, and the grinning skull of the animal shone out, clean and white: the very face of Ebola.

Being on the road in Iran is like driving down Highway 101 in California on drugs. All the basic elements are there, but they are somehow weirdly distorted and the colours are all brighter and more interesting. The driving is lunatic, the lane discipline is abysmal, yet everyone stops at the toll-booths, you always see at least one car-wreck, and you eat terrible things at roadside cafés: not totally dissimilar, therefore.

I was in an elderly Land-Rover with the head of the British Institute for Persian Studies, who used it for travelling around Iran inspecting such archaeological digs as had not been interrupted by the war and the revolution. Now, though, we were on our way to join a camping expedition in Alamut: the Valley of the Assassins. Two of the best travel books in English had enhanced my enthusiasm for the trip: Freya Stark's *Valleys of the Assassins*, of course, and Robert Byron's *Road to Oxiana*. The war with Iraq was at its height, the Islamic revolution was still crushing its victims, and life wasn't easy. All the same, the invitation was too good to miss.

We had already broken our journey at Karaj, a dormitory town for commuters to Tehran, and bought some large soft peaches, some hard pears, and a fine melon which we washed with the hose provided. After the food restrictions of wartime Tehran it seemed superb. Now we stopped at Qazvin, once famous for its grapes, its wine, and its homosexuality.

Since we were heading on as fast as possible we didn't have much time to investigate, but all we could see of this trio of specialities was the grapes: thick and butter-yellow, full of pips and rich flavour. Robert Byron had liked the local wine so much, fifty years earlier, that he bought the entire stock of the local hotel. Now, seven years into the revolution of the ayatollahs, it wasn't even a good idea to ask for any; and the penalties for making alcohol had frightened off all but the most determined bootleggers. Everything else seemed easily available: fruit, dairy products, meat. The shop where we stopped had a wide range: Japanese tuna, Soviet candles, smuggled American mayonnaise, and 'Shark' razor-blades, which Iranians say have shed more blood than all the sharks in the Persian Gulf put together. We bought our supplies for the trip, drank some white grape-juice, and headed off.

The sun had gone down by the time we found the sign that said 'To Alamut'. We were to meet up with some friends, mostly foreign diplomats, who had left Tehran ahead of us and had probably set up camp already. The trouble was, we hadn't agreed the exact place. We couldn't miss it, they'd said; which is always an indication that you will. As it turned out, the Valley of the Assassins was not a single valley at all, but an entire range of vales between hills, some of which the Assassins had fortified. I should have paid more attention to Freya Stark's title, and realized that a woman as precise about her words as she was would not have put 'Valleys' in the plural if there was only one of them.

It grew dark, and we bucketed noisily up and down these hills and vales. Sometimes we would see a light in the surrounding blackness and follow it, only to find that it was an oil lamp in the window of an isolated farmhouse. Otherwise nothing except darkness and silence. Occasionally we stopped and got out and shouted, but only the echoes came back to us. Yet we did find them in the end: a small, civilized little encampment in a fold in the hills, with food cooking encouragingly on a fire and genuine and quite decent wine to drink.

I lay out in the clear, thin, warm mountain air that night, watching the shooting stars stream across the sky as the earth entered the asteroid belt. The night was so silent it beat in my ears. In the morning I turned out my sleeping bag and a little greenish-yellow scorpion ran up towards my hand, carrying its sting like a streetfighter with a knife. We must have spent the night together. I slipped a glass over it and showed it to the others. At first I thought I ought to kill it, but my night under the stars had altered my mind about such things. I took it over to the edge of the hill we had camped on, and dropped it out of the glass. It scuttled angrily away into the rocks.

In the hard air of the morning we could see the hills camouflaged with thorn-bushes which we had toiled around in the Land-Rover the previous night. They were crossed by roads of white gravel like healed scars, and where the Shahrud River ran there were startling patches of bright green rice paddies. Up in the hills the dead bushes looked like the bleached skeletons of small animals, and crickets with blue or scarlet underwings burst suddenly out of them, flying awkwardly and without much aim. The air smelt clean. It was starting to be very hot. The closer we got to the Shahrud, the more black dragonflies we saw, buzzing around us like military helicopters on a mission. Of the castles of the Assassins, which we had come here to visit, there was no sign whatever.

Europe first heard about the Islamic sect called the Isma'ilis, nicknamed the Assassins, from the Crusaders. Nowadays it is an ultra-respectable religious group whose leader is the Aga Khan and whose cultural centre stands opposite the Victoria and Albert Museum in South Kensington, and it is hard to think that it might ever have been connected in the popular minds with drugs and murder. Yet it was so. Their first important European victim was Conrad of Montferrat, king of the Latin kingdom of Jerusalem, who was murdered by a lone Isma'ili in 1192. The popular explanation for the fanatical determination and courage of these killers was that their leader sent them out drugged with hashish. They were *hashishi-yun*, hence 'assassins'; which goes to show that the tabloid newspaper instinct has always been with us.

By the 1340s the word *assassino* was in common use in Italy to mean 'murderer'. It spread to France and eventually – much later, of course – to England. Like most tabloid terms, it was misplaced: the nickname was specifically attached to the Syrian branch of the Isma'ili sect, rather than to the Persian branch which was based at Alamut and carried out the first murders.

Alamut's founder was Hasan-i Sabbah, who was born in the middle of the eleventh century in present-day Iran – either in the holy city of Qom, or more probably in Reyy, outside modern Tehran. The legend is that he went to school in Nishapur with the poet and mathematician Omar Khayyam and the future statesman Nizam al-Mulk. The three of them made a pact that whoever succeeded in life first should help the others get on in their careers. Nizam al-Mulk went to work for the Seljuk sultan whose empire included Persia, and quickly became one of the best and most famous politicians of his age. He kept his promise to the other two, by ensuring that Khayyam would have the money to study and write and giving Hasan-i Sabbah a job in the Seljuk administration.

But Hasan-i Sabbah soon came to feel that his abilities had not been properly recognized. He plotted against the Seljuks, and then took to the mountains around Alamut where he and his followers terrorized the regime and eventually murdered his former school-friend and benefactor.

It's a great story, but it has the distinct drawback of not being true. Nizam al-Mulk was a good thirty years older than Omar Khayyam or Hasan-i Sabbah, and since they came from completely different areas it isn't likely that the two of them went to school together. Nor, in all probability, did they even meet. But it is clear that Hasan-i Sabbah became embittered by working for the Seljuk sultanate. He joined the Isma'ili sect, which was then in opposition not just to the Sunn'i and Shi'a branches of Islam, but also to the Seljuks themselves.

In 1090 he ordered his followers to infiltrate themselves into the castle on an inaccessible ridge of rock at Alamut, six thousand feet above sea level, and then he made the owner an offer he couldn't refuse: a huge amount of gold if he would sell, death if he wouldn't. The owner took the money and ran. Hasan-i Sabbah then made Alamut into an impregnable fortress with a superb library: the best, people said, in the world. There he turned his sixty or so followers into a thoroughly disciplined and highly motivated terrorist organization; and in 1092, sensing that at last they were ready for the task he wished to set them, he gathered them together and asked for a volunteer to murder Nizam al-Mulk, the Seljuk vizier.

One man, Bu Tahir Arrani, placed his hand on his heart to show that he was willing to accept the task. Not long afterwards, as Nizam al-Mulk was being carried in a litter to the tent of his wives at Sahna, Arrani approached him in disguise and stabbed him to death. When the news was brought to Hasan-i Sabbah in his library at Alamut he said, 'The killing of this devil is the beginning of bliss.'

It was certainly the beginning of a long reign of terror. Hasan-i Sabbah never again left his mountain top at Alamut. He sent out his men to murder political leaders and buy books for his library, and he spent the remaining thirty-three years of his life in study and prayer, becoming popularly known as the Old Man of the Mountains.

Alamut is a long ridge of rock, and its sides slope down sharply to a single stream in the valley far below. From a distance it is hard to spot even the outline of the castle now. In 1256 the Mongol army approached across the plain – it was said you could smell them a mile away – and under the ferocious Hulagu Khan, who had already destroyed many of the cities of Persia and would go on to raze

Baghdad to the ground, wiped out the impregnable fortress utterly. As for the greatest library in the world, that was largely reduced to ashes. The Mongols didn't hold with reading.

They must, however, have been fit. The slope that led up to Alamut, five hundred feet or more above us, was extremely steep: so much so that with my leather-soled shoes I had to cling on to clumps of grass and heather in order to make my way up. As I hauled myself wearily up the final slope, well behind all my companions, I came across a cave in which three Iranians were resting from the heat.

'*Engilisi?*'

I agreed that this was a possibility.

'*Marg bar Thatcher*,' he said conversationally; death to Thatcher.

Well, of course, I understood how he felt, but I felt obliged to tick him off.

'*Shoma biadab*,' I answered, which is ungrammatical Persian for 'You're being rude.'

The poor man was deeply embarrassed. Rudeness is not usually an Iranian failing; on the contrary, they have a tendency to be infuriatingly and endlessly polite. I suppose he thought it was a friendly gesture: the only thing you could possibly say to a visiting Brit. He placed his hand over his heart much as Bu Tahir Arrani must have done on this same rock nine centuries earlier and bowed speechlessly. I was in such a good mood at having stopped clambering up a virtual wall of scrub and grass, and at having remembered the word *biadab*, that any momentary irritation had already passed. We all smiled, shook hands and said goodbye, and the three of them ran suicidally down the slope I had just climbed.

I shall never forget the extraordinary view. The slicks of desert, the violent green of the rice paddies, the distant mountains, the rivers in their courses: it was like being taken up on a pinnacle of the Temple and shown all the kingdoms of the world. Of the Assassins' castle itself almost nothing was left except a few steps, some low walls, a path or two, and a couple of water cisterns cut deep into the rock. It was impossible to imagine where the Old Man of the Mountains had had his library, from which he could look out at this superb view.

Perhaps some of the books survived after all. The Mongols were too canny to make a frontal attack on Alamut. They just camped around the base of the rock and offered to allow the defenders to leave with all their belongings if they surrendered. They did; perhaps the smell was enough for them.

We climbed down the slope again, as alarming as climbing up it in the first place: I could see why the Old Man of the Mountains had never left Alamut. At the base of the rock we bathed our feet in the streams, and found that the children of the village had smashed the window of one of our vehicles. Now they picked up stones to throw at us, but we shouted at them and they ran away.

We drove away with an escort of running children, joking and laughing and trying to jump on the back of the Land-Rovers. But when I produced my camera and started taking pictures of them they covered their faces and ran off, howling with fear. Then we picked up speed, and the dust hid the children, and the village, and the Rock of Alamut, and we became small objects moving across the view which the Old Man of the Mountains saw every day from his incomparable library.

It was the summer of 1991. The Gulf War was over, and Saddam Hussein still seemed like a beaten man. Those of us with a sanguine turn of mind hoped he would fall within a few weeks or months. He would have fallen earlier if the Americans and British had given their support to the Kurds and Shi'ites who had risen up against Saddam at the end of the war and tried to overthrow him.

But the Americans believed that without a strong man like Saddam, Iraq would fall into its three component parts: the Kurdish north, the Sunni centre and the Shi'ite south. This, they thought, would make their enemy Iran even stronger, because it would swallow up southern Iraq, and weaken their friend Turkey, since the Kurds there would make common cause with the Iraqi Kurds. When Americans try to think in geopolitical terms they usually get it wrong. They certainly got it wrong this time.

We were bashing along a road in northern Iraq in the hot sunshine. The dust caked my eyes, and I could taste its iron earthiness between my lips. The driver, a Kurd with a complexion that looked as though borer worms had been at his face and an old rag which might once have been red and green tied round his head, seemed to be singing. Perhaps he was groaning; the objective difference was marginal. Our car, an elderly taxi which had lost most of the things that once made it a Mercedes, hit a bump in the dirt road and shot up into the air. Then it came down again, hard. My head connected with the back of the seat in front.

'Look, for fuck's sake,' I shouted.

It looks stupid on paper, and it didn't sound any more intelligent when I said it. I felt slightly better, all the same.

'What to do?' asked the driver with the worm-eaten face, looking round at me wolfishly.

His teeth, I noticed, were a remarkable yellow, like very old ivory. He had a point. We were in a hurry, the road was awful, his car was old and not very good; which part of the syllogism did I want to change?

'Well, just try and be a bit more careful,' I muttered, as though that would solve anything.

Maybe, I thought, I should be a little more emollient. The driver spoke English moderately well; and anyway, people right across the globe nowadays recognize words like 'fuck' even if they speak no other English, and resent it; one of the many things Hollywood has done to make our world a better place.

The producer, a charming and intelligent man who looked like a film director's idea of an English empire-builder, smiled at me soothingly. I could guess what he was thinking: time is running out for this film, I have taken an immense risk on setting out on this journey, the blame will be entirely mine if it goes wrong, and all this idiot can do is complain that he isn't comfortable.

I didn't like the discomfort, it was true. My knees were up against my chin, and my feet were resting on some of the camera gear; the rest of it was with the camera crew in the other broken-down Mercedes which was following half a mile or so behind us. We were making a film about how the Americans and the British had let Saddam off the hook. By that stage it wasn't possible to get into any of the areas which were controlled from Baghdad: I was *persona non grata* there, as a result of various things I had written for the British newspapers about my experiences before and during the war. There was, in particular, an article where I suggested that the best thing would be for some senior army figure to put Saddam out of everyone else's misery. This hadn't apparently gone down all that well with some of Saddam's more loyal officials.

But it was still possible to get from southern Turkey into northern Iraq, which was no longer under Saddam's control. That's why we were here. The Turks didn't like people doing this kind of thing, so we had to slip past them. There were also problems about trusting oneself to the locals; a few weeks earlier one of the cameramen who worked with me when the bombing of Baghdad started, Nick della Casa, had been murdered somewhere near here, together with his wife Rosanne and her brother Charles Maxwell, by a guide they had hired. Another reason, perhaps, not to upset the worm-eaten one too much.

The producer and I had decided that we had to film inside Iraq, but we didn't know what we would find or even where we would find it. It was a complete shot in the dark. Someone had told us Saddam's men had committed atrocities at the town of Suleimaniyeh, and that's where we were heading. It was only a hundred kilometres away, but on roads as bad as this a hundred kilometres was a very long journey indeed. I looked out at the brooding Zagros mountains which ran parallel to the road on our left; tens of thousands of refugees had crossed them in terrible conditions a few months earlier. It was there that an exhausted Kurdish woman had shouted to a BBC correspondent the bitter, accusing words that had gone around the world:

'Five million people are in this coldness and this rain. Who is responsible for this? Our house is destroyed. Some of us, we don't know where they are . . . Mr George Bush is responsible for all this. He could destroy Saddam and his army but he don't try . . .

'Kuwait is one million people. He do all this war for one million people. We are five million. Saddam Hussein bombing, helicopters destroy us. They saw this. They did nothing. Why? We are human, like you. *Why?*'

The question still hung over the landscape.

The summer seemed permanent, fixed on the sweeping country like a brilliant lacquer; unthinkable that the brown grass could turn green with rain, that the leaves could fall from the trees, that snow could damp down this light brown dust. The road stretched ahead, a yellow rutted strip in the surrounding colourless, hot landscape.

Sometimes we would pass a small, typically Mesopotamian house, built out of concrete or the grey-brown mud that gave the landscape its colour, and surrounded by bright green thorn-bushes by way of a hedge. Chickens would scatter, half-naked children would peer at us, a woman hanging washing on the line would turn to look at us. Often, as we neared Suleimaniyeh, there would be no chickens and no inhabitants and the houses would be smashed and looted. Each time we passed a house like this the driver would shake his turbaned head.

'Saddam,' he would say, and add what sounded like a curse in the Kurdish language. 'Kurds not stay together.'

He was right there. The various Kurdish movements were always linking up with each other and then going behind each others' backs to do a deal with Saddam. The last time I had been allowed back to Baghdad, I had been eating a frugal meal in the restaurant of the Al-Rashid Hotel when the Kurdish leader Massoud Barzani had come in with his heavily armed entourage to discuss their latest agreement with Saddam. Barzani was extremely nervous; not only is it a dangerous thing to accept the hospitality of someone with as bad a reputation as Saddam, but he had aroused the particular hatred of his Kurdish rivals who thought he was betraying them.

The staff in the restaurant, demoralized and despairing like everyone else in Baghdad at the time, were nervous about having to look after such an obvious target. One of them, a tall, cadaverous waiter I knew and liked, came out of the kitchen with a brass coffee pot and a dozen little cups on it. I watched him: it was plain how frightened he was of all these men with their guns on the table. Somehow, on the long walk to their table, his foot caught on something and he dropped the tray. It sounded like a hand-grenade going off.

The security men round Barzani threw him to the ground and waved their guns about wildly. Sitting not far away, I put my head on the table and waited for the shooting to start.

It didn't. The waiter lay motionless, spreadeagled on the floor in his grubby white jacket, the pool of coffee gradually spreading until it reached his sleeve and seeping into the material and all along his arm. Then one of the Kurdish bodyguards barked something, and put his gun away. Barzani picked himself up, trying to look dignified, and I raised my head. Everyone had taken his place at the table again before the poor waiter felt it was safe to do something about the spilt coffee.

Now, as we bumped and jerked our way along in the shadow of the Zagros Mountains, I saw some thin, drooping, colourless weeds which looked oddly familiar by the side of the road. It was some time before I realized that they were wild oats. The wind had sown them here. It had also sown wild wheat and wild barley. Sometimes the plants would spread out, feeble and skimpy, over wide stretches of open land; sometimes they would simply line the roadside, where the passing cars had thrown the seeds. A quarter of the size, yield and colour of arable crops, they were nevertheless the ancestors of the crops that are grown around the world. At some unthinkably distant time in human history someone must have thought that the wild wheat, barley and oats might be edible, and after that, perhaps thousands of years later, someone else tried growing them for harvest.

This dull, empty landscape with its brooding mountains had once been the hinterland of the Babylonian civilization which in around 500 BC invented the concept of the zodiac, the belt around the earth which contained the sun, moon and planets. This division of the sky led the Babylonians to divide it into 360 parts, or degrees. The Babylonians also invented seven-day periods which were associated with phases of the moon. Each of these seven days ended in an 'evil day' when particular taboos were required to propitiate the gods, and there was a full-moon day called *shabbatum*.

The Jews who were held captive in Babylon took on many of these ideas, and particularly the need for reserving one day a week for special prayers; they called it *shabat*, the Sabbath. It was a curious thought that there might be a faint connection between the wild plants beside the road and the habit of closing shops throughout the Western world on Sundays.

It took us six hours to reach Suleimaniyeh. On the outskirts of the town was a tall, conical hill: the remains of a *ziggurat*, an ancient Babylonian temple like the Tower of Babel. We climbed it, and filmed from its summit, fifty or more feet above ground-level. Below us lay an extraordinary sight: a sizeable town in which every single structure, right down to the sheds and outside lavatories, had been bulldozed down by Saddam's soldiers. The taller buildings had been neatly folded over by high explosive. Most of the houses were single storey, and the flat roofs had folded in the middle and fallen into the rooms below.

There was rubble and dust everywhere; and yet the town was still fully inhabited. In the wealthier areas people parked their cars in front of the ruins of their houses and lived in tents outside. Poor people had to live, crouched down, inside what remained of their houses. Shopkeepers traded from stalls in front of their old, destroyed premises. Children scrambled over the wreckage and played. It was a living, active, busy town which had undergone extreme punishment. Not many people had been killed, but the destruction was total.

'Saddam's men destroyed everything,' one elderly trader told us, 'because he knew we wanted independence.'

None of it came as any surprise to me. Three years earlier, in the summer of 1988, I had been taken by the Iranian army to another Kurdish town, Halabjeh, to see how Saddam treated people who were disloyal to him. Towards the end of the Iran-Iraq war the Iranians had staged an unexpected attack into northern Iraq, and the people of Halabjeh had welcomed the invading troops with open arms. A day or so later planes from Saddam's air force flew overhead and bombed them with poison gas.

I had wandered through the ruins of Halabjeh, looking at the bodies of people who had died the horrible, slow death of nerve gas or the mercifully quick one of cyanide. In one house a cyanide bomb had penetrated the room where a family of six had been eating their meal. The gas worked so fast that one of the older men was lying on the table, a piece of bread still half-eaten in his mouth. Others had died in the act of speaking to one another. Out in the streets a mother lay beside the bodies of three children: all victims of nerve gas. They were twisted in their cruel death agony, strangled as it were from within by the collapse of their breathing functions; the woman had been trying to shield them from the fumes of the nerve gas. Not far away was a truck with the bodies of twenty or more people on it. From their positions it was clear they had been trying to scramble aboard. Presumably they had survived the first gas attacks and were trying to escape when Saddam's planes came back.

What had happened in Suleimaniyeh was less savage than that. And yet to go from house to house, ordering the people out and tossing hand-grenades inside, was savagery enough. While our camera crew wandered round filming the results, I went in search of someone who could explain to me what it meant in practical, human terms. I was walking through some back streets when I looked over a wall and saw a small but beautifully kept garden: a rare thing in the workaday world of a provincial Mesopotamian town.

The door hung loose on its hinges, and I pushed it open. The house had collapsed, of course, but the soldiers had lifted off a large section of the roof and thrown it onto the little patch of well-tended grass in the middle of the garden. Rose bushes, a dozen of them, had been planted around the edges of the lawn. Most of them had been broken down or snapped off. One part of the house, no larger than a small room, had been crudely repaired, and this was where the inhabitants now lived. As the gate swung to behind me a woman in her forties emerged, smoothing down her long dark blue dress. How, I thought to myself for the twentieth time that afternoon, do people who live in this kind of squalor manage to keep themselves so clean and tidy?

She came towards me with a smile. I explained who I was, and although a visitor from the BBC must have been about as unexpected in Suleimaniyeh as an Inuit she acknowledged me without surprise. She even spoke a little English.

'I sorry for all these . . . confusion. You like tea?'

I would, I said, like tea very much. Behind her, two younger women, beautiful in the rich, dark way of Iraqi Kurds, emerged and smiled shyly. One of them began to heat some water on a stove. What had happened here, I asked, and why was the section of roof lying on the garden?

One of the daughters brought over the tea. It was strong, and heavily sweetened. We sat down on little folding chairs, as though it was a picnic, and this woman with her fine, strong features answered my questions while her two beautiful daughters, their heads down, glanced at me through their eyelashes and smiled. It was as charming a scene as any male could conjure up for himself.

The soldiers had come there, the woman explained, and had destroyed her house like all the others. She had been afraid they would rape her and her daughters – it was a difficult subject for her to talk about – but the officer in charge had said they had no time to wait for that. He had looked at the garden and ordered his men to throw the section of roof onto it and to destroy the rose bushes.

'Why?'

She spoke indistinctly, and turned her face away from me. Perhaps it was because her garden was a statement of independence; or maybe just because it was beautiful and rare. I offered to clear it for her, but she said some of her relatives would be coming soon to help. Her husband had been the original gardener here, but he had been hanged a year or so before; the Iraqis wanted to make up the numbers for a public execution. She and her daughters had kept the garden in his memory.

Not every rose bush had been destroyed. One had a single dark red rosebud on it, the colour of her daughters' lips. She snipped it off with her fingers and handed it to me.

'Please think of us.'

I have kept it ever since.

The good thing about television news – sometimes I think it is the *only* good thing about television news – is that it forces you to go and see things for yourself; no matter how far away, nor how long it takes. Once, during the run up to the revolution in Iran in 1978–9, I was in the city of Abadan, the biggest Iranian oil terminal on the shores of the Persian Gulf, at a time when the oil industry had been closed down by a strike against the Shah's government. The nearest section of the pipeline was 280 miles away across the desert, but it was clear to me that we had to have pictures of it. We also had to get back the same evening, in order to send our report to London.

My colleagues, an old and experienced cameraman, and his younger and faithful sound recordist, were understandably dubious. It was an extremely long way, the chances of breaking down or running out of fuel were overwhelming, it was far from certain that we would get any pictures that would be worth the effort. Yeah, yeah, yeah, I said, we're going anyway. Nowadays I would almost certainly agree with them; age hardens the decision-making arteries. But in my Napoleonic younger days I tended to measure the value of something by the difficulty of obtaining it. Very foolish, of course, but it does sometimes pay off. In this case it did.

We crept out of the hotel at four the next morning. I considered handing the man behind the desk a ten-dollar bill to stop him telling our competitors from ITN what time we had left, then rejected the impulse. He would tell them anyway, and by the time they woke up they wouldn't be able to catch us. Outside, the driver was asleep at the wheel. I nudged him into semi-wakefulness, and we headed off.

'I hope you know what you're doing, John,' said the cameraman, for neither the first nor the last time.

The road to the oil-fields ran due east of Abadan, as straight as a die. We stopped for nothing except petrol, a distasteful kebab which we ate as we drove, and the occasional chance to relieve ourselves. It took us seven hours to get there.

The pipeline, with its remarkable flare-off of gas reaching high into the air, was a magnificent sight. Even the cameraman agreed it had been worth the drive. We had to work fast: there were only fifteen minutes for filming, before we had to turn round and do the whole journey in reverse.

The pictures, though wonderful, were sparing; and for editing reasons which I cannot now remember the piece to camera could not have the gas flare behind me. I told the cameraman this a couple of times. I even told him again as I was about to do the piece to camera.

'The flare definitely doesn't show behind me, does it?'

He shook his head mutely; which should have told me something. He was an excellent old boy, the soul of honour and honesty. But once he had got an idea into his head for a shot, it was very hard to excavate it.

I duly did the piece to camera, and we got back into the car. An hour into the seven-hour drive he couldn't keep it to himself any longer.

'Actually, John, I did put the flare behind you in the piece to camera. It just looked so much better.'

I refused to talk to him for the rest of the journey. Twice, when I wanted to know something from him, I asked the sound recordist; who had to ask him. I see us now as if we, too, were in a film, driving across the completely flat and empty desert with the setting sun hovering huge and dark red and unstable over the road directly ahead of us, balancing on the surface of the desert like a vast bubble. The three of us, plus the driver, were entirely alone in the reddening desert; the political disturbances had kept all other traffic off the roads. We were a tiny dot with a trail of sand and dust behind us, driving towards the sun like a sperm towards an egg. In total silence.

But I was extremely fond of Bernard Hesketh, the cameraman; so much so that when he died many years later I could not bring myself to go to his funeral. Not long after the sun went down it occurred to me that there were more important things in life than whether one particular shot appeared in a television report more often than it should. I grudgingly mentioned something about this.

'They'll love it in London,' said Bernard; and he was right.

John Jockell, the sound recordist, relaxed for the first time in hours. It was difficult for him to be our go-between. The driver seemed to be the happiest of all. His face lit up in the afterglow of the headlights.

'Now talking again,' he said.

An hour later we arrived at the hotel.

The drugs business is one of the most interesting and disturbing industries of our age; not least because it is free trade at its purest. It carries no tax, and production, sale and price depend entirely on market forces. That market is, of course, endlessly buoyant. While the demand for cocaine, heroin, opium and crack is so strong in the cities of the Western world, the supply will always be there.

Peru, Colombia and Mexico tell Western governments that the problem lies with the consumers rather than the suppliers. It may seem like a half-hearted attempt to turn aside the blame, but having spent a good deal of time in the main drugs-growing areas of Latin America and Asia, I find myself in full agreement. Something very serious in Western society will have to change if the drugs trade is to fade away. The war against drugs is in the process of being comprehensively lost, and the only people who do not realize it are those who pay the cost of it: the taxpayers of the developed world.

Yet although you hear a great deal of talk about the drugs market and the buyers and sellers, scarcely any outsiders have seen these things for themselves. This is why, when the freelance television producer Rosalind Bain told me late in 1995 that she had been in contact with a Catholic priest in southern Colombia who was prepared to take a BBC camera crew to see cocaine being prepared and sold to the big cartels, I agreed very quickly.

I had worked with the whole team before in Latin America: Rosalind Bain herself, Steve Morris as cameraman, and Matt Leiper as sound recordist. I even wrote a book about our joint experiences in Peru. Now we were heading off again, this time as the guest of Father Leonel Navaez from the town of Remolino in the province of Caqueta, deep in the Amazon forest. Fr. Leonel was no small-time local figure; he had done research at Cambridge University, and was writing a dissertation on the cocaine trade. He had given us some pretty impressive assurances about what we could expect to see in Remolino, and although we had great hopes of what he would show us we were inevitably a little anxious.

There are no roads through the forest to Remolino; the only way to get there is by boat, along the Caguan River. It isn't a short journey: a little over 250 miles, with nowhere desirable to stay along the way. We would have to hire a fast boat, and do the entire trip in the hours of daylight.

The boat was easy to find: surprisingly so, until we started to find out more about the nature of trade along the Caguan. We picked it up at the town of San Vicente, a little frontier place with a single big street and a few general stores. It felt distinctly awkward to be speaking English and to be mistakable for Americans. The only Americans they knew about in this area were working for the Department of Drug Enforcement, the DEA.

We met up with our boatman, Raúl, at five-thirty in the morning. He was paunchy and sleepy, and wore a black cap backwards on his head. The sun was just coming up on the river as we packed our gear onto his boat and got everybody on board: our team, plus Fr. Leonel and one or two people he was giving a lift to. An opalescent light shone on the water, and the morning breeze wafted away the smells of the landing-stage. Even at that time a little crowd of hangers-on had gathered to watch. A dog barked dolefully as we left, and the sound followed us down the river.

The boat was surprisingly high-powered. I began to see how we could reasonably expect to do 250 miles in seven or eight hours. The bows rose up in the water, the stern settled down, the engine roared, the wind blew someone's hat off, and we skimmed along the light brown waters of the river, gripping on to the sides and hoping nervously that none of our gear would fall overboard. With the heat of the sun beating down on us it proved to be a tense and physically demanding ride.

Fr. Leonel looked like a figure from a Velazquez painting, with a round, amused face, a little pointed beard, and a white skin that proclaimed his family's European origin. I was already disposed to like him because of the Cambridge connection, but the more I talked to him the more impressive I found him. He had an indefinable air of being a risk-taker, which I particularly liked. It occurred to me to wonder, even at that stage, whether he might not be taking risks with us as well as with himself. Still, it was too late to worry about that: we were on our way. As W.H. Auden puts it,

Look if you like, but you will have to leap.

This advice has served me extremely well; indeed, the only things I have ever really regretted were the times when I didn't leap. Clearly, this was Father Leonel's motto too.

On the river banks, close to San Vicente, the forest had been cut back and herds of cows, the most destructive animals in the Amazonian jungle, were cropping the grass ruminatively and raising their heads to look in the direction of the noise we were making. The river was wide – sometimes three hundred yards or more – and there was plenty of room for other traffic. Long, heavily laden barges were travelling in our direction, with sheltered cabins at their sterns and rows of metal oil-drums and full sacks weighing the bows down. We filmed these barges, ignoring the angry shouts of the boatmen. We were, after all, so much faster than they were. But I still couldn't understand exactly what the barges were carrying.

Nor, when we arrived three hours later at the next little town along the river bank, Cartagena, could I understand much of what was going on there either. It was a Wild West kind of place, with a wide unpaved main street designed for gun-slinging. But why, in this savage place, should the general stores have so many strimmers for sale – those mechanized cutters which people in the Home Counties use for tidying the edges of their lawns? Not many lawns in Amazonian Colombia, surely?

People stopped to watch us as we passed, and in no friendly way. We were about as out of place as a television crew would have been in Dodge City, *circa* 1884, and a great deal less welcome. Fr. Leonel, who had a habit of not explaining things, advised us to go round to the police station: not to register, but to film it. It had been comprehensively shot up six months earlier, and everyone there either killed or taken prisoner. The front of the building was still pockmarked with bullet holes, and the police had never tried to come back.

The force which had attacked the police station was three hundred strong and came from the oldest left-wing guerrilla movement in Latin America, the *Frente Armada Revolucionaria de Colombia*, or FARC. I have had various encounters with the FARC over the years. It is unpredictable and varied: in central Colombia it goes in for kidnapping, in Bogota it blows things up, and in the south it is heavily involved in the drugs trade. Here it was in the process of wresting the province of Caqueta, with its massive coca plantations, away from government control. There was still an army base in Cartagena, but the soldiers stayed inside the perimeter and kept themselves to themselves. After Cartagena the government's writ ceased to run altogether.

We got back into our boat, glad to be away from such a hostile place. But from here on we were in no-man's-land, a territory where the gun was the only law – and even that was not particularly effective. All we had was Fr. Leonel's assurance that the FARC guerrillas were aware of our coming and would protect us. The river was crowded with barges now, all apparently heading for the same place we were: Remolino. It took us a further five hours under the hot sun to get there, with the forest thick on either side of the river.

Remolino proved to be a lowering little village on the riverbank, darkened by the great forest trees which hung over it. Boats of all kinds were attracted to it, like insect-life: the slow dug-outs of the local growers, the slick speedboats of the buyers from the big cocaine cartels in Medellín and Cali running rings round them and drenching them with their bow-waves. We tied up a little way away from the main landing-stage. It seemed safer that way.

It was Saturday, and Remolino was gearing itself up for the next day's coca market. We strolled through the town, grateful that the FARC knew we were here and were willing to extend their protection to us. There was no sign of them, but since they constituted the only law here no one stopped us or interfered with us in any way as we wandered along the dusty path that turned into the town's high street. The roughly built market stalls sold general provisions; one had the butchered remains of a cow hanging up on it, the flies thick around them.

'So *that*'s what happened to the last crew to come here,' Steve Morris said.

We all laughed, a little too loudly.

There were no cars here, since the only way in was by water. In Remolino you either went by donkey or you walked. After leaving our gear at the priests' house beside the little church we headed up the hill behind the town in the late afternoon heat to film a coca plantation there. Altogether 60,000 hectares around Remolino were currently given over to coca-growing, and according to Fr. Leonel this was increasing by 80 per cent a year. The drugs business was booming.

As we walked between the coca bushes I reflected how unlikely it was that this plant, with leaves the shape and colour of a Putney privet hedge, should have shaped the lives of people throughout the Western world, causing tens of thousands of murders, earning billions of dollars for the men at the top of the pyramid, and subverting entire governments with the promise of unlimited bribes and the threat of unlimited violence.

There was a buzzing sound ahead of us, and I saw at last what the strimmers were used for: cutting the coca leaves into piles of tiny shreds, reading for boiling. Here, in an open shack, lay the entire process, from the leaf on the bush to the paste which was sold to the dealers. They in turn would take it on to the laboratories elsewhere in Colombia, or in Mexico, the United States or Europe, where it would be turned into the white powder which is its final, usable form.

Two young men, pleasant looking and not particularly tough, were working in the shack. These were the *cocineros*, the coca cooks who have the unpleasant and dangerous job of reducing the leaves to powder by means of strong chemicals. The place stank from the petrol and sulphuric acid they were using: these were what the oil-drums on the barges had contained.

'We use petrol to burn the coca leaves to get the merchandise out of them,' said one of them, a young black man in a red T-shirt. He showed no anxiety about speaking to us; after all, there was no law within two hundred miles of Remolino. 'We strain it and use sulphuric acid and water to rinse it out, and then you are left with the merchandise.'

The 'merchandise' was the coca paste. An earlier consignment, already rendered down, lay in a large shallow oblong tin at the feet of the other man, who had the uncomplicated face of a young policeman. Men like these are effectively the slaves of the coca business. They are safe enough in Remolino, but everywhere else they are outlaws: so they cannot leave. They get a pittance from the extraordinarily lucrative trade of which they form the most basic level: altogether the growers and processors earn approximately ·05 per cent of the total profits of the industry.

I crouched down by the tray of thickish yellow powder like the flour you get from South African mealies. This amount, according to the young man who was smoothing it out with a spoon, was worth around $2,200. By the time it reached the streets of New York it would be worth $220,000. The big profits were made much farther up the distribution chain.

We spent an uneasy, mosquito-ridden night in the priests' house beside the church. By now everyone must have known we were here. It was a good thing, we told each other, that Fr. Leonel had obtained the FARC's protection for us.

·The next morning was hot and fine. The church house was full of the sounds of priests – there were four of them – getting ready for mass. Fr. Leonel put on his magnificent green and white vestments, and looked very different and more imposing than the smallish figure in the golfing shirt who had accompanied us here the previous day. The turn-out for mass was not large: perhaps about twenty people. The FARC and the coca-growers just about tolerated the Church's existence in Remolino, but didn't encourage it.

Outside, the weekly coca market was preparing for business and the boats were arriving in greater numbers than ever. People advertised their function in the drugs trade by what they carried and what they wore: the sellers with their plastic bags over their shoulders, the buyers with their leather money satchels, the minders who followed them, the hookers who descended on the town and paraded around, showing off their wares too. There was something for every taste: a couple of tall, simpering transvestites wobbled around uncertainly on high heels, calling out in loud voices. Remolino was packed with people, buying, selling or merely looking. The bars did excellent business in beer and Coca-Cola: the drinks of choice.

In spite of Fr. Leonel's assurances, it was a nervous time for us. There was no control here, and everyone had a gun. The FARC were nowhere to be seen. Until they arrived the market could not start. In the narrow streets between the rickety stalls and the little one-storey buildings people jostled each other and looked angrily at us. They didn't actively stop us filming them. That gave us a certain confidence.

It was noon before the guerrillas arrived. They came up the landing-stage from their boats, looking like regular soldiers in their smart camouflage uniforms and carrying new automatic weapons. For a left-wing movement dedicated to overthrowing capitalism, business was clearly booming. Two guerrillas had been assigned to escort us around, and we were told we mustn't film them. We took this to mean we couldn't show their faces, and interpreted our instructions pretty liberally. They didn't seem to mind too much; perhaps being our escorts had given them a certain cachet.

We headed back into the hot, threatening little market. By now all the tables, twenty or thirty of them, had been set out with the necessary equipment for testing the coca paste to see that it was as free as possible of water: sets of scales, spoons, cigarette lighters, rolls of pink lavatory paper. Yet even with the guerrillas to escort us, the buyers moved away whenever we came up to them. They didn't live in the isolation of Remolino: they had to show their faces in the outside world, and were anxious not to be identified. Still, the FARC's protection worked remarkably well. These were some of the most violent and dangerous people on earth, but they did nothing more than turn their faces and mutter a little when we came up to them.

Eventually, by promising not to show their faces but only their hands, we managed to persuade a group to buy some coca paste on camera. All the same, our presence had had a dampening effect on business.

'What is the price today?' I asked one particularly evil-looking character who was testing the quality of a large bagful of coca paste.

'$1500 per kilo,' he answered, a little glibly.

There was an explosion of laughter nearby.

'More like $850 a kilo,' a mocking voice shouted.

Because we were filming there, the buyers were reluctant to come forward and show their faces. Perhaps they also wanted to drive the price down by holding back.

I wandered off and left the crew to their filming. The FARC commander had arrived, together with a small contingent of attractive women guerrillas, and I wanted to thank him for protecting us.

'Don't worry,' said Fr. Leonel; 'it's not necessary.'

But I like to be polite where possible: even to a guerrilla boss in a savage drugs town. I caught up with him as he was checking out the level of sales at the market: the FARC gets 20 per cent of the total from each seller, and punishes anyone who cheats them severely.

'Many thanks for your kindness in giving the BBC your protection.'

He turned and looked at me. His face was scarred and dirty.

'I'm not giving you anything. It is a matter of complete indifference to me whether you live or die.'

'Thanks a lot,' I said, and walked away.

I could see now what Fr. Leonel had done: he had managed to persuade the buyers and sellers, and us, that the FARC wanted us to film there. It had worked, even though it wasn't true. I honoured him for the stroke he had pulled, but decided not to tell the others about it until we got away from Remolino. Assuming, of course, that we did.

By now the market was coming to an end. Even on a day when, thanks to us, sales were low, a million dollars at least had changed hands in the space of a few hours. By the time the day's coca supply reached the streets of the First World it would be worth $100 million. The toilet-rolls and weighing machines were being packed away, the tables folded up. The minders clustered round their employers to protect them from unwanted attention. Every Sunday, according to Fr. Leonel, several buyers were ambushed on their way back with the coca they had bought.

It was getting dark. Raucous laughter came from the bars. In the little huts nearby, the giggling and squealing showed that the whores were hard at work. Once there was a loud scream: altogether three people were murdered in Remolino during the night. It was an average market day.

We sat out in the courtyard of the priests' house, smoking cigars and drinking whisky and congratulating ourselves on an extraordinary piece of work. All the same, we were nervous. Everyone knew where we were, and there was no protection for us whatever; certainly not from the FARC, who had all gone back to their camp. I lay on my bunk, listening to the sounds of people sleeping, and wondered what I would do if someone came in with a gun. I was still wondering when I fell asleep.

We were up at five the next morning, and slipped quietly through the back street of the village to the landing-stage. The sky was getting lighter, but no one was around. Snoring and the occasional whimper came from the huts where so much work had been done the previous day and night. One man lay fast asleep in his grubby yellow vest on his porch. We tiptoed past him, and he turned over, grunting.

The plump boatman was ready for us, and pushed the boat well out into the water before turning the engine on. By that stage no one could catch us. As we headed out the rising sun made the water shine around us.

3

VILLAINS

Mr Kurtz lacked restraint in the gratification of his various lusts . . . there was something wanting in him – some small matter which, when the pressing need arose, could not be found under his magnificent eloquence. Whether he knew of this deficiency himself I can't say. I think the knowledge came to him at last – only at the very last. But the wilderness had found him out early, and had taken on him a terrible vengeance for the fantastic invasion.

Joseph Conrad, *Heart of Darkness*, 1902

There is a particular type of news story which takes place entirely in hotels. The journalists are staying there, and so, often, are the main participants. All the twists and turns take place in the hotel's public rooms. Major developments take place as a result of chance meetings in corridors and lobbies. The staff become strangely complicit in the whole affair, tipping you off about the movements of the people you are trying to corner and the activities of your rivals.

I usually prefer a more active, roaming kind of journalism, but there is nevertheless a curious attraction about something as neat and self-contained as the big hotel story. Oddly enough, in my career the main examples have often been associated with wars: in Kinshasa during the mercenary campaign in Angola, in Baghdad during the Gulf War, in Belgrade during the bombing campaign of 1999.

As a result, some odd relationships are engendered. In Kinshasa it quite often happened that I would have my meals or travel in lifts beside people who had threatened to kill me. We would nod curtly to one another, look pointedly away, and pretend that everything was entirely normal. I remember saying 'Have a nice evening' to one particularly unpleasant character, but that was just bravado. In Baghdad I got onto weirdly good terms with the spooks whose job it was to keep an eye on me and my colleagues, making sure with a kind of ersatz courtesy that they knew whenever I was leaving the hotel; though only, of course, when it didn't matter if they followed me.

It is familiarity which has this strange effect, of course – that, and the fact that being in a hotel makes you slip into a guest-like pattern of behaviour. Screaming, shouting, making threats, or begging for mercy are not things you do in a hotel lobby, so you don't do them even when there is every reason to. Like the Graham Greene character who knows he is going to be stabbed during a séance but cannot somehow break the convention which obliges him to carry on holding hands with the people on either side of him, you nod politely to the person you are trying to escape from, and dodge round the nearest pillar directly you can. A hotel plays something of the function of the mediaeval notion of sanctuary: if you perform the correct rituals, then you are given a measure of protection. It is, I suppose, the power of convention. Don't knock it: it can save your life.

Ever since I first became aware of him, I had tried to corner the Serbian warlord Arkan and persuade him to let me interview him. It was difficult, and one of the hardest things about it was that I couldn't find anyone who dared to act as a go-between to fix it up. Justifiably, Arkan had a very bad reputation indeed. As a result of the operations his followers, the Tigers, carried out in Croatia and Bosnia, he was indicted by the War Crimes Tribunal at The Hague in early 1999. There was obviously a degree of political calculation about this, not so much by the Tribunal as by the British and American governments which handed over secret intelligence about Arkan's responsibility for massacres at precisely the time when they were targeting Serbia. But there was nothing innocent about Arkan, even if not everything against him had yet been proven.

In 1992, just as I was leaving Sarajevo for the Croatian frontier, a friend of mine handed me an Arkan badge as a joke. I put it absent-mindedly in my pocket, and forgot about it until I was going through the metal detector at Zagreb airport. The buzzer sounded, and I emptied the contents of my pockets into a plastic tray. It took me a long time to talk my way out of that, once the security guards had spotted Arkan's curiously chubby, angelic features. I thought at one stage they were going to shoot me then and there.

The years went by, and apart from an unsuccessful attempt to contact Arkan through the priest who married him to a famously beautiful Serbian rock star, I let the idea of an interview slide. (This priest was only Orthodox in terms of religion; in every other way he was barkingly eccentric. We were invited round to his house in Belgrade, which stank of cats. He served us tea, talking with great affection of Arkan, and called his wife to join us. When she came in, she was wearing a ludicrous little-girl blonde wig, and carried a large, resentful and smelly black-and-white tomcat. It was clear why the cat was resentful: she had painted large roundels of rouge on its white cheeks.)

And then in March 1999 I found myself back in the Hyatt Hotel in Belgrade, waiting for the NATO bombing to start (see Chapter Eight). The hotel emptied out, the corridors which had been full of journalists hurrying around with equipment and suitcases became silent, and the staff were too nervous of the coming onslaught to pay much attention to the handful of guests who remained.

Arkan took to spending most of each night in the hotel. It took me some time to realize that this was not solely in order to terrorize the few remaining journalists; it was because the Hyatt was the only place left in Belgrade under the bombs where the electricity supply was assured, and where the management was prepared to serve him drinks in the early hours of the morning.

He would turn up in his black four-wheel drive with blacked-out windows, driving fast and noisily up the ramp of the hotel and followed by another vehicle filled with security men and women. Parking carefully in the no-parking zone in front of the main entrance he would jump down, help his sensationally attractive wife out, and go inside. The hotel staff would bow and scrape before him; most of them, at any rate. Arkan was not the kind of man you annoyed in Milošević's Belgrade.

A few of his men would hang around all evening by the vehicles. Others would take up positions in the lobby. At the entrance to the coffee lounge a woman dressed in black would usually stand on guard, walkie-talkie in hand. She too was distinctly attractive, but when I tried to make eye-contact with her it was like making eye-contact with a bust of Lenin.

Inside the coffee lounge, meanwhile, Arkan would be holding court. The lounge closed at 11.00 and he rarely arrived before half past, but the hotel put on extra staff to look after him. He would always be surrounded by grinning, obsequious characters from Belgrade's political and business life, laughing earnestly at his jokes and nodding at his statements. He favoured gangster chic, with dark suits, white shirts and carefully selected silk ties. After a while, when the foreign journalists returned to Belgrade and the hotel began to fill up again, he would arrive in the evenings disconcertingly prepared in case someone wanted to do a television interview with him, the pancake make-up on his face as brown and as unconvincing as an artificial tan.

Early on, when the man from CNN and I were almost the only television people in the hotel, he agreed to give his first interviews. Thinking (wrongly, of course) that CNN had a bigger audience and was more influential than the BBC, he spoke to them first. I turned up at the TV station in order to fix a time for our interview.

'What are you doing, hanging out with the McDonald's of television like this?'

I didn't just say it to irritate the CNN correspondent; I wanted to make it clear to Arkan that I would never defer to him, and that I wasn't afraid of him either. It wasn't true. Knowing what he could do, I was very frightened of him indeed; but it seemed to me to be bad for business to show it. He agreed to be interviewed the following afternoon, and would only speak on condition that the interview was broadcast live. That caused a good deal of difficulty for the BBC, and plenty of backbiting from the less loyal element at home.

I had a very narrow tightrope to walk. On the one hand I wouldn't dream of giving an indicted war-criminal an easy ride. On the other, his temper was famous. What I needed to do was satisfy the BBC's audience that the right questions were being put in a properly tough manner to Arkan, and at the same time be able to keep on reasonably good terms with him. It seemed likely that at some stage during the NATO bombing we might have trouble from the even more dangerous set of thugs in Belgrade loyal to Arkan's enemy Vojislav Šešlj, whose party had joined the coalition run by President Milošević. Šešlj had a lot of power, and he loathed the BBC. If anyone came to the hotel to take us away or murder us, it would be Šešlj's men, not Arkan's. In the looking-glass world of Belgrade, Arkan almost counted as one of the good guys.

These were distinctions which weren't obvious in London; why should they be? But there was a certain amount of disagreement about whether we should or shouldn't interview a man with Arkan's record.

'We wouldn't, after all, have interviewed Heinrich Himmler about the Holocaust,' one wiseacre complained.

Of course we would have interviewed Heinrich Himmler if we had had the chance, and Adolf Hitler too – and Joseph Stalin for good measure. We would have put the proper, tough questions to all of them, and broadcast their answers. Our kind of journalism is about placing the facts in front of people and allowing them to decide what they think. It isn't to be the cheerleaders for our side; there are enough of those already.

Arkan wasn't in the Heinrich Himmler league, though given the right circumstances he might have been. All the same, I spent much of the previous night trying to work out how I could give him a tough interview, and yet not provoke him too much. At around 4 a.m. I came up with the answer. Unusually, it still looked good in the morning.

A few hours later Arkan and I sat side by side in the Belgrade TV studio. It was swelteringly hot. There was an air raid of sorts going on at the time, and power for unnecessary things like air conditioning was heavily rationed. Arkan and I sweated away, but it showed more on him because of his make-up.

The countdown from London sounded in my head, and I introduced him by his proper name, Zeljko Ražnatović.

'May I call you Arkan? It's easier on the tongue,' I said; and for a week or so afterwards 'May I call you Arkan?' became a slightly mocking catchphrase among the staff of *The Nine O'Clock News*.

Then I produced the line I had worked out in the early hours of the morning.

'I can do one of two things. I can either ask you easy questions, which won't upset you, or I can ask the hard ones. Which shall it be?'

He twitched his shoulders in an I-can-take-anything-you-throw-at-me kind of way, and said, 'The hard ones,' as I knew he would. From that moment on I would be able to square the circle.

I asked him about the war crimes for which he had been indicted. For a time he stayed calm, reproducing the answers he had worked out and given on various occasions before.

'Any women and children who died were killed by accident. As for the Croat and Muslim men we killed, they died in a fair battle. War isn't nice, you know. But they were legitimate targets that we killed, and only legitimate targets.'

I pressed him, and he didn't like that. Sitting beside him, I could see his neck swelling and the veins standing out on his forehead. He started to shout. Slightly awkward, I thought to myself, and for a time I thought I'd blown it. Then, somehow, having talked himself up into a rage, Arkan talked himself down again. The neck, the veins and the voice all began to subside of their own accord; I didn't even have to throw him a few tame questions to calm him.

His English remained pretty good throughout, and by the time I cut him off he was enjoying himself. I felt pleased: I'd asked him far harder and more difficult questions than the CNN man had the previous day. He seemed to have enjoyed himself.

As we walked down the corridor afterwards I broached the subject of the threat from Šešlj and his men.

'The BBC will have no problems here,' he said. 'Believe me.'

I did.

Arkan was a strange man, capable of the most violent rage, and yet in other ways clever and highly rational. He had escaped from prison in Sweden, and had spent a lot of time in most of the main Western countries, involved in smuggling, gambling and other illegal things. Nevertheless he saw himself as a kind of mediaeval knight, called in to save his people from destruction. He used violence openly, yet he managed to convince himself that his methods were chivalrous. No matter how many times I put it to him that the women and children who had died had been murdered savagely by his followers, he denied it. The mental wall separating his self-image from any wrongdoing was high and impenetrable: he was totally self-convinced.

Arkan more or less invented the concept of ethnic cleansing, and many innocent people died when he and his Tigers passed through. But whereas Šešlj's men carried out their disgusting atrocities and slipped away, Arkan was mainly a showman. He couldn't resist a camera. He wanted everyone to know he was a big figure, and so when the massacres and the ethnic cleansing happened it was Arkan who gave the television interviews. Others, with worse records and names that were harder for Westerners to remember, kept their heads down, did their looting and murdering, and disappeared from the public record.

And so it came about afterwards that the man I had once tried hard to track down now greeted me in the lobby of my hotel every night when I came back from filming or doing some live broadcast. We would shake hands, though I would have preferred to avoid it. It was hard to resist his warmth altogether, though I always kept some element of mockery in my relationship with him in order to maintain a clear moral distance from him.

I am trying to be honest about this, because the easy, politically correct thing to do would be to say how much I loathed him; and there will be plenty of people whose acquaintance with serial murderers is limited to the cinema and the television screen who will no doubt feel I should have spat in his face. Instead, I fell back on humour. I took to saying, 'Hello, Arkan – good day's ethnic cleansing?' when I saw him: partly to amuse and impress my friends, but partly to show myself, and him, that I knew precisely who and what he was.

When I fell and ruptured the tendons of my left quadriceps, and had to undergo a difficult and painful operation in a Belgrade hospital, Arkan was full of sympathy; and when I left hospital and was installed in the hotel again, he showed an interest in my condition which was unwanted from my side, yet which I found somehow touching. The last time I saw him was the night before I left for the Hungarian border, having been thrown out of Serbia for saying the wrong things about President Milošević. Arkan told me he had rung the specialist who carried out the operation to find out what the prognosis was.

'You're going to be all right,' he told me, gripping my hand with both of his.

I could imagine how nervous the poor specialist must have felt, with one of the most dangerous gangsters in Serbia on the other end of the line, asking him to give assurances about my condition. But I shook Arkan's hand with some warmth, if only to forestall the possibility of an affectionate bear-hug, and said my goodbyes to him.

Within seven months he was dead, shot outside the Inter-Continental Hotel just opposite the Hyatt. He had shifted his unwanted custom there after the bombing finished. When I stayed at the Inter-Continental soon afterwards you could still see one of the bullet holes in the wall behind the reception desk, and they would show you a key-holder which had been hit by a bullet. Somewhere at the back of the lobby was a leather armchair which had been stained with blood – either Arkan's, or that of the two men with him when he died. The killer was an off-duty cop: but it was unclear who'd hired him.

I feel no great sympathy for a man who had been responsible for so much death and suffering. Arkan was a murderer, a crook and a swaggerer; but I would have preferred to see him gaoled than murdered.

My abiding memory of him in the Hyatt Hotel came not from anything I saw myself but from a word-picture drawn by my friend and colleague in Belgrade, Mike Williams. One evening Mike went down to the bar in the hotel to watch the football match between Manchester United and Bayern Munich. Arkan, who owned a soccer team in Belgrade, was passionate about Bayern Munich. He sat there in deepening gloom as it became clear that Manchester United were going to win. His guards had long since stopped watching the screen, and were watching the guests instead. Arkan, of course, was holding the remote control for the television; the Arkans of this world always do. Ten minutes or so before the match was due to end, he decided Bayern Munich was going to lose and flicked moodily to CNN.

'So what are the chances of getting Arkan and other indicted war-criminals sent to The Hague for trial?' some young woman was asking brightly.

*

We expect to know evil when we see it in people, just as we expect to know goodness. It should show itself, we think, in some kind of aberrant looks or behaviour. And yet it isn't like that, somehow. Wickedness can flicker briefly across someone's life, and leave no obvious mark whatever. If I hadn't known what Arkan had done, I should have taken him for a small-time hood; which is, of course, precisely what he was – a small-time hood who, thanks to the circumstances he found himself in, was guilty of the deaths of many innocent people.

Weakness can lead to worse things than outright wilful evil. So, sometimes, can simple efficiency, misdirected. This chapter contains cases to illustrate these points: an international organization which allowed millions to die because it couldn't quite summon up the courage to say anything about it, a man whose brainwave has brought more chaos and death to the world than just about anyone else. They are ranged alongside people who are more conventionally evil: kidnappers, torturers, murderers. I have added the case of a man who preyed on the weakness and misfortunes of others in the most despicable fashion, and who may yet have done more good than bad as a result.

In other words, these things are not as clear-cut as one might imagine. One of the most evil people I have come across – I cannot say met, since I only observed the traces of her wickedness – was clearly a loving mother, a committed Christian, and a conscientious teacher. She ran a school in Kigali, the Rwandan capital, and when the outburst of almost inexplicable race violence welled up there in 1994 between Hutus and Tutsis, she led a large gang of killers to the houses of Tutsi families whose addresses she knew because their children attended her school. In her house, alongside the school, we found a blackboard with directions to the killers: where they were to go, the weapons they were to take, how precisely they were to use them – stabbing, maiming, murdering. And in one of the rooms I found photographs of her with her own children on her knee, and others of her affectionately posing with some of the children she taught, and attending their communions.

These things are not at all simple. The pathology of wrongdoing is far more widespread and reaches far deeper than most of us would prefer to think. If the controls are lifted, people can be capable of crimes which under other circumstances they would themselves be the first to be horrified by.

In Algeria once, trying to understand who carried out the terrible massacres of the mid-1990s, I cross-examined the mayor of a little village who was one of the few survivors of an attack which had left thirty or more villagers dead, including his wife. From something one of the other survivors, a child of nine, had told us, I guessed that he knew more about the murderers than he was saying.

'So who did all this?'

'Ah, who can say? Masked men did it. I have no idea of their identities.'

'But the boy here says they came from those mountains over there, and although they wore masks he had seen them before.'

'No, that is impossible. I tell you, I have no idea at all who they were.'

'So a nine-year-old boy knows more about these men than the mayor of the village does.'

'Evidently, yes.'

'I don't believe it. I think you know perfectly well who did this.'

There was a pause for a little while, and our government minder wandered away. I tried again.

'Tell me who murdered your wife, and all the other people here.'

'All right, it was my brother-in-law. He's been in the mountains there.'

'Your brother-in-law killed everyone here, including his own sister?'

'He and his associates, yes.'

'But why?'

This time he genuinely had no answer. I could only assume that whatever fundamental control had prevented people in this area from avenging their grievances had somehow been set aside by the general climate of violence in Algeria, and that the unthinkable had suddenly become not only possible, but easy.

We throw up our hands in horror at these things, and take comfort in the thought that they happen in countries completely unlike our own, in circumstances we couldn't possibly imagine. And yet if our own circumstances were to change abruptly, and the normal restrictions were suddenly lifted, who knows what we would be capable of? In the past people used to be free in quoting Hannah Arendt's phrase about the banality of evil. But perhaps evil isn't banal so much as widely latent; and that all it takes to summon it up is a political and social break-down of the kind the twentieth century taught us was all too easy.

I once sat through the trial of a man for theft and the resulting amputation of his right hand. It was the single most shocking experience of my life: worse than seeing a trio of murderers hanged, worse than watching people die in gunfire or shellfire. What made it so horrific was the calmness and silence of it all.

The trial was very brief, and the accused man didn't deny the charges. Anyway, he had been caught with the stolen goods on him. When it ended the judge, a Sunni cleric in the whitest of robes, proclaimed the sentence so easily and conversationally that I assumed it was just another stage of the trial until his words were translated for me. The accused man had been expecting the sentence. Immediately, he rolled back the sleeve of his grubby robe and stood there, his arm bare, with stoic dignity.

There was no ceremony. The executioner, a thin, staid little man with glasses who doubled as the clerk of the court, reached into a wooden box and pulled out a large kitchen knife, then walked over to the thief, swiftly tied a tourniquet round his arm and took hold of his hand. With the deftness of considerable experience he worked the knife between the bones of the wrist, and the hand came away in his in less than a second.

The thief kept his eyes on the wall behind the judge the whole time, and made no sound. The involuntary intake of breath I gave was the only noise in the room. Then the thief's wife took him away, with as little emotion as he himself had shown. The hand was thrown out onto the dusty ground outside the court, close to a pair of feet which had been amputated earlier and which stood together, like a pair of brown shoes in the dust.

There is, in Islamic society, a clear dissociation between unbearable suffering and the agents who inflict it. Once, driving through one of the northern suburbs of Tehran, I noticed a large portrait of Ayatollah Khomeini on the wall of a building, with several uniformed

Revolutionary Guards sitting on a bench in front of it. I told the driver to stop, and asked the cameraman to get a shot of them, with me standing in front of them. I wanted the picture for the cover of a book I was writing about Iran.

They were very polite. They asked us to forgive them for refusing, but pointed out that the portrait was flaking and said it might be disrespectful if we showed it. I countered that argument, only for another to be produced: we would need the permission of the commanding officer. Soon afterwards he emerged: a gentle, unworldly, smiling man, who explained to me that it would not be possible. I argued some more. He grew more and more embarrassed, and smiled harder, and still said no. Why not, I asked?

'Because this is a special place.'

A kind of prison, it emerged. But what kind of prison?

'A prison where we— we ask people questions.'

'You mean it's an interrogation centre?'

That was exactly what he meant; and at that moment a vanload of new prisoners arrived. They looked understandably frightened, and their hands were tied. They were on their way to be tortured, and they knew it.

There was obviously no question of getting any pictures of this place. The commanding officer shook my hand with the greatest warmth, and placed his hand over his heart as a sign of affection and respect. He looked even pleasanter, and even more unworldly. Then he went back indoors, to the job of ordering the electrodes to be attached to the new arrivals.

Was he evil? Only in the effects of what he did; there seemed to be nothing intrinsically bad about him, from the little I saw of the man. It wasn't that he was merely obeying orders; he agreed with his orders, and he put them into practice as conscientiously as any SS guard.

Yet there are degrees in these things; and the lowest degree I have come across in this line was represented by a man called Raúl Vilariño, a naval petty officer who had worked for the Argentine military death squads during the so-called Dirty War of 1976–82. Thousands of people, mostly young, well-educated and liberal or left-wing, disappeared – kidnapped by the death squads, routinely tortured, and then murdered, often by being dropped out of military planes over the Atlantic Ocean. The military who seized power in the coup of 1976 thought that by these means they could stamp out terrorism and those who supported it.

I first heard of Vilariño through a Buenos Aires news magazine which he had contacted in order to make a clean breast of the things he had done. When I saw him, I was appalled by his appearance: his big, coarse features surmounted by thick, oily hair, his eyes bulbous and staring. He was in his late thirties, but looked at least ten years older. One of the main architects of the terror in Argentina, Admiral Emilio Massera, a member of the junta which seized power in March 1976, had spotted Vilariño a few years earlier, and had earmarked him for 'special duties'. He worked with a small group of others at ESMA, the Argentine Navy's engineering school. It became one of the main torture and execution centres, and Vilariño was one of its most important operatives.

Yet there is something in all of us that prefers to block out the worst of our realities. Vilariño's account of his activities always seemed to end when he delivered one of his kidnap victims to ESMA, a place where unthinkably dreadful things happened, and where virtually every one of the prisoners was later murdered. According to Vilariño, he played no part in the actual process of torture, though he knew all the names of the torturers and could even describe their hours and conditions of work. But even though he was making a confession, he always seemed to disappear from the scene at the key moment in his narrative.

As the disappearances continued, any suggestion of strategy or purpose behind the kidnappers began to disappear. The targets were no longer specified left-wingers; often they were simply picked up by mistake, sometimes because they had the same names as real suspects. Increasingly, they were just taken because they caught the kidnappers' eye, and the process became increasingly depraved.

One day the most infamous of the kidnappers, Captain Alfredo Astiz, brought in a woman in an advanced state of pregnancy together with her little daughter, a girl of six or seven. Vilariño said the little girl was frightened and upset, and that he played with her for a while until she and her mother were taken away. At that point, he said, he was sent out on a mission. When he came back he found them both suffering serious injuries. He tried to ensure that they received proper medical help, but they were taken away and never heard of again.

There were various other stories of this kind, in which Vilariño always seemed to want to help the victims yet somehow was never on hand when it mattered. One of his closest friends and associates committed suicide, leaving a note which said he could not continue doing the job any longer. Vilariño did continue, but he always maintained that his group, the original detail, would never have done the kind of things he witnessed later. It is a terrible story, and Vilariño was a terrible man, his haunted eyes looking at you as though they were seeing something altogether different, and his handshake painfully strong and yet distinctly damp. Afterwards I badly wanted to wash my hands, and when I had done it I could still feel the pressure of his fingers and the dampness of his palm. I never, I think, came across a more wicked person; and yet even he wanted to think well of himself, and doctored his account of things to ensure that he could.

'This harsh and magnificent landscape', Lord Curzon called it, 'with its harsh and magnificent people.' He loved Afghanistan, as so many British travellers have before and since. In those days he was still a young man, far less pompous than he later became. Knowing the enjoyment the people of Central Asia take in a splendid appearance, he went to a theatrical costumier before leaving London and hired all sorts of meretricious but impressive-looking orders and medals to wear when he went to visit the King of Afghanistan. They produced a sensation.

Like Curzon, I am haunted by that landscape, and am always impatient to go back to Afghanistan to see them again: even at the age of fifty-five, even at the cost of all the physical discomfort and danger which is likely to be involved. There is something about the look of the mountains and the clear thin air that make you feel somehow stronger and more effective and, I would say if such things were not so desperately unfashionable nowadays, more of a man.

I first saw Afghanistan's hills of amethyst and plains of amber in January 1980, at the time of the Soviet invasion. But I saw them only at a distance, from the Pakistani side of the border at Torkum. Nine years later, in February 1989, I crossed the border at last to report on the Soviet withdrawal. Soon afterwards I found myself trekking across it to Kabul disguised as an Afghan but absent-mindedly carrying a bag from Heffer's bookshop in Cambridge. Then I went back in the early summer of 1989 to finish off the documentary we were making.

It was hot, and the distant hills shimmered. We had driven up from Pakistan through the Khyber Pass, past the headquarters of the Khyber Rifles.

(Back in 1980 I was given lunch in the officers' mess there, and thought it the crowning experience of my life; especially when one of the officers pulled aside the obligatory framed photograph of Jinna, Pakistan's founder, and showed me a smaller, faded oblong patch on the wallpaper underneath. 'That is where the photograph of the King-Emperor used to hang,' he said.)

Now we drove along the relatively well-maintained road from the Pass to Jalallabad. It was there on the city walls in 1841 that the British watchers had seen a single rider, Surgeon Brydon, staggering towards them from the direction of Kabul, and had realized slowly that he was the sole survivor of the disaster which had befallen the British army there. Scarcely anything had changed since those days: the buildings of dried mud-brick, the turbans and long robes of the occasional passer-by, the hunters with their long *jezails*, often made at the Tower of London armoury in the early nineteenth century and adapted infinitesimally over the years to make them superbly effective for the shooting of game.

Afghanistan is one place where the modern world has scarcely touched. Before I set off for my second trip in 1989 I asked a doctor for something specific against stomach upsets.

'Don't take anything,' he said; 'just drink lots of Coca-Cola if you get ill.'

'But I'm going to Afghanistan,' I objected.

'You're not going to tell me they don't have Coca-Cola in Afghanistan,' he replied; 'just stop and get a bottle from a dispenser.'

How do I begin to explain, I thought, and decided I couldn't.

'OK,' I answered brightly, 'Coca-Cola it is.'

Knowing it wouldn't be.

We were, quite literally, looking for trouble. Jalallabad was in the hands of forces loyal to the Communist system, and was under sporadic attack from the various mujaheddin groups which controlled the countryside. Our aim was to record a piece to camera, tying our documentary together, in a place where there was fighting.

Eventually we heard it: the sullen boom of artillery, the lighter crash of mortars. We drove on, and found a group of mujaheddin in a meadow beside the road, firing randomly at the town. In the long and depressing tradition of warfare in Afghanistan, they had little interest in what they were hitting: it could have been the military headquarters or it could have been the local maternity hospital. As long as it was in Jalallabad they didn't care.

Nor did they seem to understand the fundamental value of the mortar, which is that you can move it around and so avoid the danger that the enemy will spot you, get your range, and fire back. This mortar was fixed, stationary; the meadow was a comfortable and easy place to fire from, and the mujaheddin were settled in there.

They were pleasant enough to us, and welcomed the diversion we provided. At that stage in the war the different mujaheddin organizations were more united, and here as elsewhere various groups were working together: the more moderate Jamiat-e-Islami side by side with the fiercely fundamentalist Hezbe-e-Islami. It was impossible to tell the difference between them: they all wore green turbans and *shalwar kameez*, and they all had AK-47s. Everyone in Afghanistan who considered himself to be a man carried an AK-47.

For a while we filmed them as they fired off their mortar rounds, cheering every time a cloud of grey smoke went up over their latest hit. I got ready to do my piece to camera while the firing went on behind me.

It was then that the figure in white appeared. He was clearly an Arab, not an Indo-European like the Afghans around us. His robes were spotless, and his beard sensational. He appeared to be in his middle twenties, though it was hard to be certain. His AK-47 was slung over one shoulder, and he had a nasty-looking knife stuck in his belt. His calf-length boots looked expensive.

I had a good view of them, because he jumped up on a wall beside me and started haranguing the mujaheddin, pointing to us and getting very excited.

'Problem,' said our translator. 'He wants them kill you.'

You, you notice. It was like that ancient joke about Tonto and the Lone Ranger: 'Tonto, we're surrounded by Indians.' 'What you mean *we*, white man?'

There were four of *us*, the cameraman, sound recordist, producer, and me. The mujaheddin numbered around eighteen.

The harangue went on for some time, but with a certain relief I could see the man in white wasn't getting anywhere. The audience listened carefully, and considered the merits of the case judiciously. But in the end they voted along party lines: the extreme Hezbe men in favour of the proposition, the moderate Jamiat men against. It was a good job we had chosen this particular mujaheddin post; there was another a few hundred yards up the road where the proportions were reversed, and Hezbe had a majority.

The Arab could, I suppose, have used his AK-47 on us, but the Jamiat group, with that sense of hospitality you always get in Muslim communities, had decided that we were their guests and that they were therefore obliged to protect us as long as we stayed with them. If he had killed any of us, the rules of the game would have obliged them to kill him. Very comforting.

Anyway, once that was settled we went back to recording my piece to camera. I had to kneel down so the cameraman could see the mortar firing behind me, and what with the ache in my knees and the loud explosions as each round went off, I suppose I rather took my eye off the man in white. After a while, though, I became aware of another haranguing, a little farther off. He was shouting at the driver of an ammunition truck.

'Says, come and run over infidel,' our friend translated, meaning me in particular. 'Says, he give five hundred dollars to do it.'

It wasn't much, and I felt obscurely annoyed at being priced so moderately. It certainly wasn't enough for the driver, who shook his head and laughed, and drove off in the direction of the road.

The figure in white ran off towards one of the archways under the road where the mujaheddin slept, and we followed him over there, intrigued.

We found him lying full length on a camp-bed, weeping and beating his fists on the pillow out of frustration at not being able to kill us. I almost felt like comforting him, but resisted, of course. We moved on quite soon after that: the tears wouldn't last for ever, and even five hundred dollars was a reasonable amount of money.

I never forgot his eyes, or his beard: setting one's prejudices aside, he was a splendid-looking character. We assumed he was a Wahabi, a member of the extreme Saudi Arabian fundamentalist sect which had become heavily involved in the war in Afghanistan. I had seen another member of the sect a few months earlier, as I queued up at a completely redundant Pakistani border post to show my passport before crossing into Afghanistan.

Distinctly less impressive-looking, he had hissed at me, 'If I see you across the border in Afghanistan I will kill you.'

Fortunately he hadn't seen me once we crossed the border; I was going too fast.

Nine years later I saw the face of the man in white again. The American press was full of excitable claptrap about Islamic fundamentalism, and a Saudi millionaire had suddenly become Washington's Public Enemy Number 1: Osama bin Laden. There he was in the newspaper photograph. The beard was a little greyer than when I had seen him standing on the wall lecturing the mujaheddin in their Islamic duty to butcher us, but the eyes still held that crazy, handsome glitter: the Desert Sheikh meets Hannibal Lecter.

Not long afterwards I sent him a message through a particularly good channel in Pakistan, asking him to record an interview with me. I received an answer a week or so later. The fundamentalist Taliban who now controlled most of Afghanistan were unwilling to allow him to speak in public, but if he were able to speak to anyone from the Western media, I would be the first. He himself wanted to do it, the message said, and in particular he wanted to speak to the BBC because its voice was heard everywhere.

Times change, and we change with them. This was Osama bin Laden's version of becoming mellower as he grew older. Now the genuine fanatic who once wept because he couldn't kill an infidel wanted to talk to the infidel in order to demonstrate that he was still fanatical.

It didn't happen, all the same.

Izhevsk is the kind of place any right-minded person would want to get out of from the moment they understood anything at all about the world. A thousand miles of flatness separate it from Moscow, and it is an ugly, boring, dusty little town with a few factories, a railway station, an Intourist hotel, and a main square with a statue of Lenin in it. Maybe the statue of Lenin has gone now; I'm not interested enough to want to go back there and find out.

There is only one thing which distinguishes Izhevsk from every other small Gogolesque city in Russia: from here has come the world's great Equalizer, the potential to make every bandit and terrorist and ragged volunteer a match for the best soldiers and policemen in the world. One of Izhevsk's dreary factories turns out the *Avtomat Kalashnikova*, first produced in 1947. We know it as the AK-47, and during the second half of the twentieth century it killed more good men and women than any other gun in existence. In its time the AK has convulsed entire nations: Gambia, Sierra Leone, Congo, Somalia, Sudan, Afghanistan, Tajikistan, Georgia, Bosnia, Lebanon.

I went to Izhevsk in the summer of 1988, because Mikhail Gorbachev was paying a visit there: perestroika and glasnost still meant something. It was hot, and pollen from the lime trees filled the air like snow. The local Party boss shook the great man's hand, and beamed for the photographers. As Westerners, we were there on sufferance: ten years before, if I had asked to film in Izhevsk, I would have laid myself open to accusations of industrial espionage. Now things had changed.

The security men were thick around Gorbachev, brutally pushing everyone out of the way if they came too near. One man, however, hovered by his elbow the whole time, and Gorbachev inclined his head to listen to him. He was short and stocky, and wore an open-necked shirt with short sleeves, a pair of slacks and plastic sandals. Mikhail Kalashnikov was the reason Gorbachev was in town. If it had not been for him, Izhevsk would have continued turning out second-rate guns as it had done since Catherine the Great's time.

It was only after Gorbachev had left, taking his security men with him, that I had a chance to talk to Kalashnikov. I tapped him on the arm as he finished waving goodbye. He was a very modest man, with the flat, open features of the Russian hinterland. Could I, I asked, put a few questions to him? He smiled shyly, as though he would rather be somewhere else, and then he nodded.

I asked him first how he had come to invent the AK-47. It was clearly a story he had told many times before.

'You see, I was a sergeant in the Great Patriotic War, and my tank was hit by a shell. I had injuries all over my body. So I spent a long time in hospital. And in the beds all round me were other soldiers, and they were always complaining about the same thing: the equipment they had was not as good as the weapons the Germans had.

'In particular our rifles. They jammed very quickly, and they were difficult to take apart. It needed a long time to unjam them, and a lot of our men were killed as a result. As I lay there in my bed I thought that I would invent a rifle which was simpler and better than the ones we had. I had always been interested in guns, and I was good with my hands.

'And so, even before the war was over, I began to work on it. I made each part stronger than before, and cut down the number of parts. I wanted to make a rifle you could take apart even if you were injured or couldn't see properly. And in the end I came up with the *Avtomat Kalashnikova*.

'It wasn't easy, and I had problems persuading the authorities to accept my prototype. But once they tried it, there were no more problems.'

The AK-47 is the simplest of weapons. I have seen a fourteen-year-old strip one down in Afghanistan, oil it, clean it and reassemble it in a matter of a few minutes. Because the aim is simplicity, it has fewer parts that can go wrong. It is not as accurate as other weapons, but it has a ferocious rate of fire. And it is the ultimate status symbol, more than half a century after its invention.

In warfare in the Third World, no one prefers a complex American or German automatic weapon. Afghans still trade in their foreign-made guns in exchange for Russian AK-47s; Chinese-made ones are well thought of, though they are not as highly prized as the Izhevsk models. Even a Pakistani-made version has a certain value. It has been estimated that 80 million AK-47s have been made, and that the majority of them are still in use. The Kalashnikov is the very symbol of terrorism and resistance.

'There must be times when you reflect on all the misery that your invention has caused the world.'

His answer was as well-rehearsed as Arkan's about atrocities.

'Of course I am sorry that anyone should blame the AK-47 for anything. But you see I am very proud of what I have achieved with this weapon. People say it is the best in the world; and it is not my fault, or the AK's fault, if it is used in the wrong way. Terrorists use it, I know. People often tell me that. But the people who should be criticized are those who allow them to be used.'

'You mean your own government, which exports them?'

Kalashnikov was too embarrassed by the question to answer.

At this time, he was seventy: yet he continued to work at the weapons factory which produced his brainchild, the world's best assault rifle. He had earned scarcely anything from the enormous international sales of the AK-47; his way, perhaps, of avoiding the guilt. He had an ordinary flat in Izhevsk, with one separate bedroom and a sitting room which served as another bedroom at night. He drove a Lada car, and he had a small dacha in the countryside outside the city.

His modesty was admirable; and yet in terms of the effects of what he had done – the number of people killed and the amount of misery caused – I have never met anyone worse in my life. He might merely have been in charge of designing the machinery; but it was the machinery, in its extraordinary efficiency, which did the damage. Andrei Sakharov, having been the father of the Soviet Union's nuclear weapons, became the country's leading political dissident. Mikhail Kalashnikov, one of the few ordinary Russians whose name is known in every country in the world, felt no remorse, and later went into politics on his own account. Perhaps it doesn't matter: his remorse would not have saved a single life. But the basic point is that you do not have to be evil to do evil. In an industrial and post-industrial world, it is sometimes enough merely to be efficient.

For the first time in weeks I woke up to silence: or, at least, to the silence of the guns. In its place there were other noises: the noises of a city beginning its day. The siege of Sarajevo was suspended for a couple of days, thanks to the UN. The Bosnian Serb artillery on the mountain tops surrounding us had gone quiet, and people were able to venture out of their shelters into the morning sunshine.

My camera crew and I went out with them, driving along in our clumsy armour-plated Land-Rover. Two hours of peace, and the café-owners had put out chairs and tables in the sun. Already customers were sitting down and enjoying themselves in safety for the first time in months. As for us, we felt completely liberated. We knew, as the people around us did, that wasn't going to last. The Bosnian Serbs would always claim that the Bosnian government forces had broken the truce and would start firing again; and anyway the Bosnian government wasn't enthusiastic about truces. Its main hope was to drag the United States into the war on its side, which meant impressing American television viewers with the sufferings of the people of Sarajevo. So both sides had a vested interest in making the ordinary people suffer; that's the Balkans for you.

The siege of Sarajevo by the Bosnian Serbs was the worst crime I have ever witnessed, but that doesn't make the Bosnian government entirely guiltless. I liked several members of the Bosnian government as individuals, and detested the loathsome General Ratko Mladić who organized the siege and the ludicrous fanatic Radovan Karadžić who had instigated it. But the only side I really sympathized with in this entire miserable war was the side that was totally unrepresented by any of the politicians: the ordinary inhabitants of the city.

There was no suffering this morning. You could see the enjoyment on the drawn faces of the people as they turned them to the sunlight. It was cold and there was snow on the ground, but it covered the heaps of rubble from the shelling and there was something bracing and hopeful in the air which made you feel that in spite of everything – the food shortages, the lack of power, the anxiety about water supplies, the war damage, the uncertain duration of the truce – life was worth living.

We filmed for a while, then sat down at a little outside café that had sprung up out of a previously shuttered and war-damaged house and drank tiny cups of bitter coffee with some kind of ersatz sweetener. It tasted extraordinarily good in the sharp air. Then I saw her: a young woman in her late twenties, wearing a widow's black cloak and holding hands with her two little sons. There was a look of ineffable sadness on her beautiful face. In the devastation of Sarajevo, on this bright wintry morning, she looked like the personi-fication of the city.

We invited her to sit down with her children and have a cup of coffee. There was a listlessness about the way she agreed which showed that she felt nothing in life had much meaning. She even spoke good English. Her name was Yasmina, she said, and her husband had been killed on Mount Zuć – she pointed to it, across on the outskirts of the city – six weeks earlier. Now she had nothing left but her two boys. No, she didn't object to being interviewed: why should she? What she meant was that she didn't care whether she lived or died.

'The Bosnian Serbs have agreed this truce, and it seems to be holding. You must be relieved to be able to come out into the sunshine in safety?'

Yes, she said, though it was obvious she didn't care.

'And what are you hoping for now?'

It was a tabloid newspaper question, but one that might just possibly bring some more active response.

Her face took on a sudden life, and she looked at me as though she had noticed me for the first time.

'I hope that those who have killed my husband and made me suffer will suffer ten times as much as I have. I hope they and their mothers and their wives and their children will suffer for ever.'

The cameraman looked at the translator, and I looked away. This naked intensity of emotion was something none of us could cope with, like a sudden surge of power down an electrical cable. I thanked her, and said goodbye.

'I can't somehow see you using that,' said the cameraman, as we looked for someone else to interview.

It was more than a week later before I heard from Yasmina again. The truce had broken down, and the shelling had resumed, though some of the phones seemed to be working. Directly I heard that empty, flat voice at the other end of the line I knew whose it was.

'Please, I need some help. Can I come and speak to you?'

She arrived at the hotel half an hour later, climbing as we all had to through one of the windows which had been blown out by the shelling. It was dark and freezing cold in the vast lobby, and not altogether safe. But my room was almost unbearably cold, and our office, though heated by our generator, was full of people drinking whisky. Besides, she sounded as though she wanted to speak to me in private.

We settled down on one of the garish sofas in the lobby. The gloom was so intense that I could only just make out her lovely features.

I was, she said, the only person she could think of to ask for advice; she didn't know any other Westerners, and this was a matter only a Westerner could help her with. It was clear then why she had come to see me: she wanted to get out of Sarajevo. People constantly begged the foreign journalists in Sarajevo to help them escape. Once or twice it had even worked.

It was one of the most disgraceful features of the siege of Sarajevo that the United Nations forces, which were supposedly in the city to help the inhabitants, actually policed the siege for the Bosnian Serbs. The UN controlled the airport, and refused to allow any of the inhabitants to leave the city unless they were employed by the media; in which case it was ludicrously easy for them to catch a plane and reach the outside world. UN planes would take off each day when the shelling allowed, taking soldiers, UN employees and journalists; and yet the UN would not take the sick, the badly injured or the desperate out of the city. If they had, the argument went, they would be siding with the Bosnian government and the Bosnian Serbs would regard the UN as combatants.

I could see the Lewis Carroll logic, but it seemed intolerable to me that the UN should ignore so much suffering; and I had done my part, as many journalists did, to help one or two deserving cases leave. If I had done more, I would have felt rather better with myself.

But why should this woman, who plainly didn't care if she lived or died, want to escape?

'My children,' she said. There was a short silence. 'And I cannot bear to be here, where I used to be with him. It is a worse torture than anything you can understand. Everywhere I go, he is there. I have no peace. I don't care for myself what risks I run, but I cannot take the children out through the tunnel. I must go by plane. That was what my husband told me. He said, If they kill me you must get out of here with the children. I promised him.'

The tunnel was certainly an escape route, but it had particular dangers. There was another: running across the airport in the darkness. But, to their great discredit, the UN soldiers would catch escapers and turn them back. People did escape that way, but only the young and fit.

'I don't see how I could help your children get out.'

'Oh, that's all arranged. I know how to do it. I just need someone's advice on whether it's safe.'

'Safe?'

It seemed a strange concept, under these circumstances. From time to time the journalists who were the only inhabitants of the Holiday Inn would come through the lobby and see us talking there, our breath curling up above us in the freezing atmosphere. Sometimes, too, there would be a distant explosion as the filthy war ground on, taking its daily toll of the innocent.

'I mean, will it work? I don't care what I have to do, but I'll go mad if I stay here any more.'

'It can't work, with your children.'

'Oh yes, it can. He's promised me.'

'Who has?'

And then it came out. In the UN headquarters there was a fairly senior figure who, in exchange for money, was in a position to get the necessary papers and permissions. She said his name; I even knew him slightly.

'You've seen him?'

She nodded, without looking at me.

'And he told you he would get the children out?'

She nodded again.

'I've heard that he does get people out. It's quite easy, if you've got the papers. I just never heard that he could get children out.'

'If I pay him enough, he will.'

'And you've got the money?'

'It's not just money.'

I began to see what the price might be. I'd heard the rumours.

'I must sleep with him. And pay three thousand Deutschmarks each.'

'And you're prepared to do this?'

'What do I care?'

I could see that sleeping with a venal UN official would mean nothing more to her than sitting here in the cold lobby of the hotel, talking. But it enraged me that he should take advantage of her pain like this.

'All that worries me is, will he do what he promises?'

'I'll go and see him,' I said.

'Be careful.'

She wasn't worrying about my safety.

At the old telecommunications building where the United Nations had set up its headquarters, security was in the hands of the French Foreign Legion. I drove round in the BBC Land-Rover, willing it up the steep, icy slope and letting it run into a natural parking place near a line of the strangely designed armoured personnel carriers the French drove about in. A *légionnaire* stood in the entrance to the security checkpoint, his blue helmet on the back of his head, his front teeth missing, his hands in the armholes of his flak-jacket.

'How're ya dòin'?'

No point in speaking French to him: he was from somewhere outside Belfast: County Down, I should guess. I didn't ask; with *légionnaires* it was bad form. I showed him my UN accreditation and he gave me the lightest of security checks. I wandered through. There was some shooting going on at the Jewish cemetery up on the hill above the PTT building, but nothing to worry anyone here. Not enough did worry the UN, it seemed to me. There was another checkpoint inside, where they were a little stricter. I wasn't carrying anything of interest to them anyway.

I knew the office the UN man worked in. It was, as always, full of people hanging round, waiting for something: the worst and most inquisitive of audiences. We couldn't talk about anything so private here.

'Hi,' I said, trying to sound as though I liked him.

'Hi.'

Although I knew him, I doubt if he knew me. He was offhand, as though I was the last person he was interested in meeting. Probably I was.

'I've come to see you about Yasmina,' I said quietly.

He steered me into a side-office.

'She told you about our – arrangement?'

At the thought of it, his eyes seemed to twinkle. He gave me an all-lads-together grin, self-deprecating yet proud of himself. I felt like grabbing him by the throat, but I resisted.

'She's very beautiful, no?'

I knew exactly then who he reminded me of, not physically in any way, but morally: the police chief in *Casablanca*, played by Claud Rains, who lets people out of Vichy-controlled Morocco if their wives sleep with him.

> *Policeman*: Excuse me, Captain; another visa problem has come up.
>
> *Claude Rains* [*Going to the mirror and adjusting his tie*]: Show her in.

I suppose I should have told him that what he was doing was beneath contempt, but it would have sounded pompous, and anyway he might have changed his mind about helping her to leave.

'She just wants to be certain that you'll help her.'

'Of course I'll help her. Wouldn't you?'

'Because I'll know if you don't.'

The officer laughed. 'You don't have to worry. She will be safe. She and the children will all go.'

He might have been despicable, but at least he ensured that some people could leave the city. Even if he was only in it for sex and money, he was doing what the UN itself should have been doing: breaking the siege. His colleagues were catching people who tried to escape and returning them to this hell. It was at that point that I decided finally not to mention this subject to anyone, or broadcast or write about it until the siege was over. The man was doing the right thing: it was just the price that was wrong.

I saw Yasmina very briefly on the day she left Sarajevo. I wasn't even certain whether we met by accident, or she had come to say goodbye. Did you sleep with him, I wanted to ask, but the beautiful empty eyes turned slowly to meet mine and I lacked the courage. Why did I want to know, anyway?

'I hope everything goes well with you and the boys,' I said, for the want of anything better to say.

She shook my hand and echoed, '*Well?*'

I have never been able to forget the utter despair with which she said that word.

You do not have to do anything positive to help the cause of evil; it is often enough to do nothing at all. This is the story of a group of decent, benevolent men and women who could have done something about the greatest evil of the twentieth century; and decided not to.

I came across the case in 1997, when I was making a series of television documentaries about the International Committee of the Red Cross. The experience left me with little except dislike for the ICRC, though I came to have a great deal of respect for many of the delegates who worked in the field.

Altogether we filmed in four continents. Sometimes, as when we drove up into the mountains near the city of Bucaramanga in Colombia and filmed an ICRC delegate making contact with a group of left-wing guerrillas who had kidnapped a businessman and were holding him there, I was deeply impressed by the work the ICRC was doing. The businessman was later released as a result.

But as an institution the International Committee of the Red Cross has never managed to shake off the effects of what it failed to do during the Second World War. In recent years its President, a stout and rather pompous character called Dr Cornelio Sommaruga, has spent a good deal of time touring the world apologizing for his organization's wartime record. These apologies, in the nature of things, are never quite enough to satisfy those who feel that the ICRC, through its feebleness and lack of moral courage, betrayed them and their relations.

'I am convinced my predecessors could have done more, could have been more active,' he says.

That is pretty much the extent of the apology. Big institutions, and they don't come much bigger than the ICRC, have a rooted dislike of admitting that they might have been wrong.

Nevertheless in 1997 the ICRC had become sufficiently disturbed about its reputation to allow the BBC to have unprecedented and exclusive access to its operations around the world, and to inspect its archives. As it happens – and this, too, seemed rather typical of the ICRC – it also promised much the same thing at the same time to the writer Caroline Moorhead, who is a good friend and colleague of mine. The moment when she and the documentary's producers realized that we had both been promised the same exclusive was an interesting one, but we agreed to co-exist on our projects and all turned out well. Her book, *Dunant's Dream*, was published at the same time as our documentaries were broadcast.

The ICRC's basic problem during the Second World War was that it was a wholly Swiss organization, and the government of Switzerland was represented on it. So although it had great international responsibilities, and was the only organization capable of overseeing the interests of the wounded and the prisoners of war on all sides, it was also an unofficial arm of the Swiss government. And the moment came when it was forced to choose between its humanitarian obligations and its Swissness. It chose Swissness.

The ICRC had other problems. The most energetic and effective figure on the Committee was Dr Carl Burckhardt, who later in the war became the ICRC's President. Burckhardt was a Swiss-German; and that seems to have given his sympathies a marked pro-German tilt. Like many people of his class and time, Burckhardt was terrified by Communism, and saw Nazi Germany as Europe's bastion against the Soviet Union.

In 1935 he visited several German concentration camps on behalf of the ICRC and found them 'hard but correct'. One of these camps was Dachau. His aim in going there was not so much concern for the inhabitants as the desire to demonstrate that the ICRC had the right and the ability to visit the camps. Once the war had begun and people began to die in large numbers in the camps, this was a right which Burckhardt showed no interest in asserting again.

In 1936 he went back to Germany, where he met the Nazi leadership and was enchanted with them. In the ICRC archives we found the letter he wrote to Adolf Hitler on his return to Geneva. It ended:

> What especially and permanently impressed itself upon me was the spirit of co-operation which informed everything. It opened a whole new vista and understanding for me.
>
> Your deeply devoted, deeply grateful and deeply respectful,
>   Carl Burckhardt

This, then, was one of the key figures whose intervention would soon be required if the victims of the concentration camps were to be saved – those camps which he had found 'hard but correct'.

From 1941 onwards, as the deportations began and the cattle trucks made their long journeys across the face of Europe, the ICRC archives are full of emotional letters from individuals and national Red Cross committees:

> My brother has been deported from Romania. Is it possible to find any news of him?

> We have desperately anxious relatives here in England enquiring about their family members in Occupied Europe. Please help us.

> My committee has received disquieting news that hundreds of Jews, particularly old people, are being deported from this country.

There were heartbreaking scenes in Budapest station: pregnant women collapsed during the transportation, children separated from their parents screamed and wept from fear and shock.

Thousands of Jews headed for the safety of Switzerland, only to find that it had closed its borders to them.

On the third floor of an anonymous office block in the centre of Geneva is the headquarters of the World Jewish Congress. It was in these rooms in 1942 that Gerhard Riegner, who still works there, first heard that someone had arrived from Berlin with a disturbing message. Riegner, a short, plump man now in his eighties, sun-tanned and prosperous-looking with a hoarse, harsh voice, still refuses to name the man in question, but he was an important German industrialist who had recently met Himmler, Heydrich, Eichmann and other participants at the Wannsee Conference which decided the fate of the Jews. Realizing the scale of the task they had undertaken – the entire elimination of Jews, Gypsies and other races – the Nazi leaders called in professional help: the leaders of German industry.

This man had listened in horror to the instructions he was given. He did not feel able to refuse, but at the first opportunity he took the dangerous step of leaving Germany and going to Switzerland. He sought out Riegner, and told him what was going to happen. There was, he said, still a little time: the extermination camps would not be operational until September or October 1942. Perhaps an international appeal could be launched?

The news tortured Gerhard Riegner.

'These were the most terrible years of my life. Here there was beauty, sunshine, Mont Blanc, the Lake – and a few miles from here, Hell started.'

He made urgent contact with the British and American embassies, but the diplomats there refused to believe him. His only hope was the International Committee of the Red Cross. He had carefully cultivated several of the Committee members in the past few years, and now he went to see each of them in turn, impressing on them the urgent need to do something to forestall the German plan.

There were twenty-five members of the Committee. All those he spoke to were deeply shocked by his news, and fully in favour of launching an appeal to the world on behalf of the millions who had been sentenced to death. But the weeks slipped by, and it was only after pressure had been brought on the Committee's president that he agreed to call a special session to discuss the issue.

It was held at the Metropole Hotel on Wednesday, 14 October 1942. Across the border in Germany and farther off in Poland, Czechoslovakia and Ukraine the extermination camps were already coming into operation. A preliminary sounding of the twelve members of the Committee had shown that nine were in favour of making an appeal on behalf of the civilians who were imprisoned and facing death. It seemed like a certainty.

Already, though, the revisionists had been at work. The appeal would not be made to the Germans only, demanding that they should stop the genocide of the Jews and others. Instead, it was a watered-down, generalized exhortation to all the belligerent countries to respect the rights and lives of civilians. Even so, the reason for the appeal would have leaked out, and the exercise might have done some good.

One of the Committee's twelve members had never attended a meeting before. This was Philippe Etter, a government minister who was now, according to the devolved constitution of Switzerland, acting President of the country. Etter was a curious-looking man, his ears oddly cocked back on either side of an entirely bald head. Above his habitual starched wing-collar this made it look like a large brown egg on a plate.

The meeting began at 2.30 in the afternoon, and the appeal was the only item on the agenda. The dry minutes, typed in French, took on a remarkable drama as I read them in the ICRC archive room.

They showed that member after member argued in favour of making a public statement, especially the four women on the Committee. Mme. Frick-Cramer, for instance:

> The Committee simply cannot keep silent in the face of the worsening methods of war and the extension of hostilities to the civilian population. If we keep quiet, we could risk the very existence of the Committee after the War.

Speaker after speaker agreed, until there were only two who had not given their opinion. The first was Carl Burckhardt. He took issue irritably with someone who had said that making an appeal like this was a courageous act. He couldn't see why it was so courageous. To him, it simply risked annoying the belligerent nations; by which he meant the Germans. He advised strongly against doing it.

Last of all came Philippe Etter, who was speaking with the full weight of the Swiss government. He was much more emollient than Burckhardt. He found the initiative truly noble – but he just had one or two slight hesitations about it. Firstly, he reminded them, the central principle of the International Red Cross was that they should be impartial, as between different belligerent countries; but since it was only Germany and not the Allies who were deliberately waging war on civilians, how could they possibly be impartial? The appeal was clearly directed at one side. It would negate everything the International Red Cross stood for if they issued this appeal, and it might destroy all the good they had done. Finally, there was the practical danger to the Swiss nation. Who knew? The Germans might be so angered by this one-sided appeal that they would invade Switzerland itself.

All round the table the arguments for humanity and nobility collapsed: Switzerland itself could be in danger.

Just before 5.00 it was put to the vote. Which members wished to send this general appeal? The minutes record the result in their tidy typewritten letters:

> No Members of the Committee were in favour of this.

So the organization as a whole decided to do nothing. It would continue to help prisoners of war, but it would interpret its statutes strictly and concentrate only on combatants. In this war against civilians, the civilians were on their own.

One of the key figures in our documentary was an elderly man called Maurice Rossel, who had been a delegate of the ICRC in Berlin for much of the war, and had managed to get into several concentration camps. To me he sounded rather engaging. He lived for six months of the year on his own in the Swiss mountains, studying philosophy and collecting old farm implements which he restored and displayed in a barn behind his cottage. Then, when the days grew shorter and autumn came, Rossel would return to his wife and their house in the nearby town. He had never spoken publicly about his wartime experiences. For our documentary, though, he was prepared to go on camera and answer questions.

The cottage was charming. Cows grazed in the field beside it, their bells tinkling faintly. A rabbit ran across the open ground. Bees fumbled in the phloxes and hollyhocks in front of the door. A sundial was set on the wall; *'Lente Hora, Celeriter Anni'*, it said in the usual complaint of the elderly: the hours go slowly, the years fast.

'I delight in speaking with old men, as living histories,' the seventeenth-century antiquary and gossip John Aubrey wrote, and I share his feeling. I was looking forward to meeting an old man who had seen so much and now lived the idyllic life of the philosopher.

'You're late,' complained the philosopher when we arrived.

He was in his late eighties, with the almost feminine softening of the features which some old men develop. He must have been good-looking once, I thought, with those liquid dark brown eyes and the self-consciously attractive Maurice Chevalier twinkle in them. For the time being, though, he was annoyed with us. We were too many in number, too slow, too intrusive, and I was too big and not articulate enough in French for him. He spoke to me in the deliberate, precise way you speak to children. And although he had never been interviewed before, everything he said sounded carefully rehearsed.

'I was chosen to be a delegate in Berlin. I packed a little suitcase and left for Basle, where I took the express and arrived in Berlin. Training and instruction? None. Quite simply none.'

At first I thought I rather liked him. He sounded like a rebel, and he criticized the ICRC leadership as being too pro-German. And yet there was always something faintly defensive about what he said, as though he were preparing his defences at this stage for something that might come up later in our interview. What that something might be, I didn't know.

'The ICRC had no right whatever to inspect or criticize or transmit information about civilian internees. Only people covered by the Geneva Convention: that is, military people.'

'But you had great freedom of operation in Berlin, because Geneva was a long way away and communication was so difficult. You could do whatever you wanted. You could, for instance, have condemned the terrible things you must have seen when you went to these concentration camps.'

A look of intense irritation crossed his face.

'It was extremely difficult to put in jeopardy an organization which is responsible for the lives of so many men – six million prisoners of war, to be exact. Would you want to put that at risk just to kick up a fuss and say something which the Allied governments already knew?'

I recognized the tone. It was that combination of officious timidity and defensiveness which I had encountered time and again in dealing with the ICRC – the retreat behind the rules.

Rossel described how, in order to get to the concentration camps, he would go out to the nightclubs of Berlin and Vienna with senior SS officers and bribe them to give him the necessary passes. They particularly wanted nylon stockings to give to their mistresses, and Camel cigarettes for themselves.

The thought that this strange, half-feminine old man might once have sat in nightclubs with senior SS officers drinking champagne and ogling the cabaret was a curious one. But why did he want to go to see the camps, given that the International Red Cross was not prepared to perform any useful protective function for the prisoners and he himself had made it clear it was his own initiative?

I didn't put the question clearly enough, and he didn't answer it anyway. Later I wondered if it was just in order to say he'd done it – a kind of war tourism, a professional curiosity. It seemed not to be from any humanitarian motive, since he scarcely spoke about the condition of the prisoners. At Auschwitz he got no farther than the *Oberstürmbannführer*'s office.

'Weren't you tempted to ask him what was really going on in the shower blocks at the camp?'

'Can you really envisage putting those questions to a chap you know won't reply, who will simply make fun of you? It'd be the end of the conversation, wouldn't it? Oh yes, I can really imagine it: "Excuse me, *Oberstürmbannführer*, how many thousands of people are you gassing in your showers every week, every month?" You can imagine how well that would go down. Don't forget, I had to get out of there alive. It wasn't guaranteed.'

But why did he have to get out of there alive? What was so important about going to these places where terrible things were happening, *if he did nothing about them*? What was so important about living, if he could bring no help to the dying?

We moved on to the question of his visit to the concentration camp at Theresienstadt, in Czechoslovakia. He was edgy and irritable now, and I was coming to dislike him intensely.

For some occult reason the SS decided late in 1943 to turn Theresienstadt into a show-place. It seems almost insane; the concentration camps and their horrors were something to be hidden rather than boasted about, and who anyway would believe that they were really like holiday camps?

Maurice Rossel and the ICRC did; or at least they pretended they did. The invitation to visit Theresienstadt eventually came in June 1944, after the SS had spent months easing the pressure on the hideously overcrowded camp by sending eighteen thousand prisoners to the extermination camps earlier than scheduled, and fattening up those who remained. The SS were going to make a film about the place as well.

In Israel we interviewed two women in their early seventies who had been friends in Theresienstadt and had stayed together ever since. Now they live on a kibbutz in Israel and run a small museum about the camp. Even their names are almost the same: Alisah Schiller and Alisa Shek. One is thin and grey-haired, the other is well-built and blonde. They bicker and correct each other, like all couples who have stayed together for a long time, but their friendship has endured through everything, including the extermination of all their relatives. They were both fifteen in 1944.

'We were told there was a commission coming from the Red Cross,' says Alisa Shek, 'and that the camp must look spick and span. People started to sow grass on the big square where the soldiers had exercised. They had to scrub the streets and paint the façades of the houses where the commission would go.'

The SS imposed the strictest limitations on Maurice Rossel. They forbade him to speak privately to the prisoners, and they accompanied him everywhere and at all times while he was in the camp. So why, I asked him, did he agree to go? There was no answer: just a shrug of the shoulders and a projection of the lower lip.

Rossel insisted that it was a terrible experience for him. He was shown the prisoners sitting reading in the sunshine, or listening to the orchestra which played classical music, or eating good meals.

'It was horrifying: a Kafkaesque drama which you had to live through to understand. To be there, as in a piece of theatre, when you knew that was all it was. It was a farce. And to know they were condemned to death!'

But he didn't put any of this in his report to Geneva. Instead, he described the camp precisely as the SS showed it to him.

'Some people probably thought the Red Cross would see through the whole bluff, but they were mistaken,' Alisa Shek says.

'I'm not so sure,' interjects her friend, Alisah Schiller. 'I'm not sure they didn't see through it.'

'I'm sure they didn't, because of the report we read afterwards. They said it was much better than they'd thought it would be, conditions were good.'

'Yes, but I think there were political reasons too, not only that they—'

'And it's the lack of imagination of the Swiss.'

'Ah, yes.'

The two elderly ladies carry on this way for a long time as they sit in the Israeli sunlight, disagreeing companionably. They must have had the same argument dozens of times before.

As for Rossel, he comes out of the whole episode very badly. It was one thing to meet the commandant of Auschwitz face to face and not challenge him about the thousands of daily murders. But to play the dupe at Theresienstadt seems somehow worse than playing the coward at Auschwitz.

'Why didn't you include these details in your report?'

'I knew my report would be sent to Geneva by the diplomatic bag. I knew therefore that the Gestapo would have it in twenty-four hours, and I would soon have to be making requests of them again.'

Those pointless requests, to allow him to be a tourist at yet another place of mass-murder.

'And I didn't want to get the ICRC into trouble.'

'You couldn't go to Geneva and make your report face to face?'

'It was possible but difficult. I made the journey only twice. It wasn't a piece of cake.'

At the time Alisa and Alisah, the fifteen-year-olds, thought that at least the transport of prisoners from Theresienstadt to the death camps would stop as a result of Rossel's visit. But that was in June, and by September nearly 30,000 people had been put in the cattle trucks for Auschwitz. He achieved nothing by going there, except to play the game as the SS wanted.

'Can you be proud of what you did?'

'I'm not ashamed. I could say I made mistakes back then. Of course I've been useless at times. I'm just a mediocre person.'

I didn't believe he thought this for a moment. I felt constrained by his age from following the line of questioning too heavily, but I couldn't let it peter out altogether.

'In the night, isn't there sometimes a voice in your head that says, "If only I'd told the Commandant at Auschwitz that what he was doing was horrendous"?'

'That's never happened, and it wouldn't occur to me because these people were proud of their work. They were convinced they were purifying Europe. They were proud of what they did, not ashamed of it.

'Either you get that into your head or you haven't understood anything. You know nothing about the ways of the SS. Nothing.'

By now the sly wit has vanished, and been replaced by anger.

'You are naïve, really naïve. But it will pass. You will see. Innocence doesn't last long.'

At last we came to an end. I found it hard to speak to him as we packed up the camera gear and the lights: not because I was annoyed at being called naïve, but because I was embarrassed by his cowardice and lack of self-understanding. The question I should have asked him was the question I wanted to ask again and again of the ICRC itself: if it couldn't do any good, what on earth was the purpose of its existence?

Maurice Rossel, the man who failed to tell the world about the concentration camps, waved us goodbye as we left with a sweeping gesture of his arm, as though he were sweeping us out of his life for good. He would never, he said, speak about these things in public again.

But when he sat in his cottage looking out over the sunny meadows and laid his philosophy book aside, what were the images that came to his head? The doomed orchestra playing to the doomed audience? The specially fed children playing in the sandpit? The SS men saying please and excuse me to their victims? Or the truckloads of skeletal wretches who had hoped that his visit would save them from the death camps?

How could anyone live with that much failure to stand up and say what was really happening?

4

SPIES

In a mad world it always seems simpler to obey. Wormold led the stranger through a door at the back, down a short passage, and indicated the toilet. 'It's in there.'

'Please will you explain . . . ?'

'Can't be too careful even in a Gents, when I come to think of it. A chap of ours in Denmark in 1940 saw from his own window the German fleet coming down the Kattegat.'

'What gut?'

'Kattegat. Of course he knew then the balloon had gone up. Started burning his papers. Put the ashes down the lav and pulled the chain. Trouble was – late frost. Pipes frozen. All the ashes floated up into the bath down below. Flat belonged to an old maiden lady – Baronin someone or other. She was just going to have a bath. Most embarrassing for our chap.'

'It sounds like the Secret Service.'

'It *is* the Secret Service, old man, or so the novelists call it.'

Graham Greene, Our Man In Havana, 1958

The most seductive word in English is 'secret'. On the front of a newspaper or a magazine it has something of the effect that printing photographs of Princess Diana once had.

The word has less pull in the United States, where people expect their governments to be open with them and are always surprised when of course they are not; or in France, where they assume their governments always hide everything from them anyway.

In Britain, however, we aspire to freedom of information but are rarely allowed by one of the most secretive of systems to know what is going on. Few people know the difference between the acronyms MI5 and MI6, and fewer still realize that they are not the proper names for the Security Service and the Secret Intelligence Service. But it doesn't matter. For us, the mere fact that they are secret is enough to titillate the public mind.

Originally, the word 'spy' had shameful connotations. As late as the First World War a British ambassador famously refused to open a set of intercepted letters, even though they might affect national security; he thought it ungentlemanly to tamper with other people's mail. But in the treacherous, guilt-ridden twentieth century the secret agent suited the *Zeitgeist* perfectly, with his uncertain loyalties, his questionable identity, his evasions and betrayals. Until the Soviet agent Kim Philby came under suspicion for helping Donald Maclean and Guy Burgess escape to Russia, he was tipped as the next or next but one head of SIS.

Fiction merely followed suit; and where else has spy fiction reached such high levels as in Britain? The links are as old as the English novel itself. The Restoration author Aphra Behn was a secret agent, and so in a less glamorous way was Daniel Defoe. By the First World War the genre had established itself as the natural one for clubmen, gentlemen adventurers and patriots. Somerset Maugham, and later Graham Greene, gave it greater realism. By the 1970s it had become the glum vehicle for post-imperial blues, all about betrayal and failure. And yet alongside the depressive figures from Le Carré, James Bond continued pulling in the cinema audiences, as irreflective and macho as ever.

You might assume that the real spies would find the antics of James Bond an embarrassment, and that they would prefer the apparent realism of Greene and Le Carré. Not so. Some years ago I found myself in the headquarters of the Secret Intelligence Service, commonly but not accurately known as MI6, having lunch with its boss, a charming man, bluff yet subtle, with whitish hair and sprouting eyebrows. Ian Fleming would have called him 'M', of course, but like each of his predecessors since Sir Mansfield Cumming, who founded SIS in 1909, he was really known as 'C'. This particular incarnation of the title was Sir Colin McColl, the first 'C' to be acknowledged and named officially.

We were in the new SIS headquarters at Vauxhall Cross, a post-modern office block on the south bank of the Thames which has extraordinary green touches to its façade and looks as though it might be something to do with the gardening industry. It is one of the least discreet buildings in London. Lunch was in a grand bow-fronted room overlooking the river, and was served on a crisp white tablecloth with good silver by precisely the kind of people you would expect to find serving at a British secret service lunch. A tall, discreet man poured the excellent but understated claret, and a small, plump, rosy-cheeked woman handed out the food. Neither of them looked at me much.

I was there as part of a charm offensive by SIS. The Major government was urging it to be less reclusive, and it had responded by inviting a series of editors from the media, one by one, to lunch and a chat. It wasn't the first time I had met Sir Colin; he had invited me to lunch once before, shortly after the end of the Gulf War, where it swiftly became clear to me that he knew a great deal more about Iraq than I did, even though I had just come back after almost six months in Baghdad.

That time I had been driven in an SIS car to the previous headquarters, Century House in Lambeth, a hideous and inadequate 1960s tower block, which I was mildly surprised to find staffed by precisely the kind of people you might find in any other government office: despatch riders in leathers and earrings, secretaries in their early twenties giggling in the lifts, women in late middle age carrying files, young executives wearing braces. I don't quite know what I expected, but it wasn't normality.

There had been a petrol station in the forecourt of Century House, staffed by ex-servicemen; partly to help guard the place, partly to give it protective colouring. Now, though, SIS was moving. Several departments had already gone to Vauxhall Cross, and the forecourt garage was empty. It was, Sir Colin had murmured, his greatest anxiety that the IRA would plant a car bomb in front of Century House; and once the move had been completed successfully and they were in the security of their new headquarters, he said he could sleep easily for the first time in months.

Outside on the Thames, barges made their way down-river. Rain beat against the windows. I had already explained how bad it was for a journalist to get a reputation for being too close to SIS, and that I would always want to write and broadcast about them openly – though without revealing anything that might compromise their security. Journalists and spies had one important thing in common: they both dealt in information, but their techniques were completely different. The spy's trade was secrecy, mine was openness. I would, I said, be as open as possible about my links with them; in fact I would be writing about this particular meeting. I thought they took that rather well. Then, in order to ease the atmosphere, I made some disparaging remark about the James Bond industry.

'In fact we find it rather useful in recruiting people,' said Sir Colin serenely from the head of the table. 'People equate us with the image, d'you see.'

'British people?'

'And others. More others than British, I should say.'

It was true: British intelligence has always benefited from the extraordinary myths that cluster around it. After the collapse of Communism in Russia a KGB general told me that they had studied Ian Fleming's books, all of which were in the KGB's library, for clues to the way SIS operated. Leading Nazis had also been obsessed with the British secret service, and when he was at SS headquarters Reinhard Heydrich stocked the library with dozens of trashy British spy novels: William le Queux, Guy Boothby, even the 'Berry' books. Walter Schellenberg, who rose to become the head of the Gestapo, was another addict, spending remarkable amounts of time reading and filling his head with conspiracy theories.

In the Handbook which Schellenberg and his men produced for the invasion of Britain the account of the Secret Intelligence Service is remarkably detailed (two SIS men, Captain Best and Major Stevens, were caught in Holland by the Germans at the start of the War and thoroughly interrogated) while at the same time full of foolishness. In their book Schellenberg and his men include the theory that SIS was self-financing, and got its money either from selling its secrets to the British government or else from the Anglo-Iranian Oil Company; an early form of privatization. They thought Reuter's news agency, the *Daily Express* and the YMCA were all involved with British intelligence. In fact they thought that just about everybody was:

It does not matter whether it is a junior clerk of a branch office in the middle of the jungle who tells his consul what he has observed, or whether it is a rich globe-trotting lord who reports what he has seen on his journeys round the world. It is safe to assume that these reports, like those from companies, newspapers, travel agencies and shipping companies, end up at a central office. In recent times the Royal Institute of International Affairs, located at London's Chatham House, has been suspected (see the Special Wanted List).

There is an enduring and loony quality about the SIS myth. Almost sixty years after Schellenberg, the owner of Harrod's, Mohammed Al Fayed, accused British Intelligence of murdering Princess Diana and his son Dodi by engineering their car crash in 1997. No matter that the driver was a drunk and Dodi a macho playboy who liked to taunt the photographers who swarmed around them, and that the whole thing was clearly just a tragic, pointless accident. There are always surprising numbers of otherwise sensible people who can be persuaded to believe that British Intelligence intervened to prevent the mother of the heir to the throne from marrying a Muslim.

And yet overall SIS has benefited immensely from the myth about itself. Whatever the reality might be, people around the world still believe in a service staffed by hawk-featured, silent, cunning patriots; and they volunteer their services to it, less for money than for other motives – among which can sometimes be honour and conscience. In contrast to the disaster which befell the CIA when it became clear that Aldrich Ames, one of its central figures with access to the whole range of the Agencies operations in the Soviet bloc, had been working for the Russians, SIS ended the Cold War as the most successful of the major Western intelligence services. The damage of the Philby period had long since been repaired; and in Oleg Gordievsky, who worked for them out of principle and choice, SIS had had an agent in the top echelons of Soviet intelligence.

'I will only speak to SIS,' a Romanian Securitate colonel told me, shortly after the fall of Ceauşescu; he had been in charge of liaison with terrorist groups around the world, and wanted to shop them all. 'The others – CIA, the French, they are nothing. You must help to put me in contact with SIS.'

It was clear that in defecting he wanted to obtain a touch of class for himself; and class, thanks to the work of dozens of novelists, SIS had in abundance. Alas for the colonel and his ambitions, SIS also had Communist bloc defectors in abundance now that the Soviet bloc had collapsed. With generals and government ministers desperate to get onto the payroll, a mere colonel scarcely featured. The intermediary I had contacted, the British military attaché in Bucharest, was embarrassed to have to say it, but SIS wasn't interested.

Style is something SIS fosters enthusiastically. There is a particular cult of specialism; not in terms of intelligence work, but in completely unrelated fields – the more unrelated, it seems, the better. One leading figure was an international expert on a particular type of Oriental art; another, I was told with pride, had appeared on a list of the ten best young British novelists. And yet SIS had not turned its back on the ethos of John Buchan and Sandy Arbuthnot. In a cave in mountains to the east of Kabul I heard from a group of Afghan mujaheddin how a lone SIS operative had made his way through the snow across Russian-held territory to bring two million dollars to one of the most important Afghan leaders. He strapped the money round his body, they said. They were as impressed as though they had just finished reading *Greenmantle*.

Although the invitation to meet SIS had come from 'C', I had an agenda of my own in going there. I wanted to persuade him to give some kind of access, no matter how restricted, to the BBC's cameras. It seemed to me that now his identity had been published in the press and his headquarters was in one of the most conspicuous buildings in the whole of London, he might just consider taking the next step.

He didn't, of course.

'You must understand that the entire basis of our service is trust and secrecy. Our people place their careers and maybe their lives in our hands. If they saw me appearing on television or showing you round this place, the next thing they would ask themselves was, how soon before we start publishing their names?'

Useless to say this was not what I wanted; for him, as for his agents, it would be the first step down an extremely slippery slope. But Sir Colin was a charming if subtle man, and did not care to give me an outright no.

'I will certainly reflect on it further,' he said.

More than six months later, I received another invitation to lunch with SIS. This time I took a taxi.

'Vauxhall Cross? You one of them, then?'

I wasn't, I said.

'Oh, yeah? Well, you wouldn't tell me if you was, would you?'

That's what happens when you dabble in the affairs of the secret world: it rubs off on you.

I stepped into the strange, circular airlock at the entry to the building, peering through the glass like a pickled specimen in a natural history museum. I was met and taken upstairs in the lift. Each time the doors opened I caught more glimpses of the extraordinary ordinariness of the place: offices with notice boards on which calendars, holiday postcards and the finger-paintings of infants had been pinned, cups of tea, copies of the *Guardian* and the *Daily Mail*.

I was ushered into the dining room. Same view, same crisp white tablecloth, same encouraging crystal glasses, completely different set of people. On the two previous occasions I had had lunch there, three or four other leading officers from SIS had been with us. This time there was a new 'C', and a new group of top people. Amurath had succeeded Amurath, and the old order had been swept away. But there was one familiar voice.

'Hello, John. Long time since Cambridge.'

He came forward from the window, where the light had made it hard for me to see him, and shook hands. I recognized him at once. Richard and I had been good though not particularly close friends at university, but as with so many people from those days I had lost all sight of him. Now he seemed to be the number 2 in SIS, and in due time he would become 'C' himself. The thought that I had made Nescafé for a future spymaster and discussed James Joyce with him was very strange.

Lunch was pleasant enough, but my carefully placed lures had no attraction whatever for this new shoal of fish. The window which had opened briefly and narrowly in the frontage of SIS under Sir Colin McColl had now been firmly closed. I could forget the idea of the fly-on-the-wall documentary and the interview with 'C'. I could forget everything else too, including going there for lunch again. As I left, I knew I wouldn't be invited back.

Something came of it, even so. The new management at SIS had no objection to helping me with an article for the Christmas edition of the *Spectator* about the way they regarded spy fiction, and someone briefed me thoroughly about the range of authors who have passed through SIS at one stage or another: Maugham, who was allowed to write about some of his operations and even described the first 'C' ('The thing immediately noticeable about him was the closeness with which his blue eyes were set.'); Compton Mackenzie, who infuriated them by poking fun at them; Noel Coward, who pestered them to let him work for them as an agent in the United States during the Second World War, but despite being intensely patriotic was a little too high profile to be of much use; Graham Greene, who often financed his travels by getting small donations from SIS to top up his publishers' advances, yet who never provided information of any value and at last annoyed them intensely by writing a glowing introduction to Kim Philby's KGB-inspired memoirs.

And of course there was John Le Carré. He also irritated SIS, but by being gloomy rather than disloyal: it undercut the James Bond approach. Le Carré, whose real name is David Cornwell, worked for SIS in Germany for a short period in the 1950s: 'a very dull time, with nothing going on,' said one of the SIS people. 'No big operations, no big successes. He didn't do anything important, just a bit of backwards-and-forwardsing on the Eastern side. No wonder his view of us always seems to be so depressive.'

Berlin is nowadays a building-site with some good shops and a restaurant or two worth eating in. It is quite hard in places to work out where the Wall used to run; it has simply evaporated, leaving behind nothing but a few slabs of itself as a showpiece. One evening, before I left London to go to live in Dublin, I was walking along Royal Hospital Road to my old flat in Chelsea. It was cold, and I was deep in thought; but I thought I had spotted something familiar, and walked back a few steps to check. There, outside the Army Museum, was a small section of the Berlin Wall, complete with the kind of graffiti that only appeared on it after it had been breached. It seemed to me almost like an old friend.

After that I came across small sections of the Wall in other places too; some people still have paperweights made out of it, or small chunks mounted on stands made out of barbed wire. But for the most part the breaching of the Berlin Wall has slipped into history, and most of the paper weights and just about all the bits of barbed wire were phoney anyway.

Now that we know how the story ended, I feel a certain nostalgia for the old Cold War days; much as many Russians and East Germans do. The world was a simpler place in those days. If you criticized the Soviet system you suffered for it, and someone would take up your case in the West. I myself took up many such cases, either profession-ally as a broadcaster or else anonymously as a member of Amnesty International. It was clearly the right thing to do.

It was only afterwards that things seemed a little less clear-cut. I, for instance, sent postcards in a slightly different version of my name to the Soviet ambassador in London and to the General Secretary of the Soviet Communist Party in Moscow appealing for the release of a frail elderly man called Gamsakourdia who had been treated appal-lingly in a labour camp in the Soviet republic of Georgia because of his political views. It was only after he was free and the Soviet system had collapsed that I found out more about these political views of his. Gamsakourdia was so nationalistic that he was a virtual fascist. He staged an uprising to seize power, and Georgia was convulsed for months until the extreme nationalist rebellion he headed was put down and Eduard Shevardnadze, the former Soviet foreign minister whom I had come to know and respect, was able to assert his authority.

Nowadays East Germany still seems almost as poor as it always did (apart from the cars) and the service in restaurants and hotels is sometimes reminiscent of the old days. There are fewer shortages, though Hans-Dietrich Genscher's prophecy in 1990 that it would take five years to bring East Germany up to the standards of the West has proven to be ludicrously wrong. But at least you are not followed around any longer, and husbands no longer spy on their wives or children on their parents. It is not the precise conditions that we miss about the old East Germany, but merely the sense of clarity, of fixed definition, which has now gone for ever and been succeeded by all sorts of unattractive phenomena, including a tide of street crime and neo-Nazism.

And it would be wrong to deny that there is also a certain sense of adventure which the casual visitor to Berlin, East or West, now tends to miss. In 1987, for instance, I visited West Berlin to report on the success of the East German Stasi (the Ministry for State Security) in recruiting agents in West Berlin. As part of the basic research I made an appointment to see a British army officer who was working for military intelligence. We arranged to meet in the lobby of the InterContinental Hotel in West Berlin: a large and rather undistinguished glass and concrete affair.

I spotted him immediately: he was wearing a British Warm, brown leather gloves, and a pair of rather good brogues. He was very affable and helpful.

'God,' he said over a gin and tonic, 'spying is the only serious industry in this town. You'll notice,' he went on, taking a swift look around, 'that we've got at least two people listening to us now.'

I suggested that being based in Berlin might tend to encourage a certain paranoia.

'Just because you're paranoid, it doesn't mean they're not out to get you,' he said, and laughed loudly. 'No. There's a couple of fellows you should look at. They aren't taking any notice of you – much too deep into their newspapers. But they've both got leather bags with recording gear in them, trained on us.'

I looked round. As it happened there were two men, one to the left and one to the right, who as far as I could remember had been sitting there when I arrived ten minutes or so earlier. They were both reading newspapers, and they both had leather bags beside them. Scarcely enough to accuse them of being spies, I suggested.

'Let's see if I'm right or wrong,' said the man from military intelligence, downing the last of his gin and tonic. 'There's a bit more light over there,' he added in a slightly louder voice, pointing to another set of armchairs a few yards away.

To humour him, I followed him over. They read too much Le Carré here, I reflected; they behave like this because they feel it's expected of them. We settled down in our new places.

'Now watch the leather bags.'

The man on the left was still reading his newspaper, but the bag had changed position and its end was pointing at us again. I looked in the other direction: the man there had folded up his newspaper and, with a bored look on his face, was just adjusting his bag so that it, too, pointed at us.

It was a game. The East German agents who were playing it were small fry, and there were no doubt Western agents on the other side of the Wall who were recording conversations and following people at that very moment. If the man from military intelligence had had these two arrested, something equally unpleasant would have happened to the Western agents across the Wall. The rules of the game dictated that you only took action if it really mattered. When that happened, everyone on the other side understood; even if they suffered in the process.

And anyway, the military intelligence man explained, these other things were a sideshow. The real game was played out by the Stasi against West German politicians and civil servants; and the Stasi was winning that hands down.

Soon afterwards, with a cameraman filming me, I found the wavelength on my portable radio where the Stasi broadcast coded messages to their agents in West Germany. A woman's voice, metallic and impersonal, read out a series of figures for a few minutes, until the broadcast ended and began again later on a different wavelength. My colleagues understood no German, but they found this unearthly voice as chilling as I did:

'*Sieben. Eins. Drei. Acht. Zwei. Drei. Vier. Eins. Sechs. Fünf . . .*'

To someone in West Germany this represented instructions for a meeting, or perhaps for some action to be taken. The Stasi's penetration of West German political and diplomatic life was remarkably widespread. This saved the Stasi a lot of time and trouble; a West German diplomat, for instance, provided them with West Germany's own intelligence on Britain, and when he was transferred to Tokyo he gave the Stasi everything the West Germans knew about Japan.

Britain's SIS may have been the most successful of the Western intelligence services by the end of the Cold War, but the Stasi were more successful than any agency on either side.

In 1991, after the Wall had come down and the German Democratic Republic had evaporated, I went to visit the spymaster who was chiefly responsible for this success. Markus Wolf, half-Jewish, highly cultured and subtle-minded, was now being hounded by the West German authorities in what seemed like a vendetta. No doubt all sorts of politicians and civil servants who had had trouble in the past were getting even with him.

Wolf impressed me considerably, and I wrote an article about my meeting with him in which I compared him with John Le Carré's anti-hero Karla. It was by no means an original idea, and apparently Le Carré had denied that Karla was based on Wolf in an article he had written for one of the London newspapers some years before. That I should have repeated an old *canard* scarcely reflected very well on my research, of course.

A few days later I had a letter from Le Carré which began by saying he had always rather admired me – invariably, in my experience, the prelude to some unpleasantness – but that my ignorance of the article he had written had changed his mind. He seemed to take himself and his writing very seriously.

Contrary to what most of his readers hoped and expected, Le Carré's main characters were not based on real figures from the intelligence world whom he had come across in his work for SIS. George Smiley was not Sir Dick White, or any of the other bosses of MI5 or MI6; he was just based on someone Le Carré had known. Karla was not Markus Wolf; and given that Wolf's identity was kept so secret that it was twenty years before the Western intelligence agencies even managed to obtain a picture of him, this is not surprising. Le Carré's 'Circus' was a place of the creative imagination; it bore no closer relationship to the ordinariness of Century House or Vauxhall Cross than did the world of 'M', 'Q', and Miss Moneypenny.

I had rung Wolf from London, and he gave me his address: it was a flat in a pleasant central part of East Berlin, which he had been allocated when he was one of the most important people in the country. He still lived there, even though the country had disappeared and he was being accused of crimes against a state he had not belonged to. I walked up the stairs and rang the doorbell. An attractive blonde woman in her early forties opened the door and greeted me pleasantly.

Real travelling: our vehicle makes its way over the rocks in the Hindu Kush.
In Afghanistan, only Russian jeeps – crude, uncomfortable and immensely
strong – are suitable for the roughest terrain.

The tribulations of life on the road: a group of mujaheddin examine our *laissez-passer*. Their leader is holding the piece of paper upside down, which makes it even harder for him to work out who we are and what we are doing.

Being escorted away by armed men. Arrest is an occupational hazard for the television journalist, and men in uniform the world over seem to feel the need to interfere when they see a television camera.

Top left: Coming to market: on the River Caguan in southern Colombia. The faster, more expensive boat belongs to a buyer from one of the big drugs cartels. The slower, heavily laden one is full of coca-growers hoping to sell their crops. They are all heading for the drugs market at Remolino.

Top right: Father Leonel Navaez, who got us into Remolino by persuading the drugs-growers and dealers that we had the protection of the guerrillas who controlled the area. We thought so too. It was slightly awkward to be told by the guerrilla commander that he didn't care if we lived or died.

Below: The man holding the bag is about to test the coca-paste in it for purity. The others are *tracateros* – buyers from the cartels. As far as I know, no one before or after has ever filmed a cocaine market.

The Serbian warlord Arkan, during my live television interview with him in spring 1999. The circular badge was much worn by Serbs during the NATO bombing campaign, to show that everyone was a target. A few days afterwards the studios where the interview took place were bombed with heavy loss of life; and nine months later Arkan himself was murdered by an off-duty policeman.

Osama bin Laden, the wealthy Saudi fundamentalist based in Afghanistan, who offered $500 to a group of mujaheddin to murder me and wept bitterly when they refused. I was relieved, but felt the price was rather low.

Maurice Rossel, the former delegate of the International Red Cross, who visited the Nazi concentration camp at Theresienstadt in 1944 and reported that conditions there were fair and reasonable. Understandably, perhaps, this was the only interview he had ever given about it.

Colonel Gadhafi
during our interview
in his tent in the
Libyan desert, 1998:

contemplative . . .

declaiming . . .

. . . discreetly
breaking wind.

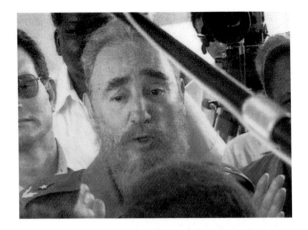

Fidel Castro telling
us how tired he is of
governing Cuba.

The allegedly
cannibalistic Emperor
Bokassa and his role
model, shortly after I
had investigated the
contents of his
deep-freeze.

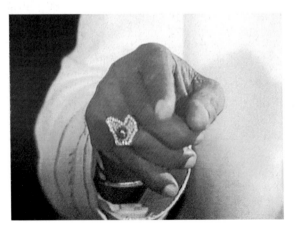

The imperial
signet ring.

Driving in style through the streets of Mogadishu with our Somali bodyguards, who were sworn to protect us with their lives (but only as long as we paid them).

Hussein, the American-educated son of the Somali warlord General Mohammed Aideed. He told me that when he was part of the US Marine force in Mogadishu he had been in daily contact with Aideed senior, who was being hunted as America's public enemy number one at the time. Perhaps the Americans thought it was a coincidence that they had the same name.

I examine a volume of Hitler's forged diaries. It seemed quite impressive, though I didn't know the ink was modern and the seal made of plastic.

A murder case of particular unpleasantness in a St Petersburg court.

'I am Andrea, Markus's wife,' she said, then called down the corridor, 'Markus, it's the gentleman from the BBC.'

She was his third wife, and a good quarter-century younger than he was. He came out from a side room and greeted me: tall, well-built, in good physical condition, with a pleasant, open countenance. He was wearing a tan-coloured suit and a maroon sports shirt buttoned up to the throat, without a tie. I thought he looked like a successful actor, now retired.

Behind him as I stood in the doorway I could see a room I would have liked to look round. Photographs and watercolours covered the walls, and there were objects everywhere from Wolf's African and Asian journeys. Too much of it was related to his secret past to be shown to an outsider, obviously.

'If you don't mind,' he said in good, lightly accented English, 'we will do our talking outside as we walk. As you say in English, Old habits die hard.'

He put on an overcoat and kissed his wife.

We headed for the nearby park where we were to do the interview, Wolf describing the case which the German authorities were bringing against him.

'It is victor's justice. They have beaten us, and now they are taking their revenge on those of us who did our duty to our own government and state. My department did particularly well, and there are many West German politicians who cannot forgive that. And of course there are some who know they have a great deal to hide, and who are talking loud in order to persuade everyone that everything in their lives will stand up to scrutiny.'

'And you still have the files to show that it won't?'

'Not the files. They were at Normannenstrasse [the headquarters of Stasi] and I don't physically have anything. Except, of course, in my memory.'

As we walked along, I felt my instinct about his actorish quality had been correct. Wolf was a consummate actor, and his speciality was playing the part of an open, frank man with nothing to hide. His handsome face took on a thoughtful expression each time I asked him a difficult question, as though he wanted me to think he was saying to himself, 'Now this is important; I must do my best to answer this one fully and honestly.' I found his company congenial, and I sympathized with the position he now found himself in; but I knew at the same time that I was meant to feel these things. Wolf was playing his part with consummate skill.

We walked once or twice up and down the little park so the cameraman could get the required pictures with the necessary mood: two men in raincoats talking about secrets in East Berlin. We sat down on a bench. Pigeons fluttered round us, and a little girl went past, pulling a toy on wheels. Wolf smiled at her absently. Le Carré and a hundred spy films had taught us to create this ambience of secrecy and deception and the dark side of government, while surrounded by the very normality which these things threatened. The cameraman and I knew our parts as much as Wolf did: it was a well-rehearsed script. But his performance was worth an Oscar.

'The Americans and West Germans always maintained that the Stasi carried out murders and assassinations. You must surely have given the orders for them.'

'Not at all. I was always totally against this kind of thing, if only because I knew that it had a tendency to backfire. No. There were of course friends of ours who did murder exiles and dissidents and so forth. I think I can tell you in all frankness that the Bulgarians did it. There were documented cases. The Russians did too. They developed a range of poisons which they let us have. Maybe I shouldn't tell you this, because it sounds like disloyalty to my allies, but I thought they were being stupid and dangerous, so I had the poisons locked away in a safe in my own office and we never took them out.'

'And what about the La Belle bombing?'

La Belle was a discotheque in West Berlin which had been popular among American servicemen. In 1986 someone planted a bomb there, which killed three people and injured a hundred and fifty others. President Ronald Reagan announced that the US had information it had been carried out by Libya, and American bombers attacked Tripoli, killing dozens of people. There had always been strong hints that the bombers had had help from the East Germans.

'It's true that some Ministry of State Security people were aware that there was going to be a Libyan attack somewhere, and that some Libyan diplomats had brought explosives into our country. But our information indicated that the man who planned the bombing had links with the United States. In these matters, you know, it is very hard to be certain.'

There was a pattern to every answer he gave me: the flattering illusion that I was getting the inside track, the real secrets. Yet it always tended in one direction: towards leaving the Stasi, and more particularly Wolf himself, in the clear.

Just as when I stood at the front door of his flat and glanced briefly into the fascinating interior, so now I was permitted the most fleeting of glimpses into the arcane complexities of the intelligence world, where no one truly knew who was working for whom, and where the official explanations bore no relationship to the reality. Markus Wolf merely put a pleasant, human face on it all.

Cold War espionage was just an industry like any other. On both sides of the Berlin Wall it had long assumed a life of its own, played out according to clear rules which both sides accepted: serious enough in their own terms, yet not affecting much in the broader scale of things. Individual lives were wrecked, places were bombed, careers were terminated, loyalties turned; yet as far as the big things were concerned, intelligence does not seem to have played a decisive part in anything serious after the Cuban missile crisis, when Colonel Oleg Penkovsky, an SIS agent inside Soviet military intelligence, kept the Americans informed about Moscow's intentions and perhaps helped to avoid a nuclear war.

None of the great turning points in the Cold War was foreseen by the intelligence agencies of either side: the building of the Berlin Wall, the invasions of Czechoslovakia and Afghanistan, the Wall's collapse. Instead, the agencies mostly fought it out on a lower level: recruiting agents, tapping into each other's systems, turning each other's disaffected staff.

As for the literature of the Cold War, it too seems diminished nowadays. Le Carré and others have done what they can to find substitutes for the old plot lines, but it hasn't worked. Reading a spy novel now is like reading science fiction about a time which has already passed: it becomes an historical oddity, which throws light on the social and political atmosphere of the time but has no wider significance. Markus Wolf may not have been the model for John Le

Carré's anti-hero Karla, but the real spymaster belongs next to the
fictional one: files in a closed account.

'Oleg D. Kalugin,' the card said; and underneath, 'Counsellor,
Ministry of Foreign Affairs of the USSR'. It was as misleading as the
other cards he must have proffered in the past: 'Correspondent,
Moscow Radio', 'Press Attaché, Soviet Embassy.' Oleg D. Kalugin
was a spy. He used to be the KGB's man in overall charge of political
intelligence in the United States, a general before he was out of his
forties. The year was 1990, and he had just taken early retirement at
the age of fifty-five; having seen a brief announcement about this in
one of the Moscow newspapers, I had phoned him for an appointment. The KGB didn't like his political opinions nor the things he
was starting to say about the organization, and it had forced him out
before his time.

At first I thought I must have come to the wrong place: a weed-
grown housing estate in the Moscow suburbs, with the usual wrecked
cars and discarded empties. I went inside one of the doorways, and a
cat yowled and ran. But there were some serious security devices on
the door, the concierge was dressed with unusual smartness, and the
smell of urine was missing from the stairwell. Scarcely a standard
block of Moscow flats, therefore.

I rang the doorbell, and a man opened it almost at once. Most
people's idea of a KGB general would, I suppose, be a squat, porcine,
Asiatic figure with hands like a boxer's. The hand Kalugin extended
to me was long and well cared for; it could have belonged to the
principal cellist of the Moscow Chamber Orchestra. Inside, I saw that
his record collection was particularly strong on Verdi, and that Sartre,
Bertrand Russell and Thomas Mann were well represented on his
bookshelves. There were some pleasant late nineteenth-century Russian landscapes of the bowed-peasant-outside-snow-laden-cottage
type; and elsewhere on the walls there were trophy heads. Oleg D.
Kalugin liked to pass his free time killing things. There were deer of
different kinds and even, weirdly, a turtle. Had he shot it, I wondered,
or wrestled it to death in the ocean? Best not to ask.

On the baby grand was a framed photograph of, yes, Kim Philby.
'All the best, old chap' he had written at the bottom of it. Kalugin

was one of his closest friends, and just as Graham Greene wrote the introduction to the British edition of Philby's memoirs, so Kalugin had done the same for the Russian edition: under a false name, of course. Kim Philby had even considered coming and living in this block of flats, but the KGB had decided otherwise.

The problem for Kalugin was that he had evolved and the KGB, like a stuffed turtle, hadn't. His shift away from the KGB had begun in earnest in 1979, when a friend of his, a dissident scientist, was framed by the KGB as an American spy. Kalugin defended him and paid the price: he was moved sideways to become the KGB chief in Leningrad.

In 1987, thoroughly disillusioned by the KGB's failure to adapt to Mikhail Gorbachev's policies of glasnost and perestroika, he set out his complaints about the organization on paper and sent them to Gorbachev himself. Gorbachev told him he agreed with everything in the letter, which didn't help him with the KGB either. Finally, he joined a group of opposition Communists called the Democratic Platform. At public meetings he pulled no punches. The KGB was the same organization it had always been, bugging, following, spying on people whose politics it didn't like. It did occur to me, of course, that he might have been doing all this in order to infiltrate the new politics on the KGB's behalf; in this strange world, who can say?

'The top men in the KGB hate what's going on in the Soviet Union now. Not all of them, of course, because there are many people inside it still who think like me. But they are not the majority, and they are military men who have to obey orders. The KGB has always had its own internal dissidents, just as the CIA and your SIS have.'

Would his friend Kim Philby have approved of what he had done?

'He would have approved of most of my ideas, but I don't think he would have liked the idea of my speaking out publicly about the service.'

Kalugin had defected, not into the arms of another country but to his own fellow-citizens. If genuine, it was a braver thing than Philby ever did.

'Is your flat bugged?' I looked at the tasteful pictures, at the deers' heads. If it had been me, I would have put a microphone in the turtle's mouth; but that was just a matter of taste.

'Probably not. For that you need compliant neighbours, and I doubt if my neighbours would be compliant.'

'But your phone?'

'Ah, certainly. I have bugged too many of my former colleagues in the KGB to imagine that they are not bugging me.'

He conceded that these former colleagues might try a little character assassination on him, accusing him of discussing the secrets of the KGB with a Westerner like myself. He was psychologically prepared for that, he said.

I shook the firm hand, and looked into the blue eyes. Was General Kalugin a little too good to be true? Was the KGB just using him to infiltrate the growing opposition? Was the courageous and outspoken democrat just another alter ego, like the counsellor at the Ministry of Foreign Affairs or the correspondent of Moscow radio?

Yet what he had said seemed unequivocal enough: 'The leadership of the KGB hates everything that is happening in the Soviet Union.'

I went back to the BBC office in Moscow and pondered over our interview. Within an hour or so the telex machine sprang into life. It was the KGB with a statement about General Kalugin.

'The State Security Committee firmly rejects such assertions by Kalugin and expresses indignation at his insults against the professional honour and human dignity of KGB personnel,' it said. 'His remarks make one question his aims.'

Maybe Kalugin had genuinely broken away from the KGB after all. And he was right about its hatred for Gorbachev. In August 1991, fourteen months after I saw Kalugin, Markus Wolf's old friend Vladimir Kryuchkov, the head of the KGB, led a coup against Mikhail Gorbachev and his liberalizing ways. It failed, and in so doing brought about the death of the Soviet system in Russia itself.

The next three or four weeks were an almost hallucinatory time, as everything which had composed the Soviet system was swept aside. The statues of Marxist-Leninist heroes were hauled away, the government was in abeyance, *Pravda* advocated the return of the capitalist system, and red stars and hammers and sickles began to disappear from public buildings.

As for the KGB, that disintegrated too. I was working with Rory Peck, the freelance cameraman who was killed a couple of years later in the aftermath of the storming of the Moscow White House. Rory was an extraordinarily brave man. I never saw better war pictures than his, and the slow upper-class drawl disguised an extremely sharp brain. He was well-dressed yet somehow faintly outmoded, as though he had studied hard to be a few decades behind the times.

The face was long, the eyes hooded, and the hair thinning in the way we associate with the British upper class. Rory was an archetypical Norman: courtly, as bold as a Plantagenet lion, yet not particularly burdened with the plodding conscience of Anglo-Saxons like myself. He was an adventurer, and I should be very much surprised if some ancestor of his had not responded in Rory Peck style to the offer of a seat in William of Normandy's boat in 1066.

Now he enlisted a friend of his, the foreign editor of *Pravda* to help the two of us gain access to the kind of places we had never previously been able to go; not even during Mikhail Gorbachev's glasnost years.

'Tell me what you'd like to see,' said Rory.

I told him. My wish-list began with a visit to KGB headquarters, continued with a trip to the offices of the Soviet Communist Party's Central Committee, and took in the dachas of the Party bosses as an afterthought.

'Don't see why not,' Rory said, and gave the list to his friend.

Later, the KGB headquarters became a regular tourist venue, the kind of place you could see for a down payment of twenty dollars. At this time, though, it still preserved its old forbidding reputation. When I had first come to Moscow, in 1978, people crossed the road rather than walk beside the building. It was a place of ill-omen, a vast yellow ochre building which had begun life as the corporate offices of a big Tsarist insurance firm, and was taken over after the 1917 Bolshevik revolution by the Cheka, Lenin's secret police.

The Lubyanka had been a prison and a centre for torture and execution. Under Stalin, tens of thousands had suffered and died there. Rumour – ill-founded, as it later proved – said that a system of underground cells reached out beneath the streets around. After Stalin died, the population of the prison shrank. The SIS agent Greville Wynne, who had been caught spying and was sentenced to a long term of imprisonment by a Soviet court, was taken out onto the flat roof with other prisoners for exercise, and if you stood in the right place you could see one of the watchtowers which guarded the exercise yard.

In the past, I had risked arrest as a spy to get a photograph of the Lubyanka for the BBC library. Now that the entire system had collapsed, I was determined to get inside the building and see for myself what it was like. Rory Peck provided me with the way in. We presented ourselves, as instructed, at the front door of the building at ten in the morning: the first foreign television team ever to be allowed into the KGB's headquarters. Rory and I were on our own: that was one of the KGB's stipulations. It had a press officer now, and he had been very helpful. His name was Pavel.

The doors were small and undemonstrative for such a large and inauspicious building: a pair of them, in the honey-coloured wood which most official buildings in Russia use. I had tried to peer in on a previous visit, but had been turned away by a policeman outside. Now there was no policeman, and no one to stop me pushing open the doors.

Immediately inside there was a flight of stone steps, quite narrow, leading up to the main floor. A couple of KGB guards in uniform stood there, on either side of a metal detector shaped like a guillotine. As Rory and I, in our approximations to Russian (his was a good deal better than mine, but spoken with the poshest of English accents) were trying to explain who we were and who had invited us there, a KGB man in a hurry burst through the main doors behind us and pushed us aside without looking either at us or at Rory's camera. He showed the guards his pass and signed a book, then went up the narrow stairs two at a time.

We waited a little longer. People came in and out. Then someone in a brown suit, a checked shirt and a blue tie came down the stairs towards us. I looked at him carefully: it was the man who had pushed by us a few minutes earlier. The KGB must be falling apart if its personnel were getting in to work so late.

'I am Pavel,' said the man in the brown suit. 'Welcome to Lubyanka.'

He was thin, and his complexion must have been pretty bad at some stage in his youth. Even now he looked greasy and unkempt. Yet there was something almost beseeching about him which I could sympathize with. He had been washed up by the tide of history, left doing a job which was no longer regarded as worthy of respect. Everything he said ended up sounding like an apology.

With Pavel to guide us, we went up the narrow stairs and into a much larger hallway. We took a lift to the third floor, and were shown along a corridor with large doorways on either side.

The place seemed empty and uncared for. No one had swept the corridor for some days, and the rooms we passed were empty. The spirit seemed to have gone out of the place. At the same time, knowing something of the Lubyanka's past, I told myself there was a sense of perceptible evil here. Thousands of people had suffered in this building, and the people who inflicted their suffering had taken their instructions from these offices.

'This is the office where the head of the Committee sits. Sat.'

'So the KGB isn't continuing any more?'

'Yes, it continues, maybe. Or maybe not.'

Pavel gave an apologetic grin. For a moment he seemed almost human.

We walked into the room. It was grandiose and yet fussy in an old-fashioned Russian way. Little glass-fronted cupboards held tea-pots and cups and the dreary valueless small gifts that big Socialist institutions used to exchange with each other. There was a plate with pictures of Markus Wolf's old headquarters in Normannenstrasse, and a silver-plated tray with some other secret police headquarters on it; secret policemen being the only people who are not frightened by their buildings, and who think there is something worthwhile about their profession. A portrait of Dzerzhinsky, the Polish prince appointed by Lenin to head the Cheka, hung on the far wall: his long wolfish face dominated by a cunning pair of eyes. A vast desk in dark mahogany dominated half the room.

'So this is where Yagoda and Yezhov sat? And Beria?'

Pavel nodded uncomfortably. Nowadays the KGB had problems reflecting on Stalin's executioners. I stood there for a little. From this desk had emanated the orders that ended in the arrest, torture, and murder of millions.

Then I walked across the thin brown carpet and looked out over the traffic in Dzerzhinsky Square. From here, past the empty plinth where Dzerzhinsky's statue had stood until a few days before, I could see the café where in 1978 I had stood in the doorway and photographed this place for the BBC, my hands trembling at the thought that someone might call the police.

And now I was standing in the office from which the KGB had been run, the first Western journalist ever to do so; and the organization itself was in a state of collapse. Seventy-four years of Marxism-Leninism had just evaporated. A single lifetime could have encompassed it all, from revolution to the terror, from war to world power, from economic decay to the triumph of liberal democracy.

'Patient endurance attaineth to all things,' I murmured, quoting a faintly remembered prayer from my childhood.

'Sorry, old boy?'

'Just reflecting.'

Rory was on his knees, struggling away at an electrical switch on the wall. He was a superb adventurer, and probably the only cameraman on earth who could have had the nous and the chutzpah and the contacts to get us in here; but the humbler side of the cameraman's job was not his strong point. He had no tripod, because he found it boring to carry one; and he didn't carry the tools of the trade either.

'Don't suppose you've got a screwdriver on you? I just need to stick the lights into the wall-plug.'

Pavel drifted off to see if he could find something. My own heightened feelings of the horror and significance of this place boiled up into irritation.

'Look, Rory, you're the cameraman. You're the one who carries things like screwdrivers. My job is to write things down. I don't ask you for pens and paper.'

'As a matter of fact, old boy, you do. You did yesterday.'

He grinned, and I grinned in reply: the moment of irritability had passed.

'Some good stuff in here to loot,' Rory mused. 'We could probably get it in the camera bag.'

I was still telling him that even now it was probably not a good idea when Pavel came back with a screwdriver.

'Don't worry, I used a couple of matches to stick the wires in the holes.'

He switched on the lights to prove it, and we carried on filming.

When the Lubyanka was an insurance office it had been a hollow square, with a large courtyard in the middle. As the arrests intensified, and the need to hold people for interrogation and execution grew, a new inner prison was constructed in the courtyard. We looked out of the windows which once overlooked the courtyard, and saw the windows of this inner shell like a smaller Russian doll inside the outer one, just a few yards away.

But we had reached the limits of the KGB's willingness to co-operate. It might be on its knees, but it was still determined to protect its worst secrets.

'I have no authorization to take you in there,' Pavel said.

We argued a little, until I realized that Pavel himself had never been allowed into this inner prison either. According to him, the cells were now used for the storage of the most secret documents from the past. Eventually, over the next couple of years, even some of these documents were shown to selected writers and journalists. In this way the world discovered how artists like Babel, Mandelstam and Meyerhold had spent their time here: the beatings, the interrogations, the sleep deprivation, the transportation to labour camps where they died miserably.

Even without these precise details, there was a powerful sense of horror about the place, which Rory and I both felt. Pavel, though, seemed largely unaffected by it.

'Don't you think this is a dreadful place?'

'I know that very bad things went on here in the past. But I am forty-three: I scarcely remember the time of Stalin at all, and after his death everything became much easier in the Soviet Union. This place is no longer a prison, for example. It became just offices for the KGB.'

He shrugged, as though he had no responsibility for the KGB, and the KGB had no responsibility for anything that had happened since Stalin: the arrests, the labour camps, the murders.

He had been authorized to take us to one last place: the KGB's museum. It filled three large windowless rooms and was a record, not of the war the Cheka and its successor organizations had fought against their own people, but of the external war, protecting the Soviet Union against foreign subversion.

'You have only ten minutes here.'

Rory hurried his shots, filming the larger exhibits: Chekist uniforms, life-sized blow-ups of photographs of Dzerzhinsky and his colleagues, and more recent ones of Yuri Andropov, the KGB's reformist head who went on briefly to become President and who promoted Mikhail Gorbachev to the uppermost levels of government. There were no pictures of Beria, Yezhov or any of the other psychopaths who once controlled the organization. I went from glass case to glass case, looking for things to film and trying to work out what the Russian labels meant.

In the short space of time available, it was profoundly frustrating. There were messages, photographs and some items of clothes belonging to Richard Sorge, Stalin's super-spy in the Second World War. There was equipment which, according to a piece of typewritten yellowing card, had belonged to Sydney Reilly, the British spy who had operated in Russia in the early days of Soviet power.

While Rory filmed this, I went to the furthest of the glass cases. The first thing I saw was a copy of Kim Philby's memoirs in Russian. As I looked from object to object I could see that the case was dedicated to the British spies of the post-war period: Philby himself, Burgess, Maclean, and someone in a sports jacket, smoking a pipe. Could this, I wondered, be the legendary Fourth Man who was always assumed to have recruited the others at Cambridge, and whose identity had been the subject of endless speculation in Britain?

The typewritten cards had been moved around, and it wasn't quite clear which one related to the man with the pipe. With my rudimentary Russian, I started to puzzle it out.

'John! Please! That is closed section!'

Pavel and the other man were running across.

'No problem, Pavel, I'm just having a quick look. What's this name here?'

'No, John, really. You must go now, you and Rory. Where is Rory?'

Rory was starting to film something else that they didn't like. They hurried both of us out. Within five minutes we were standing on the pavement outside the building. We might have been the first Western television team to enter KGB headquarters, but we had scarcely done more than lift the covering and catch a quick glimpse of what lay beneath.

The KGB would remain weak and unsure of its future for a couple of years to come. Yet it was always clear that at some stage the vacuum would be filled, and eventually the FSB was established in its place. It took over all the files, and all those agents who still remained and were still prepared to work with it, and it soon began using many of the same methods. And in March 2000 a former KGB man, Vladimir Putin, was elected president of the Russian Federation by a large majority. In Russia, Andrei Sakharov once said, the snow may drift anywhere, but the wind always blows in the same direction.

Secret policemen always assume that foreign correspondents are spies. Sometimes, no doubt, they are right, though the mental make-up of the foreign correspondent is usually a little too independent for that, and even the more slavish journalists understand that in an ideal world they should be free to write openly as they choose, and that there is something discreditable in working secretly for someone else. The most enlightened spymasters seemed to appreciate this too. When I met him in East Berlin Markus Wolf assured me (though it was only to be expected he would) that the Stasi did not use East German journalists based abroad as spies in the usual run of things, but they were expected to keep in close touch with the local embassy, and tip them off about anything they heard.

This is usual enough. When I travel somewhere, I occasionally go and see the British ambassador and his staff, and discuss any information I have come across if it seems worthwhile. But unless a friend of mine is serving there, I don't make a habit of it. The problem most diplomats face is that, in the more difficult countries at least, they tend to live in compounds, and to speak mostly to other diplomats. Journalists have access to a much wider range of contacts as a matter of course, and it is much easier for them to go and see things for themselves. Still, the relationship can be a very useful one, and a good ambassador who knows his country well is much like a good foreign correspondent who is based there. The pleasure of being a journalist is that you are, in the words of the explorer Sir Richard Burton, 'a licensed libertine'. You have *carte blanche* to wander where you choose, and find out what you can.

Which naturally makes secret policemen suspicious. To them, the difference between spies and journalists is simply that journalists report to their viewers and listeners and readers, while spies report to their governments. The methods of obtaining information are the same: observation, contacts, and the occasional leak. You can't blame them.

Often, anyway, secret policemen are a good deal more intelligent than the non-secret variety, which makes them slightly better company if they arrest you. In Romania in 1989 I had a long and quite amusing conversation with a senior Securitate officer, who discovered from his records that although I was posing as a British academic I had had a brush with his colleagues ten years earlier – when I was definitely working for the BBC.

'I think we must assume you are still a journalist, Mr Simpson,' he said.

He was perfectly pleasant. The brighter ones realize that strong-arm tactics and threats are not the only way to proceed.

'Some of you people might almost be human,' I said, and he laughed.

One evening in November 1990, a few weeks before the Gulf War broke out, I had a dinner party in a Baghdad restaurant to celebrate the fact that I would be returning home the next day. In fact, I was not in celebratory mood. I was leaving because I had been refused an interview with Saddam Hussein, and I wanted to show the Iraqis I was boycotting them. (I returned three weeks later, and stayed there for a couple of months; the Iraqi authorities finally threw me out after the war had well and truly started.)

Saddam insisted that if he gave an interview, his words would have to be used in full; no matter how repetitious or empty they might be. The BBC declared, nobly but I felt rather irritatingly, that it must always have editorial control; and that since we wouldn't give a British politician unlimited access to our airwaves, we certainly couldn't allow the same thing to Saddam Hussein. ITN, by contrast, eagerly snapped the interview up, and I booked my flight home.

Afterwards, a Dutch journalist whom I had invited to my party agreed to walk back to the Al-Rashid Hotel with me. It was midnight, and the streets were empty. Our route took us over the Jomhuriya bridge, across the river Tigris. The weather was pleasantly warm, and we stopped halfway across to look at the sluggish waters of the river and speculate on what would happen if the bombs fell on Baghdad.

'That's one of Saddam's palaces over there,' I said, pointing to the darker bank of the river. 'You can bet they'll pulverize that.'

We stood there a little longer, reflecting how hard it was to envisage a war in the peacefulness of a Baghdad night. In the distance there was sound of a siren. It came closer, and a couple of police cars appeared out of the darkness with blue lights flashing, mounted the pavement, and screamed to a halt. Four or five uniformed policemen jumped out and surrounded us, shouting angrily. I couldn't understand a word they said, but I could guess. The Dutch journalist and I decided to take no notice of them. They shouted some more, but this time into walkie-talkies. There was a pause.

Another couple of police cars drove up at speed, and stopped behind the others. Four lots of blue flashing lights; it was like carnival night. A senior policeman with a lot of gold braid and a stick sauntered over to me and screamed at me in a kind of English that unless I took my hands out of my pockets he would have me thrown into the river. The Dutch journalist was getting really nervous, so I thought I would try to set an example.

'Perhaps you could find someone who could translate that into English,' I said, much more firmly than I felt. I kept my hands in my pockets.

There was more screaming, and he waved his stick around. Another senior policeman had a quiet word with him, and the stick went back under his arms.

'I tell you what,' I said, as much for the Dutch journalist's benefit as for my own, 'British television is interviewing Saddam Hussein tomorrow. If I speak to him, I shall give him your names and complain about your violence and your rudeness.'

It wasn't strictly a lie, of course, but it was said with the intention of deceiving. The English-speaking policeman didn't understand enough to spot the weasel 'if'. He did a highly gratifying double-take, and almost ran over to his car. He shouted into his radio: I could hear the words 'Saddam' and 'television'.

Then we waited. No one apologized, no one asked if we might like to sit in one of the cars, but it was clear that, for the moment at least, personal violence was no longer on the agenda.

At 3 a.m. there was the sound of a car engine in the silent night. We looked around: an ancient brown Volkswagen Passat drew up alongside the circus of police cars, and a tired-looking young man got out. He cannot have been older than twenty-five, but his English was perfect and the senior policemen, twice his age, fawned on him.

He took no notice whatever of them, and strolled over to the two of us. His suit looked as though he had been sleeping in it, and his tie was loose. This man might be young, I thought, but in a town where secret policemen have almost unlimited power he drew a lot of water. He gave a very tired grin, but didn't introduce himself or shake hands.

'Did you really tell these guys you'd complain about them to Saddam tomorrow?'

'Something like that.'

'If I drive you back to your hotel now, will you promise not to tell Saddam?'

'A deal.'

I was worried that the senior policemen were going to kiss me in their gratitude. Instead, the one with the stick placed his hand over his heart in an attitude of respect and humble affection, and said 'Hello'; which for some reason is what Iraqis say when they mean goodbye.

We rattled back to the Al-Rashid in the Passat, which smelled of oil. There were dirty football clothes wadded up in the back. I tried to draw the secret policeman out, but he only grinned at my questions.

'Maybe some other time,' he said. 'Are you really going to interview Saddam tomorrow?'

'Not me. Someone else is, though.'

'That's what I thought. Good to know you.'

He drove off into the night, his car leaving a little cloud of exhaust smoke in the silent air.

You can see Evin Prison from the highway as you drive northwards through the suburbs of Tehran: a large compound taking in a slice of the hillside and surrounded by a high wall. There are watchtowers every so often as the wall snakes its way around. Evin is a place of evil reputation: a great many unpleasant things happened there in the early days of the Islamic revolution.

During the latter part of the 1980s, and well into 1991, each week's mail delivered to the prison contained a large buff envelope of a kind familiar to tens of thousands of people in Britain and elsewhere: the *Spectator* had arrived at perhaps the most unlikely address on earth. It was always late by a matter of several weeks, yet it always seemed to get through. Censors examined each copy rigorously, to see that it didn't contain anything defamatory of Islam, or anything indecent – pictures of women with uncovered hair, that kind of thing.

As for the prisoner to whom the subscription was directed, he would open the envelope with particular enthusiasm, since the *Spectator* was his main link with the world outside the prison walls. The ritual came to an end a few days before Tuesday 2 April 1991, when the most famous *Spectator* reader in captivity was released. After five and a quarter years of imprisonment for espionage, Roger Cooper was a free man at last.

And yet it had been clear to me for some time that Roger was a free man even in his prison cell. His occasional letters to me, painstakingly written in capital letters so the censor could see they contained no funny business, spoke of the birds he had spotted from his cell window:

> Sparrow, wagtail, two species of pigeon, rook and hooded crow . . . I did once hear the ring-tailed parakeet that used to visit my down-town garden in the old days.

They included elaborate anagrams on the names of his friends and of selected figures in the British government:

> Who 'should guard' [*Douglas Hurd*] British interests abroad? His predecessor may have made some mistakes but the hard-line Russian diplomat who said of him 'Goofer! Why is free?' [*Sir Geoffrey Howe*] surely takes the iron-like reputation of 'that great charmer' [*Margaret Thatcher*] too literally.

Roger Cooper's range of interests in prison was extraordinary.

> Lately I've been less frivolous with my time and devoted myself to English and Russian fiction, and whatever French, German

and Spanish books come my way, plus three Persian newspapers
a day and their crosswords.

I wanted to send him some books of cartoons, and knowing the
sensitivities of the Iranian clerical mind I settled on the work of Gary
Larson. Larson peoples suburbia with human-like cockroaches,
elephants, lions and snakes who wear Western clothes and often (in
the case of the females) elaborate diamanté glasses. I reasoned that
no censor could object to a female cockroach who flaunted her
uncovered hair, and so it proved.

The three Larson collections arrived back in August . . . At first I
didn't think I liked Larsonry v. much but it grows on you, and
I think the colour helps. My cell-mates including 2 Americans
were v. appreciative ('At last Cooper has got something worth
reading').

I also sent him a postcard with a Larson cartoon of two dogs
watching their mistress dishing out tinned meat into their bowls.
They are saying, 'Oh boy, it's dog food again.'

Prisoners will quarrel about anything and in fact the card led to
a huge row about whether the dogs really liked dog food again!
I was sure they didn't, but I suppose it's funny either way. There
were echoes for us, of course.

Indeed there were, which is why I sent it. What I hadn't realized
was that Roger was a remarkable cook, and was creating dishes for
himself and his fellow-prisoners which, given the restrictions, must
have been almost appetizing. I urged him after his release to write a
prison cookbook, but after all that time inside he understandably
preferred the subject of Mediterranean cuisine instead.

Westerners who insist on remaining in a country after some big
political upheaval usually run the risk of being called spies; it is a
dangerously easy accusation to make, and virtually impossible to
disprove. Roger managed to hang on in Tehran for seven years after
the revolution, doing some freelance journalism and translating for
foreign visitors. He is a lifelong Iranophile who was married to a
Persian woman and loved the country so much that when he was
released he surprised his former captors (not to mention David

Reddaway, the British diplomat who had negotiated the deal for his release) by trying to insist that he should stay in the country.

He even played for time by demanding to visit his father-in-law's grave before leaving. But the Iranians would have none of it. They were probably worried that the conservative forces which were so strong within the clerical hierarchy would hear that he was being released, and try to stop it happening. He was put on a plane in such a hurry that when he arrived in London his luggage was found to contain all sorts of things which had been thrown in by mistake, including a pair of shoes belonging to some luckless Revolutionary Guard, and several tins of army-issue potted meat ('Oh boy, it's dog food again').

Shortly after his arrest Iranian television had broadcast what it claimed was a confession by him, which on examination turned out to be a typical piece of Cooperesque word-play. He said enough to convince his captors that they should treat him with a certain leniency, while making it clear to anyone who knew anything about the subject and was prepared to examine his words with the care he would have attached to them that he was not confessing to espionage at all.

He had, he said, passed information to what he called 'the BIS' – which he said stood for 'British Intelligence Service'. When I watched the broadcast coming in from Tehran I knew at once the game that he was playing. There is no such thing as the BIS, and he was not the man to have made a mistake about something like that. He confessed only to passing information about the state of the Iranian economy to his mysterious (and probably non-existent) controllers; the kind of thing, in fact, which any journalist would have written about during those first paranoid years after the revolution.

Characteristically, it had taken him weeks to negotiate the wording of the statement with his captors; characteristically, too, they had become his friends.

It seemed to me perfectly clear that Roger was passing those who knew him in Britain a message to say that he was not guilty of the accusation, in the hope that they would draw the right conclusion and make it public. (When I saw him five years later, after his release, he confirmed that that had indeed been his intention and his hope.) Most of the British press took his 'confession' at face value; only the

BBC and *The Times* pointed out the caveats he had deliberately inserted in it. He didn't suffer in any way for this; probably, if his captors even heard of the doubts we had cast on his broadcast, they kept quiet about them.

By the time of his release I was on the editorial staff of the *Spectator*, and the Christmas issue, which came out a few weeks before his release, began with a leading article about Roger, written by another of his friends, Simon Courtauld. It was Simon who had arranged for Roger to receive the weekly airmail subscription to the magazine. He recalled that Roger had been a regular contributor from 1978–82, and it spoke of his efforts to create a better understanding of Iran in Britain.

> If it is too much to hope that Roger Cooper will be released at this season, we must pray that Iran may mark its own festival of renewal – New Year, at the time of the vernal equinox – with such a gesture, which is long overdue.

Roger was indeed released only a few days after the Persian *Now Ruz* festival. I went to the press conference he gave at Heathrow on his arrival, and was shocked, as everyone else was, to see how grey and thin and old he looked. But in his quiet, husky voice he made a joke which was repeated everywhere and won him the Man of the Year Award. When someone asked him what it had been like, he said, 'No one who has been at a British public school or served in the British army can feel entirely out of place in a Third World prison.'

On the door of the BBC correspondent's flat in Moscow was a cartoon from the satirical magazine *Krokodil*. In 1978 there wasn't a great deal for a Soviet cartoonist to be satirical about, except the Western powers. This cartoon showed two men, one labelled 'BBC' and the other labelled '*Daily Telegraph*', rowing the same boat in different directions and shouting their hatred of the Soviet Union. It wasn't very funny, except for the clothes the two men were wearing: top hats and tail coats, both rather out at elbow.

The authorities at the time hated the BBC because the correspondent at the time was brave enough to speak to dissidents of all kinds and report their views. They hated the *Daily Telegraph* because it was strongly anti-Soviet. It was typical of the atmosphere in the Kremlin that no one seemed to understand the difference between the two approaches.

I was merely a visitor to Moscow at the time. I had no camera crew, because the Russians wouldn't allow us to bring one in from London.

'Want to come to a party tonight?' my colleague asked me. 'It's round at the *Telegraph* man's flat.'

I was keen to meet him. Richard Beeston was one of the great figures from the older generation of foreign correspondents who had covered every conceivable war and crisis. He and Clare Hollingworth of the *Guardian* were the people I hoped to model myself on.

As it happened, we got to his flat first. He and his wife offered us a drink, and as I sipped it I stood with him at the window, talking.

'I don't understand,' I said. 'This is a superb place, and yet everyone tells me there's a real shortage of flats for foreign journalists. Why do they let you stay here, if they hate the *Telegraph* so much?'

'Long story,' Beeston laughed. 'Can you bear it?'

I could, of course.

It turned out that when he and his wife had arrived in Moscow, a year before, they had had a hard time from the Soviet authorities. There were no flats available, and even translators and drivers were hard to find. The Beestons were put into the Ukraine Hotel, one of that extraordinary series of Stalinist wedding cakes designed and built in Stalin's last years. Though attractive on the outside, the Ukraine was the place where the Russians shoved their Third World guests if they didn't like them. The corridors stank and the lifts were broken. The heating didn't work either.

In order to keep warm in the winter evenings, the Beestons used to go to the Bolshoi Theatre as often as they could. The tickets were cheap by Western standards, and it gave them something to look forward to. One night they were sitting in excellent seats in the stalls, and were congratulating themselves on their good luck that the three seats directly in front of them were still empty as the curtain went up.

A few minutes later there was a great deal of apologetic whispering and the clucking of tongues, and three men eased their way along the row and into the seats. Even under Marxism-Leninism, Russians had a bourgeois sense of the proprieties in the theatre, and this kind of behaviour was disapproved of.

The overture finished, and the curtain went up on a brilliantly lighted stage. Mrs Beeston looked at the back of the head in front of her, and nudged her husband.

'Dickie – look who it is.'

Dickie looked. It was Kim Philby. They had both known him well when they were based in the Middle East. When he was eased out of SIS under suspicion of having helped Burgess and Maclean escape, the *Observer* had offered him a job as its correspondent in Beirut. Philby had defected to the Soviet Union from there, and no one had seen him in public since. The men on either side of him were presumably his bodyguards.

The first act drew to a close, and the lights went up. Dickie seized the moment.

'Hello, Kim, old boy. Haven't seen you in ages.'

Philby turned round. With superb aplomb, he grinned as though they were back in the bar at the St George's in Beirut.

'Good Lord, it's Dickie. How are you both? Looking very well.'

The security men were in something of a state now, nudging Philby and urging him to get up and leave with them.

'Where are you staying, anyway?'

'Well, actually, Kim, since you ask, we're stuck in a pretty ghastly room in the Ukraine Hotel. No heating, and the place absolutely stinks. They say they can't find us anywhere better.'

'That's not very good for someone from the old crowd. Sorry to hear that.'

By now the security men were almost lifting Philby out of his seat.

'Better go now. Anyway, lots of love to you both. So glad to have bumped into you. Just like the old days.'

It made an exceptionally good exclusive for the *Daily Telegraph*.

A week or so later, the ambassador of an African country with which the Soviet Union had a special relationship was relaxing in his flat – it was by the far the nicest in the block – when there was a knock at the door. Two men from the UPDK, the organization which assigned flats to foreigners, were standing outside. They were very sorry, they said, but this flat had been reassigned with immediate effect. The ambassador and his family would have to leave. His protests, and those of his foreign ministry, were quite in vain. Soon afterwards the Beestons closed the door of their horrible room in the Ukraine Hotel for the last time, and moved into the ambassador's flat. They never saw Kim Philby again. But the Old Pals' Act had held good, even across the ideological boundaries.

5

DODGIN'

O, the candidate's a dodger,
Yes, a well-known dodger,
Yes, the candidate's a dodger,
Yes, and I'm a dodger too.
He'll meet you and treat you and ask you for your vote,
But look out boys – he's a-dodgin' for a note.
Yes, we're all dodgin',
We're dodgin', dodgin', dodgin'.
Yes, we're all dodgin'
Our way through the world.

Nineteenth-century American folk-song

It has been my good fortune – well, my fortune, at any rate – to meet a great many interesting people. You cannot tour the world at the BBC licence-fee payers' expense for thirty years and avoid them. Some – a very few – are genuinely heroic. The great majority are not. In many ways it is much easier to deal with the publicans and sinners of the world. With them, you are never disappointed, never feel let down. Indeed, if they show any spark of human feeling or generosity you are pleasantly surprised. In my job, these are the people I seem to deal with most: anxious, lying government officials, venal business-men, corrupt policemen, soldiers who are prepared to break any number of eggs to make their omelettes. The fanatics, though I have come across a good number of them too, are fortunately in the minority.

Most of us, however, are just trying to make our way as best we can: dodgin' our way through the world, as the song puts it. This is a chapter about people who are doing that in one way or another.

Some of them are conmen, others have merely found themselves in a difficult position and got out of it as best they could. One or two are outright crooks, like Robert Maxwell; yet no matter how bad they are, they don't quite seem to me to fall under the heading of 'Villains', like the people in one of my earlier chapters. One – my former translator in Afghanistan – is a true gentleman who was saved from danger by the generosity of the Irish government; but he still had to do a certain amount of dodgin', even so.

I was trying to save the licence-fee payers some money. When I spoke to the Reuters cameraman in Nairobi about the trip we were to make together to Mogadishu in Somalia, I suggested that while the BBC usually hired a particular group of gunmen as bodyguards, this time we could probably just share his own team.

There was a pause.

'You could,' he said, 'and I agree it would be cheaper. But the BBC's usual men would feel they had to kill you. It's up to you.'

Put that way, the decision suddenly seemed easy.

We flew into the little airstrip which was the only one free of fighting at the time. Our plane was bringing a consignment of *qat* to Mogadishu, and we had been sitting on the springy sacks which were packed with the stuff. *Qat* is to Somalia what vodka is to Russia, or red wine to France. It is the fuel on which society runs.

It is nothing more than the fresh leaves of a bush, and you have to chew them on one side of your mouth for a very long time in order to get the faint high which it produces. I tried it once or twice, but it seemed to me exactly like stripping a handful of leaves from a hedgerow and stuffing them in my mouth. The only high I obtained was when I gave up and spat the whole horrible mess out.

There were just two of us: Jonathan Cavender, the Reuters cameraman, and I. Somalia wasn't a safe place in the mid-90s, and the fewer people who went there the better. Jonathan was the very model of a British cameraman in Africa: dashing, amusing and footloose, and handsome in a very *Out of Africa* way. Later, in working in the Congo, he contracted some unknown disease as the result of a mosquito bite, and lost the use of his upper arms. At the time, though, he was at the height of his powers: the only cameraman I would have felt safe with in Somalia.

We climbed off the strange-smelling sacks of *qat* and out into the stunning heat of the Somali morning. The Reuters bodyguards were drawn up beside their open vehicle like guardsmen on parade. They were a remarkably tough bunch, and great-looking in a bandit-like way. Next to them, trying not to fraternize, were the BBC body-guards. They seemed to me to be less smart and more cunning, and if it had been up to me I would have preferred to have worked with the Reuters ones. But bodyguard chic isn't the only thing that counts. Living counts quite a lot too, and I could imagine that these men might well feel themselves slighted if they heard I had crept in without hiring them.

I greeted them with the enthusiasm of a man who had never had an unfaithful thought in his life.

This business of bodyguards is a strange one. I scarcely had to speak to mine; they weren't interested in conversation, just in pay-ment. It was difficult enough to recognize them among the crowds of other young, muscular men with AK-47s, and I only managed it because they never changed their clothes. The motifs on their T-shirts identified them for me. There was Adidas, and Brazilian Football, and Zanzibar, and Desert Lover.

And yet, with the magnificent stoicism of their culture, these men would have defended my life with theirs simply because I had hired them. I had heard all sorts of stories about Somali bodyguards which now made absolute sense: of whole teams wiped out down to the last man, who might have saved his life by surrendering but carried on to the death.

We drove off in style, through the red sand and the open stretches of desert, and then the huts and run-down streets of Mogadishu, where the shops were housed in ramshackle structures made from breeze-blocks piled cementless on one another, or else in containers looted from the port and set up by the roadside. I felt a sense of delight and release from the conventions of normal society. Here was a place where, for a few dollars, you could do anything at all. If I had taken a dislike to someone by the side of the road, ten dollars would have had him killed in front of me. And, presumably, vice versa.

There were no rules in Mogadishu. A Westerner who had run a

support service for the United Nations force during its ill-judged and ill-disciplined mission in Somalia had travelled southwards and supposedly been killed there. Four million dollars was found to have gone with him. Mogadishu was the perfect place to disappear, because during the worst of the rioting the British, American, French and German embassies had been broken into and torched, and all the blank passports which were kept in their consular offices were stolen, together with the necessary stamps. And if you did disappear, who was going to come to Mogadishu and take witness statements?

Jonathan and I drove in the same car, with a red open Toyota pick-up carrying his four guards in front of us, and another carrying mine behind us. Somalis have an inbred sense of style. Tall and languid, they allowed the red or white or green scarves they had tied round their heads to flutter in the wind like flags, and the arm which wasn't cradling a Kalashnikov trailed elegantly over the side of the vehicle.

We arrived at the Green Line which divided the strictly Muslim (and therefore better-run) part of Mogadishu from the part where the warlords roamed free. The only decent functioning hotel in town was here. The owner greeted us with enthusiasm; we were his first guests in several months. The hotel had its own bodyguards, and ours hung around with them in the dusty courtyard outside. Once behind the high walls of the hotel there was no reason to be afraid of anything except perhaps the mosquitoes. We ate goat-meat, drank a little carefully concealed Laphroaig, and went to bed early.

The year was 1996, and the UN's fantastic invasion three years earlier had collapsed in humiliation. The Americans were in many ways the worst contingent of all, running from the place when some of their marines were killed in a particularly untelegenic fashion. They had blasted the centre of the city without discrimination; I saw the hospital which they had attacked with helicopter gunships because armed men were wrongly thought to have appeared on the roof. For elements in the American, Canadian and Italian contingents, Somalia became a sadistic adventure playground, where they tortured and killed and destroyed as they wanted.

The cause was often frustration. General Mohammed Aideed, the head of one of the main factions whose civil war the UN had supposedly come to Somalia to stop, had been identified by the

Americans as their main opponent. The trouble was, he hadn't done what he was supposed to do. Instead of surrendering at the prospect of overwhelming firepower and accepting the UN intervention gracefully, he had resisted. He stayed one step ahead of the Americans at all times, escaping from house after house just before they were attacked, running an underground campaign which was eventually victorious.

The West saw Aideed and his followers as bandits, gangsters, murderers; Aideed saw the UN troops as another instalment of the Western invasion which began with Mussolini. I make no case for Aideed; by resisting, he was preventing the flow of aid to those who were suffering from the drought and famine in the country. But he saw the UN involvement in his country as an intrusion, and he resented it.

Now, though, Aideed was dead, and my aim in coming to Mogadishu when the UN and almost all of the aid agencies had pulled out was to interview his son, who had just taken over control of his faction. Hussein Aideed was an intriguing figure: he had been brought up in America, had served in the US Marine Corps, and had had little contact with Somalia – until he took part in the UN intervention there.

The interview took plenty of organizing. Hussein Aideed's people were happy enough for him to appear on the BBC, but things in Somalia have to be done with a certain decorum. *Qat* had to be chewed, and its price, together with the situation in the world in general and Mogadishu in particular, had to be discussed. Even the manner of our going round to visit Aideed was a matter for negotiation. We made progress, but not quickly.

At last, however, the gates of our hotel swung open and we drove out in convoy: a truckload of gunmen from Aideed's faction, Jonathan's bodyguards, our car, my bodyguards, and another truckload of Aideed's men just in case we had come out with insufficient Kalashnikovs. We drove through the shattered centre of town, through roadblocks where the gunmen swiftly stood back and waved us through when they saw who it was, past the areas the Americans had destroyed in searching for Aideed *père*, and into what must, in Italian colonial times, have been the expensive part of town. Decaying villas, the stucco falling away from their façades, showed through overgrown hedges studded with huge red and yellow flowers. Most of the houses seemed occupied by squatters: it was like being in the ruins of a city after the conquerors had pulled out.

We reached a more settled area, where armed men on every corner sat chewing *qat*, their eyes red with the drug, cradling their Kalashnikovs in a brooding kind of way. The early afternoon was not a good time to be driving around – unless you had a small army of sixteen armed men with you, of course.

One house, at a three-way intersection, seemed particularly well guarded. Our convoy stopped there, and I brushed the red dust off the white tropical suit I had worn for the occasion. I had also put on a tie. You cannot be overdressed, I have found, when you visit warlords. They like it.

The house was shuttered and the rooms cool and dark; whether out of mourning for General Aideed or as a security measure wasn't clear. We sat in a kind of passageway between two rooms. Pictures of Alpine scenes hung on the walls, to remind us what coolness was like. There was a sign for the *qibla*, showing which direction to pray in, and some very heavy mahogany furniture with clean white anti-macassars that looked as though they had been bought to please someone's grandmother. Nothing happened.

Then one of the doors opened, and two women walked through. The first was in her fifties. The other must have been in her early twenties, and was one of the most beautiful women I have ever seen: tall, languid, slender, with a perfect dark golden skin, and a thin scarf of some expensive stuff over her head. It was Hussein Aideed's sister. Our eyes met in that meaningful way that means absolutely nothing at all, and her lips parted to murmur a brief apology. Then the room was empty again, and an extremely expensive scent hung on the cool air.

Hussein Aideed came in: young, poised, thoughtful. He even looked American. Could someone like this possibly outwit the experienced schemers in his own faction? Yet when he talked I could see how intelligent he was. Brains might yet trump cunning, I thought; and the succeeding years have shown that to be correct.

We talked about the fractured situation in the country, and his

hopes of overcoming the not unnatural prejudices of the US government against someone with his name. Then I turned the discussion to
the things I really wanted to know about.

'You served in the US Marine Corps?'

'Right.'

'And you were in the Reserve when the troops were sent into
Somalia?'

'Right.'

'You volunteered?'

'No, sir. They looked me up in the records and saw I spoke
Somali, so they called me in.'

'And it was a new country to you?'

'Pretty much.'

'Now at this time your father, General Aideed, was the Americans' Public Enemy Number One. They must have realized from your
name that you were related to him.'

'Can't say anyone mentioned it, sir.'

'They didn't say, Hey, this is a strange coincidence – you've got
the same name as Public Enemy Number One?'

'No, sir.'

'And you didn't mention it to them?'

'Saw no reason to do so, sir.'

'What area were you working in when you were here with the
Marines?'

'Communications, sir.'

'So you had access to radio?'

'Yes, sir.'

'And you must have known when raids were planned to find your
father?'

'Yes, sir.'

'So did you tip him off about the raids – when they were coming,
where they going to be, and so on?'

'Prefer not to answer that question, sir.'

'All right, but did you ever talk to your father?'

'Yes, sir.'

'And he always managed to stay one step ahead of the US forces?'

'Seems so, sir.'

'Miraculous,' I said, and grinned.

A Somali would have smiled back; a US Marine Corps officer would have stayed stony-faced. Hussein Aideed stayed stony-faced.

I came to know Robert Maxwell, war hero, politician, media baron and crook, in the late 1970s and early 80s, thanks to his thoroughly dubious connections with Eastern European dictators. Whether he was actually in their pay, I could never decide. He acted as though he might be, in some ways, and yet there was only ever one cause in Robert Maxwell's mind: Robert Maxwell. It is perfectly possible that he chose to spend his time with the rulers of countries like Romania and Czechoslovakia because it made him a bit of money and he liked to get onto the front pages of the slavish state-controlled press and have people fawning over him.

He was jovial, but invariably menacing. Everything he said sounded pompous, in that loud, phoney accent of his from which every trace of the original Slovak had been surgically removed. He gave expensive parties whenever his company brought out a new, grovelling biography of some Communist dictator, notionally written by Maxwell himself. I would be invited.

'Ah, here we have the man from the BBC,' he would boom as I shook his hand. 'What lies have you been broadcasting about Romania [or Czechoslovakia, or Hungary, or East Germany] lately?'

And having insulted me, he would dismiss me from his mind. Perhaps he only did it to ingratiate himself further with the ambassador of whichever dictatorship his latest volume was about. I would usually try to come back with some quip, but it never registered with him. I was small fry: not the kind of person whose voice he listened to. If Maxwell hadn't been such an interesting, despicable character I wouldn't have gone to these occasions. But I was fascinated by him: the rumbling voice, the huge suits that looked as though they had been laid down at a shipyard, the tiny black shoes, the heavy dewlaps, the sharp, perceptive eyes as expressive as horse chestnuts under brows like an untrimmed hedgerow.

There was an old man, a good ten years older than Maxwell, who used the pool where I swam most mornings when I was in London. Victor Grosz and I took a liking to one another. He was shrewd and cultured, and had seen the world. We used to sit side by side on the long chairs beside the pool, talking. Victor had known Maxwell in his time. They were both Jewish, and had been born in nearby villages in Slovakia. In September 1939 they had set out together for France, to fight Hitler's Germany.

'I loathed the Nazis, naturally. So did Maxwell. But he was crazy. Something used to come over him when he fought them. We transferred to a British unit together when the French began to collapse, and on the way to Dunkirk we were lucky in a skirmish and captured a group of Germans.

'Maxwell went mad. He lined them up, took out his revolver and started shooting them one by one in the forehead. I tried to stop him, but he took no notice.

'Then a British officer heard the noise and came round the corner. He pulled out a pistol and told Maxwell he would shoot him if he didn't drop his gun. They had been going to give him a medal, but after that they couldn't. It was only later that he got one. Maybe they'd forgotten. Or perhaps they didn't care any more.'

The year 1989 brought the collapse of each of the dictatorships which Maxwell had smarmed up to. His grovelling books on Ceauşescu (*Builder of Modern Romania*, published by Pergamon Press in 1983), Zhivkov of Bulgaria, Honecker of East Germany and Jaruzelski of Poland suddenly disappeared from sale. His work on Ceauşescu had included the transcript of an interview between Maxwell and the great man, during which Maxwell put this fearless, searching question:

Dear Mr President, you have been holding the highest political and state office in Romania for almost eighteen years, a fact for which we warmly congratulate you. What has – in your opinion – made you so popular with the Romanians?

By comparison with this, David Frost seems almost aggressive. It took Ceauşescu a full page of the transcript to answer the question, when he could have summed up the real reason in a single sentence: I have one of the biggest and nastiest security services anywhere. After the revolution took place, and Ceauşescu and his wife had been executed by the people they were supposedly so popular with, a journalist asked Maxwell if he regretted writing about him so fulsomely.

'Haven't you ever made a mistake?' was Maxwell's engaging reply.

A few months afterwards, I went to Baghdad to cover the run-up to the Gulf War and stayed there while the bombing started in January 1991. Conditions were bad, and I developed kidney stones. After I was thrown out of Baghdad I went into hospital in Jordan for treatment.

The hospital was a Palestinian one, and was supported partly by a British-based charity. There was a good deal of bad feeling among Palestinians against Westerners in Jordan at that time, but even so I was well cared for. My reporting had attracted a certain amount of attention, and the morning after I had been taken to hospital the British press in Amman asked to come and see me.

They filed in politely, with ingratiating smiles on their faces; rather like Maxwell with Ceauşescu, perhaps. They listened without much interest to what I had to say about the kindness of the hospital staff, then started taking photographs and chatting.

'What've you got this for?' asked one of them, a man from Maxwell's paper, the *Sunday Mirror*.

He was fiddling with a Saddam Hussein lapel badge on my bedside table. One of my BBC colleagues had brought it for me that morning as a joke.

At that point I made a serious error. You should never be ironic or go into unnecessary detail when Fleet Street is around.

'The cleaners here were a lot nicer to me when they saw it by my bed this morning,' I said.

It happened to be true, but it caused great trouble. A few days later the director of the hospital burst angrily into my room, holding a press cutting which someone in London had faxed to him.

It was quite a long article, by *Sunday Mirror* standards. It described how, in exquisite pain, I had come to the hospital and had been turned away by the doctors because I was British. Then I had remembered my Saddam lapel badge, and put it on. The whole atmosphere changed, the article said. They allowed me in, and gave me treatment.

The whole thing was only smoothed over with the director of the hospital by my promising to write to the proprietor of the Mirror Group, threatening to sue. The proprietor was, of course, Robert Maxwell.

I wrote to him, suggesting that a large donation to the hospital might be in order. That gave me pleasure, since the hospital was Palestinian and Maxwell had become an ardent Zionist.

There was no reply.

I wrote again, and said how disgraceful it was that he should ignore a complaint like this. Still no answer.

By October, months after my first letter, I was enraged. But I was also baffled; how could I get Maxwell to reply to me? One day I found myself sitting with a friend of mine, who had once worked closely with Maxwell. I asked him what to do.

'There's absolutely no point in writing to him. He never reads letters.'

It turned out that the people in Maxwell's private office were under the strictest orders never to open the mail. Once, though, my friend felt that so many letters had piled up that he had to go through them. He came into the office at the weekend, locked the doors behind him, and examined the post item by item. He found, among other things, two writs and a cheque for a million pounds.

'Just ring him up. He'll enjoy hearing from you.'

He gave me the number of Maxwell's mobile phone.

I meant to ring him at once, but I kept putting it off. A week later, on 5 November, I was driving home with my daughter Eleanor after a long lunch to celebrate our trip to Buckingham Palace that day for the Gulf War honours. Eleanor fell asleep, and I turned on the radio.

'The newspaper proprietor Robert Maxwell apparently drowned last night after falling from his private yacht in the Mediterranean . . .'

That man never did anything by accident, I thought; he must have jumped. When the reports came in of the imminent financial collapse of his company, I was sure of it. Maxwell had once been a heavy cigar smoker, but had given up the habit on medical advice and had never touched another. That evening, an hour or so before he drowned, he smoked a last cigar.

Maxwell was a brute, a bully, a crook and a shameless flatterer of other crooks. But whatever else he was, he was never a coward.

*

Mr Stanley Ho would, there is not much doubt about it, have liked a knighthood from the British before they handed over control of Hong Kong to the Chinese government in 1997. He scarcely looked Chinese with those dark, saturnine features; could he be Eurasian? He gazed out unseeingly at the incomparable view of Victoria Harbour from his office on the top floor of one of the colony's most expensive buildings.

You could play indoor tennis in that office, and still have room to fetch the balls that went astray. All round the walls were photographs of Mr Ho performing charitable functions. The cupboards and sideboards were covered with trophies and unimaginably complicated carvings in jade, each one labelled with some flattering message. Mr Ho had received honorary doctorates. He had been the president of innumerable societies. He had given away more money than most of us earn in a lifetime. His enormous desk was cluttered with signed photographs from the faintly recognizable.

Mr Ho was an anglophile. He dressed in the best suits Savile Row could produce, his shoes were made by Lobb, his accent was impeccably English, and his children had been to the most expensive schools and universities Britain could boast. But he still hadn't had the only type of recognition he wanted. The British authorities had somehow resisted giving Mr Ho a knighthood. They never gave one to Robert Maxwell, either.

Mr Ho had made his money through gambling. The entire casino concession for the Portuguese colony of Macao, a little further along the coast of the South China Sea, was in his hands. Every day the roulette wheels turned for him, and the blackjack and *vingt-et-un* tables added their profits to his fortune. Mr Ho might not be happy, but he was one of the richest men in Asia. It should have helped a little, but it didn't seem to.

I liked Stanley Ho. It was partly his accent and his anglophilia, and partly the fact that he so badly wanted a bauble which all sorts of second-raters can count on as a certainty. That made him, to my mind, a romantic. But there were clear limits to his romanticism; his determination to hang on to the proceeds from the casinos in one of the fiercest and most violent places on earth being one of them.

We were there to make a film about the gangster problems in

Macao, and Mr Ho had agreed to give us one of his very rare interviews. There was some kind of intercom system with the office next door; when I explained what we were looking for, an aide in a suit which can have cost only a thousand pounds or so less than that of his boss came running in to raise a particular point.

The interview was the usual sort of fencing you always get with someone as careful and as deeply involved as Stanley Ho. No, he said blandly, there was no suggestion that organized crime was interested in the casinos of Macao. The shootings and robberies which went on there almost daily were just a part of the ordinary crime of the colony, which was unfortunately rather high; nothing, however, to do with gambling. He knew little about the Triads, and seemed to doubt, indeed, whether they really existed. Then, casting round for some other way to put the question, I asked if the American Mafia had ever shown an interest in the Macao casinos.

'Well, two American gentlemen did come to Macao, and showed a great interest in our casinos. Unfortunately, the police there are not like our police here in Hong Kong – not so well trained, you know. They put these Americans in prison for some infraction.

'And there some unfortunate things happened to them. It was all very difficult. One of them died there, and the other one had his elbow gnawed off by rats. The prisons in Macao aren't as well run as they are here, you see. Great shame. He was in terrible pain, poor fellow, so of course he had to be sent home. It was the least we could do.

'After that, for some reason, no one else came to Macao from America.'

Mr Ho looked out thoughtfully at the wonderful view across the Harbour, his saturnine face lit by the late afternoon sun. I could see now why he would never be Sir Stanley.

The weather had closed in, and Manali airport was set in a Himalayan valley, open at one end and blocked by a mountain at the far side. The incoming planes had to fly in up the valley, taking care not to overshoot. If they overshot they would hit the mountain. And since the planes had no radar, they had to be able to see the mountain if they were to land in safety. If it was too misty, they couldn't land. And now it was very misty.

Freddy, our Indian fixer, was beside himself. He strode up and down the room, fingering his moustache and looking like a character out of a 1930s film about British India.

'All I can say is that I'll do everything possible.'

Freddy had organized our entire trip. His pleasant features were suddenly a little haggard. He was perpetually over-extended, always promising a little more than he could deliver and then having to drop everything else in order to make his promise good. I had grown immensely fond of him, but I needed to get back to London as a matter of urgency. And Freddy had promised that, no matter what it took, he would make sure I got back in time.

'You see, the planes are simply not flying. They can't make it in.'

'But, Freddy, the only reason we're here is that you absolutely undertook to get me out of here by Thursday at the very latest.'

'And so I shall, my dear chap, so I shall. I'll just have to think about it.'

The moustache took a little more punishment.

We waited in Manali for another day of bad weather. Then I explained to Freddy that time had run out: we would have to get out the next day, without fail. Dawn broke over clouds which were as thick as ever in the valley. Even so, I said, the plane would have to come in.

I sat in the little departure lounge, my knapsack beside me. All around local people sat with live chickens in makeshift boxes, and bags of fruit and vegetables from the Hills which they would sell in the big city to make some money. Freddy strode off to make a phone call. A few minutes later he bustled back excitedly.

'You see, it's a friend of mine from the Indo-Pak war who is flying the aircraft. I explained one or two little things to him, and he says he'll definitely make it in.'

'Even though the clouds are still so thick?'

'He's saying it doesn't matter.'

Freddy's face, worn by the thousand extra cares of a man who has to make deals to live, broke into a grin.

Half an hour later we heard the distant note of an aircraft engine.

It came closer and closer, then seemed to veer away at the last moment. The cloud was too thick after all.

'I know, I know,' said Freddy, as I opened my mouth to speak. 'I'll get onto the blower to him right away.'

Fifteen minutes later the sound returned, and grew stronger and stronger. This time, despite the cloud, the plane landed.

'Thank God,' said Freddy.

Another task had been achieved, another promise made good at whatever cost.

I got some idea of the cost when the arriving passengers filed through the lounge. They were pale and silent, and had clearly looked upon the face of the infinite.

'Well, time for you to go. I'm glad everything worked out.'

'But what happened, Freddy?'

'I can't remember if I told you, but the pilot and I flew together in the Indo-Pak war.'

'You did tell me. But was that enough to make him land?'

Freddy coughed in an embarrassed kind of way.

'No, well, you see, cauliflowers are one rupee each here, and in Delhi they are twelve rupees. I got some in.'

I was already settled into my seat on the plane when I caught sight of Freddy again. He was loading an improbable number of boxes into the cockpit of the aircraft. Plenty more had gone into the hold. I waved to him with great affection: a man under that degree of strain needs all the support and friendship he can get.

There was no difficulty about taking off, of course: the plane merely headed out into the open valley. As it lifted off and headed steeply upwards Freddy, waving from the tarmac, became a tiny dot hidden by the swirling clouds.

Under the sudden gravity the door to the cockpit came open, and a particularly large, round cauliflower rolled down the aisle. Freddy had kept his promise.

The courtroom was dark, and someone was shouting. I couldn't understand what was going on, and I felt slightly nervous about being here; I had had problems filming in a court without permission in the past. But there was no trouble about that here. The judge didn't explode with rage that we should have arrived unannounced in his court with a television camera, and the court officials (there seemed to be only two of them anyway) sat and watched us with a certain relaxed interest.

The shouting continued. It was the man whose case was being tried. He was kept in a barred cage over on the right-hand side of the court, and ranged around and shouted incoherently in Russian. No one seemed to want to stop him.

I sent a written message up to the judge. It apologized for not having sought his prior permission, and asked if it would be possible to film this case. He was youngish, thick-set, and dark-haired. He gave me a thumbs up from his judge's throne, and the cameraman got to work.

It was 1992, and the old Soviet system had collapsed less than a year before. Russians had the feeling that now they were living in a democracy everyone should be allowed to do everything. Secret documents were being released at a breathtaking rate; we could ring any senior official, no matter how high up, and expect that he or she would speak to us frankly on camera; the Russian newspapers were revealing truths about their government and society which had been secret for ever. None of it lasted, of course. As Russians came to know and understand more about the West, they found out that there is little real freedom of information there either.

But these, for a television journalist who loves Russia as I do, were heady days. It became possible to show life there as it had never been shown before; even a trial for murder and, as it appeared, cannibalism.

We had been in St Petersburg for only a few days, and had asked our local fixer to take us to a courtroom where a trial was in progress. He had brought us to this undistinguished nineteenth-century building where smoke-encrusted stone giants strained under the weight of the upper floors, and we pushed the door open. There seemed to be no one on guard: all to the good.

The judge was openness itself. The cameraman stood in front of him, filming the questions he put to the prisoner. Then he went across and filmed the prisoner through the bars. From the little I could understand of the evidence, it was an appalling case of bestial violence. The prisoner, in a dark blue suit made for someone much shorter and slimmer, and with his neck straining over the collar of his buttoned, tieless shirt, made a half-hearted effort to get at the cameraman and perhaps kill him and eat him. The cameraman stayed out of reach. He recorded some teeth-gnashing and inarticulate cries from the accused man, then panned across to the judge.

I picked up the microphone and pointed in the judge's direction.

'What do you think of this case?'

'Well, it's only the first day, but from the evidence we've heard so far it's a terrible business. There's no doubt he's guilty.'

'But, sorry, if it's only the first day—'

'Well, the evidence is overwhelming.'

'Yes, but—'

'The man is clearly guilty as charged.'

'So what sort of sentence do you anticipate—'

'Well, I'm essentially a liberal. I'm against the death penalty.'

'What does that mean in this case?'

'Oh, in this case I'll have to sentence him to death. It's the only way.'

'But I thought you said you were a liberal.'

'Yes, but there are cases which are just too dreadful. Do you realize he killed his victim, cut out the—'

I thanked him, and moved away quickly. We went back to the prisoner again.

'I've just been talking to the judge.'

The prisoner seemed to be telling me what he thought of the judge.

'He says you're guilty, and he's going to sentence you to death.'

The prisoner went crazy, raving and trying to get through the bars at me. He wanted to eat various specified parts of me.

The judge gave me a letter for a British lawyer friend of his; he had written it while the defence lawyer was cross-examining one of the key witnesses.

As for the prisoner, he was found guilty and shot in the back of the neck a few days later. Things had changed in Russia, but they hadn't necessarily changed that much.

*

I have only once in my life been properly, thoroughly and comprehensively robbed by experts. Of course, I've had plenty of things taken off me by sneak-thieves, and sometimes been forced to hand over money and small items at gunpoint. But this time it was different. This time I played mug to a gang of trained crooks.

It happened in Prague, a matter of a few days before what everyone now calls the Velvet Revolution of 1989. I had managed to get back in after years of being banned and regarded as a national enemy (I have described elsewhere how the Czech secret police, the StB, set a rather beautiful young woman to entrap me) because it was obvious even to the immigration officials at the airport that times were changing and the old system was in the process of collapse. One of them looked at me carefully, squinted at the message which clearly came up on his computer, decided to ignore it and stamped my passport. I was back.

The next few days were wonderful. The invasion of Czechoslovakia by the Russians in 1968 had been one of the formative incidents of my life, as devastating to me as the Vietnam War; and now I was privileged to be able to watch as the whole rotten edifice which the Russians and their servants had created in Czechoslovakia collapsed in front of my eyes.

Yet the old system hadn't yet given up entirely, and to change hard currency into Czech crowns was still a lengthy, expensive and wasteful business. Much easier to do a deal with a tout on the street. It was illegal, but then so, technically, was taking part in a demonstration and demanding a free press. I decided not to worry about the law.

I wandered down into the Old Town, in the general direction of the Charles River. Nowadays Prague is thronged with tourists, the shops are full of the kind of overpriced goods you can buy anywhere, and there is an inordinate number of art galleries, selling paintings which look like someone else's. In November 1989, though, the old system was still in force. The streets were poorly lighted and irregularly paved, the shops had old-fashioned goods in them, the people were shabby and after forty years of Marxism-Leninism their faces were drawn and anxious. I loved it, all the same. If I wanted smart shops and expensive Western goods I could go to France or Germany.

Here you could see what life in a central European city must have been like for centuries.

The old part of the city was beginning to empty of people. Nowadays this is the part that stays open until past midnight, but then the streets fell quiet by eight o'clock. The shops were closing. The bells of the magical clock in the Old Town Square were chiming an elaborate quarter-hour, and the sound weaved its way through the narrow streets towards me.

It was getting late to find anyone to change money. I wandered up and down in my expensive overcoat, which signalled clearly enough that I was a Westerner looking for a deal. It began to work. A man darted out of a derelict house and walked along beside me, keeping his voice down and looking straight ahead of him.

'You interested in changing money?'

His English was good. I said I was.

'How much?'

I told him, two hundred dollars; a lot of money in Prague.

'H'm. It'll take me a couple of minutes to get the crowns.'

I walked up and down a little more. By this time there was scarcely anyone else on the street.

He reappeared at the doorway of the derelict house. It was only then that I realized the house was being renovated. Plasterers were still at work in one of the rooms on the ground floor. The man beckoned me closer.

'I'm working on the house here,' he whispered. 'Come into the hallway – it's safer there.'

I stepped into the hall. It was dark, but the light from the room where the plasterers were at work was enough for the purpose of changing money.

'So, two hundred dollars, that's a hundred and forty thousand crowns,' the man said.

I showed him the two bills. He examined them, then punctiliously handed them back to me. There is an etiquette about the illegal changing of money. He began counting out the notes: 'A hundred and twenty thousand, a hundred and forty thousand.'

At that instant there was an explosion of rage, and a heavy-set man came charging downstairs.

'Christ!' shouted the money-changer. 'It's the foreman! He's a real Communist. Quick – give me the money. Here's yours.'

He shoved a wad of notes into my hand, as thick as a brick.

'Run for it! He'll call the cops!'

I ran for it. At the corner of the little alley I cannoned into a man carrying a bag of groceries, and he swore at me. I was too nervous to say sorry. Suppose the authorities caught me: to be found changing money illegally would get me into serious trouble even in a country which was starting to undergo a revolution.

And yet there was something working away inside my head, even as the blood beat loudly in it. How come, if this was such a dangerous and illegal transaction, the money-changer had shouted out a warning to me in English? Surely that would demonstrate his guilt to the foreman?

I slowed down to a fast walk. No policemen were thundering through the side-streets in search of me. I stopped in a side-alley and pulled the wad of notes out of my pocket. There were a couple of Czechoslovak hundreds on the top, and then the rest were less familiar. I had a hollow feeling in my stomach as I examined them: they were Polish. Inflation was rampant in Poland, and the entire wad was worth about five dollars – if, that is, you could find anyone willing to accept them. I had been robbed.

I turned round and ran back. The plasterers were just packing up, and one of them spoke enough German for me to be able to understand him.

Yes, there had been a couple of men in the hallway – up to no good, probably. He'd seen one come down the stairs, even though neither of them were supposed to be there: they weren't working on the house, or anything like that. Just off the streets. He'd heard the shouting. Had they stolen something from me?

No, not at all, I said blandly; nothing like that. No, I'd just been – I'd just been asking the way.

Oh, asking the way, said the plasterer with the shadow of a grin. I hope he told you. So why did you come back?

I walked off. At first I was angry: two hundred dollars was quite a lot of money to have lost. And I felt such an idiot – such a stupid, out-of-town, innocent mark, just begging a couple of crooks to take me.

I walked on. The spires of the old city glittered in the damp evening air, and reflected on the cobblestones. John Hus, the religious reformer, stood frozen in agony on his statue in the place where the Catholic Church had burned him to death. There were, I reflected, worse things than losing a couple of hundred bucks.

And then I thought over the sting. How superb the timing had been, how believable the fear, how cleverly judged the threat from the Communist foreman. The sleight of hand as he hid the genuine wad of notes and pulled out the Polish ones from nowhere was worthy of a first-rate stage magician. I had been given a lesson in conmanship. It was an expensive one, but a performance like that certainly deserved a reward.

I laughed out loud, and people on the far side of the square looked over to see who was making that extraordinary noise in a silent city.

We stood in the street outside the International Red Cross head-quarters in Kabul, and said goodbye. It was May 1996, and the crew and I were leaving for the airstrip, to catch a plane back to Peshawar and the real world. Dr Zekria was staying behind in Afghanistan. He was a small, self-contained man, a gynaecologist with a pleasant, smiling face, and a bushy moustache, and he had been our translator during a long and particularly arduous filming trip around the country. I had come to like him very much indeed.

'John, supposing the Taliban capture Kabul,' he said, quietly so the others couldn't hear, 'would you help me get to England?'

I thought for a moment. It was a big promise to make; and even though at that stage it seemed highly unlikely that the Taliban would ever get it together sufficiently to capture Kabul, a promise was a promise. But there could only be one answer. We had put Dr Zekria's life in jeopardy by employing him at all, and an incident in the city of Herat a few days before had made everything a great deal worse.

I promised, and shook his hand.

Herat is a beautiful city in western Afghanistan which once belonged to Persia, and its inhabitants, like many other Afghans, are predominantly Persian-speakers. At this stage, though, the great majority of the Taliban were Pashtu-speakers, and when they captured Herat they were aggressive about imposing Pashtu customs on the people of the city. The women were obliged to wear the all-encompassing burka, which covers the face with a mesh of lace.

The Taliban stood out in this city like an army of aliens, in their robes and turbans, many of them wearing eye make-up, fingernail polish and golden sandals. Because their brand of Islam forbids the depiction of human or animal forms, they cut the heads off the horses which decorated Herat's most famous fountain, and they painted out the figures on some beautiful seventeenth-century frescos in the main buildings.

The mood was extraordinarily tense. As we walked down the street with our camera, watched by everyone, a couple of cars collided some way ahead of us. The Taliban police turned up, and there was an immediate confrontation with the passers-by who gathered. The entire city seemed to be seething with resentment and rebellion.

When the incident was over we got into our vehicle and drove a little way down the magnificent avenue which lies at the heart of the city, in order to get some shots of the grand mosque at the end of it. We had a piece of paper from the local Taliban authorities, allowing us to film, but we were on our own. The cameraman, Peter Jouvenal, was setting up his tripod and getting the shots while I sat in the back of the vehicle with the door open, writing some notes. I was faintly aware of someone going past on a bicycle, and then a piece of screwed-up paper hit me in the face. It turned out to be a message for us. Calling Peter over, I spoke briefly to camera about what had happened, and gave the note to Dr Zekria to translate. Peter filmed him as he read it out.

> Our lives are in constant danger. They are killing us all the time. You, BBC, must tell the world about the terrible things that are taking place in Herat.

With hindsight, of course, we should never have shown Dr Zekria's face or even allowed his voice onto the soundtrack. All I can say is that, at the time, neither he nor I nor anyone else in our team realized the potential danger for him.

When our reports were broadcast, they caused a sensation among Afghans. No one had obtained so much access to the Taliban before, nor to the parts of Afghanistan they controlled. The Taliban were incensed that we should have filmed their leader, Mullah Omar, as he held up the cloak of the prophet Mohammed to the vast crowd at an extraordinary public ceremony. But they were even angrier about the section of our film which dealt with Herat, and they blamed Dr Zekria for taking part in it.

At the time this didn't seem to matter too much, since Zekria lived in Kabul, and Kabul was firmly under the control of the mujaheddin alliance, the enemies of the Taliban. But within months, totally unexpectedly, a Taliban offensive against Kabul succeeded, and the government fled ignominiously for the north of the country. Dr Zekria's worst fears had come to pass.

It wasn't just our film that caused his difficulties. As a gynaecologist, he was a specialist in a form of medicine which the Taliban believed was tantamount to the committing of adultery. They regarded the touching of women's bodies by a man outside marriage as worthy of the death penalty.

And so when the Taliban took over Kabul they came looking for him. The International Red Cross, anxious to maintain some kind of relationship with the Taliban, were not going to give themselves even more trouble than they could already expect by championing Zekria's cause. Directly a Taliban official recognized him from our television coverage, his life was in serious danger.

Eventually the International Red Cross agreed to get him and his family out of Kabul, and they settled in Peshawar. But they were no safer there. The Taliban had close links with Pakistan: their organization had been formed in the refugee camps in Pakistan close to the border with Soviet-run Afghanistan, and Pakistani military intelligence had given the Taliban every help in getting started. Peshawar was an important centre for Taliban activity.

It was hard to forgive the International Red Cross for cutting Dr Zekria loose. They did not help him to go anywhere where he might have been safer, and they were no longer willing to employ him. After my experiences with the ICRC, and my meeting with Maurice Rossel, the delegate who accepted the charade at Theresienstadt concentration camp because he was too frightened to do anything else, this didn't come as a huge surprise to me. Nor did the fact that so many people working for other non-governmental agencies regard the ICRC with a dislike which sometimes amounts to contempt.

It was some time before Dr Zekria contacted me, but when he did I undertook to try to redeem my promise to him. A Labour government, few of whose members I knew well, had just come to office. I had, however, met and rather liked the new Home Secretary, Jack Straw; and after suggesting to Dr Zekria that he should contact the British High Commission in Islamabad, I wrote to Straw and asked him for help.

It was quite a long time before I heard anything back from him. When I did, I was so angry that I threw the letter away and cannot now quote from it verbatim. But he said in effect that he had looked into the case, and that because Dr Zekria had attended a course in Switzerland at the invitation of the International Red Cross and had not asked for political asylum in Switzerland at the time, this was proof that he could not have feared for his life. There seemed no point in arguing that Zekria had only gone to Geneva because he was confident that I could arrange political asylum for him in Britain.

In fact there seemed no point in arguing at all. The rejection seemed final. Jack Straw was punishing me, and Dr Zekria through me, for not going through the usual channels. The usual channels, I felt, might result in his death. I would have to find somewhere else for him to go.

In the spring of 1997 we went to Ireland to make our home there. Immediately I realized that the atmosphere was a great deal easier: refugees could still expect a reasonably warm welcome, and the chilly refusal that even deserving cases often received in Britain seemed unknown. At the Aliens' Registration Office, where Dee had to go because of her South African passport, all sorts of people from countries which were nowhere near as dangerous as Afghanistan were given a friendly reception. Yet the atmosphere of mistrust and hostility was spreading across the Irish Channel from Britain. The Home Office, clearly anxious that Ireland might become the back door to immigration into Britain, was putting considerable pressure on the relevant government ministries in Dublin. Once again, it seemed, my timing was all wrong.

Zekria, in the meantime, was getting into deeper and deeper trouble. The Taliban knew now that he was living in Peshawar, and he dared not leave the house by day or night. Once when he was obliged to go to the bazaar he was recognized and hunted down through the narrow streets; he was lucky to escape. Money was getting shorter and shorter, too. The relatives he depended on were themselves worried how they were going to live. Three other Afghan gynaecologists who had taken refuge in Pakistan were murdered.

I turned eventually to a journalist for help. Sam Smyth, who came originally from Belfast, is one of the best-known political commentators in Dublin, and his books on politics have a sharply witty edge to them. His column in the *Sunday Independent* and his talkshow on Radio Today are both unmissable. He invited me on to his show to talk about something completely different, and afterwards in the pub, where he and his guests always end up, I outlined Dr Zekria's case to him and asked him for help.

Even then it wasn't altogether quick: governments are rarely fast movers. But the foreign minister, David Andrews, a tall, rangy man with a pleasant, lived-in kind of face, was taken with the idea. He was close to retirement, and perhaps saw this as one way in which he could make a difference to someone's life. There was no question in his mind or that of his most senior human rights official about the merits of the case; it was, they agreed, open and shut. The problem was the fact that the British government had rejected it.

Eventually, a way round was devised; in Ireland, I have found, it always is. Dr Zekria had almost despaired of success, and had been thinking of trying elsewhere. He even wrote for help to someone senior in the International Red Cross, whose idea of helping was to contact me and suggest that I should be trying harder. At last, though, the way was clear. Dr Zekria and his family – his wife (a trained dentist) and their three children – caught a plane for Amsterdam, and Peter Jouvenal joined them there. His generosity to deserving Afghans is legendary, and few deserved more than Dr Zekria.

I waited anxiously for them in the arrivals hall at Dublin airport with a large bunch of flowers in my arms, afraid that even at this late stage they might be turned back by Irish immigration. But everything was in order: the children came running through the open doors with Dr Zekria and his wife Nadia following. We sat and had the first of many coffees while Sam Smyth arrived and met the people he had done so much to help.

I had already found somewhere for them to stay while their case was being processed. When I told one hotelier in the centre of Dublin about the family's story a couple of days before, he offered to take them in for nothing. Fortunately, though, the BBC had agreed to pay for them. Later they transferred to another hotel in Dun Laoghaire, where the children were treated like kings and the staff adopted the entire family as a kind of good cause. Peter Jouvenal and I took them to the seaside and to a mosque, where they were slightly nervous of coming across pro-Taliban Afghans. Instead they found a charming, slightly cynical Iranian.

'The Irish are delightful people,' he said. 'They believe everything you tell them.'

The first night they arrived Dr Zekria's wife and the children stayed in their hotel room while Zekria himself came out with us to dinner. He marvelled at everything: how relaxed and smiling the people in the streets were, how disciplined the motorists were at the traffic lights, how clean everything was.

The next day Peter and I took the whole family to a supermarket in the south of Dublin. I thought they were going to weep when they saw the vast orderly shelves, the enormous range of food, the politeness of the staff, and the sheer availability of everything in the First World of which they would soon be citizens.

They found themselves a house in a pleasant suburb of Dublin, rented to them cheaply by an Iranian woman, and they settled down to wait for their permission to stay permanently in Ireland. Sometimes Dr Zekria would get nervous, imagining that officialdom there might be as corrupt and capricious as in Afghanistan; but eventually the day came when his application for political asylum was approved. This was in March 2000. His fourth child was born at almost the same time. It had been three very difficult years for him and his wife, but at last everything had worked out. As I write, Dr Zekria is taking the necessary courses to ensure that he can practise as a gynaecologist in Ireland. His older children already have Irish accents.

It still seems shameful to me that the country which took them in wasn't Britain. One can only hope that those who rejected the appeal of a man whose life was in the gravest danger will never know what it is like to be driven from their country by fanatics, to stay hidden night and day for fear of the gunman and the lynch mob, and to be spurned by the callousness of uncaring officialdom.

The cities of India lift the heart as much as the landscape of Central Asia does. Pakistan seems much more pro-British, with its ubiquitous Union Jacks and the boastful 'GB's on the vehicles of those whose relatives have made it good, and with its striding hillmen in their *shalwar kameez* it resembles much more the Raj of Britain's wistful imaginings.

Yet India has far more colour and complexity: a well-ordered, peaceable country where hundreds of millions gain a precarious living in the vast web of minuscule services which constitutes everyday life in India.

I reflected on this as I walked across the well-kept park in the centre of Connaught Place, that charmingly dilapidated colonnaded circle built in the 1930s as the commercial hub of imperial Delhi. Above the ornamental bushes and trees I could see the advertisements on the buildings: 'Gupta Suitings and Shirtings', 'Exclusive Hankies', 'Modistone Tyres – They Take You Home, Safe'.

Behind me, a voice spoke: 'Excuse me, sir, but would you like your shoes shined?'

Used to ignoring the importunate, I carried on walking.

'You will not find a better shining in the whole of Delhi, sir; possibly not in the whole of India. Most reasonable, sir.'

I had to turn round then. The voice was that of a sub-continental Jeeves, but it came from a small boy, ragged and grave. If Hollywood had done the casting his part would have been played by some white-toothed, laughing Sabu; this child was dirty, his teeth were brown, and he looked as worried as a fifty-year-old with money problems. I suppose he was around thirteen.

'Where did you learn your English?'

'In the streets, sir; where else? I am Sohan, sir. No need to undo your laces, I will do that.'

It seemed I was getting a shoeshine after all. Sohan got down to work. As I sat on the harsh, well-trimmed grass an ancient leathery character in brown robes appeared from behind a bush and gripped my stockinged feet.

'Mr Ram Sebun will give you foot massage, sir; very relaxing.'

Mr Ram Sebun smiled, working away with one hand and holding out a grubby book of handwritten commendations with the other. *You don't get this sitting in Hyde Park*, Bob of Crouch End had written in it, accurately enough. Beside this was a mysterious message in a different hand: *Watch out for the ear-treatment, though*.

The ear-treatment arrived beside me at that very moment.

'Mr Lal, sir,' said Sohan, bashing away at my Crockett and Jones boots.

Mr Lal the ear-cleaner smiled a *betel*-reddened smile and produced the tools of his distasteful trade: miniature chimney-sweep's brushes, which looked almost long enough, if inserted in the right ear, to reach through to the left and clean that as well. I drew the line at Mr Lal.

Then a photographer appeared.

'Sir, just one little picture.'

'Better not, sir,' advised Sohan. 'You do not know which of these fellows may be a rascal.'

I understood then where his English came from. It was the marvellous, diverse, expressive language of the Indian press, in which 'rascal', like 'dacoit', 'dreaded ultra' and 'wicked miscreant' are part of the daily usage.

Only that morning I had found to my delight that an article of mine from the *Spectator* had been reprinted in the *Pioneer* of Delhi and Lucknow – Kipling's old paper, and the one for which Churchill briefly worked as a war correspondent. Set at the head of the text was an artist's impression of me, drawn from imagination and showing a thrusting young man with jet-black hair, instead of the etiolated grey-poll of real life.

It is a joy to sample the vitality and exuberance of the *Pioneer* and the rest of the Indian press.

Former Health Minister Narendra Singh shot the third letter to the Chief Minister Laloo Prasad yesterday. He said that the political power in the State was under the influence of a leader who had been hobnobbing with the animal husbandry mafia groups.

A thirty-year-old man was set on fire by three unidentified men who first objected and later fought him for urinating in the open. The target of the trio's ire, one Ram Niwas, has been admitted to hospital.

Kovalam beach near Trivandrum, the apple of the eye for Kerala's tourism industry, has now become a haven for suspicious foreign nationals, especially from Pakistan. One silver lining is that the Centre is seized of the matter.

The words are as vigorous and unexpected as the actions they describe. In an Indian newspaper, criminals are not arrested but nabbed, policies are not criticized but flayed, politicians are not asked for their reasons but issued with a show-cause notice, and they do not fly to conferences but air-dash to meets. Headlinese has entered everyday language, and technical terms exist to be flaunted. 'Sine die', 'suo motu', 'paradigms', 'modalities' are used without explanation, on the assumption the reader knows perfectly well what they mean. 'The PM arrived sans his entourage.' There is an instinct for the grand and the polysyllabic: 'conditionalities' is used where others might merely say 'conditions'; 'emporium' is used for 'shop'. The sweetness of disposition which leads even the police to put up signs at their roadblocks reading 'Kindly Bear With Us' also produces an emotional quality in the press: 'He expressed his anguish at the news of the hitch.'

On the way back from my shoeshine and foot massage I took in the powerful evening scents from the flowerbeds at the tidy roundabouts, and noticed how even the women who swept the streets wore chiffons of rose-red or magenta or pale green. A trishaw spluttered along like a cockroach, the words 'Horn Please' painted quite unnecessarily on its rear, and a vivid chrome yellow scarf flying from it like a flag: a woman passenger had wound the other end round her cobalt blue sari. This instinct for vividness, for the chrome yellows and cobalt blues of language, is evident in Indian English. The words are clashing yet harmonious, raw and uncoordinated, used with a lavish interest in their tone, for pure pleasure. Indian English is not a pastiche of the original; its vibrancy is entirely its own.

A friend once sent me a document from a man who was appealing against a ruling by an official at the British High Commission in New

Delhi. Mr Mohinder wanted to go to Britain to marry an Indian girl who lived there, but the official had refused his application. The document is entitled 'Humble Submission Praying for Justice and Entry Clearance', and frequently invokes 'Her Majesty Queen'. The young woman he wants to marry is, he explains, 'heart broken because of the repeated failure of matrimonial relation'. One prospective husband 'was a Don Juan and got entangled in several litigation involving women'. As for another candidate, 'It was impossible for her to bear the ill behaviour of that man, which had no bounds or leaps.'

Then Mr Mohinder met her.

> I was totally moved by the fact that the young girl was used as pawn in the hands of callous men and the intensity of the sufferings she had to tolerate at an inaugural phase of her young life. The spring of her youth was nearly spoiled. I decided to help her by reblooming her nuptial life, which was almost at the brim of in extremis. Being a young man of strong will to contribute certain good things to my society, I have taken this opportunity as God-sent to give a good life to a good soul.

I imagine the Humble Submission was written by a scribe, of the kind who might operate in Connaught Place alongside Sohan the shoeshine boy, Mr Lal the ear-cleaner, and Mr Ram Sebun the masseur of feet. A man's got to live.

I never found out whether Mr Mohinder was allowed into Britain to rebloom the nuptial life of the young girl he had taken pity on. (He wanted, he said, to 'instil a sense of safe and security into her broken heart'.) Let us hope so: our speech has become so desiccated that it, too, is almost at the brim of in extremis. Language as rich as this would do us all good.

When, in April 1985, *Stern* magazine in Germany announced that around sixty volumes of Hitler's secret diaries had been discovered, and that it was going to publish them in conjunction with the London *Sunday Times*, there was something in many of us that wanted to believe it.

No matter that, when the first extracts appeared, they were of a stunning banality; after all, while Europe was in flames and people were suffering and dying in their millions, Hitler sat in the cinema of his Bunker holding hands with Eva Braun and watching fluffy little musical comedies about shepherd girls falling in love with the heir to the throne. So to read the entry from the time of Dunkirk, 20 May 1940, for instance ('The English are worrying me. Shall I let them go or not? How will Churchill react?') or after the attempt on his life in July 1944 ('Ha, ha, isn't it laughable? This scum, these loafers and good-for-nothings. These people were bunglers!') wasn't in itself proof that the Diaries were phoney. Everyone had always known perfectly well that the evil of Nazism was banal; and Hitler himself was an empty little man whose only real talent was the diabolical energy generated by his belief in himself.

So when one of the best-respected of modern historians, Hugh Trevor-Roper, turned out to have authenticated the Diaries, that seemed to be all the evidence that was required. In 1945, in the immediate aftermath of Hitler's suicide, Trevor-Roper had been chosen by British Intelligence to write the definitive account, *The Last Days Of Hitler*, which would prevent anyone from ever suggesting again that he might have escaped from the Bunker. Forty years later his authority was immense.

Nevertheless, the doubts about the Diaries persisted; and in the days that followed the first publication of extracts by *Stern* and the *Sunday Times* several German and British historians said openly that they were fakes. But of course historians are as competitive and jealous as any other mortals, so that wasn't necessarily final. It turned out that no one had actually seen the Diaries except Trevor-Roper (now the Master of Peterhouse, Cambridge, and ennobled as Lord Dacre), the *Stern* journalist Gerd Heidemann who had discovered them, whoever it was that he had got them from, and one or two top people on *Stern* itself. *Stern* announced that Lord Dacre and Gerd Heidemann would present the Diaries at a press conference in Hamburg a few days later. I was determined to cover it.

My crew and I waylaid Lord Dacre on his way to Hamburg. He was tall, slightly gawky, with a mass of wayward, frizzy grey hair and round horn-rimmed glasses. Carrying a trench-coat, he looked like a character from one of Graham Greene's middle-period novels.

'Oh,' he said when I stopped him at the airport.

His vowels were neat and precise, and belonged to a past generation. He looked around for help, but there was none.

'You must have been shaken by all the scepticism that's been
expressed about the Diaries,' I suggested.

'Well, no, I—' He paused. Our camera light shone on him cruelly.
'I mean, of course, one must keep an open mind.'

'Does that mean you're not absolutely convinced?'

'Not necessarily, no, not at all.'

He was making things worse with every word, his head turning
from side to side helplessly.

'I mean, we must examine the Diaries properly, and be absolutely
certain about their provenance, before we can be sure.'

'But you're the one who said they were genuine.'

It sounded cruel, even in my own ears.

'Look, I'm afraid— I mean, I think I should get on. Do you think
I could—'

He went awkwardly, politely, nervously past us, and the cameraman swung round to film him walking down the tunnel.

'So what does that mean?' asked the cameraman.

'I think it means he's dug his own grave.'

I had sufficient decency to feel bad about it, as we broadcast the
interview that night.

Press conferences are usually dull affairs. The one *Stern* gave the
next day at its smart, clean, orderly offices was the most eventful I
have ever been to. *Stern's* top management sat at a long table, with
Heidemann in the middle and ten folio black-covered notebooks,
some adorned with red sealing-wax, stacked in front of him. Lord
Dacre sat on the far left, with a gap between him and the others and
a very unhappy look on his scholarly features.

At first it went as *Stern* intended. Heidemann told the story of the
Diaries' provenance. One of the last planes out of Berlin in April
1945 had crashed in what was now East Germany, close to the
Czechoslovak border, with them and other documents on board. The
Diaries had been found and hidden, and after a long search which
had involved meetings with Klaus Barbie and other old Nazis he had
finally turned them up. Unfortunately, Heidemann said, he couldn't
give more specific details, because that might endanger the people in
East Germany who were responsible for keeping the Diaries. Under

Order No. 124 of the Soviet High Command, issued in October 1945 and still in force forty years later, anyone who held on to Nazi documents was liable to prosecution. He held up some of the volumes of the Diaries so the photographers could get the pictures they wanted.

But it was plainly the glum figure of Lord Dacre which was the weak link here. I had chosen my position with care, and towered over him, ready to ask my questions.

'How did you come to make a mistake like this?'

'My view,' he answered with his usual careful courtesy, 'was that the authenticity could be established by the experts on the handwriting, who seemed to be agreed, and by the account which I then considered that I had had about the history of the text which provided a link between the crashed aeroplane and the archive. That link I must say I regard now as dissolved.'

There was a loud rustle around the press conference. The *Stern* management looked gloomier than ever.

'Do you feel your personal reputation as an historian is linked to the authenticity of the Diaries?'

'If I'm wrong, I'm wrong. If I'm right, I'm right.'

Dozens of people started shouting out questions, and Lord Dacre shook his head, bewildered at the noise and passion.

Famous historians are as open to error as the rest of us. It turned out that Lord Dacre had not been allowed to study the Diaries properly. Instead he had been taken into the vaults of the Swiss bank where they were being kept, had briefly handled them, and been assured that their provenance, though secret, was absolutely certain. He was also told that three handwriting experts had examined a couple of pages and found them genuine.

But the whole enterprise was as fragile as spun sugar: in reality it rested on the basic assumption that the Diaries must after all be genuine, because it would be such a good and profitable story if they were. *Stern* had rushed the authentication process through because it needed to publish the Diaries fast. There was a lot of money to be made. The Murdoch press had handed over $400,000 for them, and *Paris Match* and *Newsweek* had also paid *Stern* sizeable amounts.

The press conference exploded in further questions, angrier and more sceptical than ever. Then came the crash of falling bodies at the back of the press conference as the massed photographers and cameramen in the middle of the hall pushed and shoved and fought each other, and the sound of a voice bellowing in English.

The cameraman had turned and zoomed in even before I had quite had time to see who it was.

'David Irving,' I murmured unnecessarily.

Irving was the revisionist, right-wing historian who had drawn much anger on himself by suggesting that Hitler had not known personally about the Final Solution. In 2000 he lost a case he brought against an American scholar, Deborah Lipstadt, who had accused him of 'Holocaust denial' in a book she published six years before. We live in a world where it is a crime to promote anything other than the one accepted version of history, and where no others, no matter how stupid or wicked, can be permitted.

Irving had always courted controversy. When *Stern* announced the discovery of the Diaries he dismissed them as fakes in articles for one of *Stern*'s fiercest competitors, *Bild Zeitung*. Then he decided they were genuine, because the handwriting was shaky enough to support his own theory that Hitler had suffered from Parkinson's Disease. Finally, when the West German government proved them to be forged, he announced he was pleased with the verdict.

At the time of the *Stern* press conference Irving was noisily against the authenticity of the Diaries. Standing at the back of the hall with the cameraman physically fighting to get a shot of him, his large head outlined against the scarlet wall, he waved a photocopy of an extract from the Diaries and shouted that the date which appeared on one of the entries in it was in a form which Hitler had never used in his other personal writings. This caused more confusion. *Stern*'s editors tried to stay calm while they shouted back at Irving.

In the end the press conference broke up with nothing established except that we had now seen some of the Diaries, genuine or not. I asked Peter Beck, the editor-in-chief of *Stern*, who looked like an exhausted and beleaguered Bobby Charlton and had a great deal to lose if the Diaries were false, if I could film them close up. He invited me to another office to see them.

In journalese, forgeries are never described as being clever or well-crafted; they are always 'crude'. The press conference and Lord Dacre's reaction had made me pretty certain that the Diaries were forged. But if so, they were certainly not crude. When I sat down in the office, and flicked through three of the volumes while the cameraman filmed me, I was as impressed now as Lord Dacre had been in the bank vault. They looked very genuine, with the dust still thick on them, the 'A.H.' seal on the black leatherette covers, and the pages upon pages of complex, illegible writing. It was plain that the same person had written all of these volumes and presumably the fifty-seven others. It was a huge undertaking, if it really was a forgery. Moreover, you could clearly see how the writing degenerated.

As I looked at them I had no idea whatever that the capital H's in the text were completely wrong (the forger had copied them from Hitler's signature, not his usual writing), nor that the ink contained post-war chemicals, nor that the paper was of cheap East German make, nor that the red streamers hanging from the wax seals contained polyamide polyester, which was only invented after the war. I didn't think to notice that the labels on the books were all typed on the same machine, and that the typewriter seemed not to have undergone any wear between 1932 and 1945. I did see that the three volumes I saw were all written in the same ink, but that didn't necessarily seem important in itself. Altogether I was slightly rattled, and decided to hedge my bets in my report for that night's television news.

'They are highly convincing,' my script said, 'but we mustn't forget that the *Sunday Times* also bought Mussolini's diaries – and they turned out to have been forged by two elderly ladies in Italy.'

I stressed Lord Dacre's obvious doubts and the noisy intervention of David Irving, whom I described as 'a disruptive and critical element'.

Once the report had been satellited to London there was nothing more for us to do except go and have dinner. I was looking forward to it: Hamburg is one of my favourite cities. We were staying in the Four Seasons, grand and old-fashioned, and I was reading quietly in the writing room, waiting for the others to appear, when I became aware of a presence looming heavily over me. I looked up: it was David Irving. A very pretty young woman stood behind him.

'Disruptive, am I? Critical, am I?' he boomed menacingly.

Much as I had towered over Lord Dacre, Irving now towered over me. He was like Roderick Spode from the Jeeves and Wooster stories, P.G. Wodehouse's sly caricature of the would-be dictator Sir Oswald Mosley. Someone in Britain must have told Irving what had been in my report from Hamburg that night.

He spoke again.

'Well, I know what to do. I'll—'

He tossed his head angrily, and struck it a terrible blow against the wooden pillar beside my chair. Anyone more delicately built would have been knocked unconscious. Irving merely staggered away, his hand to his head, the laughter of the young woman tinkling in my ears.

The whole scam fell apart very soon, of course. Peter Beck was disgraced, Lord Dacre was humiliated, the *Sunday Times* tried to pretend it was still a really interesting story, and *Stern* took legal action against Gerd Heidemann. He in turn revealed where the Diaries had come from: not some old, deep-hidden Nazi sympathizer in East Germany who had guarded them faithfully over the years, but a small, bald, round-faced, smiling little chain-smoker with a ragged moustache called Konrad Kujau. Kujau had written them to order.

He had begun his career by forging Old Master paintings, and had gradually shifted over to manufacturing Nazi memorabilia for sale to wealthy West Germans. Perhaps Kujau didn't realize the Diaries would be sold to a news magazine; perhaps he thought the buyers were like his other clients – furtive men who had to keep quiet about their hobby and couldn't take the risk of authenticating their acquisitions.

Yet for a man with such a secretive profession Kujau was a compulsive talker. When he and Heidemann finally appeared in court he found it difficult to keep quiet. He talked to his lawyers, he talked to the witnesses, he talked to the journalists, he even talked to the judge if there was no one else to talk to. Silence was something he seemed to find threatening. Whenever an extract from the Diaries was read out in court he would sit back with a smile on his face, nodding and approving what he had written, sometimes mouthing the words, and looking round to check that everyone else approved as well.

Heidemann was his precise opposite: tall, gloomy, silent, depressed, a man who had only got himself into all this in the first place because he had had money problems – the result of spending more than he could afford on buying the yacht which had once belonged to Goering. He was obsessive about Nazi memorabilia, and in a curious way was something of an innocent. He had wanted the Diaries to be genuine, not only because they represented the scoop of his career and his way out of the money problems, but because he was a believer. For an impossibly long time he chose to ignore the clear evidence that Kujau had merely written them to order.

He was less innocent when it came to the money. The £2.5 million which *Stern*'s parent company had paid out had disappeared. Heidemann said Kujau had had it, and had put it into a bank in South Africa or somewhere else. Kujau denied it. He smiled and chattered and signed Hitler's signature as mementoes for the journalists and policemen in court.

After eleven months, during which the interest gradually faded and the public seats emptied, the trial came to an end. Heidemann, the ace reporter, was sentenced to four years and eight months in jail; Kujau, the forger, to four years and six months. *Stern*'s readership had dropped from 2.1 million to 1.6 million. As for the Diaries themselves, stripped of their purely surface authenticity, they were pretty crude forgeries after all. It was only *Stern*'s hunger for a scoop which made them publish before they had carried out the most basic of examinations. As for the entries, surely even Hitler himself would not have been quite so banal: 'Must not forget tickets for the Olympic Games for Eva'; 'On my feet all day long.'

Kujau didn't mind. Above all, he was proud of what he'd done. Not long after the trial had ended the BBC producer who'd been working on the story with me, Rory Cellan-Jones, managed to persuade the prison authorities to allow him in to interview Kujau. The warders brought him from his cell, and he hurried along between them in his tracksuit and running shoes. He was the one in a hurry, not they. He wanted someone new to talk to.

Kujau loved the attention of the camera, and spoke about the Hitler Diaries forgery as though it had been a great achievement. Sometimes, he said, it had only taken him a matter of days to write each volume.

'Will you forge anything else?' Rory asked.

'Maybe the diaries of Mao Zedong.'

He laughed and laughed at that, his little eager eyes searching for admiration.

Then he pulled out his pen for the benefit of the camera and wrote Hitler's diary entry for 3 September 1939: as banal as ever. He signed it with the crossbar over the 'Hitler' which had proved the whole thing to be a forgery:

'Adolf . . . *Hitler.*'

Then he went back to finish his prison sentence.

A good ten years afterwards I came across Lord Dacre at some function. He was still as dignified as I remembered, but more bowed, and he peered more through his round horn-rimmed glasses.

'I like your work,' he said. 'I have had my difficulties with the media, as you might imagine, but I exempt you from the others.'

He obviously did not associate the *Spectator* columnist with the younger, brasher television reporter who had stopped him at the airport and hung over him at the subsequent press conference, hectoring him into his humiliating confession. Why should he? I smiled and thanked him, and got away as quickly as I could. It wasn't a good feeling.

6

DICTATORS

Two Soviet jokes:

1st prisoner: What are you in for?
2nd prisoner: I said something nasty about Comrade Popov
in 1937. And you?
1st prisoner: I said something nice about Comrade Popov
in 1938.
2nd prisoner: And what about you, comrade?
3rd prisoner: I *am* Comrade Popov.

Q: When Mayakovsky committed suicide in 1930, what
were his last words?
A: 'Don't shoot, comrades.'

There was a lurch, and I came awake. For a moment I couldn't think
where I was. There was a strange smell, and I seemed to be trapped.
Then I knew. I was jammed into an unreasonably small bunk on a
passenger ship from Malta to Libya, and the smell was fuel oil mixed
with coffee. Breakfast was being served.

A partly fried egg with a dot of blood in the yolk looked up from
my plate.

'Somehow,' I said to Bob Prabhu, 'I don't feel hungry any more.'

We went on deck. The Libyan coast lay like a green and brown
stripe along the horizon, and the early sun was cheerful and warming.

'Good morning, Mr Simpson,' said a man in a tweed sports
jacket. He was, it turned out, a doctor from somewhere in Yorkshire,
and he was paying a visit to his parents back in Libya.

Other passengers gathered round. I have noticed that the most
ardent viewers of BBC news programmes in Britain are those who
have settled there from other countries; perhaps they are always

hoping to see some news from home. These men were gloomy about Libya. The UN sanctions which had been imposed as a result of the Lockerbie bombing had had a serious effect on the entire country. You couldn't even fly there now: hence our sea-crossing from Malta.

'So why are you coming to Tripoli?'

I explained that Colonel Gadhafi had offered us an interview.

'Maybe he's going to tell you that he'll let those Lockerbie fellows go.'

Having interviewed Gadhafi before, I doubted it. That time, everyone had expected him to make some big statement about cutting his support for terrorist groups; instead he had explained to me in some detail the intricate constitutional workings of the Socialist People's Libyan Arab Jamouhuriyah. There had been another problem too: he had spoken an English so heavily accented it was impossible to understand.

'Maybe he's been taking lessons,' Bob said optimistically. He always looks on the bright side of life.

Onshore we were met by a government official, and no one examined our bags. This was good, since I had brought a bottle of Laphroaig with me, forgetting that Libya was a dry country with unpleasant penalties for those caught carrying alcohol. The bottle clinked audibly as I put my suitcase down.

Outside the Customs post, everything had changed. Tripoli was poorer and quieter, and yet there were far more shops. Colonel Gadhafi's attempt long before to close down private commerce and replace it with monster state supermarkets had been such a dreadful mistake that he had been forced to give up the whole idea. We checked into a vast, empty hotel with tiny beds, dirty carpets, taps which came off in your hands, and a dining room which always seemed to be empty.

'If it's anything like last time, we could be here for days before we get the interview,' I said gloomily as Bob and I chewed some unidentifiable meat in the restaurant.

But it wasn't anything like last time. Gadhafi seemed enthusiastic to see us, and we were told to be ready by the day after next. We visited the Roman museum in Green Square in the heart of the old city, and were arrested by the security police because Bob took a photograph of some statuary. In Libya, it is always the security police who are called when anyone has a problem with foreigners. Within about a minute of hearing that we were in Tripoli to interview Gadhafi, though, they ushered us out in the sunshine of Green Square again. In Libya it's not who you are that counts, it's who you're interviewing.

The following afternoon a large black limousine arrived and we were helped into it. We headed out of Tripoli towards the surrounding desert.

'Where exactly are we going?'

'To see the Leader.'

'Sure, but where?'

'Ah, nobody can say.'

So that was clear.

We drove through the dusty outer suburbs, where little green flags fluttered in the sharp wind, mud-brick took over from concrete, and donkeys and camels stood outside the houses instead of cars. The desert proper had scarcely begun when we reached a vast military compound. Seeing an official car, the men lounging at the gate made a special fuss about asking for our passes, searching the boot, and checking our licence-plates.

The army base was big, and most of it was just desert. We rattled along the track, and as the sun began to decline over the horizon we finally saw Gadhafi's tent. It looked exactly as I had remembered it: the size of a tennis court, and panelled in green, red and white canvas. Inside, the ground was covered with expensive carpets.

'Fantastic,' I said.

But we didn't stop there. Instead, we were driven over to a large caravan like an American Winnebago. We followed our guide up the steps, ducked our heads, and found ourselves in a tiny room, just large enough for four people. There were no windows.

'For interview,' said our guide proudly.

'If we survive half an hour in this,' I said, 'the pictures won't be worth broadcasting. This is useless.'

'Completely,' said Bob, shaking his head.

The guide's face fell. He was a nice fellow, and easily hurt.

'The only place to do it is the tent.'

'But I don't think—'

Something about Bob's expression made him head down the steps quickly.

The tent was much as I had remembered it: roomy, pleasant, but dappled with strange colours. Bob was certain that wouldn't matter; the background of red and green panels would explain the odd colouring to the viewer. I felt that the entire experience was so weird that the viewer would be inclined to accept anything anyway.

He laboured away in the afternoon heat, setting up his lights, unravelling his microphone cables, testing the camera. It was hard work on his own. I paced up and down, trying out questions. This would be a difficult interview to structure; interviews with Gadhafi always were.

Bob was still not quite finished when the neatly suited officials who had been sitting round watching stood up and walked over to the entrance.

'He's coming, Bob,' I said warningly.

We needed some good opening shots of him walking in.

And then I saw him.

'You'll never guess what he's wearing,' I whispered. Bob was already taking his camera off the tripod.

At a distance of twenty yards, as Gadhafi approached the tent, it wasn't so much the Hawaiian shirt that seized the attention; he had been wearing them ever since he had fallen under the spell of Nelson Mandela. It was the hat, an elderly straw number, in the general shape of a trilby. Gadhafi had it on sideways, and I could even see the three little brass-rimmed ventilation holes over his forehead.

He was also on crutches. A year before he had suffered some mysterious accident, which the conspiracy-minded insisted was an assassination attempt. Gadhafi himself insisted he had fallen over and hurt his leg while playing football with some boys. Later, when I too fell over, rupturing the tendons on my left knee and hobbling about on crutches and walking-sticks for a year afterwards, I was more inclined to believe him.

Surely, I thought, one of his officials will have a quiet word and make him take the hat off, on the grounds that it makes him look barking mad. But no, they just smiled ingratiatingly and let him walk into the tent like that.

Everyone knew that Gadhafi marched to a different drummer. 'That madman,' President Sadat of Egypt used to call him. But he wasn't a savage Stalinist despot like Saddam Hussein of Iraq, nor a brutal autocrat like Hafez al-Assad of Syria, and certainly not a grand luxurious *roi fainéant* like the royalty of the Gulf. Strictly speaking he didn't govern at all, since all power in Libya was notionally vested in the Committees which were supposed to govern every level of life, from top to bottom. 'Committees Everywhere!' was the depressing slogan that faced you in the arrivals hall at Tripoli airport in the days when the planes were allowed to fly; it sounded like local government hell.

In practice, of course, his people ran everything. Gadhafi had a particularly nasty secret police organization, and no one in that vast, underpopulated country did anything that the state didn't like; except perhaps the black marketeers and criminals, of whom there were a certain amount. People disappeared or were tortured, and murdered secretly abroad; yet Gadhafi in his later years presided benignly over everything, pretending not to know precisely what was going on. Pretending not to be in power.

That, at any rate, is what I had always believed. I had found Gadhafi an engaging if oddball character in the past and felt a kind of sympathy with him now. Yet it seemed strange that none of the intelligent, Westernized characters around him would dare to suggest that he took his silly hat off for our interview. Was it because their own power and influence depended on keeping him sweet? Were they just courtiers, who were ruled by his whim as much as the rest of the country was? Was he just playing at being an eccentric?

I didn't think so then, and I don't think so now. Shortly before Bob and I arrived in Libya, I had been asked by a London newspaper to review a book of short stories which Gadhafi had written. It was an extraordinary collection: not really stories so much as homilies and parables. But the strangest thing about it was the general air of fatigue and gloom which enveloped every page. It was called 'Escape To Hell', and even with big type, small format and a long and unnecessarily respectful introduction by my old sparring partner Pierre Salinger (once upon a time press spokesman to President Kennedy, and now an increasingly eccentric figure himself) it made less than two hundred pages.

Perhaps the most extraordinary passage in this extraordinary book seemed to show that he was sick of governing his country:

> [W]hat can I – a poor bedouin – hope for in a modern city of insanity? People snap at me whenever they see me: build us a better house! Get us a better telephone line! Build us a road upon the sea! Make a public park for us! Catch oceans of fish for us! Write down a magic spell to protect us! Officiate at our wedding! Kill this dog, and buy us a cat! A poor, lost bedouin, without even a birth certificate, with his staff upon his shoulder. A bedouin, who will not stop for a red light, nor be afraid when a policeman takes hold of him . . .
>
> I feel that the masses, who would not even show mercy to their saviour, follow me around, burning me with their gaze. Even when they are applauding me, it feels like they are pricking me. I am an illiterate bedouin, who does not even know about painting houses or sewage systems . . .

Time, you might think, for his next injection. But no matter how depressed most politicians get from to time, they usually have someone on hand to stop them sending this kind of thing to the publisher. Not Gadhafi.

And now he was sitting opposite me, the bush of dark hair thinning and greying, the crevasses on either side of his nose and mouth deepening as he smiled, fussing over the arrangement of his crutches and his clothes, and keeping his hat still jammed sideways on his head. He looked, I thought, like Joe E. Brown in *Some Like It Hot*.

Then he turned his head so that the front of his hat was pointing at me, snapped his fingers, and one of the aides came over carrying a horsehair fly-whisk.

The flies were indeed a nuisance in the tent, but they were too small for the viewer to see; so when Gadhafi lashed around himself with the whisk it looked as though he was whipping himself in a pious frenzy. Maybe I should have advised him to put up with the flies, to take the hat off, to change the shirt. It wasn't that I didn't dare to do it; I have done many more difficult things in my time. It was simply that these were the outward and visible signs of an inward eccentricity which was central to the character of the man. I didn't want him to change a thing.

I still didn't know if he had a purpose in giving this interview. I questioned him on all the obvious subjects, but he was scarcely forthcoming about any of them: Lockerbie, internal politics, the attempts to assassinate him (including, a defector from MI5 had recently said, a plot hatched up with the knowledge of the British Secret Intelligence Service).

He answered all these questions absently, smiling occasionally as though he had been reminded of something particularly absurd, and whipping himself with his fly-whisk. Bob Prabhu crouched over the camera, sweating in the heat. He had been right: Gadhafi had been taking English lessons. Sometimes he lapsed into Arabic, but when I urged him to repeat what he had said in English he would always do it, smiling indulgently as though I had asked him for some rather ludicrous favour.

I was starting to run out of questions, and perhaps he realized it. As I began another one he broke in.

'I have something to say. If the two men the English government say were guilty of the Lockerbie bombing are guilty, then there is no reason why they should not be tried for it. We think they were not guilty. But there is no reason for them to stay. They can go. They want to go.'

That's convenient, I thought; but I knew now why we had been invited to interview the Leader: this was the move that would unblock the entire issue of sanctions. Gadhafi had cut the two Lockerbie suspects loose, after all the reassuring things he had said to them in the past about protecting them from the callous inequities of the British legal system. Bob and I didn't merely have an interesting collector's item on our hands, we had a sizeable scoop.

That evening, as I began to write my account of the interview, Bob knocked on my door. I know him well, and love him dearly, and could see that something was up.

'There's something funny about the interview,' he said. He'd been watching it on the portable monitor in his room.

Oh Christ, I thought: he means there's tape damage, or electronic interference. I remembered an interview I once did in a military base in Iraq, which was so crackling with electronic gadgets of different kinds that the material we shot was unusable.

'Nothing like that,' Bob said. 'Gadhafi was making noises, that's all.'

'Whatever are you on about? What kind of noises?'

'Kind of personal ones.' He looked away.

As I say, I know Bob. He is a very modest man, especially where bodily functions are concerned.

'What, stomach rumblings?'

Borborygmi can be a nuisance in a television interview.

'No, worse than that.'

'What, farting?'

Now I'd embarrassed him. He nodded, wordlessly.

'Look, that's absolutely stupid, Bob. I was sitting opposite him. If he'd been farting I'd have heard it. You're imagining it.'

'Well, listen to the tape.'

I listened. There was absolutely no doubt about it. The personal microphone which Bob had pinned on Gadhafi had picked it up very clearly. The wind passage lasted for about ten minutes of our half-hour interview. Gadhafi would rise up a little in his seat, the thunder would roll for fifteen or twenty seconds at a time, and then he would sink back into his seat with a pleased expression on his face. It may have happened to me before without my knowledge, but never, I think, in so concentrated and elaborate a fashion.

We ran the interview in truncated form on the *Nine O'Clock News*, and in full on *Simpson's World*. The wind-breaking was audible in both versions, but I thought it best not to draw attention to it in my script. With the *Sunday Telegraph*, though, I felt I could let rip.

During part of our interview, Col. Gadhafi broke wind audibly and at length.

The foreign editor, a particular friend of mine called Con Coughlin, headlined the article 'Warm Wind of Compromise Blows From Gadhafi'.

Bob and I left Libya the following day, after a trip to the spectacular ruins of Sabratha, one of the two Roman sites which, together with Lepcis Magna and what is now itself called Tripoli, made up Tripolitania, the three cities of the Libyan coast. We had come to know our driver quite well, and we decided to get him to take us across the border to Tunisia rather than face the long sea-crossing back to Malta.

The journey was tedious, and it was dark when we reached the border. There was no government official to shepherd us through this time. As we lugged our cases into the Customs Hall, large, echoing and full of flies and dirty scraps of paper, I suddenly remembered the bottle of Laphroaig. I hadn't even opened it. The customs man won't look properly, I told myself.

But he did. He delved down through my dirty clothes and found it, neatly packaged between the pair of black shoes I had worn for the interview. He pulled it out by the neck. I looked at him properly for the first time: he was big and fat, his uniform had not been cleaned for months, and he was extremely angry.

'Oh God,' groaned the driver beside me. 'One litre, one year. One litre, one year.'

I felt a strange, Gadhafi-like calm.

'Are you going to give me a year for that? Surely not.'

He made an angry muttering sound, and thought about it. It seemed to take him a long time: maybe he was reflecting on all the forms he would have to fill if he made a case out of this. Then he threw the bottle carelessly back into the case and closed the lid.

'*Y'alla*,' he said, with what sounded like a certain contempt.

As we drove across the border into Tunisia the driver's despair turned to delight.

'One litre,' he would shout, and Bob and I would reply dutifully, 'One year.'

This went on for some time. He was still laughing and saying 'One litre' when we said goodbye to him and transferred our gear to a Tunisian taxi.

'Take us to the best hotel in town,' I told the new driver grandly; after all our privations and problems I felt we deserved it.

He drove us through the belt of small boarding houses and private hotels and on into the more expensive part of town. The hotels became bigger and grander, until they reached the full five-star level. Then, mysteriously, we were back in the boarding-house zone again.

'I said the best hotel.'

'Sir, yes, no problem. Best hotel.'

We drove a little further. The road surface wasn't so good now, and the street lights were farther apart. Suddenly he turned to the right and stopped. Bob and I peered out at an ordinary, run-down house, scarcely bigger than a bungalow.

'The Best Hotel' said the board over the gate.

I pressed the doorbell twice and then once again more briefly. That was what we had been told to do.

'I'm not absolutely sure this is right,' said the languid voice beside me.

I was no more certain than Rory Peck was. And then the door opened, and both of us could see it was exactly right. The face that peered suspiciously out at us was thin and dark and nervous: a black marketeer's face. The first thing it did was to check whether there was anyone behind us. Then it raised a single eyebrow.

Rory explained in his halting Russian, half genuine and half invented, who we were and what we wanted. The face said nothing, but I had the impression that we were expected. The door opened a little wider.

It was a miserable place, in a huge decaying block on the outskirts of Moscow. One of the two rooms was filled almost to capacity with cardboard boxes from Korea. The inlaid wooden floor was coming slowly to pieces thanks to the damp, and there was a nasty smell. The passageway was dark, but he didn't turn on any lights.

The black marketeer slept in the other room. Against the wall were propped a few objects under blankets and dirty sheets.

'Painting,' said the black marketeer tersely, and pulled the coverings away. As we stood in the next room he pulled out a gigantic canvas, wheezing, and lugged it out into the passage where we were waiting.

While Rory looked at the large painting, I went into the bedroom and examined a couple of others. The first was a large unframed canvas showing Stalin walking the battlements of the Kremlin with Marshal Voroshilov, his talentless, toadying sidekick from the days immediately before the German invasion of Russia in 1941. The other was a scene from a revolutionary political meeting with Lenin haranguing a crowd of sailors. Both subjects were, of course, shot through with irony. Stalin never showed himself anywhere that he could be seen by ordinary people, and soon after the Bolshevik seizure of power the sailors from Kronstadt who had helped it along staged a rebellion against him and were destroyed.

It was 1990, and the whole Soviet system was only a year away from collapse. Yet even at this late stage, the concept that you could buy something from a freelance dealer was something the authorities could still not easily accept. By offering dollars to a Soviet citizen, even in exchange for Soviet paintings, we ourselves were not committing an offence; but the Soviet citizen was, by accepting the money. If we had been caught, it would have been confiscated, and we would have been given an official warning. Yet the police, badly paid and demoralized, would not have troubled with us even if the law on this kind of thing had been clear. The black marketeer's nervousness was merely the result of years of conditioning.

I took the Stalin, the Lenin and an official portrait of Molotov, which made the dreadful old crook ('Every time I shake his hand, I remember the thousands of people he's killed,' Ernest Bevin used to say) look rather avuncular. They cost me, as I remember, thirty dollars apiece.

Rory bought the big canvas in the passage. It was a rather good painting from the early 1920s of the assault on the Winter Palace. Its ferocity and valour were completely fictitious, since the Palace was merely defended by a brigade of (by now) mostly hysterical women, and a bunch of scared, untrained teenaged boys. Far from charging across the square under fire, as shown in Rory's painting, the attackers lined up meekly at the kitchen door which someone had left open, and there was no serious resistance. But that's the great pleasure of political art: it's as full of meaning and seriousness as a washing-powder advertisement.

Dictator Kitsch, as an artistic genre, is superbly, satisfyingly pompous and self-deceptive as well as being utterly inartistic: the equivalent of those society portraits you see in the back pages of expensive magazines, where all the sitters are beautiful, all the wrinkles have been ironed away and all the necks are smooth. Time and reality have been airbrushed out. Dictators like to believe that they are young and handsome, just as they like to believe their people love them.

At the rallies staged in the centre of Bucharest for President Nicolae Ceauşescu of Romania, the dictator's dictator, one in every twelve participants was given a placard to hold up, with the great man's face on it. Not the bad-tempered, increasingly haggard face of the late 1980s, but the young, dark-haired, thrusting face, like a premier division centre forward, from twenty years before.

At that stage, briefly, the man had been genuinely popular because he stood up to the Russians when they invaded Romania's neighbour, Czechoslovakia, in 1968. Within seven or eight years the popularity had evaporated completely, and the difference had to be made up by his public relations men. They created wonderful epithets for him, which the newspapers obediently printed and grovellers repeated during the interminable speeches which were made wherever he went: The Flag Of Our National Pride, Our Prince Charming, The Polyvalent Genius, Our Secular God, The New Morning Star.

Ceauşescu Art was the visual equivalent of all this grovelling. During the revolution a brave museum curator went round gathering up all the examples he could find: not a safe thing to do at a time when people had switched from a dull acceptance of Ceauşescu to a violent loathing for every symbol of his rule. Anyone showing an interest in conserving this frightful stuff could easily have been accused of pro-Ceauşescu tendencies and might have been lynched. The curator, a clear-sighted and intelligent man, explained that these pictures were an important part of modern Romanian history, and would one day be required when the country was capable of examining its past rationally. He showed me his collection, though he wouldn't allow my cameraman to film it in case the mob came round and burned them all. If he hadn't been so high-minded, I would have offered him a hundred dollars for anything in the collection.

To the connoisseur of Dictator Kitsch, the paintings were superb: Ceauşescu as a preternaturally handsome young man, defying some down-at-heel landlord; Ceauşescu as an aspiring Party hack addressing a rally of happy workers; Ceauşescu and his witch-like wife Elena opening a vast, environmentally destructive hydroelectric project on the Danube; Ceauşescu standing in a crowd of workers and peasants (something he never really did, of course) and laying his hand on the head of a thinly clad young boy in faintly paederastic fashion as he gently explains his theory of Building Up The Multilaterally-Developed Socialist Society to his rapt audience. As with Nazi and some Soviet art, there was the frequent whiff of sexual irregularity about Ceauşescu Art.

It is the shamelessness of Dictator Kitsch which is so attractive – the idea, which both the artist and the commissioning official know to be utterly false, that the President is a man of the people who shares the conditions of their life and is respected and loved by them. Perhaps the Great Man believes it; perhaps he is merely watching out for any sign that the people around him *don't* believe it. The portraits of dictators are on display, not simply to convince the people that they really love him (whatever they might think), but as a pledge of loyalty by the system. Dictators are rarely men of much imagination: they like to see hard evidence that the system is presenting them as they want to be presented.

Saddam Hussein's art is, if anything, worse and madder than Ceauşescu's. Every public building in every city, town and village in Iraq has its huge official portrait of the appalling barbarian, always smiling and often extending his right arm in greeting, a trademark gesture which many Iraqis privately find infuriating. In a country of ethnic and religious diversity, he presents himself as the sole unifying figure (President George Bush unwisely bought this line in 1991, and decided not to allow Saddam's overthrow); as a result his portraits show him wearing Kurdish costume, worshipping at Christian, Sunni and Shi'ite shrines, or crowned with an Arab *k'fir* and wearing a white *dish-dash*.

I had two particular favourites: in one he sported a green eye-shade and carried a tennis racket; in the other he wore a university gown and had a mortar-board on his head, while holding a set of scales in his right hand and a sword in his left. This was displayed outside the law faculty building at Baghdad University, just in case any of the students there might forget who the fount of all justice was in Iraq. The sword was a particularly good touch.

I am now banned from Iraq for the lifetime of the Saddam Hussein regime (or of the man himself, which seems likely to be the same thing), and can no longer trawl the shops and bazaars of

Baghdad for Saddam watches, clocks, scarves, ties, shirts, lapel badges and so on. Even for the five months I spent there before, during and after the Gulf crisis of 1990–91 I showed an interest in these things which the authorities regarded as unhealthy. They forbade me, for instance, to film the sixty-foot ceremonial arches composed of human arms holding crossed scimitars (the arms were modelled on Saddam's own, and were of course made by a British foundry), because they knew I was inclined to make fun of them.

This particular monument had a special brutality to it. In the roadway beneath the arched arms the architect had set, on Saddam's particular instructions, hundreds of Iranian helmets from the Iran–Iraq war. Whenever Saddam celebrated a military triumph – which was often, of course – he would drive between the two arches, his arm extended in his emperor-like gesture, passing over the helmets of his enemies like a Mongol chieftain driving his chariot over a hill of skulls. Each of the Iranian helmets had a bullet- or shrapnel-hole in it, to add to the gruesome effect; though I became a little more sceptical about the genuineness of the Iraqi show after I discovered that a friend of mine used to collect abandoned Russian helmets in Afghanistan, fire a round from an AK-47 through them and smear the inside with chicken-blood in order to sell them to American collectors.

What is not in question is the bad taste of a man who wants to drive over soldiers' helmets, under an arch modelled on his own arms. You have to have a certain cast of mind for that kind of thing: apart from anything else, it requires a major sense-of-humour bypass. This is another feature common to most dictators: they do not altogether see the funny side of themselves and what they are doing. Hitler's courtiers first tried to hide from him the fact that Charlie Chaplin had taken him off in *The Great Dictator*, and then ascribed it to the international Jewish conspiracy.

There are many fewer dictators around nowadays; the international climate no longer favours autocracy, and the World Bank and the International Monetary Fund disapprove. Like some large mammal with a valuable coat, the dictator's very existence is in question. Robert Mugabe of Zimbabwe, a man I have met and interviewed several times over the past twenty years, has all the right instincts yet permits an opposition and a free judiciary to exist; one day soon he will pack up and leave office. Dictators are not what they used to be.

Not even the American State Department defends them any more, even though it once set so many of them up. The British and French governments, who have always been able to swallow almost any appalling behaviour if they thought it would earn them a pound or two, are finding that the field of opportunity has diminished drastically. Only the Israelis habitually send advisers and sell weapons to regimes which others prefer to avoid.

Perhaps, instead of waiting to applaud when their people chase tyrants from office and kill them or put them on trial, we should tempt the few remaining dictators to go early by offering them a place in a theme park where they can stage mock executions, hold triumphant march pasts, invest their money in imaginary Swiss and Luxembourgeois accounts, and decorate the streets and buildings with their own gigantic portraits. A little careful flattery by their faithful courtiers might well persuade them that our applause and laughter represented the appreciation of the masses, and that they were still loved as much as they always had been, of course.

I have interviewed a substantial number of tyrants in my time, from Ayatollah Khomeini in Iran to General Galtieri in Argentina and P. W. Botha in South Africa. I have lunched with the head of the nastiest militia group in Lebanon, and drunk coffee at the *estancia* of a Colombian vigilante leader who boasted of the number of 'communists' (that is, ordinary peasants) his men had killed. I have listened to one of the most notorious Palestinian hijackers eat his way noisily through a *meze* in Baghdad. I have shaken hands with murderers and torturers and embezzlers, in the hope of luring them into being filmed for television. It is not something to be proud of. Still, I have discovered that you do not have to pretend to agree with such people, any more than you have to pretend to share the views of politicians you interview. Politeness and a willingness to listen are all that is required.

You are usually safe enough with the heads of established governments, because they tend to obey the rules and leave you alone.

Further down the social scale, at the level of bandits, gang-leaders and militia bosses, you can get into serious difficulty; especially if they control everything around them and have no fear of the consequences. Most dangerous of all, though, is the crazed dictator who thinks he is omnipotent.

A friend and colleague of mine made the difficult journey to Uganda in 1973, at the height of Idi Amin's reign of terror. Amin was known for his towering rages, which could be sparked off by the slightest detail; and in his compound on the edge of Kampala he could kill or maim anyone he chose.

When the crew were ushered in, they found he was powering up and down his swimming pool, displacing vast quantities of water and breathing like a sea lion. He watched them as he swam, and they decided to take the risk of filming him. At last Amin reached his final lap, and hoisted his enormous bulk out of the water. At that moment the reporter saw that one of his huge testicles, the size of a honeydew melon, was hanging out of his swimming trunks. The cameraman seemed not to have noticed, and kept the shot wide enough for the giant gonad to be visible when the pictures were shown on television.

Amin walked down the side of the pool and lowered his bulk into a chair. This, clearly, was where he wanted to do the interview. The reporter was in some difficulties. If he suggested to Amin that he might want to hoist the stray object back on board, that could spark off one of his violent outbursts of anger. They might not even survive. If, on the other hand, the cameraman continued not to see, the pictures would be unbroadcastable and all the effort and risk it had taken for them to be there would be wasted.

In the end, the cameraman himself spotted Amin's ball, and zoomed in considerably to avoid it. The interview passed off well enough, Amin denying the accusations against him with a menacing joviality. But my friend said it required an immense effort of will not to look down at the vast testicle, as it lay in front of him on the chair like a particularly fine aubergine.

Kurt Waldheim was not a dictator; he was, in turn, a Nazi bureaucrat, a notably boring UN Secretary-General, and a disgraced President of

Austria. But he had a nasty temper, and he is one of only two international leaders to have punched me. (The other, for the record, was Harold Wilson.)

It was during the Austrian presidential election of 1985, and Waldheim was holding the last rally of his campaign, in the centre of Vienna. The cameraman I was working with, a tough, extremely dependable Scot called Bill Nicol, had cleverly managed to edge his way onto the stage beside Waldheim. Standing alongside him, I could see the upturned faces glowing with pride: old faces, for the most part, with Iron Crosses pinned to their ties and sometimes an empty sleeve or trouser-leg to show what they had sacrificed for Hitler. Now they had come out in large numbers to support Waldheim, since for them no one whom the international press had accused of being a Nazi could be all bad.

Waldheim was a rotten speaker, but with elements like this in the audience even he could not fail to get a good reception. They cheered him, and part of the crowd started up a song: it could have been the *Horst Wessellied*, for all I know, but it was probably just the Austrian national anthem. In those days most Austrians still believed the convenient fiction which the wartime Allies had begun to disseminate in 1945, that Austria was Hitler's first victim. That was when they wanted to wean Austria away from Nazi Germany.

After the war, the three Western allies were careful not to go in for denazification too harshly in Austria since they were in competition with Russia, which occupied a sizeable chunk of the country. The fact that most Austrians had enthusiastically welcomed the *Anschluss* in 1938 (though there were some notable and brave exceptions) and had provided large numbers of recruits for the *Waffen-SS* had conveniently been forgotten.

Until, that is, Waldheim's past began to leak out. He was not the kind of Nazi who went round in jackboots, stamping on people's faces; instead, he had created the conditions under which that kind of thing was possible. He served in Yugoslavia, administering the German occupation. The death-warrants of resisters were signed, the torture of suspects was arranged, but Waldheim didn't have to pull the trigger or plug in the equipment himself; there were other people to do that kind of thing.

And now, after an undistinguished period at the UN (I remember the terror in his face and the way his hands shook when he met a group of gunmen during a half-hearted effort to broker peace in Angola), he was among his own people again. The crowd cheered, Waldheim held out his arms to them, Bill Nicol grunted that the camera was running, and I shouted my question over the roar of the crowd.

'Do you think you're going to win?'

'Yes, I do. You can see – zese people love me.'

He was still beaming.

'Even though in today's British press there are accusations that you ordered the execution of several British prisoners of war?'

Actually, I don't think I got that far. He punched me in the stomach, just like Wilson had, back in 1970. But although Waldheim was nastier and bonier than Wilson, I did not rate him as a puncher. Besides, I was wearing a large and rather expensive loden coat, which absorbed much of the blow.

His normally sallow face was distorted with rage, and had taken on an almost prune-like colour.

'Vy are you asking me zese qvestions? You see, ze people love me.'

He turned back to them, his face breaking into a ghastly rictus of a smile. And indeed all the old Mein Kampfers in the audience broke into a cheer, waving their empty sleeves and their crutches and hooting me for disturbing the great man at his devotions.

'You see,' Waldheim repeated, the smile giving way to fury again, and leaning into Bill's camera lens so that his face became hideously distorted, 'zey love me. I don't have to bozzer viz your qvestions. I shall VIN.'

He turned to them again, and they cheered louder than ever.

Fortunately, an American camera crew had filmed Waldheim punching me, and gave us the pictures. The whole thing caused a certain sensation, even in Austria.

A couple of evenings later, the election result was declared in a vast and hideous Franz-Josef-gothic hall in the centre of Vienna. Once again, Bill Nicol worked his way into a good position: so good that, as Waldheim and his family arrived, we were swept along with them. Suddenly, as the crowd carried us onto the platform immediately behind Waldheim, I felt an intense pain shoot up my right arm. The crush was too great for me to be able at first to see what had happened; then I realized who owned the expensive fur coat beside me, and I understood. Frau Waldheim, as tall and bony as her husband but still showing the remains of a certain hawk-like beauty, had dug her sharp scarlet fingernails into me.

'Ouch.'

'I hope you are enjoying yourself,' she hissed.

By the time I thought of an adequate come-back, Waldheim had been proclaimed President of Austria.

'Por favor, compañero, por favor.'

A stout sixtyish comrade, one of the people who watched over the place, was pulling at me, her face screwed up like a dishcloth. I looked down: my offence was to have rested my hand on a glass case containing an old, yellowing piece of folded cloth. This, according to a typed notice, was a pair of Fidel Castro's trousers, as worn by the great man during his guerrilla campaign in the Sierra Maestra mountains in the 1950s. You could see the Sierra Maestra through the museum windows. Close by, a group of tourists was being told the story of Castro's attack on this building in 1953.

In those days it had been called the Moncada barracks. From it the Cuban military controlled Santiago de Cuba, the second largest city on the island. The barracks had been a place of unquestioned nastiness, where people were tortured and shot at random by the soldiers of President Batista. Bullets encrusted with human tissue had lodged in the walls.

Nowadays the glass cases around these walls were full of relics: the contents of the revolutionaries' pockets when they made their attack on the barracks, their hats and shoes, their guns, the Pepsi-Cola bottle they had filled with petrol. Everything about this place was holy, and Castro's wisdom and revolutionary courage were praised relentlessly on every hand.

And yet the photographs hinted that the callow young man who waved at the cameras as he was released from jail a couple of years after the Moncada attack was no wiser than the rest of us; just quick-witted, charismatic and rather lucky. And he had succeeded. HISTORY WILL VINDICATE ME, ran a quotation from Fidel across one wall of this shrine. It has, because his hagiographers were in a position to write it. History used to vindicate Stalin, Ceauşescu and the Shah of Iran.

Near the barracks I met a tough-looking university scientist who had gone into politics and was standing as a candidate for the 1993 election which I was in Cuba to report on. He was a pro-Castroite, of course: there were no other candidates. What sort of a man was Fidel? His eyes took on a faraway look.

'Being next to someone of such genius is very difficult. The first thing he did was to take me by the hand and put me on the same level as he was. Of course I realize I'm not really on the same level, but it was an ethical gesture of modesty. I felt tremendous emotion, as if my heart wouldn't fit in my thorax.'

Thorax? Ah, of course, he was a scientist. I looked at his inspired, faraway eyes and the determined mouth beneath them. This boy will go far, I thought. Assuming, of course, Castro lasts.

He has lasted since 1 January 1959. Yet it was his failure rather than his success to be the last Marxist ruler west of Beijing. There had been no smooth transfer of power to a chosen successor, no plan for continuing the system into the distant future. Everything rested on Castro.

Mental rigidity had become Cuba's primary characteristic. In another part of the barracks a school had been established. Wandering round, I saw a notice on a board in the corridor:

Requirements to be chosen as an exemplary worker: ideological firmness, modesty and simplicity expressed in an austere life without consumerist habits, the energetic and intransigent defence of state property, and the fight against petty-bourgeois individualism.

Since this was a nursery school, a cut-out of Snow White was pinned above it.

Still, the old pictures of Marx and Lenin had mostly disappeared. After the collapse of the Soviet Empire their place had increasingly been taken by José Martí, the father of Cuban independence. Fidel read his writings when he was in prison, and underlined some of his leaden phrases in a book now on show at the Moncada barracks: 'A lazy soul kindles no fire,' and, more depressing yet prophetic, 'Long service obliges you to continue serving.'

We were in Santiago de Cuba because we hoped to get a word with Castro. But he is a difficult man to interview. In fact, as with other autocrats, you are never entirely sure you *want* to interview him, since he tends to go on talking for a very long time and expects that everything he says will be broadcast. That is what happens on Cuban television, and he assumes that everyone else will have the same interest. Not, of course, necessarily true. In 1998 he gave a three-hour interview to one of the big American networks, which used just nine seconds of it in their news bulletin: a usage ratio of approximately 1200:1.

Castro is not a tyrant, but he is much too fond of the sound of his own voice. I once sat through a seven-hour harangue from him, in which he rambled on about a past so distant that you had to be in your sixties to remember it properly, and lectured his long-suffering people about the need for them to make further sacrifices; as though it wasn't enough of a sacrifice to have to endure seven hours of him on prime-time television with no opt-outs.

Its human rights deficiencies apart, I love Castro's Cuba very much, and sympathize with its predicament immensely; but I find it hard to be totally enthusiastic about a man who sets so little store by the physical comfort of his audience. However, the last time I heard him speak was on New Year's Day 1999, the fortieth anniversary of his revolution; and then he galloped so fast through his speech that he finished in under three hours, and took everyone by surprise. Many of the lower Party functionaries had only just begun to settle into positions where they could nap without being noticed.

There are two perennial questions in Cuba: what will happen when Castro goes, and how popular is he in reality? Once, wandering round the old part of Havana with a camera crew, we were discussing his popularity among ourselves.

'There's only one way to find out,' I said to the producer. 'Let's just bang on any of these doors at random and film the answer.'

The producer agreed.

'So which door?'

She pointed to one: a large, eighteenth-century affair which was largely held together by its ancient layers of paint, and sported a copper door-knocker, green with age, in the shape of a woman's head. The cameraman (it was Nigel Bateson, the South African giant) said the camera was running, and I banged the knocker hard.

In a shorter time than I could have believed, a beautiful young woman pulled the door open.

'*Sí?*'

I explained in halting Spanish that we wanted to talk to her about Fidel.

'That's quite a coincidence,' she said in excellent English. 'My friends and I were just talking about him now. Come in and meet them.'

All excellent stuff, of course, except that it seemed much too good to be true. Such an attractive woman, such good English, so swift and welcoming: I knew we would have problems convincing anyone that this had not been carefully set up, like those travel programmes where everything works perfectly because it has been scripted and rehearsed time and again in advance.

It turned out that she was a ballet dancer, and her friends were also involved in the arts. They had been discussing how they could tell Fidel, whom they all admired, how hard life was and how much inefficiency and corruption you had to put up with in order to get by. Now they told us. It was superb.

'You see, we love and admire Fidel; he's like our father. None of us here knows anything else but him. And yet we want to be freer than we are. We want to be able to say what we like and read what we like and go where we like, and this is not possible in Cuba nowadays. So we have problems, and we don't know what to do.'

A few days later we went to Santiago de Cuba and the Moncada barracks. Castro himself was going there to vote, and it was pretty clear that he would say something to the assembled foreign journalists. He liked microphones.

We chose our position with some care. Nigel planted his camera tripod in the best position, where it would catch the great man's eye as he passed. I stuck a large BBC sign on top of the lens.

It grew hot. People jostled and made jokes.

'Bloody snappers,' Nigel grunted; photographers and cameramen wage a fierce world war with each other, getting in each others' shots and struggling for the best positions.

Our fixer, the television producer Rosalind Bain, who organized almost all my Latin American expeditions, thought about the question we should put to Castro if we got the chance.

'You know, King Juan Carlos offered Castro an estate in Spain recently. It wouldn't surprise me at all if the old boy was sick of all this and wanted to retire. You could ask him about that.'

'All right.'

A roar from the crowd outside warned us that Castro had finally arrived, hours behind schedule. His stature was considerable: a big, shaggy six-footer who still looked like a cigar-smoker even though he had long given up. His olive-green uniform was clearly new and clean, but in the heat it had started to take on the rumpled look which somehow belonged to him. His stomach hung over his belt, and there were patches of sweat under the arms.

He walked in a little vaguely, met everyone, stayed an oddly long time in the voting booth considering that there was no choice of candidate, then emerged to put his ballot paper in the box.

The Cuban journalists shouted out their questions, and he answered them with some care. Our sound recordist sweated in the ruck and pushed his boom microphone in closer.

'Get that fuckin' fishpole outta his face,' shouted an American voice despairingly behind us.

'*Comandante!*' shouted a Cuban.

'Fidel,' shouted someone else, more chummily.

I preferred something a little more formal.

'*Señor Presidente.*'

He turned, the heavy black eyebrows rising like the two halves of a hydraulic bridge, faint tobacco stains still visible on the beard which the CIA had once famously tried to eradicate. The dark gaze locked on to mine. In the West, I told the gaze, people were saying that the Cuban revolution was finished and that he was on the way out. Would he like to comment? Rosalind translated. He preferred her to me, as well he might: she was darkly handsome, with the flashing eyes Cubans love.

He stopped, and the crowd stopped with him. He snorted down his big nose, ran his fingers through his greying beard, and answered.

'I am a prisoner of the Revolution. I'm not a free man. If it were decided that I shouldn't continue, I would feel as though I'd been given a reward after all these years of struggle. Maybe someone else should take over in five years' time. I wouldn't feel sad.'

There was a little intake of breath around me; this wasn't the answer the crowd had been expecting from Cuba's presiding genius.

He went on for some minutes, while the crowd sweated and heaved around him, cameramen hoisting their heavy cameras over their heads and pointing them down at him, photographers forcing their way between their arms and flashing their bulbs in his face.

I kept up the eye-contact, creating a conversation between us so that he would forget the rest of the crowd who were sweating and shoving and trying to break in every time he paused for breath. I asked him if he was aware of the complaints of so many Cubans about their daily lives.

'People will have to go on fighting and working hard,' he said, though it was no answer. 'Everything changes.'

A doorstep interview with Fidel Castro lasts almost as long as a set-piece interview with any leader in the West, and the only restriction on us was the sheer impossibility, even for a man as big and powerful as Nigel, to keep focused on Castro's face under such conditions. It didn't matter; we had what we wanted.

He took a last glum look at the eager, competitive journalists in front of him, and swept on.

'Fidel!'

'*Comandante!*'

The next night my colleagues and I had dinner in the kind of restaurant Cubans cannot afford to go to. A singer, luscious and dark, approached our table.

'To live in Havana,' Graham Greene wrote in his novel about the island, 'was to live in a factory that turned out human beauty on a conveyor-belt.' She sang a corny old song for us, accompanied by a short, sweating guitarist:

> *Siempre que te pregunto*
> *Cuando, como y donde,*
> *Tu siempre me respondes:*
> *Quizás, quizás, quizás.*

'Whenever I ask you when, how and where, you always answer: Perhaps, perhaps, perhaps.' She ended the song, her eyes holding mine longer than Castro's had. Then she went away and established eye-contact with someone else.

Of course, when his term in office ran out, Fidel Castro did not head off to live in Spain; he just took another term. Everyone knew he would, especially since he had spent so much effort over the years getting rid of every conceivable political rival. Long service, as José Martí so depressively put it, obliges you to continue serving.

But what distinguishes Castro from just about every other international leader is his utter self-confidence: He is prepared to speculate about almost anything in public. Another politician would have kicked a question about his long-term future into touch. Not Fidel. In spite of the seven-hour speeches, the human rights violations, the rigidity of the system, the general atmosphere of decay, he's still managed to cling on to the shreds of his old revolutionary glamour.

As far as I can remember, I have only experienced a certain sympathy for one of the various tyrants I have come across in my career. It happened in 1986, and I was in Paris as part of a swing through Continental Europe that would eventually take my colleagues and me to Liechtenstein to report on the wedding of the Crown Prince: a Ruritanian event which seemed likely to amuse everyone.

'So,' I said, my feet on the desk, 'tell me what's going on here.'

The BBC Paris bureau in the rue du Faubourg St Honoré within a few hundred yards of the Champs Elysées and the Arc de Triomphe is the pleasantest office the Corporation maintains anywhere. Some difficult correspondents have worked there alongside the pleasanter and easier ones, but the presiding genius of the place is a bundle of Gallic energy called Ginette, with whom I have flirted and joked and commiserated for thirty years.

'John, *cheri*, I can't stand 'im,' she has said of various BBC people during that time; ''E's a fuckeur.'

She has usually been right.

Ginette works absurd hours, making phone calls to politicians and academics, cutting out articles from the French press with a huge pair of blackened steel scissors, drinking *infusions* of different kinds, and making out filing cards in red and blue biro in a distinctively French hand. While being one of the most typically BBC people I know, she is unfailingly patriotic, and explodes satisfyingly when I remind her that Paris has one inch more rainfall per year than London. But she knows everything that is going on.

'Well, we 'ave the little emperor 'ere,' she replied to my question.

'Which emperor is that? Napoleon?'

'*Ne fais pas l'idiot*, John,' she said severely. 'The Emperor Bokassa. From the Central African Empire. It's now the Republic again.'

'Didn't he eat someone? Schoolchildren? Or was it the leader of the opposition?'

It was the leader of the opposition. Ginette pulled some carefully scissored articles out of a file and showed me. There were also dozens of items about Bokassa's career from corporal in the colonial African army to captain, colonel, general, president and emperor, like an ambitious third-century Roman legionary; about his coronation, and the expensive regalia made for him in France; about his shooting down of protesting schoolchildren, and his overthrow by French troops; and about his trial, in which his French chef was the star witness. The chef explained how, whenever Bokassa felt low, he would order a slice off the leader of the opposition, whose stuffed carcass was kept in Bokassa's extra large deep-freeze. It was a story which would have delighted Evelyn Waugh.

Now, anyway, Bokassa had come to France and was spending his exile in a small château just outside Paris which he owned. It struck me as being a superb story; the chance to meet a crazed imperial cannibal doesn't come round all that often.

'*Mais enfin*, John, the *gouvernement* doesn't want anyone going to see him.'

'How can they stop us?'

'Hah!'

This was France. The authorities had dug up the road to the château on the pretext that the telephone cables needed replacing, and no one was allowed to go in or out. They had also taken away the Emperor's driving licence, and warned him that if he spoke to even a single journalist he would be sent straight back to Africa immediately. In France there is a kind of presidential trade union whereby one president protects his predecessors, even if they are political enemies. In this case the Emperor Bokassa had been saying all sorts of scandalous things about the skeletal former president, Valéry Giscard d'Estaing, and President François Mitterrand wanted to ensure that nothing new reached the ears of the press.

'But maybe there is a way, *quand même*.'

There was. Somehow, Ginette managed to do what no one else had done, and fix an appointment with the world's best known anthropophage.

We stopped at the nearby town hall to ask the way.

'Oh, you mean our little monkey,' said the official I spoke to, himself a nasty, thin little man with a wisp of a moustache; he was, predictably, a member of the National Front. 'Be careful – he may eat you.'

There were five of us – television teams were a great deal bigger in those days – and we made a lot of jokes as we drove over the trenches and potholes which the French government had dug in the Emperor's driveway, in an attempt to keep him in and the press out. We were just in time: the road was still passable. By the next day it would have been completely blocked. The house itself was unremarkable, but pleasant and compact; the kind of place a late nineteenth-century industrialist might have built for his mistress.

'Don't forget,' said the picture editor, a particular friend of mine called Mike Davies, as we got out of our vehicle, 'when he asks if you want a slice off the Sunday joint, just say no.'

We gathered round the front door, carrying the camera gear. I pressed the bell. Someone imitated the sound of an ancient door creaking open, and we all laughed tensely.

At that moment the door really opened. A little man stood there, looking like an African Richard Attenborough, short and pudgy. He was wearing a red velvet jacket embroidered with gold thread, and a skullcap. Stray tufts of beard grew out of his jaw, at angles which seemed to be purely accidental. He looked very sad. It was the Emperor Bokassa in person.

I introduced myself and my colleagues, and saw them grinning secretly to one another. The Emperor seemed not to notice. He led the way into the darkened château.

Then I spotted it, and a feeling like an electrical current went down my spine. In his hallway, the Emperor had a very large refrigerator; big enough to hold at least one medium-sized opposition leader.

I wasn't quite certain how much English the Emperor spoke, so I let the others go in ahead of me and pulled Mike Davies back by the sleeve.

'Get him into one of the rooms and keep him there while I look inside that.'

The Emperor led the way, and opened a door to the left. I caught sight of a throne, and paintings of Napoleon on the walls.

'Late King Faroukh,' Mike muttered as he went in and engaged the Emperor in some very loud but not altogether accurate French.

I stayed outside, pretending to fidget with the camera tripod. Then as Mike half-closed the door to the Throne Room I walked across the hall to the refrigerator. I was quite scared. Supposing there really was someone in there? What would I do?

It was a chest model, with the lid on the top. Glancing round at the Throne Room, I could hear the Emperor's low, gloomy voice answering some question of Mike's about Napoleon. There was no one else around. I put my fingers under the lid, and lifted. My arms were weak with nervousness.

Inside, covered with refrigerator frost, were half a dozen lamb chops, a few frozen herrings, and some packets of peas and carrots. No heads, no ears, no fingers, or anything even more personal. I leant down and reached deeper: just peas and carrots. Some ice cream. Several bags of ice. That was all. I lowered the lid, and in my relief and nervousness let it bang too loudly. The gloomy voice in the Throne Room paused for a second or two, then resumed.

Mike Davies and the others looked at me sharply as I walked in.

'I was just telling your colleagues here—'

I closed my eyes and shook my head a little. The others relaxed perceptibly.

' – about the way in which the French government has treated me.'

I made soothing noises and shook my head again, this time at the way in which the French government had treated him. The Emperor droned on, and I took the opportunity to look around.

The room was an elaborate memorial to a disordered personality.

His court in exile had sat here once a week, listening to the imperial commands, until the French government had prevented them from turning up. It was probably quite a relief for them. We sat him down with his throne behind him and the portrait of Napoleon visible over his shoulder. The cameraman, Dougie Dalgleish, shifted him around. The sound recordist, Ron Hooper (who later became a cameraman and travelled with me around Russia), pushed a microphone up the imperial jumper and pinned it to the front of his shirt. The lighting-man, Tony Fallshaw, who would one day accompany me on all sorts of expeditions when he became a cameraman himself, shone lights in his face from different angles. The Emperor Bokassa took it all with complete apathy. If we had asked him to stand on the throne and undress, he would probably have done it.

Napoleon looked out at us everywhere from paintings and engravings: life-sized ones, and for the most part bad copies, the kind of thing you found for sale, often from the Bokassa's former subjects, in the corridors of the Metro. There was a lot of gold paint on the furniture. That made it imperial, at least to his mind.

The Emperor was a fantasist, a sufferer from one of the more frequent delusions; only in his case he really had been an emperor, with the power of life and death over his subjects. I looked at him more closely. This anxious, sad little man had ordered hundreds of murders; his frown, now so predominant, had meant someone's painful death; his hands, moving nervously as though he was washing them in imaginary water, had struck those who had angered him; that mouth, now slack with despair, had closed on human meat. I was interviewing a madman.

And yet, as our interview wore on, I became more and more engrossed in his story, and found parts of it increasingly believable. I was the only one of our group who could understand what he was saying, and I missed plenty of things because he spoke so softly and his accent was so strong.

He had done many of the things he was accused of, he said, and he was profoundly sorry. He had indeed ordered his soldiers to shoot at the schoolchildren who were demonstrating against the introduction of expensive new uniforms.

'Which were made by a company owned by your own family?'

He nodded, contritely. To everyone else it had been a savage crime; to him it had been a mistake, easily enough made, which he now regretted. He would, he said, like to apologize for this. He could see it was wrong. He seemed to be looking to me to absolve him and make all the bad things go away; as though I were the Archbishop of Bangui and could crown him again, now that he had got that off his chest.

'Your critics say you're insane,' I said.

For a moment I could see the embers of the old fires. Then they died down again.

'It was only the French. They wanted to make it easier to get rid of me. Giscard was behind it, calling me his cousin and taking all the diamonds and then doing this when his brother disagreed with me over the price. And then the paras knocked down the door of my office and pointed their guns at me.'

It was tumbling out of him now, and I found it hard to keep pace with it all. It was just the monomania speaking, I told myself; and yet a certain crazy logic kept asserting itself in the mad, reddened eyes. The camera crew were getting restless, not understanding anything of the torrent that was pouring from him.

Some of it was an old story, some was entirely new. What it amounted to was this: Valéry Giscard d'Estaing had struck up a strange friendship with Bokassa – I saw letters from him in which he called Bokassa '*mon cher cousin*' – and used to visit him regularly in order to slaughter some of the Central African Empire's wildlife. Giscard encouraged his imperial mania, to the extent that French companies ran the entire mad coronation of 1977. It cost more than the entire gross national product of the Central African Empire for that year.

Giscard's brother, meanwhile, went into business with Bokassa for the mining and exportation of uncut diamonds from the Empire's mines. I saw the letters about that too, and they seemed entirely genuine. Then came the inevitable falling out over the price. Giscard's brother wanted more and cheaper diamonds; Bokassa claimed that the national interests of the CAE, which he had suddenly remembered, wouldn't allow it. You'll see what will happen, said Giscard's brother.

What happened first was the schoolchildren's demonstration, which was provoked by Bokassa's own lunacy and greed. The

violence of its suppression caused an outcry around the world, and
not long afterwards Giscard announced that France would step in to
restore order in its former colony. And so the paras landed, captured
Bokassa's palace, burst into his office, and tied him up. Then they
turned their attention to the safe in the corner of the room.

'I used to keep a little pot of uncut stones in it, sixty-eight of
them, just for myself. They were my own property.

' "You might at least tell me where you are going to take them,"
I said to the paras.

' "Fuck off and shut your mouth," the commander said – I can
tell you his name, if you want to know it. "We have orders to take
them straight to the Elysée Palace." '

'They blew open the safe, and the para commander put the
packets of diamonds into his pockets.

'And to think,' he said, knuckling away the tear which had
formed when he thought of his little pot of uncut diamonds, 'that I
regarded that man as my friend.'

Afterwards the French put Bokassa on trial. All his crimes came
out in the evidence.

'So what about the cannibalism?'

'M. Simpson, I swear to you this was a complete lie. Never have
I partaken of human flesh. The very idea is abhorrent to me. I am
not a wild animal. I did things which were bad, I know; but not this,
I assure you. You must believe me.'

The strange thing was that I did. He fixed me with his crazy eyes,
the brown of whose irises seemed to have leaked into the surrounding
whites. I nodded. There was, after all, a certain plausibility about
it all. If the French government wanted to stage something like
this, accusations of mere despotism might not be sufficient to justify
the act of taking control of the CAE in the eyes of public opinion.
And what would appeal more to the French imagination, and better
brand the Emperor as a maniac, than detailed accusations that he
had ordered his chief political enemy to be cooked?

I checked out the case later. These accusations came solely from
Bokassa's French chef. He said in evidence that Bokassa would order
him to cook slices of the frozen corpse, and specify which particular
sauce he wanted. Then he would set to with gusto. There had been
much laughter in court, and Bokassa had wept copiously. His defence

lawyer, appointed by the French, had scarcely bothered with cross-examination.

A new Central African government, more liberal than Bokassa's own, eventually allowed him out of prison, and he slipped out of the country to his château in France. By this time Giscard had long been out of office, and the Socialist, François Mitterrand, had become President. Allegations about Giscard's diamond dealings had leaked out in *Le Canard Enchaîné* and other newspapers, but Mitterrand was clearly determined that Bokassa should not be able to tell any more of his story to the press.

We all posed for photographs with the Emperor afterwards, and went into the kitchen to meet his wives: jolly, plump ladies who seemed very fond of the little man. As we made our way back to the office I tried to explain the story to Mike Davies.

'You don't believe all that, do you?'

Weakly, I pretended I didn't. Journalists are always reluctant to appear credulous, and they take refuge in an assumed scepticism which eventually becomes a settled habit of mind. But there had been something believable about the Emperor's story; and it was by no means out of the question that the French government should behave after this fashion. Why, I asked myself, should Mitterrand have gone to such extraordinary lengths to keep Bokassa quiet?

We were the only journalists, French or foreign, who managed to interview him. Later he decided, without warning, to return to what had once again become the Central African Republic to clear his name. He didn't succeed, of course. He was put away for life, and was said to howl at the full moon from his cell.

And then, since he was harmless, the government released him. He died in poverty in a hut on the outskirts of Bangui a few years later, still protesting his innocence. When the news of his death came through, I wrote an article for the *Spectator* about my visit to his château, the discovery of the deep-freeze in the hallway, and my examination of its contents. We called it 'The Silence of the Lamb Chops'.

7

ICONS

When I remember all the friends so link'd together
    I've seen around me fall, like leaves in wint'ry weather,
I feel like one who treads alone a banquet hall deserted,
    Whose joys are fled, whose garlands dead,
And all but he departed.

Thomas Moore, *Oft in the Stilly Night*

Whenever I answer questions at conferences or dinners or public lectures, the same subjects always come up. In Internet jargon they would be known as FAQs: frequently asked questions. In my case they should be AIAQs – almost invariably asked questions. Which is your favourite country, who is the most impressive person you have met, and have you ever feared for your life?

My answers vary, depending on mood, digestion, and the general receptivity of the audience. The one about fearing for my life seems to be predicated on the idea that nothing particularly dangerous happens to anyone nowadays, so it can hardly have happened to me; in fact I am always fearing for my life, usually unnecessarily. As for the others, they are just a way of getting me to talk about places and people. Depending on my mood, my favourite country can be Iran or Afghanistan or anywhere in Central Asia or Latin America: somewhere that will take people by surprise. The real answer – France – would short-change an audience which is looking for exoticism.

The AIAQ about the most impressive person I have met is altogether different. I have, of course, met dozens of people who have impressed me. Audiences like it if you answer 'Nelson Mandela', because he is the person who has made the most impact on them of a moral nature in the modern world. He is as wonderful, charming and unpretentious a person as you could hope to come across. His forgiveness, his love of his fellow-man, his breadth of vision are qualities which have enriched the entire world. And yet when he became President of South African he turned a blind eye to all sorts of corruption and nastiness going on inside his party, the African National Congress, merely because it *was* his party. He isn't, in other words, perfect; and people often seem to have a problem with that.

I write this, not to pull a great man down, but to make the point that hero-worship of the Victorian, Thomas Carlyle variety is self-deceiving. If someone as magnificent as Nelson Mandela can be less than admirable in some respects, what hope is there for an ordinary mortal who is just trying to get by in life – especially political life? The best we can do, it seems to me, is to honour the moments when someone behaves well, and try not to be surprised when they don't.

And so, after decades of watching and interviewing people at the hero-level, I have come to be grateful for much less: for glimpses of an underlying decency and humanity, for moments of courage and quick-wittedness in the face of fear and disaster, for the instinct to say or do the right and proper thing when it is inopportune or dangerous.

Some people who did the right thing when it mattered will appear in these pages. So will others who were not necessarily heroic, but who stand out in the memory as shining lights of attractiveness and fascination. Sadly, many of them are now only memories.

Close to our old flat in Chelsea, there was a very expensive restaurant called La Tante Claire. The staff treated you as though they were doing you a major personal favour by allowing you to hand them large amounts of your money, and the only time Dee and I ever went there, as the guests of our friend Jan Serfontein, we both had duck and were up all night with food-poisoning. I decided to write about the experience for the *Spectator*, but the editor warned me to be careful because the owner was suspected of being litigious. I thought about it, and finally remembered a line from an old W.C. Fields film: 'I ain't sayin' this steak is tough, I'm just sayin' I ain't seen that old horse around lately.' I wasn't saying the duck had poisoned me, I wrote; I was just saying I wouldn't ever go to La Tante Claire again.

I had quite a few letters of congratulation after that, including one from Sir Alec Guinness. 'Their pretension is intolerable,' he wrote. 'I will never darken their door again.'

They had some reason to be pretentious, though: for a time, it was one of the most fashionable places in London. On two different occasions, when I walked past, I saw Diana, Princess of Wales having lunch at one of the tables with some friends. This was interesting, because the table in question was the only one in the restaurant which could be seen by passers-by in the street. Diana had deliberately chosen it in order to be seen.

Royal reporting isn't my thing, and like a great many people I thought the hounding of Diana by the tabloid press was one of the most disgusting spectacles of modern times. And yet the defence the tabloids put forward – that she sought out the publicity – was certainly true; though it would be more accurate to say that she craved attention, not the destructive and unjustifiable prying which the tabloids went in for.

Their money lured her friends and associates (and the un-speakable people such as those who recorded her private telephone conversations and those of her husband) into betraying her. Diana was not a saint; hers was a complicated and quite fragile personality, which could not stand the strain of so much savage interference. The way the tabloids smacked their lips over the most intimate details of her personal life shamed our entire society; and sometimes journalists seemed to be the only people who did not understand this.

I first met Diana in 1989, at a state banquet at Buckingham Palace for the President of Nigeria. It was a superb occasion, and when the lights went down and a lone piper strode along the corridor leading to the hall, accompanying the waiters in full livery who were bringing in the pudding, there was an audible and delighted intake of breath all around me. They do things the old-fashioned way at Buckingham Palace. After dinner, the ordinary guests stood around in one drawing room drinking coffee, while the royal family and the guests of honour stood in the adjoining one. There was no physical barrier between the two rooms, yet no one crossed the *cordon sanitaire* without invitation.

I had just come back from a fairly high-profile trip to Ceauşescu's Romania, where I had been arrested several times. One of the royal dukes wanted to talk about all this, and once across the magic line I stayed there, chatting to other people as well. When the conversation finally ran out I stood slightly irresolute and wondering whether I should leave. Then a low, half-familiar voice spoke behind me.

'I've been looking forward all night to meeting you.'

The words carried an extraordinary attraction. I turned, and saw Diana standing there in a low-cut white dress with diamonds around her neck and in her hair. I was of course mesmerized; I suppose that was the point of the whole thing. It didn't matter to me that she must have used the same line hundreds of times before, and probably several times that evening.

We talked for half an hour, while the waiters went round with trays of superb brandy. I didn't need the brandy. Did she mind, I asked, if I didn't call her 'Your Royal Highness'? She didn't. She told me about her life, and about the way the tabloids made her life a misery.

'If you ever need any help in that department,' I said, 'just let me know.'

I didn't know exactly what I meant by that, but I was definitely in knight-errant mood.

'Thank you,' she said. 'I won't forget it.'

We were interrupted by the Duchess of York, who came bouncing up, red-haired and full of gossip. I was faintly annoyed at the interruption, but after the general starchiness of the evening there was something mildly refreshing about her approach. Until, that is, the Queen went past and said something I didn't catch, and the Duchess of York put her tongue out at her back. Maybe I was too conventional and easily shocked, but Diana looked quickly at me, frowning. The Duchess of York giggled and bounced off.

Not long afterwards the Prince of Wales came over, and after a few more words they walked away together.

'It was wonderful to meet you,' Diana murmured.

There are few things more susceptible than the heart of a man in early middle age, and I was completely bowled over. Plenty of others must have had precisely the same experience. It was too late to find a taxi, and I walked home to South Kensington in my rented white tie and tails without noticing the cold, the distance or the stares of occasional passers-by.

My unspecific offer of help was never, of course, called in. I saw her twice at a distance, driving along High Street Kensington to her favourite cinema; twice as I passed the window of La Tante Claire; and once at a dinner party which Dee and I went to, not long before her death, where we spoke only briefly. By that stage her marriage had long since collapsed, and there were endless rumours about her private life. She looked quite sensational, tucking her long legs under her on the sofa in a way no one could fail to notice.

Early in the morning of Sunday 31 August 1997 Dee and I were woken at our home in Dublin by a friend calling from Australia. Diana had been badly injured in a car crash in Paris, he said. I ran to the television set in the next room: by now the confirmation had come through that she was dead. It was devastating. I rang the BBC; they wanted me to come to London at once. We had moved to Ireland a few months before, and I had promised my boss that if ever I were wanted I could be at Television Centre within four hours. This was the first big test.

We drove to the airport without taking the time to ring ahead and make a reservation, and we were still too shocked to say much to each other. The significance of the date hadn't occurred to me until I saw the crowd that had gathered outside the airport entrance: it was the last day of the summer holidays, and we had to queue up to get inside the airport building. All the flights to cities in Britain were fully booked. It wasn't even possible to get a seat on a plane to Paris or Amsterdam or Brussels.

In the end, by paying more, we got ourselves onto the head of the waiting list.

'You'd be first,' said a charming woman from Aer Lingus, 'because we know why you've got to get back, and we're really, really sorry about that. But there's a gentleman from England whose wife is having a heart and lung transplant today, and we thought you'd understand if we let him go first in the list.'

I did understand, though it made me even more nervous. In the end, though, there were enough seats for all three of us.

'Hello, John,' said the man ahead of us in the queue. 'Amazing story, eh? Oh, by the way, I'm _____ from the _____.'

It was one of the leading tabloids. I understood now what had happened.

'Hope all goes well with your wife's heart transplant,' I said, with heavy irony.

'Oh, that.'

He laughed, pleased with his stratagem.

I thought of saying this was the kind of reason which brought the amazing story about, but decided against it. Why bother?

That evening I wrote the obituary on Diana for the main television news. I tried not to be sentimental about it: the pictures of a vulnerable, wounded young woman trying to rebuild her life, and the knowledge of where it had all ended, supplied all the emotion that was required. No need for words like 'tragic' or 'shocking'; everyone watching could supply them for themselves. And of course the tabloids were full of that kind of thing. For them, it was an amazing story.

Soon, though, it was becoming obvious that something strange was starting to happen in British society as a result of the death. The royal family had stayed at Balmoral, and the two princes, William and Harry, had gone to church on the morning after the accident in Paris, with what feelings one can only try to imagine. This was the way the British of all classes once behaved at times of great emotional strain, but by the end of the century only the upper class still did so.

The rest of society wanted to see grief, and felt robbed and let down if they did not. They expected the royal family to take the lead in the nation's mourning, forgetting how much of a trial Diana had been to her former husband and his relations, and how much criticism she had received from Buckingham Palace herself.

By Tuesday, queues were starting to form in the Mall, as people went to pay their respects to Diana in the only way open to them: by signing a book of condolence. I thought we should take this manifestation of the public mood seriously, and volunteered to go down to film the queues and talk to the people in them.

It was clear, the more I listened, that complex emotions were coming to the surface. They were not just unhappy at the Princess's death; they did not merely feel, as I did, that something of beauty and glamour had been taken away from us. They were angry. They believed that the Palace had betrayed her. For these people she had represented the new mood of British society, softer, gentler, more concerned, whereas the Palace represented the older ways: more judgemental, stricter, more in control of its emotions.

Many of the people in the queues were natural royalists, who simply wanted the Queen and her family to understand the feelings they themselves were experiencing and show that to some extent they shared them. But there was another and even more significant element: those from the more vulnerable sections of society. I quickly realized from walking up and down the queues, talking to the people there, that there was a high percentage who were divorced, or out of work, or who belonged to an ethnic minority.

There was an overwhelming sense among these people that Diana too had been discriminated against; that somehow she belonged on their side of the social divide, ranged with them against the successful and hard-nosed and wealthy – the people who showed no emotion because they felt none.

Probably none of it was true for a moment. The royal family, though most of them may well have been infuriated in the past by aspects of Diana's behaviour, seemed to be as shocked and bereaved as everyone else. But there was that two-fold, invisible barrier, much like the barrier which kept the ordinary guests at Palace banquets from mingling with the members of the royal family unless invited: the culture of the stiff upper lip, which most of the rest of society had come to find inexplicable and unnatural, and the immobility which an outdated court ceremonial had helped to create. A court where it is still frowned on to speak until you have been spoken to, where bowing and curtsying are still pretty much mandatory, has closer links with the Victorian world than our own.

'They're so cold,' one Asian woman said as she stood in the warm afternoon sun. 'They don't seem to care what ordinary people feel about it all.'

A young white man beside her nodded. 'They should come down here and see us standing here.'

Others were fiercely outspoken about the tabloid press.

'They're the ones that killed her. They never left her alone, all her life. I told my husband I wouldn't ever read a newspaper again, I'm so angry about them.'

Over the next couple of days all these feelings intensified. Once a small group of women warned a photographer from one of the tabloids that they would smash his camera if he took a shot of them, and he moved away. But it was the Queen and her family who came in for the main criticism.

'They should be down here, where she is.'

The speaker pointed with his head to the Chapel Royal, where the Princess's body was still lying.

By this time the tabloids themselves had thrown their weight behind this kind of opinion, campaigning for the flag on Buckingham Palace to be flown at half-mast, and claiming victory when a Union Jack was raised on the flag-pole for the first time in palace history, and finally came to rest halfway down it. They seemed to be trying to ingratiate themselves with the people who believed that they had been partly responsible for Diana's death.

Much later than they should have, the royal family returned to London. The kind of things the crowds in the Mall wanted were starting to happen.

And by now there was another focus for people's emotion: the heaping up of flowers at the gates of Kensington Palace. The road alongside was thronged with people carrying bunches of flowers. The florists' shops had to restock several times a day, and they were careful not to overcharge. Eventually the sea of flowers was great enough to be clearly visible from the planes coming in to land at Heathrow, and some pilots claimed that the sun reflected from so much cellophane blinded them. The whole thing was threatening to get out of hand: the crowds were growing, the public emotion was stronger than ever.

It was a kind of hysteria, of course, and it grew by emulation. The more the television news bulletins showed what was happening, the more people wanted to come and express their own feelings and leave their flowers. There was something increasingly disturbing about it all, and the messages on the bunches of flowers, like inscriptions at the shrine of a saint, often seemed to hint at inner pathologies which had become focused on Diana.

'God bless you, my darling. You understood, but they couldn't understand you.'

'Never to be forgotten in our lives.'

'You will live on for me through all eternity.'

'I always felt you knew what I was going through. Just as I knew what you were going through.'

Hysteria is infectious, and many of us who did not want to leave flowers or a message there felt the emotional pull of it all.

The funeral the following Saturday brought all the different strands together. I was asked by the *Sunday Telegraph* to write their news story about it, and was given a ticket to the press seats in Westminster Abbey. It would probably have been more sensible to have watched the entire proceedings on television, because I would have seen the coffin carried through the streets accompanied on foot by the Prince of Wales, his father, Earl Spencer, and Diana's two sons: one of the most moving sights in modern British history. I could have seen the Queen, who by tradition bowed to no one, incline her head as the coffin passed Buckingham Palace: another gesture of change in the semiotics of royal behaviour. But I had decided that seeing everything at second hand would be no real substitute for seeing one important thing for myself.

I made an early start. The morning was beautiful, with the sun slanting down between the buildings and the empty streets silent and clean. I asked the driver to stop at a garage near the Abbey, and I went in to get some paper handkerchiefs; I knew they would be needed. All the garage had was a large box of industrial-sized tissues, but I took them just the same.

The crowds were already building up outside the Abbey, and vast television screens had been erected in the nearby parks so that people could watch what was happening. A queue of invited guests had formed at the gate which led to the Abbey's north door. There were various people in it whom I knew, including the comedy actress Ruby Wax, who had been a friend of Diana's. I talked to her for a while in a muted kind of way, then took my place at the end of the queue. Behind me was an elegant woman in a black suit and stunning hat, who turned out to be the editor of one of the leading fashion magazines.

It seemed a long wait, in the early morning sun. No one laughed or spoke too loudly. A couple in late middle age, well turned out, deeply tanned and of a matching shortness, came up with apologetic grins on their faces and got into conversation with the man directly in front of me. It was plain he didn't know them, but they started talking animatedly about some resort I hadn't heard of, and he seemed to go along with it. Soon they were chatting and laughing with him, instant old friends. It was the only loud conversation in the entire queue. Finally they looked round at me with another set of apologetic smiles, and pushed their way into the queue alongside him.

'Who are the tiny twosome?' I asked the elegant woman beside me.

'Ralph Lauren and his wife.'

It occurred to me that she might not want me to speak too loudly, in case I offended them and they withdrew their advertising from her magazine. Inside the Abbey at last, the editor and I worked our way towards the front, as determined to get a good view as the Laurens were to be there at all. We finally found seats beside Gladstone's statue, a few yards from the high altar, among the court officials from Buckingham Palace: older men and women, correctly dressed and correctly behaved, determined to show a becoming reserve. These, of course, were the people whom Princess Diana had identified as her enemies; perhaps in order to avoid looking any closer at the family into which she had married.

There was silence everywhere in the Abbey, and then a sound I shall never forget: the quiet, determined squealing of rubber-soled boots on the floor-tiles of the Abbey, as six bareheaded Guardsmen carried Diana's coffin down the aisle and up the steps before the altar. With the sound came the scent of the lilies that lay on the flag-wrapped coffin, flooding the chancel like the memory of the beautiful, flawed woman whose body lay inside it. It still seemed impossible that so much ardour and elegance could have been taken out of the world.

The service began. Unlike most of the funerals that had taken place here, there could be no sense of thanksgiving for a life well spent, of achievement and honour and long service. Diana's life had been a battlefield, and she had died a pointless death, killed by the pursuit of the media, the vulgar desire of a rich man and his son to own her like a trophy, and the misjudgement of a drunken driver.

Beside me, the courtiers stiffened: Elton John was going to play the song which had echoed through the entire week, 'Candle In The Wind'. It was the first major concession to the feelings of the crowd outside, the first real departure from the traditions of a state funeral. 'Extraordinary how potent cheap music is,' says someone dismissively in one of Noel Coward's plays, and although the song characterized the entire showbusiness ethos of Diana's later life, it was indeed potent; though why Elton John should merely have recycled an old song about Marilyn Monroe and not have written something new was never explained.

Now the piano rang shrill and sharp through the Abbey, and the words which almost everyone in the world seemed to know by now filled the place. I looked covertly to my left; one of the older courtiers, a haughty-looking man in formal clothes, had tears running down his cheeks. In a sudden access of fellow-feeling, for tears were running down my own, I passed the box of paper handkerchiefs down the line. Several members of the group took one as the box went by.

Earl Spencer spoke from the pulpit. I had met him once or twice in the past, when he was starting a career in television with one of the American networks: a pleasant, unaffected young man, eager to please. Now, ten years on, he had thickened and broadened and matured. His words had real power, and the combination of passion and firm self-control was precisely what the British had wanted. Self-control alone might have been enough in the past; now they required emotion as well.

His address had the power of a Shakespearean funeral oration. It was full of open fury against the tabloids and hidden resentment against the royal family, which had taken Diana in and later turned against her because in private she had too many problems while in public she was too much of a star. Somewhere, too, was the sense that the Spencers had been the companions of kings in England when the Windsors were merely German princelings. It was angry, uncomfortable and necessary. I do not think I have ever heard a better speech.

It caught exactly the mood of the vast crowds outside the Abbey. When it was finished there was a faint rustling sound, which grew louder and louder until it swept in through the open west doors of the Abbey itself: the applause of the people in the parks and the streets, who had heard Earl Spencer on television. Inside, most of the invited guests took up the applause, row by row, until it reached the front line of seats where the Queen and her family sat, dressed in the deepest black. They did not applaud, and neither did the courtiers.

I listened to the sound of clapping and smelled the scent of the lilies and looked at the flag-draped coffin in front of the high altar, and thought how empty even the lives of people like me who didn't really know her were going to seem. I don't think I have ever passed Kensington Palace since, or driven down Kensington High Street, without thinking of the glamour that went out of London with her.

Winston Churchill did and said some fairly bad things in his time, but when the moment came he did exactly the right thing. An old Labour politician, as instinctively left-wing as Churchill was right-wing, once told me how he had slipped across the lobby of the House of Commons after the overwhelming Labour victory in the 1945 election to tell Churchill that the result didn't make any difference to the respect he and his constituents felt for him.

'Mind you,' he said afterwards, 'I felt a bit embarrassed.'

I was brought up at the tail-end of the years in which no one, left or right, had anything but praise for Churchill. My father, a Liberal at the time, queued for hours in order to walk past his coffin as his body lay in state in Westminster Hall. Yet by that time all the old pre-war criticisms of Churchill had surfaced again: his lack of stability, his excitability at the time of the General Strike, his mistake in returning to the gold standard, his refusal to countenance Indian independence, and the hoary old ones about responsibility for the failure in the Dardenelles campaign (in fact it was the awful Kitchener who was mostly responsible, but Churchill did the decent thing, resigning from the government and going to fight on the Western Front) and the Tonypandy massacre, for which he bore no responsibility at all.

In the days when I was presenting the *Nine O'Clock News*, I received an irritable letter about the way I had been pronouncing the word 'Soviet'. I was about to write a curt and self-justifying reply, when it occurred to me to look up this Sir John Colville in the reference books; the name seemed to ring a bell. *Who's Who* told me:

he had been Churchill's private secretary during the Second World War. I wrote my reply justifying the pronunciation (nowadays, of course, the very word is obsolete), but suggested that he might like to come to Television Centre and have lunch with John Humphrys and myself. He wrote back to say he would be delighted.

It was the start of a friendship that was brief but interesting. He had written three books about his time with Churchill, he said, and that was enough. A few weeks later, when we met for lunch again, he was in a state of some excitement. He had just been clearing out his attic, he said, and had come across a wartime diary whose very existence he had forgotten. It shed light on various aspects of life at Downing Street, but the best thing in it was an account of Churchill's response to the bombing of German cities. To me, having watched the modern-day equivalent at first hand, the bombing of cities like Dresden and Hamburg was a crime, and a black mark against Churchill personally.

I said this to Sir John Colville.

'Well, this is going to interest you, then. I'd forgotten all about it, but I found the details in this diary. "Bomber" Harris got together a lot of film about the bombing of German cities, and he had it put together to let Churchill see how successful the RAF was, and how well things were going. He had a showing of it in the Cabinet Rooms cinema.

'Well, Churchill loved the flicks, and so he settled himself in his armchair there, and the lights went down, and the film started. It was pretty impressive. Somehow they'd managed to get hold of some film from the ground, as well as what his photographers could see from 5,000 feet up, and there were all these splendid old buildings collapsing, and bodies lying everywhere, and people being taken to hospital. I have to say, I don't at all agree with you about the bombing of the cities because I think it had to be done, but this film rather stuck in my throat.

'Anyway, it came to an end and the lights went up, and there was "Bomber" Harris grinning all over his face with pride. I wasn't at all certain how Churchill would react – didn't have a clue. So I stole a look at him; he was sitting in the same row as me. There he was, with the tears running down his face. And he said, "Are we beasts, that we should be doing these things?"

'So that's what he thought about the bombing. Didn't half upset old "Bomber" Harris, of course. I'm going to write it up with the rest of the things I've dug out of this notebook of mine.'

A couple of weeks after our lunch, I opened the morning paper and saw that Sir John Colville had died suddenly; and his last memories died with him.

Heroes come in all sorts of forms. I found one in the form of a dried-up little watchman at the sensational ruins of Persepolis, in southern Iran. Persepolis, the capital of Darius the Great, was burned either by accident or in a fit of drunken rage by Darius' conqueror, Alexander the Great. The columns and carvings which are left, twenty-five centuries later, are quite superb. Marble blocks nearly sixty feet high tower over the double-flighted grand staircase, so beautifully proportioned that a horseman could ride up or down them with ease.

Ambassadors and captives and courtiers parade in the reliefs carrying gifts for the Shahanshah, gigantic eagles and lions defend the approaches to his throne, tribute-bearers queue up from everywhere in the Persian Empire: Aryans, Egyptians, Armenians, Brahmans, Medes turning casually to talk to one another as they climb the great staircase, Scythians from Samarkand, Syrians with their chariots, Phoenicians with golden vessels, Cappadocians with their famous cloth, Arabs with dromedaries, Bactrians with camels.

We in the Western world obtained our custom of giving presents at Christmas from this parade of gift-bearers, via the gold, frankincense and myrrh of the Magi who were themselves Persian. Persepolis is one of the wonders of the world, and if it were not so distant and Iran were not so cut off it would be as famous as the Taj Mahal.

So when a large group of earnest Islamic revolutionaries equipped with a fleet of bulldozers set out from the city of Shiraz in the first weeks after the revolution of 1979 to knock Persepolis down, the threat was a disturbing one. The ruins were a monument to the ungodly rule of the Shahs, the revolutionaries' leader announced, and they would have to go. A thousand or more people set out from Shiraz, and six or seven hundred of them were still there, thirty miles later, when the bulldozers arrived at the palace.

Ali Reza was on duty at Persepolis that day, a completely unremarkable little man in his forties. Iran is full of them: watchmen in greyish open-necked shirts, rumpled trousers and sandals, sitting in the entrance halls and gateways of office blocks and government buildings. They are there to see that the rules are obeyed, but they aren't paid to be heroic. Nine hundred and ninety-nine out of a thousand of such men, faced with a large mob of armed iconoclasts, would have opened the gates obediently and let them in.

Ali Reza was the one man in a thousand.

'We are here to destroy the palace of the Shahs,' shouted the leader. 'If you get in our way you will be serving the Shah, not the revolution.'

'I can't let you in without authority,' said Ali Reza.

'The revolution is our authority.'

'In that case show me a piece of paper that says you can come and damage these ruins.'

They could easily have forced their way past him, but his resistance stalled them at a critical moment. They looked around at the huge scale of Persepolis, and reflected that it was already mid-morning. The leader thought about it.

'All right,' he shouted, 'we can get the necessary authority and come back here. In the meantime, we can go to Bishapur where there are many godless carvings and destroy them.'

Bishapur, not far away, was the site of some remarkable reliefs cut in the rock-face by Roman prisoners of war who had been captured by Shah Sapor of Persia, in 260 AD. The Romans treacherously handed over their emperor, the unfortunate Valerian, to the Persians, and for the rest of his life Valerian was carried around in chains and made to kneel down every time Sapor wanted to mount his horse, so he could say he placed his foot on a Roman emperor's neck. Even after Valerian's death from shame and grief, his abasement wasn't over: Sapor had his skin stuffed with straw and took it with him wherever he went. The Bishapur rock-carvings portrayed Sapor's victory in all its savage glory.

Ali Reza thought quickly.

'So it doesn't matter to you that you will be destroying the likeness of the son-in-law of the Prophet's grandson?'

There was a silence. Everyone looked at him.

'One of the figures at Bishapur is that of the man who married the daughter of the saintly martyr Hosain.'

Hosain is one of the holiest figures of Shi'a Islam. He was killed on the plains of Kerbala more than four hundred years after the reliefs were carved on the rock-face at Bishapur, so it wasn't exactly plausible that his son-in-law would have been commemorated there, but it was the best that Ali Reza could come up with on the spur of the moment.

The revolutionaries went into a huddle to discuss it. The mob, though, had already made their decision: they were beginning to stream down the road back to Shiraz. Soon the bulldozers would follow them.

When I visit the ruins at Persepolis and see the rock-reliefs at Bishapur, it isn't the glory of the Persian emperors that come to mind: it's the quick thinking of an unremarkable little man in a grey shirt and sandals.

One of the bravest men I ever met was the former mayor of a nasty little town carved out of the Peruvian jungle: a drugs town, dominated by a psychopath who was in command of the local army base. It wasn't the kind of place where you would want to make a stand for any kind of principle. There would be no one to back you up, no one even to tell the outside world that your body had been found floating in the river, weighted down by stones.

The town, in the heart of the Huallaga Valley, the main coca-growing area of Peru, was called Tocache; the ex-mayor was Luis Zambrano. He was in his thirties, a teacher by profession, neatly turned out and slightly built. You probably wouldn't notice him in a crowd, unless you spotted the hint of determination which showed in the set of his mouth and chin.

The local army commander, who had the power of life and death over the people of Tocache, was deeply involved in the coca trade. Zambrano found this out, and insisted on telling the radio station which covered the Huallaga valley. Nervously, the station broadcast the interview he insisted that they should record with him. Soon afterwards Zambrano's house was firebombed, and he and his family were lucky to escape with their lives. He was expecting the arsonists back at any time.

I happened to come to Peru soon afterwards with a television team, in order to make a film about the drugs trade. We contacted Zambrano, and he agreed to be interviewed. Revealing the truth about what was going on in Tocache had been dangerous enough the first time; to repeat it now must have seemed almost suicidal.

We had been flying from town to town along the Huallaga Valley in a small chartered aircraft, keeping on the move all the time and never letting anyone know where we would be spending the night. That way, we reasoned, we could avoid a visit from the local death squads. We certainly weren't going to spend the night in Tocache. Our pilot, who may have been involved in the drugs trade himself from time to time, warned us that we would have to take off no later than 4.30. It seemed like a tall order.

We landed at 10.30 in the morning. The airstrip was well maintained, and there were half a dozen small planes parked beside it. In a tiny piss-poor place like Tocache, that showed it was an important drugs route, and that the army was heavily involved in the trade. The soldiers who were sitting around guarding the place were hostile. We were all distinctly nervous. In the intense heat we were sweating heavily by the time we reached the army tents that acted as the airport terminal. A soldier with 'NAZI' written on the stock of his rifle questioned us a little, then pointed out where we could hire a couple of broken-down taxis.

A Landcruiser painted a familiar shade of light blue was parked nearby, and our Peruvian fixer went over to talk to the two men in it. They worked for the UN anti-drugs programme, but they were far too scared to help us. They were even too scared to talk to her, and eventually wound up the window and sat there, pretending to ignore her.

There was a faint buzzing sound in the distance, like a wasp caught in a jam jar. A cloud of dust appeared at the end of the road: a man was heading towards us on a motor-scooter. It was Luis Zambrano, who had promised to lead us back to the place where he was now living. We climbed into our ramshackle taxis and followed him.

The house was small, painted grey, and had bars on the windows. It looked uninhabited. There was scarcely any furniture in the room inside: the Zambranos had lost virtually everything they possessed when their own house was burned.

We got out and looked at each other. Zambrano's white shirt was well ironed, his moustache was carefully trimmed, there were neat creases in his trousers. He looked very small and slight as he lowered himself into his borrowed armchair. But I could see at once that he had a real presence. This was not the kind of man you would want to suggest some cheap scam to; you would be too nervous of the firmness and honesty of his response.

When we had set up the camera, he started to tell us his story. He had been elected sub-prefect, or mayor, of Tocache a couple of years before in 1990, promising to clean up the town and stop the drugs trade. Directly he took office he found he was expected to attend a monthly meeting with the local army commander, Comandante Alfonso, plus the police commander and the chief prosecutor.

At these meetings the main subject to be decided was which group of drug-runners should be used, and how much it should have to pay the men round the table. The division of the spoils was clear: the other three received $5,000 each, but since the mayor had no power to interfere with the flights he received only $200. There were at least seven flights a week from Tocache. Zambrano told the others he wasn't interested in taking his share. They laughed, and divided up the extra $200 between them.

For the army, there was a huge fortune to be made from the drugs trade. Alfonso couldn't keep all the money for himself; he had to pay off his junior officers, and he also had to keep his seniors in the regional and national army headquarters sweet. But it was essential for the army to be able to demonstrate to the government in Lima that there was a continuing threat from the local Maoist guerrillas, the Shining Path (who also took a share of the drugs money). As a result the army base in Tocache had to be kept at full strength.

Murders were frequent; as far as the authorities in Lima were concerned, they were the work of the Shining Path. In fact the army had taken to killing people on commission – for unpaid debts, for adultery, for any reason or for no reason at all. The bodies would be washed up along the banks of the Huallaga River. They were usually weighted down by stones which had been painted white: the kind of stones you found at the army base. The army didn't mind everyone knowing they were behind the killings. They were the only power in Tocache.

Zambrano explained all these things lucidly, without pulling any punches. I asked him if it wasn't dangerous for him to speak out.

'Perhaps it will be; I don't know. All I know is that it is my duty to say these things. No one else will do it if I don't. This is a town where everyone is scared. I'm scared too, I don't deny it. But you cannot always live on your knees, afraid of what may happen. That is no way for a free man to live.'

His wife Daisy was sitting listening to him. She was about his age, and her face showed the strain she was suffering; but she still gave him her full support. Now their three young children came in, wearing their crisply ironed school uniforms: two girls of ten and eight, and a boy of six. As they stood there, Zambrano told them that that they must on no account let anyone know at school that a television crew had been in the house.

'Otherwise Daddy could be in trouble. All right?'

The three children nodded solemnly, their eyes on his face.

'Now hold each others' hands.'

They filed out in silence, and the door creaked shut behind them.

After that we went round to the army base to confront Comandante Alfonso. Zambrano knew what we were planning to do, but asked us not to say that we had interviewed him; he was planning to leave town for a few days, in case of reprisals. We talked our way into Alfonso's office, and sat down in front of him. He was an extremely tough character, with that occasional savage wit of the far right-winger. I told him in the clearest terms that everything that happened in Tocache now would be known around the world: meaning that if he took any action against us, or Zambrano, or anyone else we might have filmed, he would be in trouble. He must have known that our arrival in Tocache would cause him difficulties anyway. There was a distinctly awkward moment when he realized that we were secretly filming him, but we got away at last. He offered to put us up for the night at the army base but we refused. We even reached the airstrip by 4.30.

As for Zambrano, he did not suffer for speaking to us. The interview he gave us was seen in many countries, including Peru itself, and this gave him a considerable measure of protection. He stayed in Tocache for a while, and then moved to Lima.

The one who really suffered, satisfyingly enough, was Comandante Alfonso. He was shifted from Tocache, which had been such a gold-mine to him, and was transferred to a base in the obscure jungle province of Aurimac. That was the last that was heard of him.

*

> No spring nor summer hath such grace,
> As I have seen in one autumnall face.

I never had the courage to quote John Donne to Martha Gellhorn. She would have been annoyed, yet I suspect privately flattered. She did not like being old, although she spoke sometimes of her 'golden seventies', which for her were years of reflection as well as of remarkable travel. They were also the years when her books were republished, when she was honoured as she had not been for decades, and when a new generation of reporters, male and female, discovered and admired her.

'Whatever value is there in living to be eighty-eight?' she asked, curled up in her chair with a glass of Famous Grouse at her side and a cigarette in her long fingers.

'The value of seeing things through – seeing what happens at the end of the story,' I said; 'things like Communism, or Reagan.'

She snorted. 'Seeing is precisely what I can't do, darling. I'm blind and lame.'

She was neither, of course. She certainly had difficulty in reading in her last years, thanks to a careless eye surgeon who had made a mistake during a cataract operation, but she was perfectly capable until the very end of noticing that I looked tired, or had caught the sun, or was sweating because I was late and had run most of the way to her flat.

Nor was she lame; she merely had problems in getting around as fast and enthusiastically as she had throughout the rest of her life. But her impatient, essentially young spirit was deeply frustrated at all the obstacles which old age left lying around everywhere for her.

She wanted to hop onto a chair and pick out a book from the top shelf and read it; or to run out and catch a cab to the airport and fly somewhere on a whim; the old woman sitting here curled up with a glass of Scotch was merely an encumbrance to this younger self.

'Age is such a drag,' she said. 'It gets in the way of everything. Just like eating gets in the way of my drinking.'

I met her far too late in life. It was 1991, the year of the Gulf War, and the man who had been my editor at Hutchinson was organizing that year's Cheltenham Literary Festival. Richard Cohen was himself an interesting figure, a dashing Olympic-level fencer who edited the novels of Jeffrey Archer, set up his own publishing company, and eventually delivered the coup de grâce to Archer's political career by revealing that Archer had tried to persuade him to change his testimony in the *Daily Star* libel trial. At Cheltenham he set up a debate on war reporting, and invited me to be a panellist, together with Max Hastings and Philip Knightley, the author of the seminal work on war correspondents. He had, he said, also managed to persuade Martha Gellhorn to be there.

'But she must be around a hundred and fifty,' I said, with the dangerous arrogance of middle age.

'You see if you think that when you see her,' Cohen answered.

Martha was dressed up for the occasion, in a dark green coat with an expensive-looking fake fur collar and black slacks. Her hair was blonde, and her make-up was perfect. From where I was sitting alongside her she could have been sixty; from where the audience sat she must have looked about my age.

And she was sharp. She didn't like Philip Knightley because he had questioned the authenticity of the famous photograph by Robert Capa of the moment of death of a soldier in the Spanish Civil War. Capa, she told me much later, when we were on close terms, would have been her lover in Italy during the Second World War if she'd wanted him to be, and she was always devoted to his memory. Max Hastings she didn't like because he was a Tory.

She didn't take to me either. She clearly thought I was a boring establishment figure, reporting from safe places while real reporters like her wandered the battlefields of the world, unprotected by big organizations, and ignoring the official handouts which are so often the basis of news reporting; 'official drivel', she called them. She was probably right.

Martha snorted sardonically a good deal while the rest of us were speaking, pulling on the inevitable cigarette, and then launched into a sharp critique of recent war reporting; excluding only John Pilger, the left-wing writer who was always a particular favourite of hers. I was sorry to feel that she had dismissed all of us on the panel so comprehensively, because I saw she was a serious character, a writer as engaged with the present as any of us. She was a life-long radical, who had been everywhere and seen everything and yet had never lost the sense that things should be better than they were, and that there was no real excuse why they should not be.

By this stage I had locked horns with Max Hastings. Audiences like a little aggro, and although I had always liked Max, suspecting that an anarchist was buried somewhere under the grouse moor, I was prepared to give them their money's worth.

'War correspondents—' he began.

'I'm really sick of this whole expression "war correspondents",' I broke in, quite unfairly.

Then I started raving on about how journalists were just journalists, and that by calling themselves war correspondents they were congratulating themselves on something that ought to be a matter of sadness and shame. It wasn't merely said for effect: I have genuinely come to detest anyone who regards war as glamorous or enjoyable. There are plenty of them around, whether in Bosnia or Chechnya or the Gulf. They tend to wear coloured scarves round their necks and epaulettes on everything, and the suffering of the people around them means a great deal less to them than the figure they cut.

'For the first time,' Martha's cultured East Coast drawl broke in, 'someone here is speaking some sense. Wars are frightful, wicked things, and anyone who wants to specialize in reporting them is either a charlatan or else lacks any scintilla of humanity.'

The audience applauded her mightily, and poor Max Hastings, unfairly caricatured by us both as some kind of affected yet bloodthirsty *poseur*, lapsed into silence.

'I like you,' Martha said to me afterwards. 'You were quite right back there. No one but a self-regarding dolt would call himself a war correspondent. The only point in reporting on a war is to look at ordinary people in terrible situations. You must come round for a drink when you're in London.'

She had settled there in 1960, after living in Cuba, Mexico, Kenya, and various other places during the previous fifteen years. She had never entirely felt at ease anywhere since the end of the Second World War, but her cottage in Wales and her flat on the top two floors of No. 72 Cadogan Square were where she had decided to make her life for good. In the 1930s she had disliked Britain, feeling that it was too stodgy and self-satisfied; but her view of it changed during the War, as she saw how its people responded to adversity.

'I come from what they used to call good stock,' she said once, and indeed she did.

Her father George was a leading gynaecologist in St Louis; Edna, her mother, was a graduate of Bryn Mawr College. They were wealthy and liberal, great supporters of women's suffrage, and Martha (who was born in 1908) and her three brothers were brought up in a happy and stimulating environment. The three brothers were all trained in the liberal professions, and Alfred, younger than she and every bit as energetic and radical, was still in charge of the New York public health system in his mid-80s.

Martha followed her mother to Bryn Mawr. She left early without graduating, went in for a little journalism, and travelled to Europe. She told me how she had joined a delegation of French students on a trip to Berlin, where they were invited to lunch by Baldur von Schirach, the head of the Hitler Youth.

'He was of course disgusting; that goes without saying. But I endured it for the sake of the experience. It was only when his servant spilled his coffee and the brute hit him that I couldn't stand it any longer. I walked right out of the house, there and then.'

In 1935, back in America, Martha began travelling round the country interviewing unemployed people for a book which she called *The Trouble I've Seen*. It caused a sensation, not least because it was written by a woman of twenty-seven who was herself so beautiful and well-educated. The book shows remarkable powers of observation, and an unshockable pity. She not only sympathized with the people she met, she entered their lives and understood them. Her war reporting has a sparse strength and a superb ability to turn what she sees into clear expression; but *The Trouble I've Seen* still has such power that it is hard to read with equanimity.

At Christmas 1936, some months after the death of her father, Martha suggested that her mother and her brother Alfred should go with her to Florida for some sunshine. In Miami Alfred noticed a bus with 'Key West' marked on its destination board. They had never heard of the place but thought it sounded intriguing, so they caught the bus. When they got there, Edna Gellhorn spotted another interesting name: a bar called 'Sloppy Joe's'. They went in. Shortly afterwards Ernest Hemingway came swaggering into the bar and spotted Martha immediately. They must altogether have made an attractive group: Edna herself was a striking-looking woman.

Martha knew exactly who he was. He struck up a conversation with Alfred and Edna, but it was Martha he kept looking at, with her shorts and her long blonde hair; and when the others left Florida a few days later Martha stayed on, to the annoyance of Hemingway's second wife, Pauline, who was in Key West with him. When Martha left a couple of weeks later, Hemingway followed her and caught up with her the following day. They agreed to go to Spain together to report on the Civil War.

In Madrid Martha soon saw a side of Hemingway that she would eventually come to loathe. Even before they became lovers he would lock her bedroom door from the outside to prevent anyone from getting in, and when the hotel came under shellfire she was trapped inside. Soon Hemingway was telling everybody that she was the bravest woman he had ever known – braver, he said, than he was himself. There, at least, he was right.

Sixty years later, she still remembered the attraction he had had for her.

'He made me laugh. In those days he was fun. I could forgive everything else about him.'

All her life she preferred men who were content to remain her friends to those who were determined to be her lovers; the sexual side of any relationship was less important to her than the companionship, she said. But in those heightened circumstances his love of what she always called '*La Causa*', the Spanish cause, was another important element in his attraction for her. So, too, must have been his ability as a writer. His drinking, his ferocious temper, his violence – these problems were present from the start, but were less obvious then.

When I knew her, she always referred to marriage with Hemingway as 'a life-darkening experience'. It was a phrase she had honed carefully.

'He was fine until we married. Then, right from the very start, the fun left him. He became terrible. It was the act of possession which triggered it off.'

There was also the submerged rivalry between two writers. Martha described how, when they lived in Cuba, they were both working on books and would write in silence, ignoring each other's presence. The success of Martha's novel *Liana* was something Hemingway acknowledged; in a letter to his mother he said he thought Martha was a better writer than he was. But he cannot have enjoyed it.

He was savagely competitive. In *A Moveable Feast*, he destroyed Scott Fitzgerald's character once and for all, presenting him as a drunk and a weakling; and this was largely because their names were so often linked and Hemingway was determined to dominate the partnership. Re-reading the book, I found that Hemingway had shown another writer, the adventurous and free-handed Ford Madox Ford, as a ludicrous, pompous, stuffy old buffer. Why, I asked Martha?

'Oh, that's clear enough. Ford gave him his first chance – published him, lent him money, praised him. Ernest had to get back at him after that. He couldn't bear the idea that he had once been dependent on somebody.'

And yet she and Hemingway seemed enough happy at first. Eleanor Roosevelt had become a close friend of hers, in spite of the disparity between their ages, as a result of reading *The Trouble I've Seen*. Now, even though there were problems over Hemingway's divorce from Pauline and he and Martha were still not married, the conventionally moral Eleanor Roosevelt managed to persuade her husband to let the couple live together in a cottage in the White House grounds. They would often dine *à quatre*.

Years later, when John F. Kennedy was elected President, Martha was invited to his inauguration ball. She could not think why, since she knew nobody there. Suddenly there was a movement in the room, and Kennedy himself, accompanied by a crowd of others, headed over to the corner where she was standing alone. Martha wondered if he were going to offer her a job, but instead he wanted to ask her a question.

'You lived in the White House grounds; how did FDR get out at night to – you know?'

Martha, deeply relieved at not having to reject some embarrassing offer of a job in the new administration, told him about the little gate manned by bribable guards which Roosevelt had used. Kennedy seemed deeply relieved.

'You may just have saved my life,' he said.

By the time Martha left for Europe to report on the Second World War, her relationship with Hemingway was on the slide. He was often drunk, and may also have been violent, though Martha was too discreet to tell me that. She came from a class and a generation which did not talk openly about these things. Time and again she wrote to Hemingway, urging him to come to Europe. She was contemptuous of the lazy, safe life he was continuing to live in the United States and Cuba. The tide of the war had long turned by the time he finally bestirred himself to make the trip.

The hotel from which the international press covered the British end of the war was the Dorchester, and Hemingway insisted to the management that he must have a safe room there. He found one on the protected side of the hotel, on the second floor. A wealthy elderly lady was living in it already, but Hemingway demanded that the hotel management should get rid of her. Martha, demonstrating her dislike for him and her contempt for what he had done, moved up to the exposed top floor where *Collier's* magazine, whose roving correspondent Martha was, now rented a permanent room for her. She would come back after weeks away in Italy or Normandy and stumble into the room, only to find that someone from the Free French or the Free Poles had borrowed it to spend the night with his girlfriend. Martha would have to find somewhere else to go, and come back the next morning.

Many of the wealthier inhabitants of Mayfair had also moved into the Dorchester because they had had to close up their own houses for want of servants. The Hon. John Gilbey was the head fire-warden, and the family firm provided him with his own non-rationed supply of gin. There would be parties on the roof so that Emerald Cunard and other stars of London social life, fuelled with Gilbey's gin, could watch the bombing. It was from there that Martha watched the first V-2 missile to hit London fly eerily along the line of Park Lane and crash into the much less select Cumberland Hotel at Marble Arch, a couple of hundred yards away.

The smaller news organizations could only have one accredited front-line correspondent in each theatre of war. Hemingway, knowing this, approached *Collier's* and offered to write for them about the war in Europe. This meant that Martha would automatically lose her accreditation, with its honorary rank of captain; but she wandered around the front lines of Europe without it for the rest of the war, finding that her looks and courage and intelligence were enough to get her accepted everywhere.

'With all those soldiers about, you must have had some problems, surely?'

'Never. Maybe things were a little different then; there was more idealism, I suppose, and people still understood the concept of behaving like gentlemen. But I never had a single night's difficulty.'

Because Hemingway was now *Collier's* accredited correspondent, he was taken secretly to a staging area before the D-Day invasion and watched the landings from an attack transport off the Normandy coast. The first Martha heard about it was at a briefing given some hours after the landings had actually begun.

She immediately left for the coast and managed to smuggle herself on to an unarmed hospital ship that was leaving the following dawn. The nurses on board adopted her, and hid her in a lavatory when the security men searched the ship. Getting to the Normandy coast was an extremely dangerous business: the hospital ship had to make its way through a mined channel under heavy shellfire. On the night of 7 June Martha slipped ashore with the stretcher bearers, and stood on the soil of Europe only forty hours after the first landings, the first American journalist to do so.

Hemingway, who had had to watch the landings from his transport ship, went into a frenzy of anger. He insisted that *Collier's* should bury Martha's story at the back of the magazine, and for the rest of his life he insisted that she must have lied about going ashore since she hadn't had the necessary accreditation. In fact the American authorities arrested her on her return to England for being on the hospital ship without permission, and put her into a camp for

American nurses. That night Martha climbed over the wire and made her way to a military airfield where she told a pilot that she was desperate to see her fiancé, who was based in Italy. The pilot let her stow away on his aircraft.

That was the end of her marriage to Hemingway. Martha had nothing but dislike for him now, and he had begun an affair with someone else anyway. Martha was the only one of his wives to have left him; he never forgave her for it. Throughout the rest of his life he reserved some of his worst spite for her.

In the summer of 1997, less than a year before she died, she told me she was going back to her cottage in Wales to sort out some correspondence. She had lived there for most of the 1980s with a couple of cats, swimming every day in the single-lane pool she had installed in the garden.

I noticed the note of finality in her voice. What correspondence, I asked?

'I'm going to burn everything Ernest sent me.'

I tried my hardest to dissuade her, but it was quite impossible. When she got back, I went round and saw her again. Had she, I asked, really burned everything?

'Everything. It made me féel a lot better.'

I remembered seeing a letter signed by Hemingway for sale in New York for $5,000.

'How many did you burn?'

'Oh, I've really no idea. Dozens, maybe more. He used to write such a lot.'

The life-darkening experience had finally been dealt with. She was putting the last part of her life in order, and getting ready for the end.

It was a great sadness to me that I hadn't known Martha when she was a little younger. When after her death a friend of mine, the novelist Nicholas Shakespeare, quoted some of her letters to him in a charming article he wrote, I was consumed with jealousy. 'Sweet Shakespeare', one of them began. By the time I first met her, her eyesight was going and she no longer wrote letters.

Yet she remained magnificent to the end, heading off abruptly to Egypt or anywhere else hot in order to snorkel. I even joined her for a day at her hotel in Ras Mohammed, on the Red Sea. When she was 87 she travelled to Rio and reported on the fate of the street children who were being murdered by the police at the request of shopkeepers. It was precisely the kind of subject which Martha relished: difficult, dangerous and morally clear-cut. She was unhappy with the long article she wrote about it, although it seemed to me to be excellent. I would have been very pleased with myself if I had been able to write anything so crisp and clear.

Going to see her was a pleasure I hoarded up in advance. She didn't always like the wives and girlfriends of her disciples, but she became very fond of Dee. She even came with us to dinner at the Dorchester; the first time, she said, that she had been back there since 1945.

Martha had known so many people in her life: Picasso, George Orwell, Greta Garbo, Diana Cooper, Duff Cooper, Chiang Kai-shek, Chou En-lai. If you worked hard you could even get her to talk about them. I relished everything about my visits to her: the way she would say 'Come up, darling!' over the intercom, the heavy front door, the small, varnished, unsteady lift, the open door of her flat. I would kiss her, and see her bright unlined face looking enthusiastically yet never quite uncritically up at me, and I would accept the first Famous Grouse of the evening.

'Now,' she would say, pushing a bowl of crisps or nuts towards me, 'tell me everything about it.'

'It' might be the Congo, or the Amazon, or Afghanistan; it fuelled her own imagination and her own extraordinarily wide-ranging memories, and she would ask the kind of questions that showed she was there in spirit. Although she did plenty of travelling for herself still, I felt that in my adventures she relived her own.

'Tell me again about the Taliban,' she would say.

She loved the idea of bearded, turbaned warriors with Kalashnikovs who put on eye make-up and gold high-heeled sandals and painted their toenails red.

But it was always better and more interesting to listen to her stories.

'No one cares about that sort of thing any more,' she would say; but I could see it gave her pleasure.

Each time I went to see her I would determine not to drink so much whisky that I would forget what she had told me. Each time I succumbed, and duly forgot. Perhaps that was her intention.

Her own papers have been lodged with an American university, and cannot be opened to the public until twenty years after her death.

'By that time everybody alive will have forgotten that I ever lived.'

Inconceivable.

Sometimes, when I was writing a book, Martha would ask me to read a passage to her. She was a tough critic.

'I have to be able to feel it. I need to see the colour of the walls, and what the people are wearing, and the view out of the window. You aren't giving me enough of that.'

I despaired of ever matching that powerful, reserved, perceptive tone of hers, which was so like the rhythm of her speech that even now she is dead I only have to read a couple of lines out loud to hear her voice in the room. She was the clearest-headed of observers. 'I gave up trying to think or judge,' she wrote about the Second World War, 'and turned myself into a walking tape recorder with eyes.' She went to Dachau shortly after its liberation:

> I have not talked about how it was the day the American Army arrived, though the prisoners told me. In their joy to be free, and longing to see their friends who had come at last, many prisoners rushed to the fence and died electrocuted. There were those who died cheering, because that effort of happiness was more than their bodies could endure. There were those who died because now they had food, and they ate before they could be stopped, and it killed them. I do not know words to describe the men who have survived this horror for years, three years, five years, ten years, and whose minds are as clear and unafraid as the day they entered.

Dachau, you recall, was one of the camps which Hitler's 'deeply devoted, deeply grateful and deeply respectful' Dr Carl Burckhardt, who became President of the International Committee of the Red Cross, had visited in 1935 and pronounced 'hard but correct'.

Whether writing about bugs in a Depression-era house (*The Trouble I've Seen*, 1936), or taking a plane into German-occupied Prague (*A Stricken Field*, 1940) or attending open day at an African leper colony (*Travels With Myself And Another*, 1978) Martha was always wonderfully fresh and funny and sharp. She was, she said, a journalist first and a writer second, and a woman only third. She became something of a hero to the feminists, but that irritated her: 'As though somehow we're a different species from men.'

She had been ill for some time with cancer, but she always insisted to me that it was an ulcer. I believed her, because I wanted to. Her eyesight was fading quite fast, and her recent travels had been a disappointment. In Corsica, where she had gone snorkelling a few months earlier, she had been mugged. For a free spirit like hers, the options were becoming too restricted.

She had, the last time Dee and I saw her, stopped taking whatever tablets it was that she had relied on, and said she felt easier as a result. I looked at her very carefully, but could see no signs of anything different: no obvious pain, no anxiety. Somehow or other Dee and I had managed to get our previous appointment with her wrong, and Martha had got up from her bed to make us dinner and we had not appeared. I felt terrible, and apologized grovellingly in letters and with flowers. Her annoyance quickly passed.

Her brother Alfred was there, leaning over her chair, and the two of them made a superb picture of elderly elegance. I knew something was going on, but I couldn't work out exactly what. Suitably, since she was one of the great travellers of the twentieth century, we used the language of travel.

'Don't go away,' I said quietly to her at last over my glass of Famous Grouse, with a sudden sense of urgency and alarm.

'Darling,' she said in that lovely upper-class American voice of hers, 'I'm not staying around for ever.'

Three days later she died in her sleep. She was, her son said, smiling.

Arthur Penlington is not the kind of person you would immediately spot as a big media hero. He doesn't go to body-building classes, nor does he wear knee-high suede boots, nor does he talk very loudly in restaurants. Big media heroes don't often seem to be called Arthur, anyway. And yet if you had to draw up a list of the heroic efforts some people will make to ensure that the news reaches our television screens, Arthur Penlington's name should certainly appear on it.

At the time of the Gulf War in 1991 he was a producer on the Nine O'Clock News, and was sent out to Saudi Arabia. When the coalition forces liberated Kuwait City, the BBC team there needed fuel for its portable generators; and so Arthur had to drive a ten-ton truck loaded with oil-drums along the mine-infested road from Dahran to Kuwait, at night and on his own. When he arrived he attracted attention even in that city of battle-weary, unwashed people because he was so spectacularly dirty. He offloaded the fuel and some tyres which he had also brought, then loaded up his truck with satellite equipment which had to be brought back fast to Dahran. On the way, he persuaded the Americans to make him a temporary officer in the British army, so he could fill up his tank with petrol. The round trip took him thirty hours, and he did not stop for a break at any time.

Many people put in long hours in television news, though rarely as many as that. But what earned Arthur his place on the list of heroes was that, during his return trip to Dahran in the middle of the night, the tarpaulin covering the satellite dish broke free and blew away into what was probably a minefield; Arthur went in, grabbed it and tied it back onto the satellite dish. And when someone asked him why on earth he should have risked his life in this way he answered that it was BBC property, and he didn't like to leave it there.

There is a definite touch of the public corporation about that, a sense that there will be an inevitable rendering of accounts, which makes it a characteristically BBC story. 'You do not seem to have returned your Mark IV-A canvas-type tarpaulin, issued on 20.1.91,' some administrator would unquestionably have written to him. 'Unless you do so, the full amount of its value will be deducted from your next pay cheque.'

After my book *Strange Places, Questionable People* was published, a very nice lady in BBC administration wrote to me that she had read it, and had a question to ask me. I had described in it how I climbed the mountain in Afghanistan where the world's best lapis lazuli comes from, and had given a Sony Walkman as a present to the mujaheddin commander who was in charge of the mines there. Was this Walkman, she asked, BBC issue?

We who have grown old in the BBC's service know that tone very well. Such people are the Arthur Penlingtons of administration: they will do their duty doggedly, no matter what adversity they have to face.

Many television organizations now give credits at the start or finish of their news reports, listing the people on the technical and editorial side who have worked to get the item on the air. It is a useful reminder that the people the audience sees do not assemble the pictures alone, and therefore do not deserve all (or sometimes any) of the credit.

Soon after the Gulf War was over, and the refugee crisis in the Kurdish part of northern Iraq built up, a BBC picture editor headed off with the cassette of his team's report into a heavy snowstorm. The journey to the satellite-point took him three days altogether. He had to wade across an icy river, hitch lifts from wild-looking characters, and sleep in a shepherd's bothy. Another set up his editing machines in a hotel room in Beirut which regularly came under fire from the valley below. To get to his editing room he had to crawl along the corridor, below the level of the windowsills. Once inside the room he had to stay on his knees throughout the entire editing period – two hours or more – and reach above his head to work the controls of his machines.

'What was that?' the correspondent with him asked nervously as something came through the window.

'Just a bullet,' replied the picture editor absently, and carried on.

I was the correspondent.

Bob Prabhu, the cameraman, was in Tblisi filming a demonstration. The rushes are quite remarkable; you see a group of gunmen driving up and opening fire into the crowd. The man standing beside Bob on the podium is hit in the arm, and Bob himself falls to the ground and rolls over, still filming. He was determined to keep his camera running, he said, because if he were killed he would want people to know what had happened to him.

A sound recordist I know let himself be struck with an iron bar on the shoulder in order to protect the cameraman he was working with. Facilities engineers, mostly quiet, undemonstrative people, drive their equipment along appalling roads in places like Bosnia and Chechnya, setting up their satellite equipment in the middle of a war zone.

The transport manager of the BBC, a man who could perfectly well have stayed in London driving his desk, preferred instead to drive the BBC's armoured vehicles in and out of Sarajevo. Once he saved the leg, and perhaps the life, of a photographer friend of mine who was injured in Sarajevo. He drove her all the way through the shelling and the roadblocks to hospital in Ljubljana. Cameramen excepted, there are no prizes for these people when the television news industry hands out its carefully allocated awards each year. They take the risks because it is part of the job; and they are men and women who prefer that kind of job to one in an office.

Television news very largely subsists nowadays on the efforts of freelancers who do all the technical jobs themselves: filming, lighting, recording sound, editing pictures. In the management-speak of today's television this is known as 'multi-skilling', though we used to call it 'one-man-banding'. During the 1990s, with the growth of all-news stations and television news agencies, Australians, New Zealanders and South Africans have taken over much of this area, travelling everywhere with equal cheerfulness and enthusiasm.

Another, slightly more organized group called Frontline offers its services and its pictures to television companies around the world; especially those which occasionally feel the need to do some reporting from the world's more dangerous areas but which lack camera teams with the experience or enthusiasm for the job. Frontline is an agency which is run by a small core of full-time shareholders, who market their own work and that of other freelances.

It began with a small group of self-taught ex-army people, often from 'good' regiments, who wanted something more exciting than a new career in the City. In the early 1980s they gravitated to Peshawar, on the north-west frontier of Pakistan, and began to cover the war in Afghanistan. Various crooks and charlatans were doing the same thing, with the financial encouragement of the CIA and other intelligence organizations, and some highly dubious pictures were appearing on American television in particular.

Pictures of what were said to be spectacular mujaheddin successes against Soviet troops were on occasion filmed in Pakistan. Once an American network showed what it said was a bombing raid by Soviet aircraft; only the aircraft in question were clearly Pakistani and the bomb explosions were cut in from other footage.

The Peshawar group set out to offer a genuine alternative to this kind of thing. Men like Peter Jouvenal, Rory Peck, Ken Guest, Vaughan Smith, John Gunston and Chris Hooke competed with each other to get the best pictures of fighting between the mujaheddin and the Russians, and their work carried its own guarantee. Peter

Jouvenal, formerly of the Royal Horse Artillery, was a central figure in this group, and no one made more trips into Afghanistan than he did. Bearded and wearing Afghan dress, he looked like some nineteenth-century player of the Great Game.

Peter's speech is famously clipped. Once, when he had been driving me though the Hindu Kush for two unbroken days and nights, we found ourselves stuck in thick snow on a narrow mountain road with a line of broken-down trucks on one side and a stark precipice on the other.

'What's the worst that could happen?' I asked, nervous that we would have to spend the night there and I would miss my connection back to London.

'We could always go over the edge,' Peter replied.

Vaughan Smith is another figure from something of the same mould. A former officer in the Grenadier Guards, he used his army background to talk his way unaccredited into Saudi Arabia during the Gulf War. There he borrowed bits of uniform and equipment to make himself look the part of a serving British officer, but realized that just about every other officer had a jeep and a weapon of some kind. He stormed into the office of a harassed American officer in simulated anger and demanded to know what he planned to do about his vehicle which (he claimed) an American soldier had just totalled, and the side arm which had been in the back of it at the time. The officer gave him a new jeep and a new weapon.

Vaughan was present, with his camera hidden in a bag, at the final briefing given to the British forces the night before the assault on the Iraqi lines, when the general commanding warned everyone to look out for a cameraman disguised as a British officer. He then talked his way on to an American Bradley fighting vehicle, where he persuaded the rest of the crew that he was senior in rank to all of them, and filmed the allied advance and the attack on the Iraqis from the Bradley's turret: the only decent television pictures of front-line action from the entire battle.

To get the pictures back, he jumped on the first military plane out, and found it was going to Sicily. There the US authorities were much more suspicious than in free-and-easy Saudi Arabia, and he decided to rent a car to drive to Germany. He was bathing his bleeding and blistered feet in the sea near Palermo when he turned and saw a group of thieves stealing the equipment from his car. The tapes he had shot were gone.

Shoeless, he hobbled up the beach and drove to the office of the chief of police. He demanded help, leaving some impressive blood-stains on the floor. The chief of police told him that if he were prepared to offer a large cash 'reward' the return of the pictures could be guaranteed that night. The video cassettes (though not the camera) were duly returned on time, and the chief of police insisted on a photocall as he handed them over to Vaughan. The pictures of the climactic battle of the Gulf War eventually made it on to the air.

Of all these cameramen, Rory Peck was the most laid back, and often obtained the most extraordinary, though sometimes distinctly careless, pictures of all. I came across his *dragoman*, a wild figure with a scarf tied round his head and a weapon stuck in his belt, while filming the violent revolution in Bucharest with Bob Prabhu and his then sound recordist, Paul Francis. With intense gunfire breaking out all round us, I asked the dragoman where Rory was. He pointed to a vast stone building opposite, every window of which was belching flame.

'Outside?' I asked.

'No, inside,' said the *dragoman*.

Rory had managed to beg an asbestos suit off the firemen, and was filming from the heart of the fire: the pictures of the main staircase collapsing were unforgettable.

Rory was an entrepreneur as well as a cameraman. In the immediate aftermath of the collapse of the Soviet system he put in a bid to buy the beautiful, early nineteenth-century building in Moscow which houses the museum dedicated to the Bolshevik revolution: the exhibits included vehicles used in the famous attack on the Barricades, and the blood-stained coat Lenin was wearing when an attempt was made to assassinate him. The authorities, unclear whether anyone would even want such a museum in future, now that Communism had come to an end, were attracted by the price Rory was offering. They agreed, on condition that they could find somewhere to house the collection. The negotiations fell through only because no suitable building could be found.

Soon afterwards, anyway, Rory was dead: shot by a special forces gunman at the main Russian television station, Ostankino, while he was filming the crowd which went to attack the building in the immediate wake of the storming of the parliament building by pro-Yeltsin forces in 1993. Bob Prabhu, who was also there, was lucky to escape.

I recognized Rory's body from the pictures: his prematurely bald head was instantly recognizable as he lay beside his camera. The German television company he had been working for at the time, ARD, tried to get out of making any payment to his widow and family, but the BBC (for whom he had so often worked in the past) agreed quickly to give them a large amount. ARD was shamed into adding some money, but it was only a fifth of what the BBC paid.

On a blustering rainy day I watched as Rory's body was buried in the family grave at a small Church of Ireland church just outside the city of Londonderry. Peter Jouvenal was one of the pall-bearers, and Frontline was strongly represented.

As a way of celebrating Rory's buccaneering life, a prize was instituted in his name for people like himself: freelancers who go to the worst places and take the greatest risks, yet had never received the proper credit for it. Not being an enthusiast for committees or organizations myself, I quickly slipped out of my responsibilities to the Rory Peck Trust; but it still gives me pleasure to be associated with his name.

There are, of course, many other absent friends to be recalled over the past thirty years:

Tony Fry, a BBC reporter who died as a result of a car crash on his way from Derry to Dublin in 1972, and whose funeral I had to arrange in another Church of Ireland graveyard, in County Meath; Ted Stoddart, a BBC sound recordist who died after stepping on a mine in Cyprus; Peter Begin, one of the most experienced and successful of BBC cameramen, killed in a road accident near his home; George De'ath, a freelance cameraman killed by a mob during political rioting in South Africa; Bernard Hesketh, the brilliant but controversial cameraman who was the oldest man to take an active part in the Falklands War on either side and filmed more wars than just about anyone else, but who died in his bed; Andy Skripkoviak, a cameraman who was murdered for his money by the mujaheddin group Hezb-e-Islami in Afghanistan while he slept; Norman Lowes, a BBC picture editor who was killed in an accident at home; Keith

Skinner, a cameraman who was injured in rioting on the Broadwater estate in London (where his sound recordist, Robin Green, lost an eye) and who later died in retirement of heart disease; Nick della Casa, who was murdered together with his wife Rosanne and her brother Charles Maxwell while they were working as a camera team for the BBC in the Kurdish part of Iraq (Rosanne's body has never been found); Mohammed Amin, one of the most famous of freelance cameramen, who lost his arm when a munitions dump blew up in Addis Ababa in 1991, and his sound recordist, John Mathai, who was killed. Mo Amin was later killed when a plane he was travelling in was hijacked and crashed into the sea; Brian Hulls, a quiet, gentle and extraordinarily brave cameraman, who lost his battle with cancer; Tihomir Tunukovic, known to us as 'Tuna', a freelance cameraman who died when his car was hit by an artillery shell in Bosnia; John Harrison, a particular friend of mine, who was the BBC correspondent in South Africa (he hired my future wife Dee to work with me in the 1994 election which brought apartheid to its final end) and died in a car crash; Pete Martini, a young, happy and enthusiastic young producer who was in a car hit by a drunken driver on the road from Moscow to St Petersburg and died of his injuries before help could come; John Schofield, equally young, a talented radio reporter who was shot and killed by Croatian troops on his first tour of duty for the BBC to the Balkans; and Abed a fearless driver from the BBC's Beirut bureau, killed, perhaps on purpose, by the Israeli army in southern Lebanon in 2000.

There are others, of course: these were just my own colleagues and particular companions. They are not and will not be forgotten. Other friends and colleagues of mine, too, were injured in wars: Roy Benford, Chris Morris, Tim Llewelyn, Don Legget, Oggy Lomas and Don Nesbit, but they all fortunately survived.

And there was Ian Smith, charming and easy-going, a correspondent who had a skiing accident and died without regaining consciousness after being in a long coma. Ian was a good friend of mine.

One night, as the duty reporter in Belfast, he was wakened with the news that there had been a big explosion in, I think, the Springfield Road. He hurried into his clothes, met up with the camera crew, and found the only eyewitness, an elderly lady with a powerful

Belfast accent. She described what she had seen, in a shaky voice bound up with all the impenetrable vowels and diphthongs of the area. She was quite incomprehensible.

'So what happened next?' Ian Smith drawled, in his familiar public school tones. 'Or have you already told me?'

8

BOMBING

> To a surprising extent the war-lords in shining armour, the
> apostles of the martial virtues, tend not to die fighting when
> the time comes. History is full of ignominious getaways
> by the great and famous.
>
> George Orwell, *Who Are The War Criminals?*, 1944

In March 1999 I went to Belgrade to report on the coming war.

It wasn't easy to get there. The Serbian authorities disliked the
BBC, and my reporting from Sarajevo during the siege by the Bosnian
Serbs had been regarded in Belgrade as anti-Serbian. Nevertheless in
February I had invited the foreign minister to be the guest on my
programme for News 24 and BBC World, *Simpson's World*. I gave
the minister a hard time, and was worried at one stage whether I
hadn't merely irritated him further. Apparently not.

'No one else from the British or the American media has asked us
for our point of view,' his adviser said afterwards. 'They just seem to
want to tell us what we think.'

So we were able to be there for the big crisis after all. I flew in to
Belgrade only two days before the airport was closed for good. The
situation looked bad; and now, with the benefit of hindsight, it is
clear that this was the intention. You do not have to be pro-Serbian
– and I am no more pro-Serbian now than I was anti-Serbian in
Sarajevo – to realize that the Kosovo crisis was a set-up. President
Clinton, badly damaged by the Monica Lewinsky affair, had decided
with his Secretary of State, Madeleine Albright, that there would only
be one outcome to this particular Balkan crisis: Milošević would have
to back down, or be bombed into submission. The draft agreement
the Americans offered him at the Rambouillet conference at the start

of February was packed with elements he could never have accepted. They wanted him to say no.

None of which makes Milošević or his backers in any way the innocent party. The latest crisis had erupted because Serbian para-militaries had entered the village of Racak in Kosovo on 15 January and murdered forty-five people. Milošević was the closest thing in Europe to Saddam Hussein: for a decade he had deliberately stirred up ethnic tension, ensuring thousands of deaths in the process, had lost every piece of territory he fought for, and had clung on to power in an area of operation which was getting smaller with each new crisis.

Something, people felt, had to be done about him. President Clinton and Madeleine Albright thought that bombing his country was the best way. This had been Albright's solution to the Bosnian crisis; now it was her solution to the Kosovo one. She failed to notice that Bosnia was much less important to Milošević than Kosovo, which Serbs regarded as the cradle of their culture. It would all be over in a matter of days, she said. She turned out to be absolutely right: 78 days.

President Clinton agreed, but insisted that there could be no question of putting American servicemen's lives at risk. In doing so he automatically sentenced five hundred or more Serbian civilians to death, since the bombing would have to be high-altitude and that meant it would inevitably be less accurate. Clinton's policy also ensured that large numbers of ethnic Albanians would lose their homes or be killed too, since there were to be no NATO ground troops to protect them, and the Serbs were thirsting for revenge. The British went along with all this, as did the other NATO allies. To have failed would have been to desert the United States at a critical moment. It would never have been forgiven.

As for me, I stayed in Belgrade throughout those 78 days, plus a little more. Part of this time I spent with my leg in plaster, for reasons I shall explain, and I was thrown out, rather absurdly, after the conflict was over. I kept a diary, of which these are some extracts. I have interpolated some explanations to make it clearer, but I have resisted the temptation to embroider the facts in my favour.

Tuesday 23 March 1999

Richard Holbrooke, the American negotiator, is trying to persuade Milošević to do what Washington demands of him. I like and admire Holbrooke. I had lunch with him once, and was much impressed by the breadth of his reading and his knowledge of the business of diplomacy. From time to time he comes back to the Belgrade Hyatt, where he always stays and which has become the main press hotel. The dozens of television crews and reporters who are covering the crisis fall on him, shouting their questions. I hang around at the back on these occasions: you never get anything worth having under such conditions.

In the late afternoon I go round to the British Embassy. The people there have the reputation of being the best informed of the Western diplomats.

'The signs aren't good,' says _____. 'If it all breaks down the bombing will start pretty much at once. And it'll be hard.'

How hard, I wonder? I reflect that diplomats like him will be long gone, but we'll be under it all and the Serbs will want to revenge themselves on someone.

He explains: the infrastructure of the country will be progressively stripped away, giving Milošević the opportunity to stop it any time he chooses. The chances are that Milošević actually wants to back down now, and that he is looking for the opportunity to do it. If so, he will be able to tell his people after a few days that they have fought heroically, but that they simply cannot hold out against the greatest military alliance on earth indefinitely and must give in now.

'Does NATO have the nerve to keep on bombing until that point is reached? Or the cohesion?'

'I understand what you are saying, but we think it does.'

I drive back through the quiet streets, looking at the gloomy buildings and wondering how many will still be standing in a few weeks. On the other hand, I tell myself, I have been through this before. Baghdad was hit with more high explosive than any city in the history of warfare, and yet we survived perfectly well. The trouble is, you never know beforehand how bad it is going to be this time.

Back at the Hyatt Richard Holbrooke arrives, tired and gloomy.

He is a servant of his government, but he is also a man who knew the former Yugoslavia well; I have the impression he would have liked to avoid a war if it were at all possible. It clearly isn't – not given the ultimatum Clinton and Albright have ordered him to give.

I corner him near the lifts:

'Our mission has failed. I will now be flying to Brussels to consult the alliance.'

The war is about to begin; it simply requires the final agreement of the NATO countries, which is a foregone conclusion. The huge crowd of journalists breaks up and streams away. In the lift I grin at a producer from one of the American television networks, whom I remember from Baghdad.

'So we're in for it again.'

He rolls up his eyes.

'Food shortages, water shortages,' I intone. 'Soon we'll be able to tell which rooms are occupied because they'll smell so bad.'

'So you'll stay?'

'Won't you?'

'Doubt it. The White House'll probably try to get us to pull out.'

That, I reflect, is the reality for many American journalists now. When the big, dangerous stories come up, they are the first to leave. In Belgrade there are only one or two Americans who are prepared to stay. We'll no doubt be left, as we usually are in bad situations, with the old firm: the Brits, the Aussies, the French, and the occasional Italian or Spaniard or Dutchman. But for the most part you can forget the Germans, the Japanese and the Americans.

Wednesday 24 March

'The first bomb that falls on Serbia, you Westerners will suffer. And so will the Albanians. We'll kill them all.'

It's just a hotel employee talking, but he reflects a genuine level of feeling here. Things could get very nasty directly the bombing starts. It gives me great pleasure not to give him a tip.

The government have been making their preparations in characteristic fashion. The independent radio station B-92 was closed down this morning. So was the satellite operation run by the European

Broadcasting Union and Reuters Television. Several people were punched and slapped about, and Nikki Millard, a BBC cameraman, had his camera stolen by the secret police who carried out the raid. It won't be returned, of course; these people are a law unto themselves, and they'll sell it abroad somewhere.

Civilians who prepare for war always have a look of utter disbelief on their faces, and their preparations are half-hearted and badly done, as if they don't really expect that anything will come of it. In the security and familiarity of their own streets and houses they can't imagine what it'll be like to have huge quantities of high explosive falling out of the sky. Nor can I.

We are filming the arrangements which the shopkeepers are making in the centre of town when my mobile rings. It is Jonathan Paterson, the BBC producer who is working with me.

'Can you talk?'

'Yes.'

'We've just had word from Brussels that the first NATO planes have taken off.'

'I'll be straight back.'

It is a curious feeling to think of those immensely powerful bombers heading towards us at 500 mph, and that no one around me yet knows it. It reminds me of Barbara D____, a family friend who worked in Military Intelligence during the War and had a nervous breakdown because she could not tell anyone about the V-1 and V-2 rockets which she knew would soon be landing on London.

We drive back over the main bridge towards the hotel. In the evening sunlight people are queuing as usual for their trams home. No panic, no sign even of nervousness. They don't know what is coming their way. If it's anything like Baghdad the bridges will go early on.

Dragan Petrović, our Serbian producer, is driving. He is a powerfully built man of thirty, with a head as shaven as that of any Arkan supporter, and no one messes with us if Dragan is there. His appearance belies his character entirely: he is a thoughtful, serious-minded and gentle man, and I have come to rely greatly on his advice and information. His English is superb, but he does a particularly good angry-Serb-speaking-English impression. 'For why you criticize my President?' he asked an American correspondent who had been sounding off about Milošević. 'Tell me your name.' The correspondent almost went down on his knees to apologize.

Now, checking my watch, I ask Dragan to stop in a side-street near the hotel. The first bombs will fall very soon now, and I want to be out in the open when it happens, so that I can see them more clearly.

The sirens begin to wail, first one, then another, then right across the city: a sound I haven't heard for nine years. That was on a different continent. But the smart bombs and the missiles will be the same, and I'm not nearly as nervous about them as I was in Baghdad in 1991; then I thought we would all be killed in a savage indiscriminate carpet-bombing of the city. Instead, their accuracy was phenomenal, and there is safety in that. The real danger for us will be the reaction of the local thugs: their desire to revenge themselves on anyone from the countries that are bombing them.

Now we sit and wait: it is already some way past the time Jonathan told me to expect the first explosions. Then there are two flashes on the distant horizon, and the sound follows some seconds later. I call London on my mobile and go live into the six o'clock radio news: 'The air attacks have started.' But I am surprised that they are no nearer than a dozen miles from Belgrade. This is not going to be a savage all-out attack after all: the bombs will grind us down slowly.

That evening power-generating plants and some factories on the edge of Belgrade are hit, and the television cameramen stationed on the roof film the distant explosions.

'Not much of a shot,' one cameraman grumbles, peering through the eyepiece at the sudden upsurge of fire on the horizon.

I record a piece to camera and take the cassette downstairs with me to edit. While we are still busy someone comes running into the room.

'They've arrested all the guys on the roof and taken them away.'

Kevin Bishop, our other producer, was there, with Gig (Peter Gigliotti, an Australian cameraman who's working for us). It's a bad moment. There are at least forty other camera crews up there. We have no idea where they have been taken, nor what will happen to them.

Thursday 25 March

They spend most of the night at a police station, being questioned and having their full details recorded before being released. No one seems to have threatened them, perhaps because the hotel security staff went with them. They also brought them sandwiches and coffee at three in the morning. Modern warfare is a strange business: our countries bomb this city, we watch it, and some of the victims regard it as their first duty to make sure we're properly looked after.

The atmosphere has become a great deal nastier, all the same.

'We have to take certain measures,' says someone at the Foreign Ministry warningly, when I ring to complain about the treatment of our staff and the theft of our camera by the police.

Arkan arrives in the Hyatt coffee shop with his gang of minders in black leather, and settles down to watch the foreign journalists with a menacing look on his pudgy young face. Christiane Amanpour, CNN's best correspondent, whose outspoken documentary detailing Arkan's crimes has just been rebroadcast and who is a strong advocate of bombing Serbia, is marched through the hotel lobby to the front door in the middle of a crowd of heavies. It was brave of her in the circumstances to have come here at all. She looks strained and frightened, and the heavies have been brought in by one of the Western embassies to get her to safety across the Hungarian border.

I panic, though, thinking she has obtained an exclusive interview with Milošević and is being escorted off to do it. It is only when I see Brent Sadler, another of the CNN correspondents, celebrating that I realize she must have been thrown out of the country. I'm sorry she's gone, because I admire her and like her. But I'm also relieved, because she is serious competition. Things should be easier for us now.

All the other journalists crowd round to the Information Ministry. It's like Angus cows queuing up at the roast beef trolley in Simpson's-in-the-Strand. Vuk Drašković, formerly an opponent of Milošević but now his vice-premier, is flushed and his speech slurred: it is 11.30, and the day's first bottle of slivovitz must have been going around.

'You are all welcome to stay,' he says.

But at another press conference elsewhere in Belgrade the Serbian information minister, a nasty, pasty-faced little man who looks like a character out of Dickens and is a faithful supporter of the extreme nationalist Vojislav Šešlj orders all journalists from NATO countries to leave the country at once. There is panic at the Hyatt as the news spreads. The BBC group gathers to talk it over, and they all want to go. I would rather stay, but decide to go too; what can I do here, entirely on my own? The thugs would pick me off in ten minutes.

My stuff is already in the vehicle when I hear from Jonathan that Greg Wilesmith of ABC Australia is staying. On an impulse, I tell Jonathan I'll stay as well. At least I'll have company. I dig my case out of the vehicle again and say goodbye to the others, feeling scared yet oddly justified. 'I think you're doing the right thing,' says Kevin Bishop. It's nice of him – but I think the chances are I'm destined for some obscure and miserable fate. Even so, I feel liberated. It's a great feeling to be shot of all that pack journalism stuff and to be on my own.

I take over a suite – why not, under these circumstances? – and phone the office. Malcolm Downing, the foreign editor, sounds relieved. I also phone Dee to explain. She is calm and resigned, which makes me feel a lot better. She knows she's married to a lunatic, I suppose. I pour myself a generous slug of Laphroaig, light up a big, fat Upmann no. 2, and start broadcasting. This, I feel as I look out of the window, is the life. Let's hope it is.

Friday 26 March

As the bombing intensifies, so do the demands. I never knew there were so many BBC news programmes. By the evening I have done 167 live interviews. By the time the crisis finishes, three months later, I will have clocked up 190 hours of calls on my mobile. Any researcher wanting to know if this is dangerous merely has to give me a brain-scan. Our phoneline is cut several times: the security police are listening carefully to everything I say. If the questioner or I begin to criticize Milošević, they pull the plug. The hotel is entirely silent, though the nearest bombs are still a few miles away. This is not turning out to be anything like Baghdad, where I stayed in 1991 when the Gulf War bombing began. It's a lot lonelier, and a great deal more scary. There we were afraid of the bombs. Here I'm afraid a mob will storm the place and get me. And yet I still feel really good about staying. Even if something really bad happens, I think I will have done what I was paid to do.

At 2 a.m. the tannoy in the room orders everyone into the air raid shelters. I ignore it: this is my chance to get a couple of hours' sleep. Someone bangs on the door: 'Open, please!' Convinced it's Arkan's Tigers, I leap out of bed stark naked and hide in the gap between the curtains and one of the windows. Pressing the cheeks of my backside against the window and holding my hands strategically in front of me, I prepare to sell my life dearly. It's only the hotel security men. They suspect I am around somewhere, and keep calling out variants of my name, going through the cupboards in the various parts of the suite, but for some reason ignore the curtains; though one man passes close enough to make the material move perceptibly.

They catch me later, slipping into the room after I have fallen asleep. It is a relief to look up and find it's not a mobster dressed in black with a gun in his hand. Politely, the security men usher me downstairs. I find one or two other stay-behinds there, including Dave Williams of the *Daily Mail* and his equally relaxed and pleasant photographer: good company, I feel.

Saturday 27 March

I can't operate entirely on my own much longer. I need to know what Serbian television and radio are saying, and I can't find out because I can't speak the language. I also have a desperate need for some contact with life outside this hotel, in order to be able to report what is going on. Simply describing the explosions I can see from my window won't be enough soon.

I ring Dragan and Vlad Mirjanović, our other local producer, on my mobile. They are both entitled to be nervous and resentful, since I am breaking their cover and it could be extremely dangerous for them. Instead they are courteous and friendly. Surprised, though; they had assumed we had all gone. Dragan insists on coming straight round. He is a magnificent character: the best.

'It could be really dangerous for you, *Dragane moi*.'

'I'm coming anyway,' he says gruffly.

We throw our arms round each other when he walks into the room.

Later the phone rings. It is Peter Gigliotti, our Australian cameraman, who travels on an Italian passport. (Italy is still regarded here as a friend.) He has managed to get back to Belgrade. Now we can start operating again in earnest.

Sunday 28 March

We drive out to see the wreckage of the US Stealth aircraft shot down near Budjanovći. A wing lies in a field, and there is such competition to get a piece of the anti-radar fabric that a local photographer jabs his knife at me when I get in his way. Mostly, though, the Serbian journalists co-exist easily with us. An old woman brings out glasses of *rakija*, ferocious home-made brandy, and hands me one.

'If they drink this, they won't fight any more,' she says.

I down it, and understand why.

The pilot has been rescued by an American helicopter team. This really is an extraordinary war. No doubt the Stealth aircraft had engine problems, and the bullet-holes we can see in it were inflicted when the plane was already coming down. But that isn't, of course, how the Serbs see it. Soon they will be printing stickers reading 'Sorry, we didn't know it was meant to be invisible.' They regard this as a sign that NATO is far from being invincible, and that if they can hold on and inflict a few more losses like this NATO's will to continue may start to fade.

If the British diplomat was right, and Milošević's real intention was to carry on resisting for a few days and then to hold up his hands and say 'They're just too overwhelmingly powerful for us,' then that entire strategy has come a serious cropper. Now the Serbs think they're more than a match for NATO. We could well be in for the long haul here.

Monday 29 March

Dragan and I venture out for the first time to the centre of Belgrade.

'Don't say anything and don't make eye-contact,' he warns me.

I walk around with my eyes firmly on the ground. There are some very unpleasant-looking characters hanging around, and the cultural centres of Britain, France, the US and Germany have all been comprehensively trashed and looted, with obscenities spray-painted on the walls. It makes me angry (bourgeois habits die hard, I suppose) and I start to exclaim and shake my head.

'John,' Dragan hisses beside me, 'you'll get us both killed if you don't shut up.'

He's right; but I hate the sight of all those books burned and destroyed.

Tuesday 30 March

Mike Williams, from the *Today* programme, manages cleverly to get a visa back to Belgrade. He has a difficult and dangerous journey back in, and has to stop at the main army barracks outside Belgrade for a while. This is probably the worst-bombed building in Serbia.

Mike is excellent company, witty, sympathetic, widely read; he also takes a large share of the burden of radio and television interviews off me. 'What's the mood on the streets?' and 'What are the Serbian people being told about all this?' we are asked again and again. It is easier to bear now there is someone to complain to.

Wednesday 31 March

Things are still very dodgy: gangs of nasty characters hang around the hotel and the centre of the city. Someone in London won't take no for an answer and keeps asking me to go into the RTS studio for a fatuous interview down the line instead of doing it over the phone. To them it's nothing: just a matter of the look of their programme. It could be really difficult for me. But I'm in business to broadcast, not to stay silent; so in the end I reluctantly agreed.

I refuse to put Vlad or Dragan in the spot, so I decide to go on my own, full of self-righteousness and not a little self-pity. Fortunately the spare car is sitting in the hotel car park, and the porters have the key. I am quite scared as I drive through the empty streets. If anyone catches me, I have no documents or passes and could be in trouble. I reach a police roadblock. The cop peers in, and I pretend to struggle with the window then give up helplessly with an 'aren't-I-stupid?' gesture and a grin. He looks bored, and waves me through. Outside the TV station I park carefully: I may need to make a quick getaway. I remember the BBC correspondent in Northern Ireland who was chased by an angry mob to his car, and snapped the key off in the ignition in his anxiety. The army had to rescue him.

The television staff are the same as ever: not friendly, but not hostile either. I don't care about them; it's the gangs outside who are the problem. I sit in the sauna-like studio (fan not working again) and hear all the comfortable sounds and voices at the other end. The technical staff in London are always friendly and jolly, at any rate.

Then on comes the questioner. There is testosterone in his voice.

'How does Slobodan Milošević think he's going to get away with committing crimes like this?'

I start to answer in emollient fashion. No good: the line is cut by some angry Serbian control freak.

'Oh dear,' says testosterone-voice, 'we seem to have lost John Simpson there in Belgrade.'

'I wonder why,' I think.

I sit there for a bit, listening to the line noise, but we're obviously not going to be reconnected. I storm out into the control cubicle.

'Who the hell cut our line with London?'

Shrugs and embarrassment all round: oh, was it cut? Nothing to do with us. Must have been some technical fault. Or maybe the bombing. They know as well as I do that the censors were listening, and would have pulled the plugs immediately if there was something they didn't like.

I'm too irritated to be nervous as I storm out of the studio and cross the road to my car. Three nasty-looking characters are hanging around nearby, but nobody had better mess around with me at a time like this. I glower at them and get in, remembering not to snap the key off. They take no notice of me anyway.

In the afternoon we visit the University Clinic, which lies right in the middle of four or five natural targets for NATO: the Security Police ministry, parts of the Ministry of Defence, etc. etc. The director and his staff tell us of their fears that if NATO attacks these targets the hospital will be hit. He is a gentle man, who has clearly watched the pictures of suffering refugees from the borders of Kosovo on Western satellite television and feels profoundly disturbed by them. 'You must not think we are barbarians,' he murmurs.

We meet several doctors, liberal-minded people with close links to British and American medicine, who tell me anxiously and with passion how their stocks of drugs has been depleted as a result of the outside world's sanctions against Serbia. How can the West presume to dictate to Serbia about humanitarianism when it restricts the supply of medicines to the sick?

In the end I can't keep quiet any more. 'And what,' I ask, 'did you do when the Bosnian Serbs were besieging Sarajevo, and the main hospital was down to two surgeons who had to operate on patients without anaesthetics by candlelight?'

There is bewilderment in their faces: this isn't a version of history they have come across; and to them it must just sound like the kind of arid point-scoring which habitually goes on here.

Thursday 1 April

Interview with Arkan [see p. 71]. It's going to be difficult, and I am determined that no one can accuse me of giving him an easy ride, as they did over CNN's interview with him yesterday. But it's one thing to be criticized for a feeble interview, and another to be criticized for doing the interview at all. Quite a lot of people in London seem to feel there is something wrong with interviewing those on the other side of the line. That, I'm afraid, I simply don't understand. How can more information be a bad thing? Are we so insecure about our own approach, so scared of hearing anything else, that we dare not allow people to hear the responses of an out-and-out thug?

Friday 2 April

NATO goes downtown. At 2 a.m. two MUP [interior ministry police] buildings are hit in the city centre, right beside the University Clinic hospital where we filmed on Wednesday. We dress and run out of the hotel; by now there is no one to stop us. Dragan is driving. Mike, Gig and I stay very quiet when we reach a police roadblock. The policeman turns us back, but Dragan finds another way to the city centre. We park, leaving Gig and his camera in the car for safety's sake, and tell him we will come back and get him if it's OK.

Mike, Dragan and I creep silently through the dark streets, avoiding police patrols. The flames light up the sky, and we have to be even more careful as we get nearer the MUP buildings. Now we are starting to get inquisitive looks from the people who have gathered to watch, and from the police. Not far from us, cameramen and photographers – all of them Serbs, working for Serbian organizations – are being roughed up and arrested. There is no question of getting Gig out of the car with his camera. While the others hang out in the street I dodge into the front garden of a block of flats and do a couple of live interviews for BBC World and News 24 on my mobile.

Afterwards we slip round to the University Clinic, to see if any damage has been caused there. We find the mothers in labour and those with young children have been moved into the basement – several dozen of them. A lot of fear and anger here. The director we spoke to – the one we interviewed on Wednesday, who was apologetic over what the Serbs were doing in Kosovo – hurries in from home to inspect the damage to the hospital. He shakes my hand almost with distaste. I ask if we can go in to film the women in the basement. He breaks away and hurries inside. 'No, you may not,' he calls out angrily over his shoulder.

Belgrade has been at the heart of ethnic cleansing and outright war for years, while scarcely suffering in any serious way. For the most part this city's people know only what their government has chosen to tell them through the state media about the suffering which the rest of the former Yugoslavia has endured as a result of President Milošević's policies. Now, for the first time, they are suffering something of what their President has inflicted on everyone else, and they don't like it.

Wednesday 7 April

The army press centre takes us to Priština, where NATO has hit a row of houses and killed some civilians. We drive for hours through the silent countryside of southern Serbia and Kosovo, looking at the torched houses and the paramilitary thugs lounging at the roadblocks. Priština is eerily empty, cleansed of most of its Albanian inhabitants. The Serbs mostly stay indoors. The only sounds are the crows in the trees and the barking of abandoned dogs. Terrible things have gone on here.

Friday 9 April

I start to notice something intriguing. Time and again, the Serbs seem to know where the next bombing is going to happen. Until now this has been just a suspicion, but today it becomes near-certainty when we receive information from Kragujevać, south of Belgrade, where the big Zastava car factory is situated. The workers in most big industries have been staging sit-ins in order to deter NATO from bombing them. This human shield tactic developed from the concerts held each night on Belgrade's main bridge.

Last night, representatives of the local authorities in Kragujevać went round to the Zastava factory and told the work-force there to end their sit-in, because NATO was about to attack. The workers moved out of the factory and into the car parks and waste ground beside it. Not long afterwards the bombers arrived. The plant was destroyed, and 124 people who had strayed too close were injured. The Kragujevać authorities, we're told, are delighted: their warning worked.

So how did they know? Either NATO is leaking information to the Serbs about what they're planning to hit, in order to minimize civilian casualties, or else there is a spy within NATO. This second possibility is completely outside my range of knowledge, but the first is certainly worth considering.

Since television news is not a good medium for floating theories, I decide to launch my trial balloon in my weekly column for the *Sunday Telegraph*:

> A pattern is emerging which suggests that the Yugoslav government may be receiving prior warning from NATO about some of its planned air-strikes, in an attempt to minimize civilian casualties. There are signs that as more and more Serbs join sit-ins to protect their places of work and their cities from air-strikes, Belgrade has had word beforehand so that the human shield can be lifted.

Not, perhaps, the strongest introduction to a story I have ever written, but it's as far as I can go without having any informed background material or confirmation from this end.

[A year later, the BBC broadcast a documentary about the war which demonstrated from reliable sources in the US forces that the Yugoslav government was indeed receiving prior information from NATO. But I was wrong to suggest that NATO as an organization *intended* to give it to the Yugoslavs: it came from a spy. There were various possibilities: the Greeks and Italians, though members of NATO, maintained contacts with Belgrade throughout the bombing; France was continually intervening to prevent air attacks which would cause particular damage or loss of life; there was unprecedented doubt and dissension within the Alliance about the entire strategy of bombing the Serbs, which may have led some individual to a unilateral act of betrayal; and the Russians seem to have begun their espionage efforts against NATO again, so that the leak could have come from them. Or the Chinese, whose embassy was later bombed, may have been monitoring NATO communications.]

Monday 12 April

We are allowed to film at a special session of the Yugoslav Parliament. Before it starts we can wander around on the floor of the house, and I approach Vojislav Šešlj, who is in his seat with the rest of his party members to the right of the speaker. I offer to shake hands with him.

'Fuck off, BBC,' he says, scarcely looking at me.

'Thank you,' I say as smoothly as I can manage, 'can I use that?'

Šešlj's men were some of the worst during the earlier fighting, and he remains the most dangerous figure in public life here; which in this gangster-ridden place is saying something.

We need to interview people in the streets: the voice of ordinary Serbs has so far been lacking. It is certainly going to be dangerous, because feelings are running so high. Just three of us will go: Gig, Dragan and I. We joke in the car, but we are all anxious.

'Let's just do it here,' I say when we get to the main pedestrian area.

A couple of policemen stroll past. Dragan asks them if they'll hang around in case of trouble.

'BBC? Fuck off,' the policemen say, and walk away laughing. It seems to be becoming a habit.

Already people are gathering angrily around us. I scarcely need to ask them any questions: they're shouting before I've got the words out. Spit lands on my face.

'We used to like everything from West. Now we hate you.'

'We are all for Milošević now, even if we didn't like him before.'

'You British are the fucking slaves of fucking America.'

There is a real sense of violence here, yet in the end by listening to what these people are saying and arguing with them politely I find that I can talk them round. They don't really hate us at all; they are frightened and resentful of the bombing. I end up on friendly terms with one of the stall-holders who sells patriotic lapel badges and postcards of the bomb-damage. He loads me down with presents as we leave.

We have a powerful story, and we have escaped without getting our heads broken. I've never had so many 'fucks' to blank out in a report before.

As we are editing in our hotel suite a couple of secret policemen arrive: big men. They are polite enough, but unyielding – Gig must get out of the country within 24 hours. I should have guessed: the Angel of Death was sitting in the hotel lobby when we got back. She is a big, blowzy woman from the security police, who dyes her hair a brilliant and unlikely red, and seems to come here as a back-up whenever someone is thrown out of the country. I ring a senior official in the hope of getting the decision reversed, but he is adamant. It's a punishment for our hostile reporting.

Tuesday 13 April

The foreign journalists have started coming back to Belgrade in large numbers, and the hotel is filling up again. I'm glad, in that it gives us a lot more protection: no one can just come round and pick us off now. Even so, I rather miss the quietness of the hotel and the sense of being free of pack journalism. Jacky Rowland, the BBC correspondent, has managed to get back too, and has taken a lot more of the burden of reporting off my shoulders and those of Mike Williams. I am fond of her, not least because she reminds me of my daughter Julia.

Wednesday 14 April

A column of Albanian refugees is hit close to the border. Various suggestions are proffered in Brussels: it was a military convoy; enraged Serbian soldiers shot the refugees; it's all an invention of the Milošević propaganda machine. Here the immediate assumption is that it's NATO. I say in a *Nine O'Clock News* interview that if the Serbs feel confident that NATO did it they'll take us down to see the place where it happened. If not, they'll quietly forget about it.

Thursday 15 April

Fury in Whitehall at my reporting – both the filming in the street and the 9.00 studio interview. Unnamed officials tell lobby journalists I have been guilty of accepting the Serbian version of events. I am gullible, I am being used by the Serbs for their propaganda purposes, I am pro-Serb. Tony Blair has told the Commons that I am working here 'under the instruction and guidance of the Serbian authorities'. Some MP (Labour, I think) called out 'Shame!', God bless him. If Blair repeated that outside the privilege of the Commons, I would sue him and win; the Serbs aren't instructing me, and they certainly aren't guiding me; and I take it as the greatest insult. For his part, Alastair Campbell, the Downing Street press spokesman, apparently thinks our interviewees in the street only said what they did because they were frightened of the secret police. He should have been there.

But it had to happen: when the going gets tough in wartime (the Falklands, the bombing of Libya in 1986, the Gulf War) the first instinct of British governments is to attack the people who are reporting the unpalatable. There's already been a harbinger of it all, a Labour MP called Ben Bradshaw. Downing Street have set him up to attack me because he was apparently a BBC correspondent – a stringer in Berlin, someone tells me – before he was elected to Parliament. It's a spiteful attack, quite personal. When someone from one of the British papers rings me for my reaction I say, grandly but perfectly truthfully, that I had never heard of him, either as a BBC correspondent or as an MP. The quote is taken up.

A phone call from a friend at Westminster: the MoD has been much worse and more insidious than Downing Street; Alistair, whom I've always quite liked, was merely bluff and irritable. It was a couple of senior MoD people who were putting out the real poison.

This time, though, there is a big difference from all the other occasions in the past. The newspapers rally round, MPs object, support flows in. The BBC is more robust than I have ever seen it: I get calls of support from Sir Christopher Bland, the BBC Chairman, Sir John Birt, the director-general, Tony Hall, head of news and any number of others. In the past the BBC would have caved in at once. Nowadays it's developed some real lead in its pencil. Maggie O'Kane, the *Guardian* correspondent in Belgrade, slips a note under the door: 'For what it's worth, I've always thought your reporting was completely independent.' It's worth a good deal at a time like this.

Friday 16 April

Interviews with Russian, Japanese, French, German, Italian, American, Swedish, Greek, Turkish, Dutch and Spanish journalists. By now the story, much exaggerated, has gone round the world: the British government is trying to silence the BBC. Opinion abroad is genuinely shocked, and I find myself defending Tony Blair and trying to explain the BBC's independence of the government; it doesn't sound very convincing, in the light of all this. The Serbs are jubilant, of course. That's the worst of all – they think we're as bad as they are. I refuse to be interviewed by their newspapers or television on principle, and explain why.

The fact is, I can say most of the things I want here. It is true that our videotaped reports have to be passed by the censor [by the end of the war my reports had been more censored than those of any other correspondent in Belgrade] but the security people no longer seem to be listening to our phones. Whenever the censors cut something out, I simply repeat it over the phone.

We have to be careful, all the same. There are passionate advocates of the Serbian cause listening in London to everything we say, and reporting back to Belgrade; especially a ghastly little man with a bald head like a penis who pops up all the time on BBC World and Sky. His name is Garsić, pronounced Garsich, but we call him Arsić. If you are sensible, do not go in for name-calling (Milošević a fascist dictator, etc. etc.), and can substantiate what you say, then you are likely to survive here. But if we find a good story that is likely to get us thrown out, I have made it clear to everyone here that we will use it and damn the consequences.

Goran Matić, a smooth, cynical government minister and a confidante of Milošević's, is amused by my troubles with the British government. 'They should have complained about _____,' he says, naming another Western organization. 'We call them Serbian Television.' Interestingly, Downing Street has backed off completely. Now, apparently, they're falling over themselves to say they don't know how anyone got the idea they were critical of my reporting. Respected figure, doing a good job under difficult conditions, etc. etc. It's all very amusing, really. It just shows that if the BBC stands up for itself against the politicians, it will always win the day.

Sunday 18 April

Robin Cook, the Foreign Secretary, still hasn't got the message. Shrilly, he tells GMTV I should get out of Belgrade. Clare Short, the overseas aid minister, compares my reporting from Belgrade with reporting from Berlin in the Second World War; that makes me a Nazi sympathizer as well as being pro-Serb, I suppose. _____, a political friend of mine, rings from his mobile without giving his name. 'Watch George [Robertson],' he says. 'You won't find him slagging you off. He's advising the others to stay cool. Cook and Short don't count for anything anyway, and they're only attacking you in order to show how super-loyal they are. As for Tony, he's really embarrassed about the way it's all backfired. Your lot have come out of all this rather well, I thought.'

Much more seriously, one of the last voices to be raised here against Milošević has been silenced. Slavko Curuvija and his wife came home this afternoon from a walk in the spring sunshine, and two gunmen shot Curuvija dead. He was a complex and interesting man; not an angel, certainly, but someone with real moral courage and an independent spirit. He had helped to found *Dvevni Telegraf*, The Weekly Telegraph. There is a gangsterish quality about this place: anyone can be shot at any time.

Monday 19 April

Dragan and I sit in our car in the car park of a dreary housing estate, watching out for policemen or other official busybodies, and wait for a tall, gangling young man in his early twenties to come and find us. 'This is him now,' says Dragan, and flashes the headlights. His name is Balša, and he is a young cameraman, recently out of film school. We have to be careful: even the fact that we are meeting him can turn out to be very awkward for him. If the Serbs throw out our accredited cameraman to punish us, what might they do to a young bloke who is just starting to make his way in the world?

'You'll like him,' Dragan says, and I do: he's quiet and brooding, but there's an earnestness about him and a determination to do the job to the best of his ability which pleases me. He knows a picture editor, too: Bata, a sensitive and gentle man, also in his early twenties. They are very different in character, both from each other and from Dragan, the mainstay of our whole operation here. But their company keeps me going in this depressing place: they lark around, and bring an air of real life into our reporting, something better and more decent than the gloom of Milošević's regime.

Tuesday 20 April

We set up shop in the hotel. Power cuts are frequent now, but one of the advantages of having a suite is that for some occult reason the razor socket in the bathroom still works when the entire rest of the hotel is in complete darkness and the generator is at its lowest capacity. Bata and Balša think we can run our editing machines, which (thank God) I told Gig to leave behind when he was thrown out, from this socket. We hired the room next door to mine for the edit suite long before, and Bata and Balša sleep there each night. (Dragan has another room, which he shares with his girlfriend Daniela, a beautiful and delicate Montenegrin girl. He brought her here because of the bombing, their own flat being on the top floor of a nearby block and unpleasantly vulnerable to passing missiles.) So the wires snake their way across my suite, gaffer-taped down to prevent anyone tripping over them. The hotel security people have warned us not to run anything off the razor sockets in case there is a fire; but the work comes first. We successfully run about eight different machines off this tenuous link with civilization.

Balša suggests we should film at the KGB Café in central Belgrade. Young people, sick of the war and of their rotten government, come here as a refuge. Talking to them is deeply refreshing: like the Belgrade of the old days. It's a relief to find a bedrock of people here I like and can sympathize with. There are one or two older ones here too, getting away from all the hatred and stupidity outside. It feels like a real refuge. Thank God someone in this city is sane and decent.

Wednesday 21 April

We try to go to Curuvija's funeral, but are specifically told that if we do we will be thrown out of the country immediately. I don't like giving in to threats, but decide eventually not to go: staying here for the long haul is more important.

This week's edition of Curuvija's paper came out today: there were the usual nudes, a vicious attack on the BBC's reporting, a lot of rhetoric about gallant Serbs and neo-fascist NATO aggressors – and no mention whatever of Curuvija's murder. The press has learned its lesson.

At the funeral another brave man, Professor Jarko Korać of Belgrade University, told the mourners, 'Slavko was the toughest critic of the government. His assassination was a political message, and some people are asking themselves if this has opened the process of settling scores with those who think differently.'

Slobodan Milošević's Yugoslavia is a place where any dark crime can occur.

Thursday 22 April

At around 3 a.m. I have just got into bed when an explosion, terrifyingly close, almost knocks me to the floor. I bundle the blankets over my head and roll into the bathroom just as another gigantic explosion rocks the room, knocks things over, and makes every window in the place bulge inwards. I wait a moment or two, but I know what it is: the Usce building, three hundred yards away. It's where the radio and TV stations belonging to Milošević's family and friends is based: a great ugly 60s block which used to be the Communist Party HQ. I creep over to the window and poke my head through the curtains, as though that will protect me. Half the building is in flames; and just as I look, a third smart bomb hits the roof and drops down through the building. It's an extraordinary moment. The place is on fire throughout, and yet there are sections of the building where the electric lights are still on. At last they go out.

The transmitting tower stays upright on the roof of the Usce building, however. Some nights later there is a fantastic whirring sound overhead: the noise of a cruise missile's motor. It strikes the transmitting tower, which can only be seven or eight feet across, and knocks it over the edge of the building where it hangs like a crumpled wire coat hanger. The thought that a missile fired from five hundred miles away could be so accurate is extraordinary.

It's beginning to feel uncomfortable here: the bombs are close, and the threat of the murder gangs hasn't gone away.

'Oh, you'll be safe enough,' says ――――, a colleague from London, rather patronizingly. 'They won't hit your hotel with journalists there.' Glad he thinks so; they managed to hit the Al-Rashid [in Baghdad].

Friday 23 April

I have just got to sleep when a tremendous explosion nearby rocks the room. It is 2.13 a.m. RTS, the State television service, has been hit. I turn the TV set on: just hash and line noise. NATO threatened to do this before, but Jamie Shea, the NATO spokesman, gave the strong impression it wasn't a target. I must say, I always assumed it would be. I've been going round there night after night with Vlad to satellite our material, and every time we walked out afterwards I wondered whether the place would still be standing in the morning. We've had warnings from the BBC in London for two weeks now, advising us not to go there. What can you do? Here, you could get killed just lying in bed.

[Some months later, one of the most senior people at CNN told me that he'd been called by the Pentagon and warned that the TV station was going to be hit that night. He rang everyone he could in Washington to advise them not to go ahead with the attack, and later heard that the plane in question was turned around half an hour before it reached the target. Afterwards, though, the decision was reviewed, and the Americans decided to go ahead with the bombing. Richard Holbrooke was a particular enthusiast: RTS was Milošević's main propaganda weapon and had to be taken out, he said. If only these people knew a little more about the way television works. The Serbs had planned everything out in the event of an attack on the TV station, and they were only off the air for a few hours. If NATO had had the wit to attack the transmitters, no one would have been killed and the TV service would have been off for much longer. When they try that later, it works.]

We decide it is too risky to drive round to the RTS building right away; there will be gangs out on the streets. Instead we will go at first light. The sight of the place, still burning and with rubble strewn everywhere, is really depressing in the cold chill of dawn. Firemen are clambering over the heaps of rubble, listening for the sound of human voices.

A government minister arrives: he is remarkably sprightly and jolly with us, and his face only becomes serious when we interview him. I start to believe the stories which have been going the rounds, that the government told RTS to ensure that the station was fully manned every night. It makes excellent propaganda for them if people have been killed.

They let us in, and we walk along the corridors which have become so familiar over the weeks; only now they are smashed and burned, and our feet crunch on rubble and broken glass. We peer into a studio where I have done a lot of interviews: all wrecked.

'Somebody here,' says our guide.

I know this little room: it's where the overnight make-up lady worked. Her foot is sticking out of the rubble at an angle. It is encased in a dusty shoe, and there is a razor cut over a bunion. Nothing I have seen in this city so far is worse than this.

What kind of war is it, where NATO targets a make-up lady, and the government is glad to see her killed? The television staff came here because they assumed they would be safe. They should have noticed that the top management never came in at night-time.

By 7 a.m. RTS is broadcasting again: it had cost fifteen lives to keep it off the air for four and three-quarter hours. Serbian Television is indeed part of the central nervous system of President Milošević's control over this country, just as NATO says. It has made it far easier for him to ensure public complaisance over the stripping out of Kosovo's ethnic Albanian population. It has, by judicious editing and selection, managed to give its viewers the impression that only NATO's governments are in favour of the war, while ordinary opinion abroad supports 'this small, brave country'.

It has buoyed them up artificially with the belief that Russia is about to enter the war on their side, and has hinted that the Russians have been supplied with all sorts of secret weapons. It has assured them that dozens of NATO aircraft have been shot down. For years now it has hidden from them all information about the terrible crimes that people acting in Serbia's name have committed in the former Yugoslavia.

By any measure of honesty and decency, Serbian Television is the tame instrument of a nasty system. That made it a natural target for NATO bombs and missiles. But should the television station, as opposed to its transmitters, have been hit? Should the make-up lady have paid the ultimate price for the propaganda of people so high up in the system that she would never have been allowed to put powder on their foreheads?

Monday 3 May

I decide to make a move over the whispering campaign against me a fortnight ago. I write a fierce letter to Alastair Campbell, but make it clear I will take no legal action if he gives me an undertaking that the government has no criticism to make of my professional conduct here. The letter sits in my word processor for a while: this will really be a declaration of war, if he refuses to play ball. Then I e-mail it: let the chips fall where they may.

Thursday 6 May

Real signs of war-weariness by now. 'If only this were over,' someone says to us in a street interview. Later President Clinton, visiting Europe, says NATO can do a deal with Milošević. As a result Milošević gets a new lease of political life, ministers here are jubilant. Clinton, who promised there would be no ground war, has now given Milošević further reason to hold out.

Tony Blair says this is a war for international morality. People here call it the War of Two Penises – Clinton's and Madeleine Albright's.

Friday 7 May

Receive an emollient letter from Alastair Campbell. Not an apology, certainly, but then I didn't expect one: governments never apologize. But he's sorry it happened, and I get the impression he feels it was all a foul-up from their side. The assurance I was looking for is clearly there. Should I make the letter public? It's marked 'private and confidential', so I can't. But in the afternoon I get a call from the *Sunday Telegraph*: somehow they've heard about it. I confirm the version they've received, correcting the odd detail. Strange feeling, being a spin-doctor on my own behalf against the headquarters of spin-doctoring. Stranger too to win.

Saturday 8 May

Wakened at two-fifteen by a God-almighty bang close by. Mike Williams rings: 'They've hit the Chinese Embassy. We're going round there – are you coming?' To my great and lasting shame I say no. I've had only a few hours' sleep over the past week and I'm too lazy to roll out of bed once I've got into it. 'Stupid bastards,' I mutter. 'Tell me what it's like when you get back.' Serious dereliction of duty: this is of course one of the biggest stories of the war. While everyone is hanging round outside the embassy in the darkness there is another missile attack nearby. The hotel where Arkan's Tigers are based has been hit. Typically, NATO seemed not to have got any of them, while killing three poor Chinese people.

How can they conceivably have mistaken the Chinese Embassy for another building? It's right out in the middle of a stretch of open ground. It doesn't even look like anything except a Chinese Embassy, with its curved gables and its typically Chinese surrounding wall.

Much later, in America, _____ (a former American diplomat, who at one stage had close links with the CIA and the rest of the intelligence community) told me that the bombing was the work of a small rogue grouping within the CIA, who switched the maps which the US Air Force needed for bombing the ministry of military procurement in Belgrade. The ministry is near the embassy. Mistakes always happen in war, of course, and the Chinese were known to be passing information about NATO to the Serbs.

The conclusion the Americans draw from this war is that you can't fight an intelligent campaign with 19 nations involved. My conclusion is slightly different: the stupidity factor in Washington is higher this time than it has ever been. That's saying something.

Sunday 9 May

I read the *Sunday Telegraph* front page on the internet. 'Downing Street Apologizes To John Simpson', says the headline. Not entirely true, but close enough to be satisfactory. I don't think this government will try to call the BBC to heel again. Maybe, if we're lucky, no future government will either. If you're weak and feeble, it's an invitation to these people to hit you again. If you punch back (and especially if you fight dirty, as I have) they'll look for another target.

But the day is a special one for other reasons. Dee arrives. She has battled her way through Romania in order to get to the Yugoslav border. Dragan warns me not to, but I can't resist climbing on a concrete bollard to wave to her. She waves back. The border police come running over and threaten me with all sorts of things. I'd forgotten quite how beautiful she is. She looks sensational in her pink sweater and coat. Dragan purrs approvingly beside me. We drive back to Belgrade, and I cannot stop talking, trying to show her everything as we go. She is amazingly gutsy about it all, viewing the ruins of the different government buildings and the Chinese Embassy with a calm interest. We discuss at length whether we should take a safer room, further away from the bombs. Dee says no. Life for me has suddenly become a great deal better.

Wednesday 12 May

Cluster bombs land in the centre of Niš. These are disgusting weapons, which should be outlawed along with landmines. Mike Williams describes the way they parachute down slowly and explode, killing and maiming people over a wide area. _____ contradicts him flatly on air, sounding exactly like a NATO spokesman. What prats some of these people are: as though, just because the rules say cluster bombs can only be used under certain circumstances, NATO is only using them like that. My impression is that the Americans in particular are taking more risks with civilian lives now. Maybe they've noticed how quickly, once NATO has made its formal apology, the mistakes are forgotten. Every Serb you speak to believes now that civilians are being deliberately targetted. It's not true, but this war is already worse than the Gulf War in terms of casualties. As for Milošević, he must be delighted; loss of life among his own people has never held him back.

Friday 21 May

Not a good day. After a swim with Dee in the hotel I am walking down some steps near the pool when I slip on the wet tiles and land badly, rupturing the tendons that attach my left thigh muscle to the knee. It's much worse than breaking the bone, and pretty painful. A doctor comes and gives me an injection, which lasts for a while. Thank God for Dee, and Dragan too. He lifts me up as gently as a father.

Eventually an ambulance takes me to hospital: the University Clinic, where we have filmed before, and where we were turned away after the bombing of the secret police headquarters next door. Great place to be. As I am being lifted out of the ambulance in a certain amount of pain, an oafish paramedic starts haranguing me about NATO and Blair and the bombing: I tell him to fuck off, and feel slightly better.

As a couple of nurses take my details, the air raid sirens begin to wail. They glance at each other, and then at me. One seems about to say something unpleasant, but the other shakes her head.

The registrar explains what has happened: the tendons connecting the thigh-muscles of my left leg have been ripped away from the kneecap. It's something to do with being in my fifties. People who are younger or older would have broken a bone. At my age, it seems, the tendons are briefly weaker than the bones. As I lie on the stretcher, trying to think what I should do, Dee uses her mobile to consult a specialist friend of hers in South Africa. (What a strange world, that she can ask someone in Jo'burg for advice in the middle of an air raid in the darkest Balkans.)

This will be a very difficult operation, he tells her, and if it goes wrong I won't walk again. His advice is to catch a plane for London at once. The trouble is, there are no planes here to catch. It will take a good twenty-four hours to get to London, probably more. We talk about it between ourselves about the advisability of having the operation done here, as rationally as though we are deciding where to have lunch, but both of us know how important our decision could be. I'm impressed by Dee's calmness. This moment will decide her life as well as mine.

The registrar listens to our discussion – what must he be thinking, given that if even he is injured he cannot leave the country? – and points out that if the operation is delayed the tendons in my leg will shrink and recovery will be even longer and harder. He explains the operation in the kind of detail I don't really want to hear: drilling holes in the kneecap and tying the tendons to it. It'll take me a long time to recover, he says.

There are two dangers: that the hospital, which has already been hit once and is right beside all sorts of NATO targets, will be hit again while I am here; and that the quality of the surgery won't be high. Then I remember what one of the specialists said when we filmed here a few weeks ago: 'The only good thing about Yugoslavia's recent history is that all these wars we have been having have provided us with excellent experience.' As for the hospital being hit, that's a danger everyone in the city faces. Only yesterday we filmed at the neurological ward of another Belgrade hospital which had been hit during a NATO attack on an army barracks nearby. Three patients were killed.

'All right,' I say, 'we'll do it here.' I feel better immediately.

I'm not leaving Belgrade at this late stage in the war: I want to see how it all ends. Dee and Dragan both seem relieved, and beam at me.

The operation takes place in the afternoon. I am determined to be as conscious as I can, and opt for an epidural injection. 'Be nice to the anaesthetists,' said a medical friend of mine once. 'They're the ones who kill you; the surgeons just maim you.' It is easy to be nice to the anaesthetist here because she is a very pretty blonde, and she is really nice back, which makes me feel better. Although groggy and moving in and out of consciousness, I manage to watch a surprising amount of the operation reflected in the shiny steel of the overhead lamp, as they slice open my knee and pin back the flaps. It lasts about 45 minutes. While it is going on, the charming young surgeon tells me afterwards, two people come up to him and say he shouldn't be wasting his time on a Brit when NATO is killing Serbs every day. Thank you, Hippocrates. Fortunately he tells them where to get off.

When it is over, I am brought into the intensive care ward for the night. This is far worse than being under the knife. To lie in a silent hospital ward in the blackness of a power cut, unable to move, watching anti-aircraft fire arcing into the air and listening to the engines of the NATO planes as they come in for the attack, is to share the fears of everyone else in this city. Up at the Hyatt we aren't particularly safe – windows have been broken, and some of the bombs have fallen uncomfortably close – but the thick double-glazing protects us from the noise of it all. Not here. Especially not here. This hospital has already been hit, and it is surrounded by military buildings which NATO has already targeted. Each of them is within fifty to a hundred yards of where I find myself tonight. And if something happens, I can't even get out of bed. I can scarcely even move.

Saturday 22 May

They shift me to another room, away from the other patients, many of whom have been injured in the bombing. I feel a bit of a fraud: all I did was to fall over in the swimming pool of a five-star hotel. I hadn't planned to write my *Sunday Telegraph* column this week, under the circumstances, but now I feel a bit clearer in my head I change my mind. I ring the foreign desk: they sound surprised. I scribble my report into a notebook and dictate it to copy. It runs easily enough, since I'm just telling the story of what happened to me. The key part was last night. Dominic Lawson, the editor of the *Sunday Telegraph*, once said to me, 'You're the kind of person who'll be writing descriptive pieces on your deathbed'. If so, he was right.

Dee, Dragan and Mike Williams come round with food and presents. Mike has made something for me to illustrate the old First World War joke, which he taught me, about military communications at the front: 'Send reinforcements, we're going to advance' becomes 'Send two-and-fourpence, we're going to a dance.' He's mounted coins to the value of 2/4d in pre-decimal money in a frame, with a little note. I'm very touched. To be able to look at the three of them and feel the warmth of their affection is better than any medicine. I sit here like a kid with my toys after they have gone, playing with each in turn.

At night, though, things don't seem quite so good. Dee, Dragan and Mike have left (I refuse to let Dee stay with me, in case the hospital is hit) and virtually all the specialists and doctors head for home. Just a few nurses are on duty. I can hear the other patients snoring or muttering in their sleep, or calling out '*Sestre!*', 'Nurse!' But the nurses are exhausted, and usually sleep through the calls.

Pain and the discomfort of this fiendish cast keep me awake. The lights are switched off directly the air raid sirens sound, and I wait for the night's fireworks. If you are immobile, you feel especially vulnerable. Who will come to help me if a bomb lands on us? What will I do, given that I can't even shift this heavy weight, my leg?

The whoosh of the anti-aircraft rounds, the whining of the jet engines as the pilots search out their targets, the deep rumble and shake as the bombs hit – not far away, that one: these are noises I never heard at the Hyatt. Now I'm getting the *version originale*, as they say in the French movies.

The cause is just, I tell myself as I wait for one of the neighbouring buildings to go up; those are our boys overhead. Somehow, though, lying in the darkness unable to move, it's hard to be convinced.

Friday 28 May

I've been back in the hotel for four days now, lying on the bed in our grand suite and trying every now and then to learn how to use crutches. A ferocious-looking but charming physio comes over from time to time to torture me.

'For you, Tommy, ze war is over,' says Dee.

I'm determined it shan't be. I have put too much into it to leave now, and although my left leg is in plaster from ankle to groin and I stay in bed for large parts of the day, I shall soon be able to get up and go downstairs to record a piece to camera. I have scarcely told the BBC about my problems, nervous that they will go Auntie-like and try to medivac me out of here. Most of the programme presenters who interview me over the phoneline clearly know nothing about it; though you would think they might read the newspapers. One presenter asks me what I see when I go out onto the streets. I answer as briefly and truthfully as I can, without saying 'I've been lying in plaster for a week and can't even stand up, you daft bimbo.' Which is, of course, what I would like to say most.

For the rest of my life I shall probably have a slight limp, and sometimes be forced to use a walking-stick. My knee will always remind me of my time in Belgrade. Still, my chances of playing rugby for England were getting pretty slight anyway, and there are worse things than limping. The memory of a poem about these things stirs faintly, but I won't be able to track it down until I get back to Dublin. It turns out to be by W.E. Henley, more excitably imperialist than most:

> What if the best of our wages be
> An empty sleeve, a stiff-set knee,
> A crutch for the rest of life – who cares,
> So long as the One Flag floats and dares?

Which has nothing to do with my emotions whatever, and anyway mine was a pretty ludicrous accident, scarcely glamorous or self-sacrificing. I did the job I was sent to Belgrade to do, and don't worry too much about my stiff-set knee as a result. After all, I could have done it coming out of Finnegan's bar on a wet Saturday night in Dublin.

The hotel management is a problem. The last time the ambulance-men carried me through the lobby on a stretcher, we were told we must go through the back route from now on. It upset the guests to see me, they said. Bastards.

I am, thanks to the efforts of Dee, Dragan, Mike, Balša, Bata and Vlad, managing to keep going. I lie on the bed in the editing room, cutting my reports, and then Dragan wheels me down each night to the front of the hotel and props me up so I can do my obligatory piece to camera. Often I am standing at a slight angle, I notice; no one else seems to. I can watch ghastly Serbian television, and BBC and Sky and CNN, get BBC On-Line on my laptop, and have room service to bring me anything I want, and enjoy the company of my wife and friends around me. Really, I have been in worse wars.

Thursday 3 June

At long last, it's coming to an end. It has lasted far, far longer than Madeleine Albright promised the Clinton administration it would take. In Washington they're calling it 'Albright's War', and the knives are out for her. But she will of course survive, like some waddling turkey that has become a household pet and cannot be cooked for Christmas. Tony Blair was right to advocate the sending in of ground troops, because that was the only way the lives of innocent refugees could have been saved and the war brought to a speedy end. But Clinton apparently told him in as many words to shut up about it.

All that has happened in Albright's War is that NATO has expended vast quantities of money and much of its prestige dislodging the Serbian police militias and the MUP [Internal Ministry] troops so the Kosovo Liberation Army can take their place and start doing precisely the same thing to Serbian civilians that the Serbs have done to Albanian civilians: killing them, torturing them, forcing them to flee. This is a country where the tribe counts above everything. You are not an individual here, you are a representative of your people and therefore available for attack and murder in the event of trouble.

Serbs who have grown up in the friendliest way with their Albanian next-door neighbours set fire to their houses and drive them out at gunpoint with nothing; and Albanians do it to Serbs.

'You are bombing us,' people say to me every time I take a camera out into the streets. 'What do you mean?' I reply irritably; '*I'm* bombing you? You're not getting bombed any more than I am.'

What they mean is that my tribe is bombing theirs.

All Madeleine Albright did was to get involved in a nasty little local conflict, and then try to persuade the rest of us that one side was uniquely evil while the other was uniquely innocent. The whole-sale clearance of ethnic Albanians from Kosovo was an act of wickedness, sure. But that's what the Serbs do: if they're being hit by someone they dare not hit back at, they will take their revenge on some weaker party. We set it all up for them so that they would take out their anger on the ethnic Albanian civilians of Kosovo.

This has not been a moral crusade, it's been a practice exercise for bombers which were in no danger themselves and took insufficient care about the lives of others. And since those others didn't count in terms of American politics – they were foreigners, after all – then no one was counting. As for NATO's claims about destroying Serbian military equipment, they have turned out to be absurdly wrong. Finally, the man who's responsible for the whole evil mess in the former Yugoslavia, Slobodan Milošević, is bound to be left unchallenged in power at the end of it. NATO has not scored a lot of points out of three.

Anyway, it won't last much longer. Today the Serbian Parliament has accepted NATO's terms. It is a beautiful sunny day, and I am far too excited to stay indoors. Dragan carries me down the car and we drive to the city centre, where I sit at an open-air café reporting to London on my mobile. People around about me listen, but no one interrupts me or threatens me; those days are long gone. No one here cares about anything any longer, except just to get it over with as fast as possible. While I sit here in the sun, Dee, Dragan and the crew are interviewing people in the street. Again and again the interviewees say they want to get rid of Milošević. In the new climate here, we won't even have any problem satelliting this kind of thing tonight.

Tuesday 8 June

The bombing ends, but no cars drive through the streets, honking their horns. No flags are waved. No one is holding a street party. The headlines in the newspapers and on television faithfully report what they have been instructed to: that this is all a remarkable achievement by Serbia, that Belgrade has succeeded in keeping *de jure* control of Kosovo, that its army is undefeated. In some ways, depressingly, it's true.

In the open-air cafés people sit and read *Politika* and *Blic*, and draw their own conclusions about who has won. People here are going through the motions, exactly as though nothing has happened. Their feelings and emotions are on autopilot. The girls saunter along in their skimpy summer clothes, the young men laugh with their friends, the older people hurry to jobs they are lucky enough to have kept, or worry about finding enough food to buy.

I am taken to the hospital, where one of the surgeons examines my leg. I ask him how he feels, now that there will no longer be any bombing to disturb his operations. He goes over to the window, looking out at the sublime summer's day.

'I don't know whether to be relieved or depressed,' he says, and there are tears in his eyes.

The last victims of this war were three poor so-and-sos killed on a farm in rural Serbia which NATO hit by accident. By this stage, no one seems to care. The journalists in Brussels do not ask NATO for an explanation, and there is no apology.

In the evening, Bata, thoughtful and long-haired, is sitting at the editing machines, putting the final touches to our report about the end of the bombing. Dee sits on one of the beds directing him. I am lying on the other bed, my left leg in plaster from ankle to mid-thigh, recording the commentary on a microphone like Peter O'Sullivan at the Derby.

There is a knock at the door. Two secret policemen, the politest I have ever met, are standing apologetically in the doorway.

Dragan goes over to speak to them, and listens to them gravely, while I shout into the microphone as though the Derby is in its last furlong.

'They've come to throw you out, John,' Dragan says when the race is over. After thirteen weeks in Belgrade without a single day off, my temper, never particularly good, is at a record shortness.

'Tell them to bugger off. We're busy.'

It doesn't faze them. Polite as ever, they offer me all sorts of indulgences: someone else can bring my passport to be stamped with a 24-hour exit visa, and it can wait until tomorrow morning. But it will have to be done. I have apparently upset the Serbian Information Service in London – those experts on objective reporting – by something I have said about Milošević. Maybe it was Mr Arsić, the man with the head like a penis.

For the next few hours we argue and pull every string we can collectively think of; and by emphasizing the medical problem we manage to get the deadline extended by a week.

Tuesday 15 June

Dee and I leave at 9.30 a.m. for the long drive to Hungary. After eighty-eight days I wave goodbye to Dragan, Mike, Balša, Bata, Vlad and the rest. They have become like my own family.

We stay overnight in an expensive hotel in Budapest, where the food is a great deal better than anything we have had for months, and watch a video. We should be extraordinarily relieved and happy; instead we both feel a little low.

Wednesday 16 June

The boss himself comes to Heathrow to welcome us back: the BBC's equivalent of getting the Victoria Cross.

It doesn't come as an enormous surprise when we get home to read in the newspapers that after 79 days of bombing, 40,000 or so sorties and untold tens of thousands of tons of bombs, smart and stupid, NATO managed to hit only 13 Serbian tanks in Kosovo. It claimed, of course, to have knocked out up to 40 per cent of the 280 or so tanks which the Serbs were believed to have deployed in Kosovo, plus nearly 60 per cent of their artillery and mortars.

What NATO really hit were canvas and wood replicas. Colleagues of mine reported seeing some of these in Kosovo after the bombing was over, together with old armoured personnel carriers, broken-axled and rusting, which the Serbs had carefully left out in the open for NATO's pilots to target.

As for me, I always knew I would get a lot of grief for sleeping with the enemy; or at any rate living, working and to some extent suffering with them. When I go through the mail, I find the full extent of it: large amounts of hate-mail from people who didn't want to be told what it was like on the receiving end of NATO's bombing. The clinching argument always seemed to be the same: would the BBC have had a correspondent in Berlin from 1939–45? ·

Well, of course we would, if only it had been possible. What's the problem about wanting to know more, rather than less, about what is going on? That, surely, is what we should all want. Slowly, as I go through the letters, I understand that what these people dislike is the reminder that under NATO's bombs there were ordinary men and women like themselves. They would much rather not know; they wanted to believe that every bomb reaches its target, that every casualty is someone who deserves it. Well, I'm here to tell you it ain't true. Sorry.

The hate-mail merchants will probably say I am the victim of the Stockholm Syndrome, whereby prisoners come to love their captors. But lying in my hospital bed, listening to the groans and snores and the cries of 'Sestre!', I understood that we were all in this together. If a bomb had hit the hospital during the nights I was there, we would all have suffered: the English patient along with the Serbs. When it really counts, your tribe doesn't really mean anything. But try telling anyone in the former Yugoslavia that. Or the people who write me hate-mail, for that matter.

9

GUIGNOL

C'est à travers de larges grilles
Que les femelles du canton
Contemplaient un puissant gorille
Sans souci du qu'en-dira-t-on;
Avec impudeur, ces commères
Lorgnaient même un endroit précis
Que, rigoureusement, ma mère
M'a défendu d'nommer ici.
Gare au gorille! . . . .

Georges Brassens, 'Le Gorille'

Grunting, the pilot nudged me and pointed. I had come to dislike him intensely, so I tried to ignore him, scarcely glancing out through the windscreen. Then I looked again. He was pointing at Beirut. It lay ahead of us, jutting out into the lapis lazuli waters of the Mediterranean like a newel post.

From the air I could see all the things I remembered about it from the past: the port, the ruined buildings, the red earth, the racecourse, the unused beaches. A big column of dark smoke drifted across the airport, a strip of black on the right-hand side. Oh Christ, I thought, they're bombarding the runway.

'Only burning rubbish,' the pilot said with a smirk, as though he knew what I was thinking.

He bent forward. A gold cross disentangled itself slowly from his chest hair and swung in space.

'Coffee,' he called out to the Madonna-faced stewardess, and then, holding out his plastic cup, 'Put it there.'

Gently, obediently, she did what she was told. Then came a

wonderful moment: in passing another cup across, the pilot's hand collided with the co-pilot's and the coffee spilled into the undercarriage controls.

'Jesus, Mary, Joseph,' cried the pilot.

He had just finished explaining to me how my life wouldn't be worth a snap of his fingers when we reached Beirut, so now I laughed coarsely. He and the co-pilot fell to inserting bits of Kleenex into the slots in the controls, and as he extracted each one, wet and brown, he glared at the stewardess as though it had been her fault.

It was certainly her fault that I was in the cockpit. The MEA plane was almost entirely empty, apart from my colleague Brian Murray and me, and the stewardess had lowered her face close to mine and suggested that we might like to meet the pilot. We agreed.

Now the plane was on a line with the runway, the coast and the shattered buildings flashed underneath us, we headed into the smoke, and the pilot started praying loudly.

'Put your hand here,' he called out urgently to me, and I threw my weight on to the undercarriage levers.

The plane hit the tarmac heavily and bounced along a little way. Then it was all over, and the pilot was laughing again.

'If you and your friend are dead by tonight, don't blame me,' he said as he shook hands with us. 'I am Christian. They don't look for Christians any more. They want foreigners.'

A big, friendly bear of a man, Brian looked at me and shrugged. He was a picture-editor, and the only person the BBC could find to come with me on this trip. The staff cameramen had all been unaccountably busy.

There was only one reason why I had come to a place as difficult as this. I was still under a cloud as a result of being sacked from reading the *Nine O'Clock News* two years earlier, and I was looking for a way of salvaging my reputation. There were very few foreign reporters in Beirut now. As the pilot said, the Shi'ite fundamentalists were looking for Westerners to kidnap.

The Israeli army was still occupying the south of the country, and different factions inside Beirut shelled each other every day. On the day we arrived three gunmen walked into the bank next door to the hotel where we were staying, made the staff and customers lie on the floor, robbed the tills and the vaults, and then murdered everybody before sauntering off. Firepower ruled Lebanon; without it, you were naked.

Now that Brian and I were here, it was hard to think what we would do. I had told the foreign desk I would find a cameraman when I arrived, but sitting that evening on the edge of my bed in the Commodore, I couldn't think how.

The next morning, with bright sunlight slanting down into the narrow streets, we went out for a coffee. The BBC's three drivers, all unarmed but trying anxiously to give an impression to the contrary, fanned out around us so that no one would be able to pull us into a car and drive off. I have rarely felt more conspicuous. People would stop to watch us as we walked, and cars slowed down to get a good look. We drank our thimbles of fierce, black, scented coffee, thanked the proprietor for his generosity in giving them to us for nothing, and went back. I hadn't known a hundred yards could seem so far.

Once inside the BBC office, though, we felt safer. I started ringing round to find a cameraman. Half an hour later, I had got nowhere.

'Maybe—' I began gloomily.

Then we heard someone whistling in the corridor outside. I recognized the song at once. It was a satirical Georges Brassens number called 'Le Gorille': funny, cynical, rather nasty, about an escaped gorilla. The whistling stopped, and there was a knock at the door. A tough-looking, stocky, southern European type in his mid-forties, with a badly broken nose and grey hair *en brosse*, stood there. He was wearing a particularly handsome leather bomber jacket and jeans.

'Jean-Claude,' he announced with a kind of flourish. 'I am cameraman. French,' he added, as though he thought it might be necessary.

As I talked to him, I worked out what had happened. Jean-Claude had fallen out with the French television network he worked for, and had sued them successfully for a sizeable amount of money. He had invested it in a television camera and editing gear of his own, and had decided to set up in business in the one place no one wanted to be: Beirut. He had arrived a few days before us. The trouble was, he couldn't make his editing machines work. Did we know anyone who might be able to help? Brian grinned and pulled out his set of screwdrivers.

Jean-Claude and I were natural partners: exiles from our past, prepared to take risks in order to rebuild our careers. He was a Corsican, witty, hard-boiled and completely lacking in any kind of idealism: a political carnivore. His political opinions were savage, and could scarcely have been more different from my own herbivorous view of things. He would tell me of his appalling doings as a soldier in Algeria and elsewhere, then listen seriously to my protests, nodding his cropped grey head as though his better nature almost, but not quite, compelled him to agree with me. He was one of the bravest people I have ever met, and he believed in only two things: will-power, and the medicinal powers of a glass of Ricard.

We talked a lot about our respective pasts. He had covered more wars than I had, and seen more action; yet some of my experiences had been nastier and more dangerous than his. His had left him physically unmarked; I had only one scar, an inch or so long on the side of my face, which at that time was less than three years old and had been inflicted only a mile or so away, in another quarter of Beirut. It was the result of telling a gunman in Beirut not to be rude to me. Jean-Claude liked that, so I told him the full story.

I had come across a group of paramilitary figures trying to liberate a jeep with a heavy machine-gun mounted on it from a lock-up garage in West Beirut; there was a lot of military hardware hidden away in the city in 1982.

'What are you doing?' I asked.

The question may have been otiose, but I was perfectly civil.

'Fuck off. It's none of your business,' the men's commander answered in rather good French.

He scarcely looked at me. This was a city where the possession of a gun was all the repartee anyone needed.

'There's no reason to be rude,' I said. 'I was polite enough to you.'

I suppose it was a tactical error to have called him *tu*. His face went a distinctly infarctive colour and, screaming to one of his men for an automatic weapon, he jabbed it into my face and said he was going to kill me. There was a pause for a moment or two, and I stood there with a little trickle of blood running down my cheek. Then it seemed to me that the purple began to fade from his face.

'*Zut alors*,' I said, not knowing what else to say.

I turned and walked down the street.

'If I see you here again I'll shoot you,' he shouted after me.

'Yeah, yeah, yeah,' I replied; but this time I had the sense to keep it under my breath.

I also avoided that part of West Beirut for the next few days.

Jean-Claude laughed for a long time.

'*Connard*,' he said. '*Espèce d'ordure*.'

He didn't mean me. I never could understand why, when ordure means little more than 'rubbish', 'species of rubbish' should be a serious bit of bad language, not to be repeated in front of your aunts. As a cameraman, used to making his way through the nastiest troublespots without a weapon of any kind, he had contempt for men who relied on guns to give themselves stature and authority.

Lebanon had changed a great deal in the three years since I had picked up my scar. Now the Israelis were trying to extricate themselves from the mess their defence minister, Ariel Sharon, had got them into, while trying not to seem weak. They were withdrawing from Lebanon sector by sector, and were currently at the Litani River, about a third of the way up the Lebanese coast from the Israeli border.

The Shi'ites who constituted the majority of the population in the area were in open revolt. There were almost daily attacks by fundamentalist suicide squads, who drove cars packed with explosives at the roadblocks and barracks of the Israeli troops. The Israelis responded with open brutality. I suggested to Jean-Claude that he and I should travel down there together and do a little filming. He agreed even before I could finish speaking.

The Litani River crossing was just a rusty Bailey bridge over a weed-grown stream. Even at this time of year the atmosphere was stifling, and the rich greenery seemed in danger of taking over the bridge altogether. It seemed a small, unimportant, out-of-the-way place. Yet this was one of the great trunk roads of history, running north to Sidon and Beirut, and south to Tyre, Acre, Jaffa and Egypt. The Pharoah's armies, Jesus Christ, Mark Antony, Richard Coeur-de-Lion and St Louis had all crossed the river here. Now it was the frontier between occupied and unoccupied Lebanon, and twenty bored Israeli soldiers were in charge of it, sitting on looted, broken chairs, snacking on potato crisps and listening to heavy metal on a ghetto-blaster. The inhabitants of the area were forbidden to cross the border. So were television crews; a CBS team had been shot dead by the Israelis here a month before. If they had been Americans there would have been a big fuss about it. As it was, they were Lebanese, and the fuss quickly subsided.

A hundred yards north of the Litani, in Lebanese-held territory, there was a fork in the road which led from Beirut. The main route went on to the bridge; off to the left was a small dirt track southward through the marshes and the high bamboo of the river bed. The Israelis forbade anyone to take this side-road, but rather than go through the delay and humiliation of the border crossing Lebanese people of all ages thronged down it, pushing carts and riding donkeys in full view of the soldiers, fifty yards away. With casual brutality, the Israelis raked the lane with automatic fire every twenty minutes or so. They usually hit someone.

Jean-Claude and I had left Brian back in Beirut to gather any picture material he could find, and keep a general watch over the situation. One of our drivers had brought us down and dropped us a little way from the fork in the road, just out of sight of the Israelis. We waved goodbye to him, each wondering when we would meet again, and trudged off with the camera gear towards the forbidden side-road.

The sun was hot, and insects sang loudly. We joined the flow of several dozen people, all heading in the same direction, but no one looked at us. An unpleasant quiet hung over the place, as everyone listened for the sound of gunfire. I was carrying Jean-Claude's tripod, which must have looked unpleasantly like a rocket-launcher from a distance of fifty yards. Jean-Claude carried everything else. He was quietly whistling the Brassens tune.

We had timed it reasonably well. Torpid in the heat, the Israelis held off as we passed. I could see them clearly enough through the thin cover of the bamboo, and the sound of their music came to us faintly in the heavy air. We were through the exposed stretch of lane by the time the next burst of automatic fire came. If anyone was hurt that time, I couldn't see. People were panicking and running all round us, old men and women, children, and young men who could well

Martha Gellhorn with Dee in Trafalgar Square in 1996, on the day Nelson Mandela received the freedom of the City of London. Martha has brought her Second World War binoculars to get a better look at him.

Luis Zambrano, the mayor of Tocache, a violent little drugs town in the Huallaga Valley in Peru. He had the courage to say publicly that the head of the local army base was heavily involved in the drugs trade and in torturing and murdering local people.

Dr Zekria Bakhshi, who acted as our interpreter in Afghanistan, translates an appeal for help against the brutality of the Taleban which has just been thrown into our car in the city of Herat.

When our report was broadcast, the Taleban recognized Dr Zekria from this picture and hunted him down. The British home secretary shamefully rejected his request for asylum; but thanks to the generosity of the Irish foreign minister he and his family were finally allowed to make a new life in Dublin.

Top left: Bob Prabhu at work in the Libyan capital, Tripoli. The mild-mannered scion of an Indian warrior-caste, Bob is famously brave and famously lucky. Soon after this picture was taken, he and his wife won the Lottery in a big way.

Top right: Nigel Bateson, an amiable South African giant who is usually treated with respect by the nastiest of gunmen. His trenchant good humour and immense physical strength made him a perfect companion on our Millennium Island journey.

Right: Tony Fallshaw, the quintessential Londoner: witty, clever, and full of unbounded energy, in the shadow of the ayatollahs with Dee in the Iranian city of Isfahan.

Markus Wolf, head of the East German espionage service and the most successful of Cold War spymasters. Interviewing him after the fall of the Berlin Wall, I felt sorry that he was being prosecuted by the West Germans. Then I realized that was what he intended me to feel.

Inside the KGB's secret museum. In the days immediately following the collapse of the Soviet system in August 1991 it was briefly possible to penetrate even here – but our KGB minder got nervous and stopped us just as we were trying to film the section about KGB penetration of Britain.

The car which the French cameraman Jean-Claude was driving in southern Lebanon when an Israeli army officer fired at him from close range. Only someone as tough and quick-witted as Jean-Claude could have escaped alive: he threw himself sideways and steered the car lying down.

Rhodesia/Zimbabwe, 1977: our report on a British mercenary and his tracker searching for poachers in the bush got me a job with television news.

Above, left: With Dr Marko Kardija, the Serbian surgeon who operated on my knee in a Belgrade hospital during a NATO air raid. Without his skill, I might not have walked again.

Above, right: Dragan Petrović, the mainstay of BBC television's operation in Belgrade during the NATO bombing of 1999, looking remarkably benevolent. One look at his imposing stature and close-cropped head usually calmed any hostile Serb at once.

Below: Dee with our Belgrade crew, Bata (centre) and Balša.

Celebrating Christmas on board the MS *Matangare* with Mike Donkin, Simon Wilson, Nigel Bateson, and Dee. I am holding the patent collapsible camping glass which my daughter Julia gave me; a week later it became the first receptacle on earth to celebrate the new millennium.

Millennium Island in the Pacific Ocean, on the penultimate dawn of 1999.

Dee in her millennial hat.

Me in full *Simpson's World* flow.

have been Shi'ite volunteers. Jean-Claude and I, realizing we were pretty much out of the Israelis' line of sight by now, took shelter in an olive grove, behind a low wall of crumbling grey brick. It looked like an ancient fortress. In this continuum the Egyptians could have built it, or the Crusaders; or it could just as easily have been put up by the Turks, less than a century ago.

The spring sun shone magnificently through the grey-green leaves, cutting down through the thick air. Underneath me I could feel the pebbles and the shrivelled remains of last year's ungathered olive crop, while small greyish ants clambered over us much as we had just clambered over the fortifications.

'*Gare au gor-l–l–l-ille—*'

'Don't you think you should sing a bit quieter?' I asked nervously.

'*GARE AU GORI–l–l–ILLE—*'

He raised his left fist in the direction of the Israelis, chopping the edge of his right hand into the bend of the elbow.

'You know this song of the gorilla?'

'Describe it,' I said with immense cunning, knowing that he talked quieter than he sang.

Jean-Claude summarized the verses for me. Georges Brassens' gorilla, gripped by an uncontrollable sexual urge, escapes from a zoo. The local inhabitants flee, except for a judge who thinks the gorilla couldn't possibly mistake him for a female.

'You know what the song says then? "The sequel proved him wrong."'

We only stopped laughing when there was another burst of fire, particularly long and loud, from the Israeli position at the bridge.

Jean-Claude nudged me, and pointed to a local tough who had taken cover behind an olive tree. We had come across him on the pathway, and he had stuck with us in the hope that we would protect him. He refused to help us carry the gear, though.

'He thinks the tree will protect him.'

' "The sequel proved him wrong!" ' we shouted in unison, and the youth watched us with weak hatred as we laughed at him.

But he was right to be afraid. The Litani crossing was only the start of it.

We cut back to the main road again, having skirted round the Israeli position. There was a line of Lebanese taxis from Tyre, a few miles to the south, waiting there to pick up those who had made the illegal crossing. We drove into the city which Dido had founded, a major cultural and scientific capital of the ancient world, where pictograms of ox-heads and snakes and houses were transformed into the alphabet from which every European script derives.

Now, though, it was just another featureless Third World town. Its jerry-built concrete blocks were half-destroyed by war, its streets stank of rubbish. If there was a building which was unmarked by shells and bullets, I didn't see it.

Everything in Tyre was silent: shops closed, houses shuttered. The Israelis had imposed a heavy curfew. We persuaded someone to rent us an ancient Volkswagen, noisy and ill-maintained; it was our one chance of getting up into the mountains behind Tyre, where the resistance to the Israelis was strongest. No camera crews had yet filmed there.

Jean-Claude drove. The silence was frightening, and the streets were almost entirely empty. A solitary man, nervous and hurried, came past on a bicycle.

'How do we get to the mountains?'

'You're crazy. No one's getting to the mountains. The Jews are everywhere.'

'And if we wanted to?'

'Up that way.' He pointed to a narrow road between orange groves on the slope above us. 'But you're going to be killed.'

Jean-Claude gunned up the engine, and it echoed like a shout in an empty church. We reached the outskirts of Tyre: a suburb of big, deserted mansions set in untended gardens. These places had mostly been abandoned during the civil war a decade earlier. Our Volkswagen turned into an open area, and a jeep leaped towards us from between two houses.

'*Merde alors!*' shouted Jean-Claude.

He spun the car through 90 degrees. Orange dust welled up around us, and the engine died. There was a burst of automatic fire. Grey fragments trickled from new bullet-holes in the wall above our heads.

A huge soldier got out of the jeep and walked over to us, his Uzi pointed at us. Yellow letters in Hebrew stood out on his olive-green fatigues. He was hairy, and very ugly.

'*Gare au gori–i–i–ille*,' Jean-Claude sang quietly. Even at a time like that, I smiled.

The gorilla screamed at me to get out. He kicked my legs apart and pushed me face down on the bonnet of the Volkswagen. When I protested, he kicked me harder. He wrenched at my clothes, searching for weapons.

He treated Jean-Claude the same way, and hit him when he kept on whistling. Jean-Claude didn't stop; he merely whistled under his breath.

When the gorilla saw our television gear I thought he was going to wreck the car with his bare hands. For him, television crews were as much an enemy as suicide bombers. We had no papers, so we had no rights.

'Now I'm gonna kill you,' he said.

He meant it.

The sheer ordinariness of everything came flooding over me: the cinder-block wall with the tatters of an old poster on it, the white Volkswagen clicking in the heat, the smell of dust and oil, the reddish earth. No, I thought; dying is important and significant and special. It can't happen somewhere as ordinary as this. Not to me.

And then another man got out of the jeep: younger, smaller, listening to a Walkman. He came and stood between me and the gorilla with the gun, and put his headphones over my head. I could hear familiar, silly music.

' "My Word," ' said an announcer's voice. 'A radio panel game, in which people whose business is words—'

It was the BBC World Service.

'No killing today,' said the soldier, and took his headphones back. 'Come, Shimon.'

Shimon lowered his Uzi reluctantly.

'Next time,' he rumbled.

I thought of the Lebanese paramilitary officer who had cut my face. This kind of thing seemed to happen rather too often to me in Lebanon.

We were held prisoner for a few hours, then released: the senior Israeli officers had more important things to worry about. Israel was getting ready to withdraw from Tyre. We drove off, found a useful vantage point, and filmed their preparations. We also filmed them blowing up a car bomb they'd discovered. These were excellent pictures, and I decided I had to get them back to Beirut in order to send them to London that night. I told Jean-Claude he should stay behind and get more pictures.

He thought I was pulling out and leaving him.

'I'll be back tomorrow,' I said.

'Sure.'

'Look, I mean it.'

'Sure.'

He grinned, and tried to show he didn't mind.

He drove me to the spot where the forbidden side-road met the main road north out of Tyre, just out of sight of the soldiers on the bridge over the Litani.

Jean-Claude shook my hand, gripping my elbow with his left. We had grown close as a result of our day's experiences. I stood in the red dust and watched the battered white Volkswagen turn and drive back to Tyre. Jean-Claude waved for a while, his arm sticking out of the car window like a railway signal.

I made it along the path in safety. There was the sound of distant shooting, but it didn't come from the soldiers on the bridge. They stayed quiet as I made my way nervously past them through the bamboo plants. After a difficult journey back to Beirut, I handed the videotapes to Brian Murray. He greeted me as though I had returned from the dead. We edited our report, and sent it by car to Damascus where it was satellited to London. It was a big success: many other television organizations around the world picked it up and broadcast it.

At midnight Jean-Claude phoned. He had been trying to get through for four hours. He told me that directly he had driven off in the Volkswagen he had come across an Israeli patrol. They apparently had orders to fire at any unaccompanied driver in a car, on the grounds that he could be a suicide bomber. At thirty yards they must have seen the big Press sign we had made and stuck to the windscreen, but they fired anyway.

The first two bullets had entered the car low down and on the right. Jean-Claude threw himself down on the seat, and another bullet which hit the windscreen directly in front of the driver's seat also missed him. His handsome leather jerkin, which had been lying on the back shelf, had a bullet-hole through the shoulder. The Volkswagen ended up in a ditch, but apart from a bruised knee Jean-Claude was fine.

I had always intended to go back the next day anyway, but this settled it. The journey down the following morning was just as difficult as before: the shooting, the nervous walk down the forbidden side-road, the problem of finding a taxi into Tyre. It was worse doing it on my own.

Once I reached Tyre, I had a great deal of difficulty locating Jean-Claude. Eventually, though, I came across someone who had seen him filming a few minutes before. My taxi took me round there. Jean-Claude hadn't been expecting me to come back, and he gripped my hand with sentimental warmth. Then he showed me the bullet-holes in the Volkswagen. They were much worse than I had imagined. Each had been intended to kill.

'*Gare au gori–i-i–ille . . .*'

The day was glorious. This time no one stopped us as we drove towards the mountains. Larks hung in the scented air, bees clambered into the heavy orange-blossom like mountaineers. We filmed everything we wanted: the villages destroyed by Israeli reprisal raids, the casualties, the young volunteers being trained for further suicide missions. They had never seen a Western television team here before, and there had been nothing like this on Western television. Jean-Claude was at his best, cheerful, inventive, funny. He sang the gorilla song all the time.

'You know,' he said, 'two things make me happy – beautiful women and beautiful pictures.'

'You sound like a really bad French film director,' I said.

We tried to get back that evening, but things had changed. The road from Tyre to Beirut had been blocked below the line of the Litani River. There was a long line of trucks waiting to cross. The Israelis had made the drivers stand in a line, and when one of them had stepped forward a soldier shot him dead. We got there before the blood was dry.

Going back to Tyre in the fading afternoon light was particularly dangerous, and the man who was driving us was terrified.

'Allah,' he groaned.

Jean-Claude laughed unsympathetically. 'You're getting a hundred dollars for this,' he said. 'You should be happy.'

'Allah.'

He was a decent man, though, and offered us beds for the night. His small, bustling, shapeless wife made us dinner and, as we ate the *tabouleh*, the *fule medames* and the mutton, his two daughters, dark and silent, watched us.

Jean-Claude watched them.

'My night may not be undisturbed,' he said as we finished. 'You know the song of The Gorilla?'

'I'm starting to by now.'

'When the gorilla comes out to violate the town, it isn't only the judge who stays. There is also a centenarian lady. She says, "To think that a gorilla would attack me is impossible, and besides it's completely unhoped for." When I was stationed in Oran a group of us got drunk one night and—'

'I don't want to hear this,' I said forcefully.

I decided that we must get a message back to Beirut to explain why we hadn't returned. Already, as I guessed, the word had gone round that we were missing, and people thought we had either been shot by the Israelis or kidnapped by fundamentalists. Soon the story would reach London.

During the day, to cover their retreat, the Israelis had destroyed the already tenuous phone links between Tyre and Beirut. Now, someone said, the only way of getting a message through was to get the Lebanese civil defence force to put it on their citizens' band radio.

Stumbling over the broken pavements in the utter darkness of the night, anxious about Israeli patrols in the curfew, we found our way to the civil defence headquarters. The volunteers were sitting in their hot staff room playing cards. A picture of Lebanon's evanescent President hung on the wall: the civil defence force was the only national organization left in being in Lebanon, in these fractured days.

They had a real *esprit de corps*, though, and seemed glad to do something useful. One man fetched me a pad and pencil to write my message, and the other got on to the radio to the next post up the coast. Their CB radio sets, they explained, had only a short range, but the message would be passed from one post to another until it reached Beirut. I decided to keep the message simple:

'*I am safe in Tyre. Returning tomorrow. John.*'

That night I slept well. Whether Jean-Claude did, given the two dark daughters, I didn't know. None of them would look at each other over the breakfast table the next morning.

' "Completely unhoped for?" ' I asked.

Jean-Claude guffawed, but didn't answer.

Our trip back to Beirut was easy enough. There was only intermittent shooting at the Litani bridge, and the faithful BBC driver was waiting for us on the other side.

'Always knowing you come, Mr John,' he said, but he seemed relieved.

Back in Beirut we were heroes: the only journalists to have seen the Israeli withdrawal from Tyre and to have met and filmed the Islamic resistance.

'Got your message,' Brian Murray said, giving my hand a particularly enthusiastic shake. 'I liked the pun.'

'Pun?'

He picked up a grubby piece of paper, the result of five or six rounds of Chinese whispers up the coast of Lebanon, and handed it to me.

'*I am safe and entire,*' it said.

Our trip was effectively over. Brian and I began packing up, and we said our goodbyes to Jean-Claude.

'You might be a fascist bastard,' I told him, 'but I had a great time.'

' "Completely unhoped for", perhaps.'

'Not at all.'

He pulled off the leather jerkin with the bullet-hole in the shoulder.

'This is yours. You must keep it.'

I put it on, and watched the tough, compact figure walking away, turning occasionally to wave. He might be cynical and unsentimental, but I knew I could always rely on him. Besides, we were two of a kind: at odds with the world, determined to get back on terms with it. For both of us, our partnership had been an important part of that process.

A few weeks later I was walking through the newsroom in London when the foreign duty editor called out to me.

'Isn't this your mate?'

He held out a piece of agency copy.

It was a despatch from Beirut. A French cameraman, Jean-Claude Ortoli, had been kidnapped at gunpoint near the Mayflower Hotel in the western part of the city. Islamic fundamentalists were thought to be responsible, but so far no ransom demand had been made.

As I stood there with the piece of paper in my hand the thought flashed across my mind: I'm sorry for those poor swine; they don't know what they've taken on. Then immediately I corrected myself: No, it's Jean-Claude I should be worried about. I started drafting an appeal for his release, which I sent to his former employees in French television. They were distinctly uninterested. The BBC didn't seem particularly enthusiastic either. Freelances can't expect much help from big, comfortable organizations if they get into trouble; maybe they prefer it that way.

On the third day the foreign duty editor handed me another news agency despatch from Beirut: 'A French television cameraman Jean-Claude Ortoli who was kidnapped by Islamic fundamentalists outside his hotel in West Beirut three days ago reappeared this morning. He had escaped from his captors during the night.'

Over the next few hours more details emerged; I had been absolutely right to worry about the men who had captured him. Under cover of a violent thunderstorm Jean-Claude had prised a cinder-block from the wall of the outhouse where he was being held. He had made the hole big enough to climb through, and had then crept up behind the man who was supposed to be guarding him and smashed his head in. As I say, Jean-Claude was a tough character. He stopped a car and turned up at his hotel, wet through but still laughing, half an hour later.

I sent him a telex of congratulation, and received his reply the next morning:

'The sequel proved them wrong. Fraternal regards. Jean-Claude.'

I knew what he meant by 'fraternal': we might be down on our luck, but we were both fighting back.

*

A lot can change in five years. I became the head of the BBC's foreign reporting, turned freelance, and wrote for the *Spectator*. When Saddam Hussein invaded Kuwait I made my way to Baghdad and based myself there.

One afternoon in November 1990, two months before the Gulf War broke out, I wandered over to the Baghdad Sheraton to see what, if anything, was happening there. In the foyer stood a fountain in neo-Saddamist style: Soviet realism crossed with Babylonian mysticism. It was dreadful. The goddess Ishtar, life-sized, poured the water of life into the fountain's basin. When it worked it was noisy, and the water wasn't of the cleanest. It wasn't working now. I preferred the Sheraton to the Al-Rashid, where the government insisted we had to stay. It was easier to tell who was doing the spying in the Sheraton, and which rooms had the microphones.

As I walked in, I saw a man sitting on the edge of the fountain, reading *Paris-Match*. There was something distinctly familiar about his bullet-shaped head with its low scrub of grey hair. The head turned: Jean-Claude Ortoli's reflexes were still as sharp as when he had been a para sergeant in Oran. A lot of hand-shaking and shoulder-patting followed. All around the lobby, eyes watched our reunion.

He had done as well as I had. After his coverage of Tyre and the escape from the kidnappers his old television company had offered him another contract; not just as a cameraman, but as bureau chief. An attractive young Lebanese woman came up and fussed around him.

'My assistant,' he said.

'So I see.'

We laughed.

It didn't take long for us both to establish how our fortunes had improved. Somehow after that the conversation dried up, like Ishtar's fountain. The watchers turned back to their copies of *Al-Thawra*.

'Remember this?' I asked, to break the silence. I whistled a few bars of *Le Gorille*.

'*Gare au gori–i–i–ille*,' he sang, and the *Al-Thawras* were lowered again.

'The sequel proved him wrong,' I said, nodding to the big mandatory portrait of Saddam Hussein on the far wall, and we laughed again while the spooks watched us and the beautiful Lebanese girl, mystified, picked up the empty coffee cup by his side.

'I've been thinking of trying to get down through the desert to Kuwait,' he said after another moment or two of silence.

'Me too,' I said.

'We might be able to do it together.' His forefinger pointed to me, then back to himself. 'It'd be great. Just like in the past.'

But I knew it was a different world from 1985 in Lebanon. You do that sort of thing when you have nothing to lose; both of us had plenty to lose now.

A young Frenchman came up, loaded with television equipment. Jean-Claude had someone else to do the camera work and carry the gear. The attractive producer murmured something about an interview which had to be done, and Jean-Claude nodded. We shook hands with the same old warmth, and promised to keep in touch.

It was the last time I saw him.

A few months later I was walking across Hyde Park, on my way to the Hyde Park Hotel for a little something to cheer me up. In fact it is something of an exaggeration to say that I was walking; I was crawling along, dragging my heels and feeling as you do feel if you are recovering from the combined effects of kidney stones and some cracked ribs. These things were the result of working in Baghdad during the Gulf War.

'Great to see you looking fit and well,' said a cheery voice.

I moved my head with a certain difficulty and focused slowly on the voice's owner. Thin chap, handsome but elderly, disturbingly active. He kept hopping from one foot to another, and seemed to be wearing a tracksuit.

'Middle of my fifth mile,' he confided. 'Big tennis match this afternoon. Queen's.'

'Ah.'

'Extraordinary coincidence, meeting you like this.' He kept on hopping. 'Been talking to a scriptwriter about your thing in the *Guardian*. Ages ago.'

'Article?'

'You wrote about your time in Lebanon, getting taken hostage, escaping, all that kind of thing. Gorillas featured a lot.'

'Well, that wasn't really me. It was more the cam—'

'So Ralphie and I have been turning it into a film script. Need your permission, of course.'

He was still hopping. Bursting with energy, as though he'd found a way of syphoning off mine as well. The accent was upper-middle English, with a side-order of upper-middle American.

'Got the money. Well, I say got, the backer's given us all the necessary undertakings. You know how it goes.'

I might have guessed, but I didn't. The thought that someone might think me interesting enough to make a film about swept away what was left of my critical faculties like the Severn Bore. I suddenly felt quite active and inclined to hop myself. Rejuvenating business, the cinema.

'You'll have heard of the films Ralphie and I have made.'

He listed five, of which I had only heard of two. But those were really quite big, and still got an occasional showing.

'If you agree, send you a treatment. Oh, and a contract of course. Worth a good quarter mil to you.'

I wrote down my address and phone number, with an energy I thought had left me for ever. Two minutes later I could still just see his dark blue tracksuit between the distant trees.

He did get in touch, and we had a script conference.

'Rented this place for a few days, knock things around.'

I hadn't known people lived like this. It was quite superb: one vast room with a beautiful kitchen, a bathroom with marble and gold, a small gym and a large bed all in different alcoves. The Emperor Caracalla would have felt well set up here; and indeed a bust of him – Parian marble, not plaster – presided suitably over the sleeping area.

We knocked things around; which meant that the two of them put forward suggestions about presenting my story for the screen, I objected, and they went ahead and wrote them down.

'So the cocaine dealer—'

'Well, in Lebanon it's really more heroin. Dope too, of course.'

'Of course. Good thinking. Point taken. Absolutely, eh, Ralphie?'

'Sorry?'

'John's point.'

'Oh, yes, totally. One hundred per cent. Heroin and dope. Quite right. But my point was that the cocaine dealer should get involved in kidnapping foreigners. One of those big groups, you know the ones.'

'Hamas? Hezbollah?'

'Whatever. Mixed up with drugs anyway.'

'Well, they don't really—'

'Because you see it needs something a little more up-to-date for the US market. All this hostage stuff, you know, highly important and all that, but needs something for an American audience to get its teeth into.'

'Or nose.'

'Ha, ha. Very good, that. We're agreed, then?'

'Well, I—'

'Who would you like to play your part? Day-Lewis? Too type-cast? Mikie Douglas does a very good English accent. Cost us, of course.'

'I—'

'Always sort it out later.'

It was plain the serious work could only start once I'd gone. I'd scarcely got stuck into the oysters and smoked salmon before Ralphie was letting me know they'd send me a copy of the script treatment directly the brainstorming was over. It wouldn't, clearly, be my brain which was to be stormed.

The finished product arrived a couple of weeks later. Outside, it was sensational: a kind of marbled antique Italian work, of the kind you get in shops off the Piazza San Marco. I kept it for years, to put old receipts in. Inside, the typing was beautiful. But as an account of my adventures in Lebanon with Jean-Claude, it lacked a certain verisimilitude.

It turned out that I (or Jack Halliday, as my character was to be called) was having wife-trouble. He lived in the Nash terrace at the end of Portland Place. ('Handy for Broadcasting House. Oh, I thought you worked there. Well, no matter, the audience won't know. Most of them won't have heard of the BBC anyhow. No, probably not London either. Ha, ha.') One night, alone in the gorgeous drawing room and listening to Brahms ('Or Mahler, perhaps. Your thoughts, Ralphie?'). Jack hears a car draw up, and looks out of the elegant Regency window. ('Lamborghini, we thought: puts it into the right context.') A gorgeously stockinged leg appears, as the driver gives Jack's wife a last, lingering kiss. This, it seemed, was the treatment of the break-up of my marriage in bourgeois Wimbledon. ('Bit, well, how shall we say, *everyday*?')

I forget now how the rest went on. Jean-Claude was American, of course. You don't often find Americans working as cameramen in dangerous places nowadays, except in the movies. I think it ended badly for him and well for me, though it might have been the other way round, and there was a beautiful sultry woman in it somewhere.

Then things changed. A French billionaire put up some cash for the film, and Jean-Claude was back in. For a while, at any rate.

I had quite a lot to do with the athletic Maurice afterwards, none of it good, and he never said a word to me about 'A Song for Gorillas' again. Life, for him, was a Darwinian selection of deals, one or two of which occasionally came up while the rest collapsed. Prospects of success and money and fame flickered for a while on the screen of his existence, and were succeeded by something else. That I never saw a contract goes without saying.

In a way, I felt quite good about it all. I wasn't going to be a cinema hero, but all this had made my life seem positively sane and down-to-earth by comparison.

The Romanian revolution was over, and the ruins had ceased to smoulder. Nicolae and Elena Ceauşescu, executed in a hail of bullets by twenty panicky soldiers on Christmas Day, had been in their cold graves for six nights. It was New Year's Eve 1989, and I was going to party.

I strode alone across the cobbles of Georgiou-Dej Square in Bucharest, my feet crackling on broken glass and bits of smashed brick. This was where the camera crew and I had rolled in the gutter, bullets cracking and hissing a few feet above our heads, while the fighting was at its height. Much later I came back and discovered, by talking to some of the key figures of the revolution, that everything had been carefully organized behind closed doors beforehand, and that most of the bloodshed had been entirely unnecessary. At the time, though, the violence had seemed genuine enough, and we were lucky to have escaped uninjured. More cameramen and reporters were killed during the few days of the Romanian revolution than at any similar period since the end of the Second World War.

I looked back. On the other side of the darkened square the ruins of the National Library stuck out jaggedly into the night sky and I could see the stars through the burned roof beams. Heaps of broken brick, fallen stone and ruined books lay on the cobbles in front of it: as gloomy and disheartening a sight as it was possible to imagine. Yet I chuckled to myself as I remembered how angry I had been at the sight of army tanks firing from close range at the library. Apparently someone thought a sniper might be firing from the roof.

'Stop that at once,' I had shouted at the officer commanding the tanks, like a passing busybody wading in to stop children fighting.

The officer, his eyes red with sleeplessness and strain, screamed in a spray of saliva that he would shoot me if I continued to get in his way. I made angry noises in order to preserve a certain dignity, but I slipped off quickly. In that time of lawlessness and violence, anything could happen.

Now the city was silent, and more or less safe. All the same, I had to walk carefully: the cobbles were frozen and covered with a thin layer of snow. I remembered a line from a guidebook about this square, written when Ceauşescu's hold on Romania was so total as to make any suggestion of revolution seem an impossibility. It described this with remarkable prescience as a brooding sort of place, waiting for a coup d'état to happen: which is precisely what did take place in December 1989.

Ahead of me I could see the magnificently seedy Athenée Palace Hotel, its windows throwing out golden light onto the square. It looked so welcoming and warm that I could almost forget its bad reputation. There must have been a bigger concentration of secret policemen, spies and informers in the Athenée Palace than in any comparable building on earth in its day; and its day had ended only a week before. Now, though, the spies and informers were all desperate to show how they had always been democrats at heart; and they grovelled to the kind of people they had previously preyed upon.

We could, I reflected as I pushed my way through the handsome 1930s swing door, expect decent service tonight.

Not that I left my coat, scarf and hat in the cloakroom in the magnificent art deco entrance hall. The revolution had been a time of unprecedented theft, and it wasn't over yet. The man on duty at the door to the restaurant looked at me with old-fashioned Central European disapproval as I carried my things over my arm, regarded as an uncultured thing to do in every European city east of Berlin, but he remembered himself and his position, and turned unctuous. The Western journalists who had once been his natural prey might, after all, turn out to be his protectors. His dark yellow teeth showed in an informer's smile.

The heat and noise, the cigarette smoke, the smell of food and sweat and damp clothes combined in a single powerful force, battering my cold face, assaulting my senses, so that at first I felt like pushing my way out again and getting back into the silent, dark street. A small band was playing Christmas music, and across the main part of the restaurant was draped a vast scarlet banner of the kind that would once have proclaimed one of Ceauşescu's empty slogans.

Carelessly produced, this now warned us in the Romanian language, that mixture of dog-Latin and Esperanto, to have a felicitous Noel; it was the only official Christmas in Romania for forty of the longest years in human history. For the first time in the memory of any Romanian there, except perhaps the oldest of the hobbling waiters, there was a Christmas tree at the far end of the restaurant. It was decorated with red bunting also borrowed from some Communist purpose, and the red stars on it were Marxist ones.

The tables were jammed. People with greedy, sweating faces sat squeezed together, laughing coarsely: diplomats, foreign journalists and Romanian black marketeers, a few hookers, an army officer or two. No one else could afford to be there. To me, still cold from the silent world outside, it felt like stumbling into a Berlin nightclub in the 1920s. It had cost the organizer of our party tonight thirty dollars (a lot of money in Ceauşescu's Romania) merely to get a table for us, but for once there was enough food. A few days earlier the special stores of the Communist Party and the secret police, the Securitate, had been thrown open to the people.

The waiters edged their way between the tables with the care and skill of toreadors, trays high above their heads, avoiding the careless movements of elbows and arms, turning neatly. The lead violinist in the band was playing the first few bars of 'Rudolf The Red-Nosed Reindeer' when, through the blue-grey atmosphere of cigarette smoke, I glimpsed a couple of my friends sitting at the far end of the restaurant, and pushed through the diners to join them. It took me a while.

I recognized only three of the eight people sitting round the table, but there was an easy relationship between journalists in those dangerous days which transcended the differences of nationality, age and general attitude. We had nothing much in common except that we all worked for television, and had spent the last few days huddled together from the bullets, or trying to force our way into places where we weren't wanted. One of the people there had stayed with my producer when she had had to cross an open space near the television station over which a gun battle was being fought. Another had asked me to take his video cassettes back to the hotel for him when he was filming a lynching. A third was one of my own colleagues.

They greeted me warmly and ironically, and I shook hands with the rest, who grinned at me. I could see from their faces that a bottle of the evil colourless spirit produced in Romania had already gone the rounds. Only one man, a stocky Flemish cameraman in his early thirties, with a carefully tended and mildly absurd moustache, said nothing and scarcely looked at me as he mechanically took my hand. His eyes turned back to the red and green table decorations.

'*Pas la peine de lui poser des questions,*' said a dark, unshaven, saturnine Frenchman whose car I had shared on the drive from Belgrade to Bucharest a week before. He indicated the Flemish cameraman with his chin. 'No point in asking Dirk anything. He's lost his best friend.'

The table went quiet. A Turkish correspondent had been shot at a roadblock a night or two earlier, and a French photojournalist had died under the tracks of a tank not long before that. There had been others.

'His camera,' the Frenchman finished off.

When the laughter finally died down, Dirk was still silent. No sign of amusement.

'*Ce p'tit type,*' said the Frenchman pitilessly, putting his arm round Dirk's shoulder, 'has just watched a thirty thousand dollar camera break into pieces before his eyes.'

Another cameraman winced audibly. The rest of us, correspondents who had no professional equipment beyond a small tape-recorder or a portable computer, shook our heads in sympathy. For the first time since I had arrived Dirk looked round the table, and when I looked into his face I remembered I had seen him in action in one or two places; the moustache was unforgettable. He was a morose man by nature, inclined to push others out of his way and disinclined to say sorry. He must have been good, though, judging from the places I had seen him. No one hires a cameraman to go to Tiananmen Square unless he has proved himself. His voice was harsh and low, and I had to lean forward to catch what he was saying above the shouting and laughter from the tables around us.

'That camera had become evil.'

His English was thick and heavily accented, but like most young Flemish people nowadays he spoke it colloquially.

We avoided each other's eyes. 'Evil' is a word you associate with religious fundamentalists, rather than television cameramen. It has not become debased with over-usage, like 'wonderful' or 'incredible' or 'appalling'; it still means what it says. In this atmosphere of carelessness and indulgence it was an embarrassment.

Dirk seemed not to notice the sudden awkwardness. I had never heard him say more than twenty consecutive words before, but now it became impossible to stop him; not that we would have wanted to. The sweating waiters continued to labour around us, the surrounding racket from the other diners was as loud as ever, and the band had moved on to gypsy music; but as in a film the background noise seemed to dip down below the level of Dirk's thick, quiet voice as we listened to him.

His story was a curious and rather horrible one, but I knew enough about some of the details to feel certain that it was broadly accurate. Here I have had to change some of the details: too many friends and relatives of the people involved are still alive. But those who sat with me over dinner that night at the Athenée Palace Hotel in Bucharest and listened to him will understand the alterations I have made.

'I loved that camera.'

Dirk arranged his waiting dinner plate absently, so that the blood-red bust of Athena decorating its rim was exactly at the top.

'It was the first one I ever owned. I had to re-mortgage my house and lie about my life insurance to get it. Nowadays I've got a Beta SP, which is a whole lot better. But I've always brought the other one along with me when I come on a big story like this. Maybe the new one will go down, or maybe I can hire out the old one. There's always someone who needs a camera, and it makes good money for me. Made.

'But after I went to Haiti I started to change my feelings about it. We were interviewing the President, the one who came after Baby Doc, I don't remember his name, and I had to leave it with the guards for twenty-four hours so they could check it for security. When it came back it was changed. I don't mean it was covered in chicken's blood or anything stupid like that. I know it must sound weird, but it felt *heavier*. Even though when I weighed it at the airport it was exactly the same. But when you carry something around with you all day you get to know these things. It was changed, that's all.

'And another thing: something had happened to the electronics. It would shift into wide-angle, or stop down, or do other things I didn't mean it to do. And yet the pictures were great. They were just different from what I'd intended. Can you understand that?'

Maybe some of the others who were sitting there listening to him so intently did; I couldn't. Still, you could see that Dirk was utterly certain of what he was saying. His moroseness had somehow dropped away now, and there was an urgency about him which was almost touching: as if he really cared that we should understand what he was saying, and had to follow him detail by detail.

Our elderly waiter broke in to ask if we wanted another bottle of the thick, sherry-like red wine. Someone nodded at him impatiently. We were starting to lose our appetites now, though our plates with the head of Athena on them were still empty. Our attention was concentrated on Dirk.

'I first realized there was something seriously wrong with the camera when we were working in Nicaragua. We were up north with the Sandinistas near Jalapa, and there were Contras in the area. Lots of them. You remember those days, how bad that could be.

'There was a woman in charge of the Sandinista patrol, and she took us up a hill near the Contras' camp. The others stayed behind, but she crawled forward with me through bushes, and we saw half a dozen Contras only a few yards away, sitting round a fire. They weren't taking any notice of us – I guess they were preparing a meal.

'I switched on and focused up.'

His hand, on the table, made the movements instinctively.

'The camera was running normally. I was looking through the viewfinder, nothing more. I didn't touch anything. And then it just ejected the cassette. You know how much noise that can make.

'They started firing at us in a moment. The Sandinista girl was hit, and I took a bullet in the arm just as we got back into the bushes. The rest of our patrol gave us covering fire and we were all right. Got some good pictures after that. But it was weird.

'Everyone kept saying I must have pushed the wrong button, but I knew I hadn't. You know about those things – you can feel afterwards in your fingers if you've done them. When I got back to Brussels a friend of mine looked at the camera, and he said there was some kind of electronic stop to prevent the camera ejecting, and it was still operating. But he said he thought the camera felt kind of heavier than it should. He stripped it down to the board, but couldn't work out why.

'The girl? Oh, she was fine in the end, just hit in the hand. She'd got plenty of scars anyway. She was great about it, believed me when I said it wasn't anything to do with me, though the others didn't. They didn't like television anyway. We went back to Managua to get my arm seen to – that wasn't too bad either, though it's still stiffer than it used to be.'

He stretched it out, and showed us the scar: an inoffensive little white dent in the forearm.

'The other thing I think about that camera is that it always seemed to make you do the wrong thing. It fooled you in some way. And it made other people do the wrong thing too. Did I tell you that, when I was lying on the ground with the blood pumping out of my arm, everyone just left me there? Even the other journalists.

'The Sandinista girl starting screaming and saying they had to get her to hospital, even though she just had a slight graze on her hand, and everyone just went off and forgot about me. I managed to make

a tourniquet out of one of my camera leads and get it round my arm
and stop the bleeding, but it was difficult. And I was really frightened
the Contras were going to find me lying there.

'In the end everyone came back, and the Sandinista girl said how
sorry she was, and how she couldn't think what had come over her.
But it started me thinking: so many things going wrong, so many
people doing what they wouldn't normally do. And I thought,
suppose it was the camera? Crazy thought, but I couldn't get it out
of my head after that.

'Anyway, when I was in the hospital in Managua a friend of mine
from Dutch television came and asked me if he could rent out the
camera. Well, these things were still just ideas, just suspicions; I
couldn't be certain. And money is money. So I said OK.

'He and his sound recordist went to Salvador. They had some
hotshot correspondent with them, who always had to stay behind
and make phone calls when they went out on patrol with the army.
Afterwards he used to do his here-I-am-in-the-middle-of-the-firefight
stand-up in the bushes round the back of the hotel.'

For the first time since Dirk had started talking, there was
laughter round the table. Most of the cameramen there had worked
with people like that, or felt they had; it was part of the cameraman's
self-image to see himself as the only one who was really prepared to
take risks. I laughed because the others were laughing, and I could
see that the same was true of the saturnine Frenchman. Our eyes met.
I thought I could read into his something of the same feeling of
disturbance that I was experiencing myself. The trouble with Dirk's
story, absurd and fantastical though it was, was that it seemed rather
plausible. What next, I thought? Haunted television studios? Polter-
geists in the word processor?

The waiter interrupted us. He carried an enormous, battered
metal tray over his head and put it down on the table in front of us.
There were dishes of carp and red cabbage, and potatoes done in
some way that the Athenée Palace prided itself on. I suppose it was
all really good, yet I scarcely glanced at it. Nor did anyone else round
the table. The waiter dished it out for us and went off muttering.
Dirk didn't even look at his plate.

'Anyway, this Dutch crew were ambushed by the guerrillas when they were out with the army, and got some beautiful stuff. They were filming a soldier lying beside them, and he rolled over just like in a Hollywood film to change his magazine, and a line of bullets cut up the ground right where he'd been lying. The look on his face should have got them an award, the sound recordist said.

'And then, just as the army was telling them it was time to move out, the cameraman said, "No, I'm getting some great material here." And he stood up and moved out of cover.

'The sound-man told me afterwards that he was still hooked up to him, and he could see there was nothing to film. Nothing whatever. Just a few rocks and some scrubby trees. The guerrilla positions were completely hidden. Of course the sound-man tried to pull him back – well, you can imagine – but he kept on going.

'He was hit eight times in all, and the bastards from the army ran for it and left him there. The sound-man stayed with him till he died a couple of hours later: the guerrillas didn't do anything to them, just stood round and watched. They didn't have any medical gear with them, and even if they had, there's not much you can do about a man with no stomach and not much of a head left. In the end they let the sound-man go. They even let him take the camera with him.

'I was making enough money to get another camera by now: my Beta SP. I was starting to get really superstitious about the old one. Maybe you can imagine. But somehow I couldn't just get rid of it: earning too much money from it, I suppose. I didn't use it myself, I just rented it out. I know what you must be thinking, but I still couldn't prove anything. Sometimes people behave in a crazy way. It doesn't have to be because they've got a camera with them that's somehow gone wrong. And anyway I didn't hear of any other problems with it. I suppose I thought it had all been my imagination anyway.

'Well, I got here the day Ceauşescu went out on his balcony and got howled down. I was just working for myself – hadn't got anything fixed up by the time I reached Bucharest, though within half an hour I had half a dozen calls from people desperate for pictures. Especially the BBC.'

I grinned, remembering just how desperate we had been before my colleagues and I arrived. There was a murmur of amusement around the table: everybody there had competed with, or worked for, the BBC at some time, and as a result they didn't always like us. Dirk didn't smile; he never did.

'So I was standing in the lobby of the InterCon, thinking that someone would ask me to do something. And the first person who came along was a guy from Turkish TV. It turned out they were staying on the same floor as me, and they'd seen that I had two cameras. Theirs had developed a fault in some way. They needed another one badly, so I rented my old one out to them. I don't suppose you think very much of that, any of you.'

No one answered. We knew now what was coming.

'Anyway, because I knew what the camera could do, I said I'd go with them. I don't know why: just a bad conscience, maybe. This was a few nights ago, and we were out filming near the TV station. You know how bad it is round there: each time I've tried to get in there the soldiers have threatened to shoot me. They're totally paranoid and really scared – especially the young ones.

'There was a house opposite that was burning, and the Turks wanted to do a stand-up, a piece to camera, whatever you like to call it, with the house in the background. That's what they wanted my camera for. I'd mounted a light on top of it, but I said to them, "Don't switch it on because you'll get us all shot." They just laughed; you know how gung-ho those bloody Turks can be.

'Well, it was really creepy there, with the fire still burning. You couldn't see them, but there were soldiers everywhere, and maybe Securitate snipers in some of the empty houses as well. That's what the soldiers thought, anyway. You could feel the glass crackling under our feet as we walked along. You never know how much noise to make – whether to creep around so they won't notice you, or make a racket so they'll all know you're there. I can tell you, I was getting pretty scared. And I kept feeling, there's nothing for me to do; I'm only here to make sure the camera doesn't do anything wrong.'

Dirk paused. He had completely ignored the food on the plate in front of him, and the rest of us picked at ours. The carp was fine: it was just that you couldn't concentrate on eating when a story like this was unfolding. The gypsy violins were squealing in a schmaltzy way, and the people at the next table were singing a drunken Christmas carol in competition.

Our table was completely silent. Dirk began to speak again, more slowly now, his pale blue eyes fixed on the plastic roses in the vase in the middle, among the half-finished dishes. He was back there, in the darkness and the cold outside the television station.

'The Turkish correspondent was a good man. He started speaking to camera, holding the mike in front of him. I remember he kept asking whether the logo on it was visible, and brushing his hair back because of the wind. The flames from the house behind him were starting to die down, but there was still plenty of light from them to show his face properly. The cameraman told him it was fine, that there was still plenty of light from the fire, but he'd better hurry up.

'I guess he was nervous. That's understandable. I couldn't understand what he was saying, but he fouled up several times, and each time he got more upset with himself. Finally he looked over at me as I was standing there next to his cameraman, and said, "Sorry, this will be the last one." I suppose he didn't feel he had to say sorry to his own crew, but he did to me because I was an outsider.

'So he started again. He'd got maybe fifteen seconds in, when the camera light came on. You know how brilliant that is. It blotted out everything else in that darkness, even the burning house. I knew the cameraman couldn't have switched it on: I'd have seen him reach up and do it. It had just come on of its own accord.

'There was only one shot, and it came from quite close by. The correspondent went down in a heap. We were all shouting and screaming, and the cameraman switched the light off. He kept saying, "It wasn't me, it wasn't me," meaning the light, I suppose. He didn't shout or anything. There was kind of a surprise in his voice, like he couldn't take in what had happened.

'The soldiers stayed where they were, and didn't do anything to help. They knew he was a journalist, that he hadn't been threatening anybody, but they shot him anyway. He died right there on the ground in front of us. Can you imagine what it felt like, to be listening to him, a nice, easy-going young guy like that, while he choked and drowned on his own blood, looking up at us as though we could do something to stop it? And to *know* why it had happened?'

Dirk's face was white and strained, his eyes were still on the plastic roses, and his hand was clenching and unclenching on the unclean tablecloth. I just thought two things: the first was he'll never get over that moment, and the second was thank God it wasn't me that died.

'I picked up the camera and just left them all there. They could deal with the correspondent – he was their man, they didn't need me to help them. I went off carrying the camera. I wanted to find a way of destroying it, grinding it down to nothing, so that whatever was in it would die with it. I wanted it to be vicious and painful. I wanted revenge of some kind. And maybe I wanted to feel absolved too. You see, I knew it was really my fault. I had to pay for what I'd done.

'I had no idea what to do, so I started walking to the centre of town. The camera felt heavier than ever, and I had to keep shifting it from hand to hand. You'll think I'm really crazy now, but I felt it knew it was going to be destroyed, and it was fighting back. There really was something that had got into it: something evil, with a mind of its own. Into a thing like a television camera: can you have any comprehension of that? Even now I wonder if I wasn't just mad. But there was the evidence of all the things the camera had done, and lured other people into doing. That wasn't my imagination, even if the weight of it was.

'It was getting harder and harder to carry, and I started to be afraid that it would make me do something suicidal. I knew I had to keep tight control over myself, not to do anything sudden, not to throw my life away because the camera had identified me as its enemy. Now I really do sound crazy. But I promise you that's how it seemed as I walked along.

'Well, I got to that aviation monument in the middle of the boulevard, with the woods on one side: you all know it. And there I heard tanks coming. They were heading into town, along the boulevard. Suddenly I didn't feel afraid of anything any more – not the army, not even the camera. It came to me what I had to do, and I didn't care if I was killed doing it. I was just angry.

'As the lead tank in the column came alongside me, I ran out and put the camera down in the road, directly in the path of the tank-tracks. I thought for a moment I wouldn't be able to get there, the camera felt so heavy; but I did, and I threw myself back onto the pavement, out of the tank's way.

'I don't suppose the driver even felt it. And with all the grinding and squealing that the tank-tracks made, I couldn't hear the noise when it got crushed. But a weird thing happened: as the track went over the camera the lens jumped out into the air, as though it had been squeezed out of it. It must have gone up at least as high as the top of the tank. Then it came down and smashed on the ground, right by my feet. I moved away fast, I can tell you, because I didn't want to get even a sliver of it on me.

'Three tanks went over the camera altogether; it wasn't much more than powder when they'd gone. I stood there looking for a moment or two, but it got too quiet and I was scared. Angry and relieved too, and guilty. I suppose I'll always feel guilty now. But anyway, that's what happened to my camera.'

Our meal was utterly spoiled. What was left of it lay cold and congealed on the plates. Dirk pushed his away. The old bald waiter, hurrying over, clucked his tongue and offered to take the serving dish away to heat it up again. It wasn't any good, someone told him: none of us was interested in food now. But he hadn't heard Dirk's story, and he couldn't think of anything else except feeding us.

No one wanted to talk about the various people who had died, I noticed. I suppose we thought it was bad luck, or bad manners. The only questions we had for Dirk were technical ones. What, I asked him finally, did he think might be the physical explanation for the heaviness of the camera?

'I wouldn't know. I'm only a cameraman. I just switch the thing on and off.'

He got up and shook hands with each of us in his Belgian way. Maybe he felt better for having got the story off his chest. He seemed a little easier, a little less burdened. Then he headed through the happy, sweaty, noisy crowd of diners, under the sign that ordered us to have a felicitous Noel, and went into the silent world outside.

10

ABSURDITIES

> Many of Corker's anecdotes dealt with the fabulous Wenlock Jakes . . .
>
> 'Why, once Jakes went out to cover a revolution in one of the Balkan capitals. He overslept in his carriage, woke up at the wrong station, didn't know any different, got out, went straight to a hotel, cabled off a thousand word story about barricades in the streets, flaming churches, machine guns answering the rattle of his typewriter as he wrote . . .
>
> 'They gave Jakes the Nobel Peace prize.'
>
> Evelyn Waugh, *Scoop*, 1938

If ours is a mad world, and it is, the madness is not so much outright insanity as a constant state of absurdity.

Once, in Peru, I interviewed a group of coca farmers. They grew the raw materials which were then processed and sent on to the dealers of the First World either in the form of cocaine or of crack. There it became a genuine danger to the structure of Western society.

I had assumed that these coca farmers would be vicious, dangerous characters. On the contrary, they were quiet, gentle, intimidated men, easily frightened by the dreadful *tracateros* who would turn up, often stoned and always armed, to buy their coca leaves at the lowest possible price.

'If I could grow anything else, I would,' said the spokesman for the group, himself a little shrimp of a man, dressed in a torn and faded T-shirt. 'I don't want to have to deal with evil men like this. And you never know when the government or the *nortearmericanos* will come and arrest us and burn our fields. But if I went back to growing maize, like I once did, I couldn't sell it anywhere. When you go to the market in Tingo Maria' – he pointed in the direction of the nearby town – 'you find maize being sold there for half what it costs me to grow it. They buy it from North America, and it is very cheap. The only thing I can grow which will bring me a decent return is coca. So that's what I do. And if you ask any of us here, they will all say the same thing.'

The others nodded intently. They were coca's slaves, condemned to a life of fear and criminality by the habit of Western countries – in this case the United States, but it could equally well have been the European Union – of dumping their surplus produce on the un-defended markets of the Third World. This in turn stimulates the drug industry, and Western countries are obliged to tax their citizens more in order to pay the high social costs of addiction and crime. Could anything be more absurd?

But in this mad world my own trade, journalism, exists in a climate of permanent absurdity. Journalists, knowing this, are con-stantly amazed and disturbed to find that other people take their work so seriously. They know how thin the ice they skate on really is, how unreliable the evidence they adduce. Anyone who has been present at some news event knows how unrecognizable the versions of it in the next morning's newspapers are. Even journalists who are not expected to twist their copy to suit the political slant of a proprietor find it hard to reach total accuracy: shortness of time and the confused nature of events tend to prevent it.

I watched the full course of the revolutions in Czechoslovakia and Romania in 1989 from the streets without realizing that both were in their different ways set-up jobs; especially in Romania, where it later turned out that nothing we had assumed at the time was really correct, and that the entire affair was planned by a small group of conspirators. The notion that journalism is the first draft of history has never been one I have subscribed to; though the later drafts of history have often seemed just as flawed as well. 'A shot in the dark' is more the phrase that comes to mind.

A journalist I once knew who worked for one of the big American news magazines was invited by the information minister of an African country to come and see the appalling drought which was building up there. The journalist really did mean to go, but his plane was cancelled. It was plain that he could not reach the area of the drought in time to write for the next edition, yet his editor was expecting the story.

So he sat in his hotel room in a different country and wrote an eyewitness story on the basis of what the information minister had told him. It was very strong stuff: the stick-like limbs, the pathetic children, the flat breasts of the women, the staggering skeletons. The magazine splashed the story on its cover with pictures obtained from the country's information ministry, and decent people all over the world sent in their money to alleviate the problem.

A friend of mine who knew the country well went there a few months later and found that, although indeed it hadn't rained for two years, the nomadic population traditionally expected droughts to last four or five years at a time, and did what they could to prepare themselves. He found no evidence that people's lives were in serious danger; but he did notice that the information ministry and other government buildings seemed to have had a lot of money spent on them recently.

None of this means that journalists who write about genuine droughts and famines make it up, nor does it spring from any deep-rooted suspicion that humanitarian disasters are really invented by unscrupulous ministers of Third World countries as exercises in money-making. It is merely that journalism is the kind of profession where mistakes happen constantly, but are so thickly covered over with a varnish of apparent seriousness and sincerity that they are rendered acceptable to the world at large. Politics is just such another. So is the law.

It would be harder for a television journalist to do what this American magazine journalist did, not because television is of its nature a more truthful medium – it couldn't be, given the amount of editing and selection which goes into it – but because faking it on a big scale is pretty difficult: you not only have to have pictures and interviews, you would also have to rely on the silence of your colleagues. There have been a couple of examples where television documentaries were faked with the collusion of everyone involved; but in television news, in my experience, this does not seem to happen much. The chronic shortage of time makes it difficult, and so does the fact most television journalists work with teams which are constantly shifting and changing.

Most important of all, the culture of television news (certainly in the English-speaking countries) is one where, whatever its other shortcomings, this kind of thing is deeply disapproved of. Television's self-image, like that of the British broadsheet newspapers, is one of truth-telling; in the offices of many British tabloids, by contrast, anecdotes of clever or witty inventions are passed around with admiration.

When at the beginning of 2000 ITN sued the clever, iconoclastic magazine *LM* for alleging that some of its pictures had been misleading (ITN's boss said, with presumably unintended irony, that the case had been brought in order to defend freedom of speech) much of the ITN case was taken up with statements from its own employees about how good and reliable its reporting had always been; which is true, but not necessarily to the point.

The case touched the heart of the problem with television news, which is the interpretation of pictures. Everything depends on the impression they are allowed to give the viewer. ITN's reports from the Bosnian Serb prison camp at Trnopolje in 1992 were the most famous television news pictures of the decade. An emaciated Muslim in a crowd of other prisoners stared out at the camera from behind a barbed wire fence. Right across the world people who saw these pictures thought they knew exactly what they meant: Trnopolje was a concentration camp along the lines of Auschwitz or Theresienstadt. In the United States people campaigning for intervention in the war between the Bosnian Serbs and the predominantly Muslim Bosnian government seized on these pictures as proof that the Serbs were today's Nazis.

Yet the pictures weren't quite what they seemed. The emaciated man had only arrived at Trnopolje that morning from a far worse camp elsewhere. At the trial, there was much discussion about whether the barbed wire which in the pictures seemed to be surrounding the prisoners, was not in fact surrounding the reporters. Trnopolje wasn't Auschwitz or Theresienstadt at all; it was essentially a transit camp where people like the skeletal figure they filmed were taken before being released or moved on to other, worse camps. Unpleasant things could certainly happen to prisoners there; no Muslim in the hands of Bosnian Serb captors during that evil war was entirely safe. But that didn't make Trnopolje what most viewers assumed it was.

The ITN reporters were careful not to call Trnopolje a concentration camp; but when their pictures were shown around the world other television organizations were much less meticulous. Again, they thought they knew what the pictures showed. The judge in the ITN-*LM* case seemed to support the key point that the barbed wire ran around the camera crew not the prisoners, but he accepted the word of the reporters that they had not realized this. Unfortunately the videotape 'rushes' which might have proved this one way or the other could not be found. *LM* lost the case, and was driven out of business by huge damages. Thus was the cause of free speech defended.

It was certainly true that there was a powerful pro-Muslim lobby among the British and American journalists in Bosnia. Reporters from well-known newspapers habitually wore the badge of the Bosnian government in their lapels when they were in Sarajevo (though I imagine they took them off when they went among the Bosnian Serbs). There was great competition at the time among the journalists to uncover more and more evidence of wrong-doing on the part of the Serbs, which was very considerable, and not all the facts were checked too carefully.

It's at times like this, I've found, that you most have to keep a clear head. The need to be completely honest in your commentary about what is going on in the television pictures is more pressing than ever. The danger still exists that other television organizations, including those whose journalists do not speak English well enough to understand all your caveats, will use your pictures to promote some false idea of what they mean. But at least your hands will be clean.

There are, of course, plenty of honest mistakes in television news, caused by ignorance or stupidity. A classic mistake is only a breath away for all of us who work in television. For months the government of India made an enormous degree of fuss about an occasion when someone on BBC World accidentally played some library pictures of Kurdish refugees into a story about Kashmir. The BBC graphics department, asked to produce a silhouette which would look mysterious for a story about suggestions that there was an unknown spy for the Russians working in the British government, picked out a photograph at random and blacked it out. On screen it was still recognizably Robert Maxwell, and we were lucky to escape a writ.

The worst mistake I ever made was during the Israeli invasion of Lebanon in 1982, when what was left of the Lebanese parliament gathered on the outskirts of Beirut to elect a new president. Bashir Gemayel, the thuggish boss of a particularly nasty private army, the Phalange, was the favourite. At that stage I had never met him, and had no idea what he looked like. Nor did the cameraman I was working with. The result was declared, and the Gemayel party appeared triumphantly out of the barracks where the election had been held. We hurried over.

'Now you've won, what are you going to do?' I called out.

'Our main policy is to restore peace to Lebanon,' Gemayel said.

We satellited our report that evening. It was only the following morning that I found out that the man I had identified as the new president, and had interviewed, was Bashir Gemayel's brother Amin; Bashir had decided at the last moment not to turn up. Two weeks later Bashir was killed by a terrorist bomb, and Amin was elected president in his place. I made the obvious joke that I had simply broken the story first; but it wasn't one of my better moments.

Journalism is a curious way of making a living. It can be a licence to lie, or a commitment to the most rigorous honesty. Yet it seems to me that a great deal of what you read in the newspapers or see on television is not so much wrong as depressingly stylized. Journalists often seem to think only in terms of stereotypes: innocent victims, great leaders, evil killers, vicious dictators, tragic children, vengeful wives, love rats. Under this kind of treatment the complexity of life, which is its truth, evaporates almost instantly.

Television news may not be good at putting over detailed information, but it is unrivalled at giving an overall sense of what is going on. A word, a gesture, an image lasting no more than a second can fix an atmosphere permanently in the viewer's mind. All the more need, then, to get the atmosphere right. During the Gulf War of 1991, when a few Iraqi missiles were aimed at Israel, some of the foreign correspondents in Tel Aviv appeared in front of the camera wearing gas-masks. It gave the completely unjustified impression that there was a serious threat.

'We're ordering you to take cover,' called out the anchorman to one showman.

'No, I'm staying here while I still can,' the reporter shouted back.

Then the ten-minute live satellite slot which his company had been allocated ran out, and a colleague of mine, Brian Barron, appeared in his place, standing perfectly calmly in front of the camera and explaining what was really going on. To those of us who were watching, his coolness and unexcitability came as a great relief. Look-at-me television, where the reporter becomes the event, is as much of a falsification as an outright lie.

The Irish politician and intellectual Conor Cruise O'Brien once said that the attention of the media was like being picked up by some giant skinhead, examined at horribly close quarters, handled with great roughness, then dropped painfully and abruptly. Life can never be quite the same afterwards; every part of the process is damaging. Even in my section of the television news business the danger exists that merely selecting a particular incident or a particular country to report on will distort people's perceptions of it for good.

At the end of 1999, I made a film about international crime and corruption. Looking round for somewhere particular to focus on, we spoke to Interpol. The people there were in no doubt that the clearest example of these things was currently Hungary. We went there, and found it was true. Politics, the police, business, the civil service had all been affected by an original scam in 1990, as a result of which oil from Soviet army dumps in the former Warsaw Pact countries was smuggled into Hungary and sold. For me, the most impressive thing about our report was that policemen and politicians were prepared to take the risk of speaking to us on camera.

When the report was shown by BBC World, it caused a sensation in Hungary. The government accused the BBC of deliberate distortion and said it was considering suing it; under what law was unclear. Anyway, the government's position was rather undercut when a spokesman accepted that there were no factual errors in the report.

What offended many ordinary Hungarians, as well as their government, was that at a time when they were hoping to join the European Union, someone should have gone and opened this particular dirty-clothes cupboard. It had, many people felt, been done deliberately, to sabotage Hungary's membership application. A former BBC employee wrote me an e-mail containing the phrase 'Hurt national feelings aside . . .', which meant of course that he had not been able to set his hurt national feelings aside at all.

The problem comes with singling out a country like Hungary, as though Poland and the Czech Republic and all the other former Soviet bloc countries were not also suffering a tidal wave of organized crime; and as though corruption doesn't exist in almost every Western society. But television isn't good at generalization; its strength is in clear example. Our example, the clearest one available, was Hungary. That doesn't make it any easier to digest for the people whose country has been singled out for treatment; and it can indeed affect the perceptions of the outside world for years to come.

In a post-Communist society, the idea that there must be a clear agenda behind everything the media does and says is a difficult one to shake off. The purpose of newspapers, radio and television under Marxism-Leninism was to be the voice of the state, and it isn't always easy for people to understand that things aren't that way in a free society. The *Sunday Telegraph* columnist Christopher Booker, an anti-European, is convinced that the BBC has a firm policy to push the Euro onto an unwilling British public. It does no good to explain that this isn't true, and that if it were many of us would resign noisily and publicly; not because we were necessarily anti-European, but because it would have violated the BBC's basic principles. Sheer waste of breath: it merely provokes a greater flood of accusation.

You can't please everyone. All you can do is make sure your conscience is as clear as a profession full of compromise and uncertainty will allow it to be.

A group of two or three men or women who know nothing of one another and have sometimes never previously met gather in the departure lounge of the airport, shake hands, introduce themselves if necessary, and for a week or ten days they live in the closest possible proximity to each other, perhaps sharing rooms, certainly listening to each other's stories, depending on each other's skill and energy for their professional reputations and (just occasionally) for their very lives. All news reporting is strange, but reporting on foreign affairs for television news is a great deal stranger than most.

Companionship can keep you going under the most difficult circumstances. A television reporter and a producer I know, under arrest in Africa, were ordered to clean out the prison lavatories. They kept up each other's morale as they did this unthinkably unpleasant job by telling jokes and singing spirituals. Sometimes, of course, merely being together has the opposite effect. I have known television teams which have ending up trading insults or refusing to speak for days on end. I have also known men and women who, working together on the road, have had affairs or begun lifelong friendships.

These, though, are exceptions. For the most part, people who work together for television just get on with the job, putting up with each other's quirks of behaviour as best they can, pretending they haven't heard the stories before, trying not to be irritated or offended. And then the time is up. They shake hands in the arrivals hall, go back to their homes, and put the whole episode behind them.

In the past, when television teams were large and I travelled the world with a producer, cameraman, sound recordist, lighting man and sometimes a driver/despatch rider, I was allowed no say whatever in the matter of who they might be. Merely to suggest that since I was going to Germany and since X spoke good German he should perhaps go with me was enough to ensure that I would be given a cameraman whose skills barely included focusing a lens, while the crew I had asked for would be assigned to stand outside Downing Street for weeks to come, as a punishment for being good. In those days, assigning crews represented a small but very definite degree of power; and power like that is never surrendered easily.

Television news teams, like everything else in British society in the 1970s, were still constructed on the class principle. The correspondent was the senior officer, dressed differently, educated differently, speaking differently, interested in different things. The producer, though often the same age or older, was unquestionably junior in rank: the adjutant, whose job it was to ensure that all the arrangements were properly made. The cameraman was the sergeant, the backbone of the service. The correspondent might wander off or have a fit of the vapours, the producer might go mad, but the cameraman was expected to make sure that everything worked correctly and the job was done.

'What would you do,' the editor of BBC television news asked a would-be cameraman at a selection board, 'if the president's office rings and says your interview is going to happen at once; and when you knock on the correspondent's door you find he's dead drunk?'

'How's that different from any ordinary day?'

He got the job, of course.

The sound recordist was the corporal, who had to do the donkey-work. There were some to whom sound was the most important thing in life: genuine artists, who weren't interested in promotion and whose work could make the difference between an ordinary report and a brilliant one. Most, though, were apprentice cameramen, learning the trade. Like all apprentices the unpleasant things came their way: lifting things, staying up later and getting up earlier, watching the cameraman's back, carrying more than their share of the gear. There were sound-men who, within minutes of arriving somewhere, would have organized food, drink, a vehicle, and a decent place to spend the night. Such people are superb to work with. The lighting man was like the radio-operator: there primarily for a single technical skill, and much abused if there was a problem with it.

Of course it was never quite as clear-cut in practice. The camera-men were sometimes better educated or brighter than the producer or the correspondent; the sound recordist could be the wit of the team, producing some of the best ideas for news reports; and I have spent long, pleasant journeys being driven by lighting-men or despatch riders, discussing the serious things of life. Essentially, though, the system was a hierarchical one, and everyone knew their place in it.

The BBC used to get many of its cameramen from the old cinema news agencies – Movietone, Gaumont and the others. They had a particular glamour for me, and I could never hear enough of the stories they told.

'So Derby Day comes round again, and I'm thinking how Movie-tone had forced my car off the track last year and made me miss the finish. So we put our heads together, and hired four blokes with mirrors to stand round the finishing line. And when the Movietone van comes powering along, filming the leaders in the last furlong or so, the four blokes get their mirrors out and focus the sun onto

Movietone's lens. It did the trick, but we had to get out sharpish when they came looking for us.'

My own life seemed so tame and safe by comparison; and I would look at these distinguished middle-aged gentlemen in their suits and ties and well-shone black shoes with admiration and envy.

I adopted their jokes and catch-phrases; 'it's compulsory', for instance, said with a Belfast accent. It arose from the experience of a cameraman who was on a long tour of duty in Northern Ireland, and who like the rest of us was given a heavy breakfast each morning at the Crawfordsburn Inn, just outside Belfast.

He ordered an Ulster fry, one of the great cholesterol-rich dishes of the world.

'I want two fried eggs, fried bread, fried mushrooms, fried bacon, fried tomato, fried black pudding, fried kidneys. But I don't want any sausages, darling, OK? Because I don't like sausages.'

'So no sausages, right?'

'Right.'

She disappeared into the kitchen.

Fifteen minutes later, she brought out a huge heart-stopping plateful. Two large pork sausages were nestled in the middle of it.

'Look, darling, what's this? I ordered two fried eggs, fried bread, fried bacon, fried tomato, fried mushrooms, fried black pudding, and fried kidneys, and no sausages. What are those?'

'Sausages.'

'Take it back, darling, and bring me what I ordered.'

The plate disappeared. Two minutes later it was back. The sausages were still there. The girl looked at him defiantly.

'Chef says the sausages are compulsory.'

Now, of course, everything has changed: the world, society, television, we ourselves. There are few sound recordists left in news, and therefore no period of apprenticeship. Cameramen, as a result, are usually in their thirties rather than their fifties, and working on their own has made them more self-sufficient. Lighting-men and despatch riders have vanished utterly from television news. The jobs they once did are either done by the cameraman, or are not done at all.

All the same, television news is still a group activity. As a result, television people keep with their colleagues from the same organization, working together, eating meals together, taking time off together if there is any to be taken. Journalists working for newspapers, who operate on their own, tend to form ad hoc groups for the sake of company and cost-cutting. They share cars and information and translators, often agree on 'the line' to be followed, dislike the separatism and elitism of television, and are in turn disliked – or, worse, ignored – by the television people.

As a result of all these factors, working for television has its own difficulties, its own pleasures, its own demands, which are quite unlike those of any other medium.

And it generates its own anecdotes, which are also *sui generis*. The mistakes of television news are particular to television; so is the kind of embarrassment it gives rise to. Some specifically television stories follow: none of them particularly edifying, but altogether characteristic of the medium.

Bob Prabhu wanted to have dinner at a fish restaurant. That was part of the problem. The other part of the problem was that the fish restaurant was a long way from the centre of town. How Bob had come to hear of it was a mystery to me; he is one of those people who does come to hear of things.

It was 1988, and we were in Chile to cover the referendum on whether General Pinochet should continue in power. In those days Bob was still a sound recordist: a clever, complicated, deeply loyal man born of Indian parents in Aden, and therefore as much of a child of the British Empire as I was. Nowadays he is one of my favourite cameramen. He is also starting a new life: married to his second wife, a beautiful Russian girl, and the almost absurdly proud father of a bouncing new baby. Only men in their fifties who have been through the mill know how golden this second life can be. It may have helped that only about a month after the birth of their child Bob and Valya won three-quarters of a million pounds on the lottery.

I felt I had to humour him about the fish restaurant. He and the cameraman he was working with, Steve Morris, had had a bad time of it ever since we arrived in Santiago. Pinochet was not going to give up without a fight, and his police force were enjoying the opportunity to crack a few heads. Twice we had gone out at night to cover the impromptu demonstrations in favour of a 'no' vote in the referendum, and filmed the riot police attacking the crowds with rubber truncheons. They also particularly enjoyed smashing television cameras.

Behind the riot police came big unwieldy armoured trucks on which hoses like the guns of a tank were mounted. These hoses squirted a high-pressure jet of water mixed with tear gas and sewage at the remnants of the demonstrations. You could always tell when they had passed, and if the water was sufficiently charged you could sometimes tell when they were approaching. The men who drove these behemoths took real pleasure in their work. They lingered over it, picking out individuals and following them down the street with the jet, knocking them down and rolling them into the gutters.

The first time we came across one of these water trucks we had little idea what it could do, or how foul the water it squirted could be. Steve and Bob were drenched, and their camera was wrecked. By chance, the main jet missed me. I was struck by a few drops, which smelled bad enough and made my eyes hurt, but that was all. The second time, they filmed it from between two cars which were parked by the side of the road, lurking in the darkness and then standing out suddenly as the truck came closer.

The men in the truck loved that. They took careful aim and covered Steve and Bob from head to toe with stinking, burning water. Steve, knowing what to expect, had put a rain-cover over his new camera and it was protected. They weren't.

As for me, I have strong feelings about correspondents who let their crews take the heat while staying safe themselves. On the other hand, it seems to me, this applies only to bullets and nightsticks; I do not feel quite the same obligation to share their suffering when it comes to sewage laced with tear gas. Directly the water truck spotted us and opened up, I moved sharply back onto the pavement and took refuge behind a phone box. The filthy stuff, searching me out, slammed against the glass and dribbled disgustingly down it; I may not have been proud of myself, but at least I was safe and dry.

Which is why I felt I had to humour Bob in the matter of the fish restaurant a few nights later. There was to be a big demonstration at nine o'clock in the centre of Santiago, near the Carrera Hotel, and it was clear there would be serious trouble. We wandered round filming the preparations, and the way the riot police hissed obscenities at us and struck the palms of their hands with their truncheons showed that they were looking forward to the evening's entertainment.

We weren't. I stood the others a bottle of champagne in a nearby bar, feeling that the BBC's licence-fee payers would probably approve, and as the light was beginning to fall we headed out to the place Bob had heard of.

It turned out to be a long way away. Santiago is pleasant enough but slightly featureless, and as we drove through the suburbs I was already starting to worry about getting back in time for the demo. We found it eventually. What distinguished this place from the restaurants round the Carrera was that the service was much slower. It took a good hour before the fish was cooked, and another hour to eat it and get the bill. Then we had a thirty-minute drive back to town.

Even given the general lack of time-keeping in Latin America (*hora ingles*, English time, is the usual expression for punctuality, dating back to the period when the British built the railways) it was clear we were going to be on the late side. As we drove I grumbled incessantly about Bob's choice of restaurant, preferring to forget that I had agreed to it. Eventually we reached the square where the demonstration was to have been held. The cobbles were wet and stinking, CS gas still hung unpleasantly in the air, but everyone had gone: demonstrators, riot police, even the water trucks. I was furious.

We went back to the Carrera. In the lounge at the top of the stairs, overlooked by some huge, rather excessive art deco *conquistadores* and *caciques* inlaid in marble, journalists and photographers lay exhausted and filthy in the armchairs, with solicitous waiters moving among them with trays of drinks and cloths. Everyone looked at us with a certain contempt; everyone, that is, except a Chilean cameraman who was a good friend of mine, Raúl Cuevas. Cuevas, the hero of a hundred such demonstrations, had worked with us in Chile before, and knew that we would not deliberately avoid something like this.

'They were really bad this time.'

He wiped his filthy face, and I tried not to show what I thought of the smell. It made me feel very clean and very safe.

'They must have had orders to go for the television cameras. They had iron bars.'

Several cameramen had had their arms, their skulls or their collar-bones broken. One or two had been seriously hurt. The people we found in the Carrera were the lucky ones, who had escaped relatively lightly. We, the luckiest of all, quickly went up to our rooms. I might feel embarrassed, but something inside me was also distinctly grateful to Bob for giving us the excuse to avoid injury.

The next morning we had to edit a report from the pictures which Raúl and the other agency cameramen had shot the evening before. There was one rivetting sequence which lasted for a minute and a quarter, an eternity in news terms, which showed a press photographer being attacked by the riot police, falling to the ground, being beaten again, picking himself up and running, being attacked again, falling, being kicked, escaping again, and so on. Each time the batons landed on him you could feel the pain yourself. In the end the photographer managed to get away, and everyone who watched the pictures with me cheered.

It caused a sensation at the BBC in London. That evening we received a message from the *capo di tutti capi*:

Congratulations your magnificent report. Please take greatest care. Nothing is worth getting injured for.

Later there was a move to enter the report for one of the main television awards, but fortunately I managed to stop that. While the photographer was enduring his savage beating we had been miles away in Bob's restaurant, eating some rather good fish.

The year was 1979, and it was the old world still: the world of superpowers, the Non-Aligned Movement, the Organization of African Unity. The Shah of Iran had just been overthrown, Margaret Thatcher had been in office for a few months, the Soviet Union seemed to be at the peak of its strength and the United States at the depth of its weakness. Third-Worldism, which tended to mean that a few corrupt, undemocratic characters could demand a bigger platform than they deserved, appeared to be a serious force. It was not yet clear that the tide of apartheid was starting to turn in South

Africa. Rhodesia – where an absurd and wrong-headed effort was made to return to a chapter of history which was finished – still remained to be sorted out.

We were in Lusaka, the capital of Zambia. The weather, gentle and warm, was a delight, the reddish colour of the earth was even more pronounced than it was farther south, and the delicate purple blooms were starting to appear on the jacaranda trees and to burst audibly underfoot as you walked along. Lusaka was to Salisbury, the Rhodesian capital, what Salisbury was to Johannesburg: a sleepy country cousin.

It had recently erected a statue to the martyrs of Zambia's independence struggle against Britain. Since independence had been freely offered to Northern Rhodesia almost as quickly as it had been demanded, it was a little hard to know who these martyrs might have been; it turned out that some people had been tear-gassed during a demonstration about something else. But President Kenneth Kaunda, a charming man whom I came to know quite well, and who would one day surprise his OAU colleagues by stepping down voluntarily when he lost an election, wanted to play his part on the wider Third World stage. Zambia, therefore, needed a retrospective independence struggle. The statue solved the problem: it was like buying history off the shelf.

The Commonwealth Conference, a biennial event, was being held in Lusaka that year, and as ever the Queen came to open it. The year before, I had left the job of BBC correspondent in Johannesburg and gone back to work in London, but my heart was still in Africa: it was something to do with the warmth of the air and the redness of the soil and the sight of the jacaranda trees, and the gentleness of the people. And I was able to work with friends and colleagues again.

The cameraman assigned to me was François Marais, a liberal Afrikaner of Huguenot descent, as broad as he was tall, who enjoyed the good things of life and eventually left camerawork to run a wine-farm in the Cape. With him was a tall and beautiful blonde sound recordist called Carol Clarke. Between them, François and Carol had got me my present job as BBC TV's diplomatic correspondent. Two years earlier, when we were on one of our trips to Salisbury, Carol had invited a susceptible old gent called Boss Lilford to tea at Meikles Hotel. There she had convinced him to let us go and film on his farm in the south-east of the country, where he was employing British mercenaries to kill the guerrillas who were infiltrating his land and killing his cattle for food. Boss Lilford later met a strange and unexplained death, but at this time he was the real power behind Ian Smith and the Rhodesia Front party.

As he sat among the chintz sofas of Meikles' tea room, tall and gaunt under his wideawake hat, he looked like a combination of Cecil Rhodes and Marlon Brando playing the Godfather: only thinner and bigger. Boss Lilford had an intense dislike of everything to do with modern-day Britain. And he loathed the BBC.

'You twist every bloody thing we say: bloody shower of bloody Communist pooftahs.'

He didn't quite say these things in the genteel atmosphere of Meikles, but plenty of white Rhodesians did say them, and Boss Lilford must certainly have thought them as he sat opposite me. I had put on a dark suit and my most sincere expression, in order to show how trustworthy I was.

Boss Lilford wasn't taken in by the suit or the expression; he scarcely looked at me anyway. But he was defenceless before a pretty face. Carol played the Southern African card – her parents had, it seemed, known the Lilfords in quieter and easier times – and by the time the Darjeeling had been poured out and the cream was on the scones he had agreed to let us go.

The job itself had its problems. Mick Whitehead was a former para who lived in Croydon, and had been recruited by some shady outfit to work as a mercenary in Southern Africa. He was sharp enough, but found it difficult to understand our rôle in all this.

'We'll be lying in ambush down there.' He pointed to a flat rock where the path curved. 'When the terrs come along, I'll give the word and you switch on your camera-lights. That way I'll be able to see them, and you can film them going down.'

I did my best to explain, but it wasn't easy.

'We're just observers, that's all. I don't want to take sides in this.'

'Seems to me that by coming down here to film me you've taken sides already.'

'I don't want to be a party to any shooting, I mean.'

'So you don't want to see any action?'

By this time, he was right: I didn't.

Carol stayed behind at the house, and François and I set out with Croydon Man and his African tracker.

'This man passed about one hour ago,' said the tracker, kneeling beside a footprint in the red sand. 'I know this man from his takkies. He will come back.'

'Takkies' is southern African for running shoes.

As the sun began to go down we lay on the flat rock and waited for the ambush to happen. François and I had made it clear that he wouldn't be switching on his lights to help in the business of killing the guerrillas, and Mick had shrugged. His opinion of the BBC and of me was roughly Boss Lilford's, I should imagine. He shifted his AK-47 in his hand irritably.

It was a long, silent wait for the biggest game of all. The light finally died out of the sky and the stars came up: the startling, low-slung stars of Africa. I could see the constellations with a clarity I had never had before. An occasional satellite sped over, and the constellations shifted with the movement of the earth.

Insects found me. I had never been fond of insect-life, but since I could not move on the flat rock without making a noise and getting a warning look from Mick I had to let them go where they wanted. For the most part they merely regarded me as an obstacle in their path, something to surmount. Ants formed lines over my legs; spiders stalked slowly across me. Why not, I thought? They live here, and I am merely an intruder, a passer-by. No doubt, as the cold stars shift in their courses, the white settlers in Africa will pass through as well, and maybe mankind as well; and the ants and spiders will still be marching across this rock when we and all our works have gone.

'Nine o'clock. They won't be coming back this way now.'

I was profoundly grateful: getting mixed up in an ambush arranged for our benefit would have caused some serious ethical problems. As it was, we interviewed Mick in the darkness about the reason the guerrillas had not come our way, and his plans for the future, and walked back to the farmhouse feeling much better about the whole business. François' pictures were haunting and evocative, and our report convinced the editor of television news back in London that I should be brought back there as diplomatic correspondent. I owed it all to François' and Carol's powers of persuasion.

Now, a couple of years later, I was working with them in Lusaka.

We all lived for the three weeks of the Commonwealth Conference in a rented house, together with the other BBC people and a nest of African killer bees. I used to sit on the *stoep* in the morning playing the flute, and the bees, possibly enraged by this, gave everyone a fright by attacking François, who was allergic to bee-stings; his life was only saved by an injection at the main Lusaka hospital.

The Queen arrived, and did the rounds. Kenneth Kaunda was always said to be one of her favourite Commonwealth presidents, and he treated her with great respect. 'Her Majesty the Queen', he invariably called her, with the courtliness that southern African leaders seemed to reserve for the monarchy.

Early on in her visit she was due to open the Lusaka Show, an agricultural occasion of a type familiar wherever the British have set their foot across the globe: women in big hats and white gloves, men looking uncomfortable in suits, mud, plenty of livestock, and steaming heaps of awkwardly placed dung. We were warned to be at the ground an hour beforehand, but there was a good deal of other filming to be done and we arrived late. The officials in charge were unwilling to let us in this late.

'Her Majesty is here already, you understand.'

Carol, however, looked at them and smiled, and they took us down through the stands to the edge of the pitch. There, it was clear, our problems were only starting. The Queen had taken her seat in the northern stand, and the rest were packed to capacity; the stadium seated seventy thousand people. The band was playing in the centre of the field, in the middle of an enclosure where the prize bulls and cows were to be paraded. All the other journalists and camera crews were there already. The enclosure was made of barbed wire, three feet high.

'You'll have to climb over that. It's to stop the animals getting out and troubling Her Majesty.'

I assumed he was referring to the journalists, but he could have meant the cattle.

It was a long walk across the grass. Carol attracted the attention which a blonde five feet ten tall carrying television sound gear might expect. The barbed wire seemed very high. François and Carol made it easily enough, but I have always been clumsy and awkward. A stray prong of wire stuck out and caught me in the seat; the action of lifting my leg over the fence ripped my trousers open from top to bottom at the back. I was wearing bright blue underpants, I remember. They were torn as well.

At first, probably only ten thousand people noticed. They were the ones who had been watching Carol. The way they applauded me attracted the attention of the rest. Slowly, rippling round the stands like a Mexican Wave, the crowd, seventy thousand strong, got to its feet and applauded me. For a moment or two I stood there, appalled. Then I realized I had to get into the shelter of the camera crews in the centre of the enclosure, forty yards away. It seemed a great deal further. I raised my fists in the air as a gesture of triumph, but it was pretty feeble. My trousers fell away to reveal the blue underpants, mooning the Queen directly. People said afterwards she thought it was funny.

Huddled in the centre of the crowd of journalists like a rugby player whose shorts have been torn off in a tackle, I stood while Mike Nicholson from ITN pinned the torn edges together with borrowed safety pins and consoled me.

'One good thing, it doesn't matter what happens to you in future – you'll never be more embarrassed than you are now.'

'I'm not embarrassed.'

But I was. The crowd cheered me off the field at the end, and for days afterwards people came up to me and spoke about it. At the dinner the Queen gave some days later, we were off to the side filming. Her gaze settled on me, and it seemed to me she started smiling. Or maybe not: it was a feeling I had quite a lot at that time.

Russians, under their apparent roughness, are a courtly people. '*Ne kulturniy*', uncultured, is one of their worst insults; and, as I found when I used it on an airline official at the Aeroflot desk when I was trying to get from one godforsaken part of the old Soviet Union to another, it is something which should only be used under the most extreme circumstances. No one you have called *ne kulturniy* is ever likely to help you again. I was stuck in Minsk for a day and a night as a result.

In particular, invitations to dinner have to be kept in Russia. Eating, like being cultured, is taken seriously. People do not understand Western casualness about such things.

Nor do they like it if you try to explain that you have something else to do, like work.

There were five of us: Olga Mersherikova, the best fixer in Russia, whom I always like to work with when I go to Russia; Bob Prabhu, who had by now been a cameraman for ten years; Paul Simpson, my producer, whom most people assumed wrongly was my son (when Dee travels with us the assumption becomes a certainty); and the large but quick-witted Vasili, our driver. We headed out of Moscow to a place which, only a few years before, had not appeared on the maps. It was quite a sizeable city, named after one of the least attractive early Communists, and it had been closed to foreigners because secret electronic equipment was manufactured there. In those days the Soviet authorities did not want Westerners going there and trying to buy up their secrets. Now, seven years after the collapse of the Soviet Union, the authorities were only too glad if Westerners wanted to buy anything.

We were there because of the mayor, a rising star who was already being spoken of as a possible future President of Russia. He was clever, had a clear understanding of the direction in which the country had to go, and looked good on television. The trouble was, we were a good hour late for our appointment with him, and the light was starting to go. We had to do as much filming now as we could; if we went to see the mayor first, we wouldn't have enough light to film the town. And since we had to satellite our report to London that night, we would have serious problems. Olga, who has superb manners and the general attitude to life of a Tsarist princess, was distinctly unhappy.

'We must go and tell them why we're late. Otherwise it will be very rude. And if he becomes President he will remember it. You will see: the BBC will suffer.'

'The BBC always suffers,' I said; but I agreed.

We filmed for an hour or more. It was a depressing place, built in the 1950s, with deeply rutted streets which harboured deep puddles of slowly thawing ice. You could find yourself in freezing water up to your shins if you misjudged it. I misjudged it at least once.

Bob was enjoying himself.

'Just one more shot. Really. We need to see this.'

'Bob, look, we've got to get going.' I felt like a parent.

'We've got to have this. The sun reflecting in the puddles. It's beautiful – you'll love it. Just a moment or two more. This old woman – look at her. You know.'

I knew. 'All right. But we've got to be finished here in ten minutes.'

'Sure, no problem. Just another couple of shots.'

'Ah, "*just*"; the quintessential television word': I could hear the voice in my head, even though it had been ten years since I had heard it. I had been interviewing an old German-Jew who had survived the camps and had come back after the war to live in Berlin. I had lured him to meet me at the heap of rubble on the site of the old Gestapo headquarters in West Berlin, where he had once been taken in for questioning. (With true German attention to detail, the rubble did not itself come from the Gestapo headquarters. The building had been flattened and the rubble taken away, and rubble from *different* places had been trucked in to cover the site. The idea was that there would be no possibility of souvenir-hunting, since no one would know what a particular brick or piece of stone-work was a souvenir of.)

Again and again I had asked him to climb the rubble with me, so that the cameraman could shoot us from different angles.

'Would you mind doing it just once more?'

'Ah, "*just*". That is the quintessential television word. "Just once more." "Just a minute or two longer." "Just" is designed to make innocent people like myself think that this will be a very brief experience, that it will take only a moment of my time, that I will only have to do something one more time. Whereas I know from experience that I will still be standing here in half an hour, doing things I would rather not be doing.'

'Oh, I wouldn't say that.'

But he turned out to be right; and I could tell I was right now, as I stood in the main street of this once-secret Russian satellite town. It was not going to be a quick business.

Finally, as the light went, we made our way in the chilly twilight to the mayor's office. For myself, I dislike lateness and am covered with embarrassment if I keep other people waiting. As a television reporter, on the other hand, I am not only used to it, I feel perfectly justified as long as it is the demands of a difficult job which have made me late. So, as we pushed our way through the yellowish wood doors, hanging loosely on their hinges like every outer door of every official building in Russia, I wasn't too upset. Bob Prabhu had been quite right: the pictures came first, and the interview, which would be indoors anyway, could wait. The key to reporting for television is to recognize which of a series of demands is the most urgent, and act accordingly.

The mayor was short, tough, thickset, fair-haired, warty of face, and distinctly annoyed. As I shook hands with him and explained our problem, I could see he wasn't at all convinced. Nevertheless he waved us towards our seats, and settled down at his desk to talk to us. As with all former Soviet offices, there was a place where the portrait of the Party boss used to hang; Gorbachev latterly, but before that a succession of characters, great or small, terrible or merely ferocious, who were now represented by a paler patch on the wall. An inferior painting of some birch trees didn't completely cover it.

In front of his desk was a smaller table, sideways on, with three chairs on either side of it, so that the whole arrangement made a capital T exactly as in Communist days. He had two telephones in front of him, one red and one green: the kind of bright, unconvincing colours that made them look like kids' toys. They weren't. The red one must have been linked directly to the Interior Ministry in Moscow.

I repeated my apologies, and could see I was wearing him down. Suddenly I understood that his main emotion was disappointment: he had been boasting about the arrival of the television team from the BBC, and we had made him seem less important than he wanted. He had lost face in the eyes of his staff. Now he needed to be built up.

We built him up. Bob and Paul Simpson rearranged his office in the way television people always do: mystifying ways, which meant that all the things he might expect us to want in the background were shifted aside, while everything he hadn't felt was important or interesting was moved forward. The red phone – the single most important object in the room as far as he was concerned – was put on the floor, out of sight.

Sitting there chatting to him while they laboured away moving things, I reflected that merely to work for television was a licence to mess people around and cut them down to size. Once, at a European summit in (I think) Dublin in 1980, I grew so irritated with the way Margaret Thatcher was laying down the law before our interview began that I interrupted her in mid-flow and made her shift the microphone on its little clip up and down the lapel of her dark-grey pinstriped jacket until I felt that a balance of power had been re-established between us. No wonder she disliked television. No wonder she disliked me.

The mayor seemed not to dislike me. In fact, the more I apologized the more he warmed to me. I could see my technique was working. Our interview went very well, and he said all the things an aspiring politician would want to say: boastful things about his time in the town, modest things about his longterm aim to be a candidate for the Russian presidency after Boris Yeltsin. Olga beamed: she had spotted this man's potential long before. At Paul's suggestion, I asked an extra question to end with. Bob switched off his camera and started replacing the divots.

'And now I invite you all to a banquet with me and my officials.'

There was an awkward pause. The four of us looked at each other. Television news is a demanding master, and has no qualms about making its servants miss their dinner. I ran through the timings quickly in my mind. We would have to satellite our report at 11.50 p.m. local time that night, it would take three hours to edit the pictures, and it was an hour and a half's drive back to the BBC Moscow office. The time now was 6.50: we would have to be on the road within thirty minutes, and here was the mayor inviting us not just to a banquet, but to a Russian banquet. I began to frame a polite refusal, but Olga discreetly shook her head. I thought quickly.

'Could we maybe just have a cup of tea?'

The mayor was not thinking of a cup of tea. He was starting to look irritable again. Olga moved in quickly.

'We're going to have to leave in half an hour, but maybe we could have a quick banquet.'

The warty face beamed again. He led us out of his office and towards another building where the banquet, and his officials, were waiting. There was serious face to be saved here, I could see.

A smiling old lady in a headscarf who looked as though she was in a wart competition with him shook hands and gave a little curtsy. The entire table was covered with the most delightful-looking *zakuski*, cold snacks which would constitute a heavy meal in themselves but were merely the start of the banquet. I could see goose, chicken, tongue, beef, ham, fish, caviare of four different kinds, and a long row of wine bottles. Eight of the mayor's officials were standing around, waiting for the signal to get their heads in the trough. They shook hands politely, and we warned them how soon we would have to leave. The officials looked at each other, and the old lady looked at the mayor. The phrase *ne kulturniy* seemed to be forming in their minds.

The solution to our difficulty came in the most natural way possible: through alcohol.

'A toast!' called the mayor, as we laid into the goose and the caviare. It had been a long, hungry and thirsty day for us.

Tumblers appeared in our hands: big tumblers. Vodka filled them to the brim.

'In honour of our visitors from the esteemed BBC!'

We emptied the tumblers, anxious to be as polite and authentic as possible. I could feel the passage the vodka was burning down my oesophagus, and swayed a little. Someone was already refilling our glasses. I started to open my mouth, but Bob Prabhu's Russian was good and he got in first.

'We drink to the people of this town and its mayor!'

And so we did.

'To the friendship between our fraternal peoples!'

Someone moved forward with more vodka, and we downed the third tumbler. Now, I thought, we must go. Someone blocked my way. He seemed to be dressed in black, and he was holding a vodka bottle.

My mouth seemed a great deal bigger than usual, and my tongue was made of – could it be mohair, I wondered? A silence had settled on everyone. Faces were turned to me: red faces, smiling faces, faces suffused with drink. I watched little beads of sweat appear on the mayor's forehead. I had plenty of time for these observations, since everything had suddenly switched into slow motion, like pressing the jog switch on an editing machine. It was my turn to speak, I knew. But what should I say? Perhaps I should slap them all on the back and ask them for some ideas. That was funny, I reflected, and laughed quite loudly: louder than I had expected. Everyone else was laughing too. Friendly people. Nice people.

'To the nice, friendly Russian people! Long may they drink vodka! Long after we have left tonight.'

I downed the fourth big tumbler. By now it was like drinking some anaesthetic liquid – Thawpit, I thought. Do they still make Thawpit? The mayor seemed uncertain on this point. He was holding out his hand to shake mine, but his aim was definitely off. Thawpit, I tried to explain to him while our hands sought each other, had been much used for removing stains from clothes when I was a boy. Not so good to drink, though. The mayor agreed about that, and offered me another tumbler, though not in words. Words were in short supply now.

Our hands met eventually. Big hands. I wanted to explain to him that we really were all brothers, but it was hard to speak while laughing. He was laughing. Everyone was laughing. They still had a lot of vodka ahead of them.

Ahead of us was a long drive. We waved a good deal through the windows, and they waved back. They were still laughing, and so were we.

'Fraternal,' I tried to call out, but I said 'Flat-earth' instead. It didn't matter: the mayor couldn't speak English anyway.

'That banquet lasted exactly twenty minutes,' Olga said crisply. She had avoided the vodka.

So, fortunately, had the driver. He behaved as though nothing whatever had happened, but neither of them thought we were very cultured.

'And more than half a bottle each.'

We laughed about that for a while. Then we realized I would have to write a script to go with all these pictures of the town, and that it would have to be written and recorded within two hours. There was silence in the car while we each reflected on that. I certainly couldn't enunciate words by now, but my hand worked after a fashion and I was able to write. Big letters, but readable. I started to write, sitting in the back seat. The fumes shifted around my head, parting at times to allow a thought or a name or a memory to come through, then meeting impenetrably behind them again.

By the time we reached the outskirts of Moscow I had the thing written. The Thawpit concept had tried to work its way in at one point, like King Charles's head in Mr Dick's memorial, but I had managed to fight it off. My tongue was still several sizes too large, as though I had bought one in a butcher's and had tried to fit it inside my mouth, and I couldn't read my script out loud. We laughed a lot about that. All of us except Olga.

By the time we reached the office we weren't laughing so much: we were up against it. In the cutting-room, with a picture editor who had had no vodka whatever, I was able to record a version of the script. It sounded as though I had just had most of my teeth out with a powerful anaesthetic, but it was something the editor could start working on.

By the time the job was finished, just under two hours later, my tongue had shrunk to almost its normal size. I was still swaying, and only managed to hold my head on by an act of great will; but I could manage sibilants without putting an 'h' with them, and even avoided speaking with that terrible precision which marks the recently drunk.

'It'll do,' Paul said. 'Just.'

His 's's were getting better too.

The mayor loved it, as it turned out. They were still talking about the twenty-minute banquet in his once secret town for a long time afterwards.

The heat was stifling, even for Lagos. We were standing in an open courtyard, but we might as well have been crowded into a tiny windowless hut. My shirt, unwrapped crisp and neat from the hotel laundry an hour before, hung on my shoulders like an old chamois leather. Flies, stupefied by the temperature, blundered into my face. There was an open puddle in the middle of the courtyard, bright green in colour, and mosquitoes rose hungrily from it. I was coming to loathe the whole place.

'What a dump.'

We were waiting for a couple of British prisoners to arrive for a court appearance. Some time before they had sold a helicopter to some Nigerian company which had failed to pay them. After a long period of waiting and remonstrating they had seized the helicopter and tried to fly it out of the country. Unfortunately they had been caught and charged with a list of serious offences.

Alongside us were other television crews including ITN, whose correspondent was Michael Brunson. The competition between the BBC and ITN in those days was extremely fierce, and Brunson, who was a man I had always rather admired, kept as close an eye on me in the airless courtyard as I was keeping on him.

So now, dripping with sweat, we waited for the prison van to arrive and tried to work out where to get the best shot. It was worse for the camera crew than it was for me. Chris Marlow had to carry the camera, while Roger Snow was loaded down with the sound gear. I was lugging the tripod with me, that Sisyphean burden of the television correspondent: four feet high, balanced with a particular wrongness, and with various projecting bits to get humiliatingly caught in things. The only thing worse than having to carry the tripod is not having a tripod to carry. I have worked with Italian and French crews who find the tripod as much of a nuisance as I do, and who prefer filming from the unaided human shoulder instead: with the result that no shot is ever still or steady.

There is a gadget called a monopod, an extendable leg to rest the camera on; but that too lends itself to wobbling. In 1986, when Margaret Thatcher paid a triumphant visit to Moscow, I was carrying a monopod when she went to see an Orthodox monastery just outside the capital. The crowds were huge, and when the KGB men were not pushing elderly women or young children around they were sticking their great hands into the lenses of the foreign camera crews: the self-appointed role of the security man the world over, it seems.

One large and aggressive figure, built along the general lines of a concrete pillbox and with a hat perched on top, was giving our cameraman a particularly hard time, and the more he pushed and punched him the angrier we became. The crowd swirled around us, separating us from him slightly. That gave me my chance. I pulled out the monopod to its fullest length, insinuated through the press of bodies in the crowd, and shoved the head of it very hard into his groin. It was like potting a billiard ball. It was so crowded that he couldn't double up, but his eyes went very red. He tried to get through to me afterwards, but my colleagues always stood between him and me. The monopod has its uses.

Through the Nigerian heat came the sound of sirens, as sluggish as though it was wrapped up and unable to breathe, like us. Brakes squealed, and the prison van drove fast into the courtyard. What it must have been like for the two poor men inside was hard to imagine. The ITN crew and we jostled and shouldered each other like footballers anticipating a corner kick, but as the prisoners were taken out and brought across the yard to the stairs to the courtroom Chris Marlow managed to get ahead of them, and went backwards up the staircase, filming them while I asked them questions. ITN had to film from a step or two behind. First blood to us.

'What are we going to do when we get to the top?'

Chris's whisper was loud enough to be recorded on tape. So was my answer.

'Just keep on filming.'

A soldier was standing by the door of the courtroom with a rifle. He looked as surprised to see us as I was to see him.

'Now what?'

'Keep going. It'll be all right.'

It wasn't one of my more accurate predictions.

The soldier said nothing more; he was too amazed to stop us. We were swept in through the door, Chris and Roger and I walking backwards, the two prisoners and their escort coming next, and ITN following at the back. I could see the cameraman looking questioningly at Michael Brunson, and Brunson doing what I would have done: urging him on to follow the opposition.

We were in a big, dark room. As I began to look round and my eyes grew accustomed to it an enormous bellowing broke out at the far end of it.

'You there! Whatever do you think you're doing?'

'It's all right,' I whispered to Chris Marlow. 'Just keep filming.'

It was my second big mistake of the morning.

Peering down towards the source of the bellowing I made out an enormous scarlet shape topped with white, like some kind of gigantic pudding. Then the extent of my mistake became obvious. We were standing in the well of the court, and the scarlet shape was a judge in full robes. Complete with Old Bailey-style wig.

Now the words became clearer, yet if anything louder.

'Who the devil are you, and what do you think you're doing with that camera in my courtroom?'

'I'm very sorry. Sir. I didn't understand where we were. It's entirely my fault – the others just did what I told them. I can't apologize enough, sir.'

I thought it sounded rather handsome: sincere but not grovelling. The judge felt differently. He exploded with scarlet wrath.

'Would you dare behave like this in an English court? Would you? Would you?'

'No, sir, I wouldn't, and I greatly apologize. All I can say is that I didn't appreciate where we were, sir.'

It was like being a schoolboy again; but I thought that if I went into auto-grovel we might at least get out of the place as free men. Still, something strange was going on: the more I abased myself, the more sorry I said I was, the angrier the judge became. I looked around me in despair. What else could I do?

The British consul was sitting on a bench not far away, and he was mouthing something desperately at me. Yet it was as though there was a glass panel between us: I couldn't understand the twisting shapes his lips were making. I turned back to the judge.

'I am the one who was solely responsible for this act of rudeness, sir,' I found myself saying. Of course, I would have liked to blame ITN, but this might have strained the judge's credibility too much.

The bellowing started again. In his rage the judge was addressing the other people in the court.

'This man comes into my court, ignoring all the rules and conventions, and he proceeds to insult me by refusing to use my proper title. Would he call an English judge "sir"?'

At last, at long last, I understood. That was what the British consul had been mouthing: Call him M'Lord.

I called him M'Lord.

At once the atmosphere became a little easier: I might even get out of this without being arrested, I told myself.

And indeed, given what a British judge would have done to a

Nigerian camera crew which erupted onto the floor of Court Six at the Old Bailey, the judge in his magnificent scarlet robes treated us with extraordinary leniency. He insisted, however, that we should hand over our cassettes. I could see that Chris Marlow and the ITN cameraman were both taking the tapes out of their cameras, and, with a sleight of hand practised often over many years, were exchanging them for blank tapes which they had previously fished out of their bags. Michael Brunson and I took the virgin tapes up to the judge, bowed humbly, and handed them over. I imagine Brunson was thinking exactly what I was: I pray he hasn't got a machine which can play professional videotapes.

Close up, the judge was a great deal less terrifying. Under other circumstances, I thought, he might be rather jolly. He let us go with another warning, and that evening we received our cassettes back. The two British pilots were soon released from prison, though I never heard whether they received their money.

In time I came to love Nigeria, even though during one visit I was arrested five times in one day in Lagos, merely for trying to film in the streets. It is a nation of people who behave with great courtliness, and even in the worst slums they are remarkably well-informed, thanks largely to the Nigerian press, which is one of the liveliest and most competitive in the world. The next day one newspaper wrote up our courtroom intrusion as follows:

> The two British newshounds breezed into the court and started taking snapshots with great abandon. One of them, Mr John Simpson, the head of BBC media, got into trouble with the judge for incorrect appellation, but he deeply apologized and was allowed to leave relishing his freedom.

Perhaps the press, like the judge, let us off lightly: it didn't, for instance, make any of the misprints for which the Nigerian newspapers are famous. For years the staff at the British High Commission kept a cutting from one Lagos paper on their notice board. It described the arrival back in Lagos of the Nigerian foreign minister:

> He bounded down the steps of the aircraft with a smile on his lips and a rose in his bottom-hole.

As I say, with journalism the absurd is never far away.

11

PLEASURES

This bearer, Captain Henry Bell, returneth home fraught
like a traveller more with observation than money.

Letter from Sir Henry Wotton,
British ambassador to Venice, 4 May 1618

In 1877 a reporter for the London *World*, a Victorian forerunner of
Hello magazine, went to visit the explorer Sir Richard Burton and his
excitable wife Isabel at their home in Trieste, where Burton was the
British consul. It wasn't small.

Captain and Mrs Burton are well, if airily, lodged in a flat
composed of ten rooms.

The place, according to the reporter, was absolutely crammed
with objects, and was divided between the Cross and the Crescent.
The Catholic part, which was Isabel's, had an altar and was filled
with her devotional paintings, crosses and little lamps burning in
front of the figures of saints. The much larger Islamic part was
Burton's.

The rooms, opening into one another, are bright with Oriental
hangings, with trays and dishes of gold and silver, brass trays
and goblets trays, chibouques with great amber mouthpieces,
and all kinds of Eastern treasures mingled with family souvenirs.
There is no carpet, but a Bedouin rug occupies the middle of the
floor, and vies in brilliancy of colour with Persian enamels and
bits of good old china. There are no sofas, but plenty of divans
covered with Damascus stuffs . . . Every odd corner is piled with
weapons, guns, pistols, boar-spears, swords of every shape and
make, foils and masks, chronometers, barometers, and all kinds

of scientific instruments . . . Idols are not wanting, for elephant-nosed Gunpati [Ganesha?] is there, cheek by jowl with Vishnu.

And so was Burton's library of 8,000 books on every conceivable subject, many of them ones which Isabel preferred not to know about. (Once, when she was having a tea-party with some of her friends, Burton stalked disapprovingly into the room without saying a word and threw a manuscript down on a side-table before walking out again. The ladies clustered round excitedly to find out what his latest book was about. Its title was 'A History of Farting.')

Dee and I know a little of this business of collecting things. Our flat is also jammed with objects: spears and feathered headdresses from the Amazon, clay figures from China, swords from the Middle East, masks from West Africa, prints and oils from South Africa, boxes and astrolabes from Persia, carpets from Afghanistan, gun-metal busts of Lenin, Stalin and lesser Soviet heroes, and a thousand other mementoes from the 120 countries we have visited between us. There is the wind-up gramophone I bought in the Baghdad *soukh*; a silver *buzkashi* whip from Jalalabad; a French stereoscope from Bogota; totems from Nigeria. There is even a painting of an archangel from colonial Peru. Archangels, being super-powerful, must naturally have been armed; so ours, impressively winged, holds a flintlock musket.

This mania for collecting things has brought its problems. By the fireplace, for instance, is another musket, made in 1825 at the Tower of London armoury for the East India Company's army, then sold or captured by Afghans and turned into a *jezail* of the kind that put a ball into Dr Watson's leg and made it ache on those November evenings when he went to see Sherlock Holmes. I went to enormous trouble to get a certificate for it in Kabul, and another in Peshawar across the Pakistani border. Then I wrapped it up again and checked it in with my luggage for London. There was no question of disguising the shape: no need for that, anyway.

We arrived at an appalling hour of the morning, and all the other passengers had taken their luggage and left by the time my musket came around on the carousel. As it did so, I heard the sound of running feet. Three policemen wearing flak-jackets and carrying the latest automatic weapons surrounded me.

'This firearm yours, sir?'

I agreed that it was. The policemen became very worked up. They checked me for other guns, as though I might have had a spare AK-47 somewhere.

'Clean, sarge.'

That was a relief.

'Do you have a permit for importing a firearm to the United Kingdom?'

We went through this question at length. After a while it turned out why they were so excited: the previous day a man had gone into a school at Dunblane and killed several children. I was a man, I had a gun, *ergo* I too might go into a school and kill people with it.

'I think you'd better look at the gun a bit more closely.'

They looked at it.

'You *say* this is an antique. Can you prove that?'

I looked at the original flint-lock, which still had its flint in place, and shrugged. There was a pause.

Then the police armourer came striding out in a what's-all-this, don't-you-know-I've-got-serious-work-to-do kind of way and picked the musket up. He looked like a younger version of Q in the Bond films.

'I say, what a fantastic example! Excellent condition. Look – Tower markings there, the lion. Lock in working order, too, I shouldn't wonder. Superb! Where on earth did you get this? It's a museum-piece.'

'It's a dangerous weapon.'

'Oh, yes, very, sergeant. If this gentleman fired it, someone would almost certainly die.' He winked at me. 'Him.'

At last, reluctantly, the policemen decided that maybe after all they hadn't captured another potential mass murderer. I was allowed to leave the airport without a stain on my character.

At Sheremetyevo Airport in Moscow, it was always war. This is where a smiling KGB man had once put my briefcase containing a filmed interview with the dissident Andrei Sakharov into a kind of infra-red oven before handing it back to me. The idea was that the interview would be magnetically wiped, but Soviet technology ensured that the interview was scarcely affected.

In 1991, after the failure of the coup against Mikhail Gorbachev and the resulting collapse of Marxism-Leninism, I went through Customs with a suitcase filled with gunmetal busts of Soviet big-shots: Lenin and Stalin, of course, but also rarer figures like Kirov, Dzerzhinsky, Sverdlov and Frunze. No one wanted these things at the time, and I had picked them up from shops and stalls all over Moscow. There were fourteen of them.

There was no law against taking them out of the country. They were without any intrinsic value, and had mostly been made after the Second World War. All the same, there did seem to be rather a lot of them. I had found it impossible not to buy every one I saw; who knew, after all, whether they would even survive this latest flip of the Russian wheel of fortune?

'What is?' asked the Customs man, looking at his X-ray machine.

I went round to look: Sheremetyevo is the kind of place you can do that. Fourteen little heads were looking at me out of my suitcase. I was fascinated: you could see Frunze's beard, Dzerzhinsky's buttoned-up tunic like a dentist's white coat, Marx's perennially hectoring finger, Lenin's outstretched arm. They were all higgledy-piggledy, as though they were taking a turn in a washing machine. I looked at the Customs man. He didn't share my interest.

'You cannot take these things out of the Soviet – out of Russia.'

'They're paid for. And it isn't illegal; they're all modern.'

'You cannot take these things out of the country.'

We swiftly got into the old 'Show-me-where-it-says' and 'Because-I-say-so' routine. Customs men always, in my experience, win these contests; they have the rule book on their side, and you can't inspect it.

'Why do you want these things?'

It sounded as though he thought I was a secret agent: maybe I was going to copy them and flood the world with phoney Lenins.

'Because I'm interested in history.'

'Hm.'

I reflected for a moment; he had a certain look about him. A Communist look, perhaps.

'You see, not everyone wants to forget the Soviet days. Do you, for instance?'

'That's my business, Mr History Man.'

Now we were getting somewhere.

'If these things stay here, God knows what will happen to them. If I take them, I will always protect them.'

He looked affectionately at the faces which were staring out at him in the X-ray: faces of the crooks, the idealists, the fanatics, the time-servers who had brought this poor suffering country to its present crazy pass.

'Look after them well, Mr History Man.'

In 1997 I went back in Beijing for the first time since the massacre in Tiananmen Square, eight years earlier. The Chinese authorities had been reluctant to let foreign journalists who had witnessed the massacre return to China. And as time passed, and the memory of the events of May and June 1989 started to fade, the Chinese authorities increasingly tried to give the impression that there had been a great deal of exaggeration about what had happened. Some, including the defence minister, blandly denied that anyone had died at all in Tiananmen Square; and, as with all big lies, there is always someone who is foolish enough to believe it. Maybe it appeals to the little man's instinctive distrust of what he is told, and of the motives of those who tell him.

Nowadays people quite often ask me, especially in the United States, whether anyone genuinely witnessed any deaths – or was the Tiananmen Massacre just an invention of the Western media? Since I myself saw a number of people shot down by the army that night, including a young woman and a Korean photographer who was standing on the balcony next to mine in the Beijing Hotel, my answer has always been fairly crisp.

Not every Chinese official was quite so barefaced about what had happened. Some were inclined to speak of 'the tragedy', without being more specific. They had to be careful: in 1989 a great many government officials in Beijing had come out openly in support of the students and their month-long demonstration in the Square, and they were as appalled as anyone else at the murder of the students. But they had their careers to think about, and they quickly pulled their heads below the parapet again.

One of the great pleasures of being a free journalist is that you don't have to toe anybody's line. The Chinese foreign ministry was kind enough to invite my colleagues and me to a banquet at one of the best restaurants in Beijing, and it proved to be a very jovial affair. Until, that is, the moment was reached where, with amazing delicacy, the question of the BBC's reporting of Chinese matters was raised. I smiled politely, and waited for the knife to be slipped in.

Eventually it was. What a pity, said the chief official, that our reporting of events in China wasn't more objective. All this business about human rights – so unnecessary.

I laughed, in as phoney a way as I could manage.

'Well,' I said, 'speaking as someone who could, if he chose, sue the Chinese government for appalling professional defamation in any of a dozen international courts—'

It was the kind of thing that had to be explained, and I told them how the Chinese government had sent video cassettes to their embassies around the world in the immediate aftermath of the massacre, showing their side of the story; which was that foreign agents like me had given money to the students to buy weapons for their uprising against the authorities. Someone gave us a copy of the video, and we used it in a report for BBC Television News. In one sequence you could see me handing a piece of paper to a student: cash, said the voice-over. Cut to students unloading rifles from a lorry: these were what the students had bought with my money.

There were lots of secret policemen hanging around in the Square with video cameras throughout the month-long demonstration that ended with the massacre. One of them must have filmed me signing my autograph – every foreigner who was there was asked for his autograph; it was a fad among the students – and another of them filmed the mysterious arrival of a lorryload of rifles in the Square. The driver of the lorry had screeched to a halt and ran off, and the students discovered the rifles in the back. They unloaded them and handed them over to the police. End of story.

Imperturbably, the senior official was in the process of passing me some choice morsel as I spoke; but it was noticeable that at the moment when I suggested suing the government his chopsticks paused momentarily in mid air before resuming their movement towards my bowl of rice. We talked about other things after that.

Even eight years after the massacre it was still difficult to get into the Square with a television camera, but we managed it. I looked for the bullet holes on the steps of the Monument in the centre, where the students had gathered at the end, but they had all been expertly filled in; just a faint discoloration, perhaps. Otherwise there was no sign whatever. On the anniversary the newspapers and the speeches of senior politicians made no mention of the massacre. The most critical moment in Chinese history after Mao Zedong's death seemed to have been entirely forgotten.

I was beginning to feel like that character in Stendhal's *Le Rouge et le Noir* who fought at the Battle of Waterloo but had told the story so many times afterwards that he began to wonder if he really had been there after all, or had only heard about it from other people. I looked at the stretch of gutter in Chang'an Avenue where I had lain while an armoured personnel carrier passed close by me, blasting away. Over there was the place where I had seen a woman take a shot in the back, before some of the bravest of the onlookers rescued her and rushed her off to hospital. And that was where the man with his shopping bags stood in front of the column of tanks. Or did I just see that on television? Surely not.

It was hard to think, though, that any such thing had ever taken place in this busy street. A traffic jam had formed. Eight years earlier, cars had still been almost a rarity and most people had got around on bicycles; by the late 1990s bicycles were on their way out in Beijing. I wandered through the Square, remembering all the things that had happened to me there, and all the people I had met, and the acrid smell of cooking, and the harsh taste of pancakes which a few enterprising stallholders had hawked around from tent to tent, and the crackle of broken glass and bits of wood under my feet. And the smiles. There was real innocence in the smiles.

I hailed a trishaw: one of the few around now. It was a trishaw driver who had stood on the unstable seat of his vehicle and ex-plained his reasons for bringing students here to the Square free of charge. Some people laughed at him, because of his ungrammatical Chinese.

'All right, so I'm a humble man,' he shouted. 'But I have the dreams of an emperor!'

Those were sublime days. And now the Square was clean and empty and heavily guarded, and every third or fourth person here seemed to be a policeman.

> The Empire is destroyed, yet mountains and rivers remain.
> In the city, it is spring; the grass and trees flourish.

It is one of the most famous couplets in Chinese poetry, written by Du Fu in the 760s, after the utter destruction created by the rebellion against the great T'ang dynasty emperor Sywan Dzung. The words express a dull feeling of surprise that life should still continue after all the fixed points of life have been overthrown. In 756 An Lushan, the commander of the Chinese army, felt his position was being undermined by the growing influence of the beautiful Yang Gweifei. She was the Emperor's favourite concubine, and in his adoration of her he utterly ignored his imperial duties. Yang Gweifei had used the Emperor's favour to get her relatives into some of the top jobs in the administration. Her beauty, heavy and voluptuous, set the standard for Chinese womanhood, and the paintings, sculptures and clay figures of the next century or so reflect her features.

The civil war which An Lushan unleashed destroyed China's economy and fatally weakened the T'ang dynasty. The national tragedy was mirrored in a personal one: the Emperor and Yang Gweifei fled the capital, Chang'an – what we now call Xian – and were pursued by the rebels. The Emperor's own men, still loyal to him but bitterly angry with Yang Gweifei who they believed had brought the disastrous rebellion about, refused to go any further unless she was put to death on the spot. The Emperor had to watch while she was strangled by the roadside with a silken cord. The place where this happened is still pointed out, twelve hundred years later.

My time in China during the Tiananmen period had given me an abiding interest in Chinese poetry and art, and I had begun to collect some of the cheaper clay figures of the T'ang period: especially those which echoed the beauty of Yang Gweifei.

'Liu Li Chang,' I said to the trishaw driver; but since my tonal values were non-existent he couldn't understand me for a while. Then, 'Ah, Liu *Li* Chang.'

Liu Li Chang is a little enclave, part phoney and part very attractive, not far from Tiananmen. For centuries it has been the antiquities market of Beijing, and the houses and alleyways have remained as they were in the Qing dynasty period. Many of the things that are for sale there nowadays are modern imitations: there are factories all over China where antiquities are manufactured, then buried in the earth for a set period of time so that they will have the right smell and appearance. A good judge of T'ang dynasty clay figures can often tell at once whether a piece is old or faked; but with the best and most important the only way to tell is to have them tested in a laboratory; a company in Oxford is the one which the serious dealers in Hong Kong use.

I wandered along, remembering the times I had been here in 1989, and the people I had met then. I went into a tea house and sat through the usual ceremony, but it seemed quicker and more perfunctory than when I had last been here, and the tea lacked the extraordinary lingering scent which it had had before. The girl from whom I had bought a mandarin's hat with a crystal button on its crown, and a curious fish carved out of some strange green and red stone, had gone; now the shop sold cheap imitations of Chinese landscape paintings.

In a thoroughly melancholy mood I caught a trishaw back to my hotel: one of the enormous, faceless places with identikit names which have sprung up with sometimes questionable money in every large Chinese city. In a corridor just off the lobby I had noticed a dark shop, tucked away around a corner. In its window were some figures which looked as though they might just possibly be genuine, and were certainly worth investigating. There was, for instance, a Yang Gweifei figure which might or might not be genuine, her hands clasped, her plump, lovely face turned slightly and looking upwards. There were all sorts of other things too: busts of Mao in porcelain and metal, Little Red Books, some vases which might have been genuine Qing but probably weren't.

The man behind the counter scarcely bothered to look up from his paper. He was thin and gaunt, perhaps in his early thirties, with a beard which looked like a plant struggling in thin soil. Then he put the paper down quickly. I could feel his eyes on me as I looked at a rather charming mounted figure in clay, with traces of paint on it. Surreptitiously I licked the tip of my finger and touched the clay: the moisture sank in at once. It isn't an infallible sign of age, but it can sometimes be an indication. Smell can be too. I lifted it up and sniffed it discreetly.

The man laughed. 'First time in my shop, but not first time we met.'

I stared at him.

'I know you. You forget me.'

I looked for a clue: if we had met, it could only have been in 1989. Surely he was too young to have worked here then?

He walked round me and closed the door to his shop. He was surprisingly tall, I found. He turned back towards me.

'We were very many, you not. This is why I remember.'

So he had been a student in the Square. But did he really remember me, or was it someone else he recalled?

'You are from BBC. Was very bad rain. I give you coat.'

Surely not, I thought. I struggled to remember his face in the savage storm, but all I could remember was what he did, not what he looked like. It was in the last stages of the protest in the Square, just a few days before the savage destruction of 3–4 June. The sky had darkened apocalyptically, and the rain had dropped like a flood. I was wearing a light tropical suit which was soaked through in an instant, and a fountain pen in the inside pocket exploded as though I had been shot and bled black blood.

The cameraman with me did his best to protect his camera – there was no chance of filming anything anyway – and we tacked across the empty square towards the shelter of the underpass a quarter of a mile away, blown to and fro by the violent wind. It was suddenly very cold, and I shivered uncontrollably as the rain leaped up at us from the paving stones.

Three figures tacked their way towards us like little wherries, students who were trying to make for the tented camp, or what was left of it. The air was thick with bits of flying debris – tarpaulins, boxes, bits of plastic sheeting. As the three students came alongside us one of them stripped off his thin raincoat, made of some lightish rubbery material, much worn by the poorer students; we used to call them body-condoms. He held it round my shoulders and it whipped in the wind.

'You remember?'

I did; but I wanted to test him, just to be certain. 'What did you do when you gave me your coat?'

'Ah, you think I not know. I kiss your hand.'

He had, too: he went down on his knees onto the rain-drenched pavement.

'Why?'

'Because you were still there. You and others. I was glad for all of you.'

It wasn't just me, he meant, in case I regarded myself as being worthy of particular worship. I didn't, knowing I wasn't.

His name, he said, was Li, and he had had a hard time of it at the end of the Tiananmen protest: hunted out of the Square by soldiers, lucky to remain alive. He had headed off to the provinces, like so many of the students, and worked quietly on a farm for a year or so. The local authorities knew who he was – in a society like China, where everyone has a work number and an internal passport, there is no escaping them. But he hadn't been a student leader, so they chose to ignore him. Eventually he had come back to Beijing, went through the necessary self-criticism, finished his studies, and was in the process of taking over this shop from an elderly relative.

We shook hands enthusiastically, two survivors of the past.

So what, I asked, did he have to show me that was interesting? He laughed. The mounted figure I had been looking at was good: it had been brought to him from a Sui dynasty tomb somewhere near the Great Wall. But there were much better treasures: a porcelain saucer so thin you could see your hand through it, a pot that he said was from the early T'ang dynasty, a scroll by a particular master whose name I could not catch. And this, he said, reaching under the counter and bringing out a red box that might have held a cake. Instead, it held a head: the head of a general, discoloured from its time in the ground. It was clearly a portrait. I could never have afforded that, or any of his other treasures. I looked again at the clay figure on horseback.

'This really is genuine?'

'Sure.'

He said it in an offhand way that made me uncertain.

'But that would mean I couldn't take it out of the country.'

'I give you certificate to say it's copy.'

So he won both ways: he sold it to me as genuine, and yet the documentation said it was false. I shook his hand, and he bowed me to the door. The idealist who offered a stranger his raincoat out of respect now sold cheap fakes and swore they were real. And yet, hidden away under the counter, he still had something that was genuine and unique and truly valuable. Not everything had been spoiled; not everything had been entirely forgotten.

One of the best foreign correspondents of the twentieth century was – is – a lady of a certain age with thick glasses, an extraordinary range of contacts, and a clever line in presenting herself as vague and helpless. Clare Hollingworth worked for most of the British broadsheets from the end of the thirties to the present day. She watched the first German tanks roll into Poland to begin the Second World War, and woke her senior colleague in Berlin, Hugh Carlton Greene (later to be the director-general of the BBC) to tell him. He insisted she must have been mistaken, and suggested that she should go back to bed.

In the course of the war that followed she obtained an exclusive interview with the Shah of Iran at the beginning of his reign, and nearly forty years later she carried out the last major interview with him, after he had been chased out of Iran by Ayatollah Khomeini. At a dinner party in the 1970s she charmed the captain of a Soviet nuclear submarine and made him promise to take her on board. He did, and it was the first time any Western journalist had ever seen one from inside.

In East Berlin she spotted a new type of Russian tank standing unguarded, climbed up onto it, and got a good look at the dials on the dashboard. An angry Russian soldier caught her, but she explained that she was lost, and had merely climbed onto the tank to see how she could get back to West Berlin. The next morning her newspaper carried an exclusive report on the maximum speed and range of the new Soviet battle tank.

Clare Hollingworth is perhaps most famous for her reporting from China during the latter part of the Cultural Revolution and the death of Mao Zedong. Life was very hard for foreign journalists then. A friend of mine from one of the big international news agencies who was there at the same time told me how he and his colleagues took it in turns to speak to ordinary Chinese people.

'You dreaded it when your turn came. You had to sidle up to someone in a queue or standing in the street, and try to get in a question. Even if they answered, it would only be a minute or so before the police would come and beat you up or arrest you. Then the only good thing was the thought that it would be four weeks before you had to do it again.'

Clare's Chinese translator, appointed by the authorities, was hostile and reserved, an older woman who had lived in Beijing before the Communists took over. She was fiercely committed, never missing an opportunity to criticize Clare or tell her of the superiority of Maoist thought. It was only after they had slowly reached a basis of friendship that the translator would describe to her what life was really like for middle-class people like herself. In particular, and under conditions of the strictest secrecy, she told Clare a story.

Once every year, on their wedding anniversary, she and her husband would make sure that their children went to bed early in the tiny apartment where they lived. Perhaps they would give them something to sleep soundly: during the Cultural Revolution children were often the greatest danger, since they were indoctrinated with the need to inform on their parents or grandparents if anything of a counter-revolutionary nature were said or done. The translator knew that she and her husband could be imprisoned or even killed if they did anything of the kind. Even so, directly the children were asleep they would lift the floorboards in their bedroom and bring out a box which they had hidden there.

Inside the box were a ball gown and a suit of evening clothes. In complete silence the couple would put them on. In complete silence they would take hands. In complete silence they would waltz around the small space in the centre of the room, careful not to knock anything over. She would rest her head on his shoulder, and they would hold each other tightly for a moment or two, remembering other days. Then the orchestra in their heads would cease to play, and they would slowly, reluctantly, sorrowfully move apart. It was time to take the clothes off again and pack them carefully away in the hiding place below the floorboards. The ceremony had lasted for perhaps fifteen minutes, and was the most dangerous thing either of them ever did. But this secret pleasure gave them the strength to continue for another year with the terrible charade of living with and praising the absurd and terrible system created by the twentieth century's worst dictator.

One of the greatest pleasures of travelling in the Islamic world, and they are many, is to visit the bazaar. The brightness of the sun cuts as suddenly as a film to domed and vaulted passageways thronged like the runs of an anthill. The racket of voices shouting and chanting wares engulfs you:

'A white sweet lemon, fruit of the gardens!'

'How fragrant, O mint leaves!'

'Spices for your rice!'

'Clothes for your back!'

'Fine leather, fine leather!'

'Whatever you lack, come to my shop!'

A push in the back can come from an old man bent double with the weight of two dozen carpets, or from the nose of a laden donkey, or from the front wheel of a motorbike easing its way through the crowds. Boys slip between the lines of shuffling people with brass coffee pots, or kettles and little cups: '*Chai, chai, chai*,' 'Coffee hot and well-spiced.' The incessant sharp clatter of the *nahassin*, the coppersmith, as he turns his wares around on his knees, hammering out little dips and depressions in the soft metal, rings through the alleys. In Tripoli they make the crescents for the tops of mosques; in Baghdad they knock out trays and cooking pots; in Bohkara they make enormous pots for weddings; in Isfahan, exquisite plates with delicate designs on them, working away in the light of hurricane lamps.

Medical shops, especially in Damascus, sell dried lizards, snakes, salamanders and chameleons, mostly to improve potency. There are cucumbers which help with stomach pains, turtle shells which, laid on a child's chest, prevent frightening dreams, and dried hedgehogs which prevent baldness. Sweetshops sell every variety of local confection; in Isfahan they specialize in *gaz*, which is lighter and better than French nougat and contains pistachio nuts, while in Qom, the religious centre of Iran, they sell *sohan* in tins like old film cans: it is a brown disc, six inches or more across, incredibly yet satisfyingly sweet, made from oil, flour, sugar and some kind of herb which no one has ever quite managed to identify for me.

In the Tehran bazaar Dee and I searched for an azan alarm clock, a frightful mosque-shaped object in pink or baby-blue plastic which wakes you with an electronic cry like a *muezzin*. These things are kitsch in the extreme; perhaps that is the attraction. Yet there is also something about being wakened by the sound of the azan which, no matter how artificial, makes you feel for that first conscious instant that you could be in Mashhad or Samarkand or Khiva.

I saw one at a stall filled with plastic junk, and we pushed our way through the river of customers and sellers and stood in front of it. The man behind the counter was about my age, with a grey handlebar moustache and a dirty suit. His eyes lit up when he saw Dee.

'I would like one of your azan clocks, please.'

'Ah – a Muslim!'

'No, but I enjoy being wakened like one.'

He liked the quip. 'You are English.'

One of the pleasures of being in Iran is that there are so few other Westerners around: you are a rarity, something of genuine interest. I explained that I lived in Ireland, which was a place he had never heard of. But he knew all about the British; everyone in Iran does. Everyone also thinks they still direct affairs in Iran through the medium of the Americans, whom they regard as being the stupid tools of the subtle *Ingilisi*.

' "If you trip on a stone," ' he quoted, ' "be sure an Englishman has left it there." '

'But I will not put a hat on you,' I said, trying to remember my scanty stock of Persian proverbs. Putting a hat on someone means you are deceiving them; something like pulling the wool over their eyes.

He was delighted by that. He thrust a second azan clock at us, and would have given them both to us for nothing if I hadn't insisted on paying. But we had to have tea. Dee drank hers like a Persian, holding a cube of sugar in her mouth, and that enchanted him even more. He was still waving as we launched ourselves back into the river of people and lost sight of him.

Women pushed by us, their faces covered, swathed in all-embracing black cloth, yet with the hint of some brilliantly coloured fabric underneath which would only be revealed in the privacy of the living quarters. Strangely for a society where it is illegal for men to touch women in public and where women cannot wear clothes that show their figures, brassieres and panties hang from stretched-out wires across the fronts of innumerable stalls, and men sell them appraisingly to the women who pass by.

But the bazaar is still fundamentally a male preserve. In a city like Tehran, where the merchants of the bazaar are a powerful economic force, the shop is usually just a front for dealing in other commodities. So a shopkeeper who sells pencils and exercise books for school-children will use his treasured telephone (to buy one and have it connected can cost a great deal of money) to trade in wheat futures or pistachio nuts or the export of sheep meat to Thailand. The *bazaaris* are regarded as a conservative and religious group, and they certainly played an important part in bringing down the Shah. But in Iran as elsewhere these things are fading. I have met *bazaaris* whose children go to university in Britain or the United States, and who want an end to the religious dictatorship which has damaged the Iranian economy so seriously.

I have never yet come across a woman who owns a shop in the bazaar; not even in Iran, where women have more rights than in most other Islamic countries. The only bazaar where I have seen women selling things was in Istanbul. In the tea houses, dirty and fly-blown and lit by noisy flickering neon yet nevertheless havens of delight, men sit under pictures of the President or the King or some cool green landscape puffing meditatively on water pipes – *qalian* in Persian, *narghileh* in Arabic – reading newspapers and discussing the news of the day, and drinking tea from small glasses or coffee tasting of cardamom from even smaller cups.

The tea came originally from China, which gave it the name *chai*, and the coffee from Kaffa in Ethiopia and thence to Mocha on the Red Sea, where Shaikh Ali ibn Omar al Shadili offered it to a group of Portuguese adventurers in the early sixteenth century. For a long time Islamic scholars were deeply opposed to coffee, and in some parts of the Turkish Empire the penalty for drinking it could be death; but by the end of the seventeenth century it had become accepted. A man has to drink something as he sits smoking apple-flavoured tobacco in his *nargileh*. Not that tobacco or the *nargileh* are as old as coffee or tea; tobacco arrived in the Middle East from the New World at the start of the seventeenth century, and the water pipe is merely an invention of the eighteenth century. The charcoal is stirred in its little cup on the top of the *nargileh*, the water bubbles inside the glass, the mouthpiece (nowadays plastic, and removable) is held at the side of the mouth, and the fragrant smoke billows cheerfully upwards.

In a popular tea house there is always the clash of dominoes or backgammon pieces. Throughout the former Turkish Empire dozens of variants of backgammon are played, with a speed and a ferocity which the outsider can never grasp. Young boys take your shoes away and clean them in the courtyard; occasionally – just occasionally – a *hakawati* or storyteller will wander in and gather people around him.

The stories they tell are the kind you come across in *A Thousand And One Nights*. The only *hakawati* I have listened to at length was an old man in the holy city of Qom in Iran, who declaimed his account in a sing-song voice about a princess who turned into a bird and back again. Many of the stories you hear deal with the ancient theme of the ruler wandering around among his people in disguise, to listen to what they are saying. Maybe the idea persists because so few rulers in the Middle East have traditionally cared anything about their people's grievances. Haroun al Rashid was the first and most famous of them, strolling around the Baghdad *souk* at night-time and getting into all sorts of trouble and adventures. That was in the Abbasid city of Baghdad, constructed as a vast circle, which was destroyed so utterly by the Mongols in the thirteenth century that scarcely a trace of it still exists, except for a wall or two.

The succeeding city was built farther down the bank of the River Tigris, and includes the oldest university in the world and some wonderful antique shops like the one which belonged to a Kurdish friend of mine. It had once been a Turkish official's house, and carpets and camel bags hung over the rails of the balcony that ran around the four sides of the central atrium. Scimitars hung on the walls, and there were showcases of jewellery, silverware and glass everywhere. I used to go there to buy memorabilia of the kings of Iraq and the presidents who succeeded them: medals with the head of King Faysal I or King Ghazi, cigarette lighters with President Qassem's face on them, cups and saucers decorated with the gentle features of the young King Faysal II, murdered by a Baghdad mob in 1958.

After the death in 1999 of King Hussein of Jordan, Faysal's cousin, I interviewed the new Jordanian king, Abdullah II: a straight-backed, fine-looking young man whose mother was English and who had studied in Britain and the United States. The paintings of his Hashemite ancestors hung on the walls of the audience chamber where our interview took place, and the sad eyes of the young Faysal II looked over us as we spoke.

'Tell me,' I asked him, 'about these trips you've been taking round the place in disguise – the Haroun Al Rashid bit. You've obviously enjoyed them hugely. But do they have a serious purpose, or are they merely theatre?'

'Obviously in this position the greatest fear I have is of being isolated, so going out in disguise was really to be able to keep that link with ordinary people that I'd had previously. It's not good enough for me to call up members of the government and say I've been told by so-and-so that there's a problem, because people will think I don't know how realistic that is. It's given people in the civil service the inspiration to do the right thing—'

'Because they think it could be the King walking through the door?'

'Exactly. So in a way they begin to treat every citizen like the King, because they don't know when the King is going to appear next. It's taken on a life of its own. I sort of joke that it's a bit like Elvis: there are sightings all over the country.'

Various other Arab leaders have tried the same thing, though rarely as successfully as King Abdullah, who has disguised himself sometimes as a doctor and sometimes as a member of a television crew, putting on a false beard and wearing dark glasses. In the past

Saddam Hussein tried the same technique in Iraq, but for entirely different reasons. King Abdullah wanted to improve the quality of care and service for ordinary Jordanians; Saddam wanted to demonstrate how popular he was. He would turn up in a huge convoy of security men and courtiers, accompanied by at least one and often two television crews, and would descend on some poor Iraqi family, who had to pretend they had no idea that this heavily moustachioed character surrounded by armed guards was the man they see every night for an hour on their television news reports.

The results of one such episode were shown on television in Iraq in 1990. Saddam asks some ancient characters whether his pension is enough for his needs.

'Who raised the level of your pension? Who do you have to thank for that?'

'Why, our leader, President Saddam Hussein, of course. We're very grateful for everything he's done for us, I can tell you.'

Then it was his wife's turn to join in the pantomime.

'Look who it is, husband! Don't you recognize him?'

'Me? No, who is it?'

'It's our wonderful President, Saddam Hussein himself, that's who!'

'Oh God! Let me kiss your hand, sir.'

It went on for a good half-hour, and was the lead on that night's television news. It was, in its stagy way, highly entertaining; Haroun Al Rashid, strolling around the Baghdad *souk* disguised as a merchant, was never quite like that.

The greatest pleasure of the bazaar is the buying of carpets. Whenever I go to Iran or Afghanistan or Pakistan I set aside part of an entire day to visiting one or other of the carpet dealers I know: not to buy, but merely to look at the stock and learn more about it.

There was a time when I would be greatly embarrassed if a carpet salesman invited me into his shop; I had that British reluctance to put someone to any trouble when I knew I was not seriously interested in buying, and carpet sellers go to a great deal of trouble. It takes two men to lift up each carpet and lay it out while you sit on cushions on the floor drinking tea and inwardly rejecting everything you see. A carpet seller in the Tehran bazaar who had lived and sold carpets in, I think, Manchester once explained to me the reality of these things.

'You see, I know now that English people just feel bad about seeing all these carpets being laid out and not buying. But our mind is different. You sit there saying "Oh yes, how nice" but not showing any real interest, and we think "Oh, he is just looking for a better price." But if we realize that you aren't interested anyway, it doesn't matter to us.

'It always looks good to other carpet sellers if there is a European in the shop, looking at the stock. It shows that we can get people in, even if they don't buy. And of course they don't always buy. A carpet is like a painting – you have to live with it, so you must like it. We know that. It is enough for us to be showing you. The tea costs nothing, the trouble the men go to is nothing.'

I long ago cast my Anglo-Saxon attitudes aside, and learned to regard my visits to the bazaar as part of my education in carpet-lore. I quickly spotted the aniline colours of the last ten or twenty years and rejected them in favour of traditional dyes: pomegranate seeds for the darker reds, cochineal and madder for the lighter ones, delphinium for yellow, indigo for blue. Fortunately carpet makers are increasingly going back to the older, natural colouring now. The method of weaving carpets, with the weft and warp going at right angles to each other, has remained unchanged since the earliest days; the British Museum has examples of weaving which probably date from the sixth millennium BC.

The basic materials, too, have remained unchanged for thousands of years; warp and weft are made of cotton, while the pile is made of wool. In the twentieth century silk was sometimes added to the wool, or took its place. There is a natural fineness to a silk or part-silk carpet which I personally prefer above all others; but you know that you are not getting something that is really old when you buy one. The quality of the carpet is dependent on the fineness of the knotting, and the hands of young girls, being delicate and small, are best for making the finest knots.

Many Westerners quite properly have moral difficulties with this idea, since it ensures that girls will not be educated properly and can have little chance of leaving the house, where the carpets are by tradition made. Nevertheless it is a balance of evils; in most carpet-making countries the choice is not between forcing a girl to make carpets or sending her to school. An investigative journalist I know produced a report on the way girls as young as eight or nine were obliged to join their mothers and fathers in the family carpet-making business. As a result, the international demand for carpets from that country dropped immediately. The result in many cases was that girls who had formerly made carpets were forced into prostitution in order to maintain the family income.

Classical Persian carpets from Qom or Tabriz or Mashhad are magnificent, with their elegant, restrained, stylized patterns derived from rose-gardens or trees of life. Nowadays these patterns are usually based on *vagirehs*, paper cut-outs which are cut up and mounted for the carpet weavers to follow. Village carpet makers often use *vagirehs* too, though sometimes they work their way through the design by memory and imagination alone. Older carpets were usually made with the help of a man called a *salim*, who would sing the pattern of the knots for the makers. There are said to be some *salims* still working in the remote carpet-manufacturing town of Shahr Kord in the Zagros mountains, south-west of Esfahan.

Personally, I prefer the kind of carpets which are made in the villages of Iran, Afghanistan, and Central Asia. These are often eccentric, much less regular in design, yet bolder and sometimes stunning in their sense of colour and their pattern. When I first visited the carpet sellers of the Tehran bazaar, twenty-one years ago, I examined dozens of silk Qomis and drank at least six cups of tea, but my heart lifted immediately when the seller told me he would like to show me just one 'tribal' carpet. It turned out to be a superb yellow silk with a stylized pattern of a house on it, and there was a blessing implicit in its weaving.

But it was at least an hour before I bought it. I insisted on seeing every other tribal carpet he had, and set aside several of them, and some Bokharas with their characteristic large oval motifs as well, before making my final choice. But the carpet seller knew, and I knew, that the yellow silk tribal carpet was what I really wanted; and it was only when he had sent away the silk Bokhara which was my second choice to be backed with a couple of strips of leather that I at last made a serious offer for the yellow one.

The Anglo-Saxon mind dislikes this process, preferring a straight-forward price tag which can be accepted or discarded according to the depth of the purse. Yet the bargaining process is so enjoyable to a seasoned carpet buyer that merely to buy a carpet off the pile as you do in Europe seems a dull way of doing it: almost as boring as buying something machine-made. There are the traditional haggling techniques: you can disparage the goods on sale, pretend that you have no interest in the one carpet you like, and walk out in the hope that the seller will come running after you. He usually does, of course.

Yet I find this is not to my taste. I don't like telling the seller that his stock is poor and threadbare, or that there are faults in the carpet's make and stains on its fabric. I always make a particular show of checking the pile, if the carpet is presented to me as being an old one, to see whether the colour is the same all the way through; sometimes carpets are washed with strong chemicals to make them look a little faded and old. I also examine the back carefully for signs of repair.

But I have never enjoyed the thought of walking out and having to come back. The technique I developed for buying something in the bazaar is different. I work out in advance how much money I am willing to spend, and either carry exactly that much with me or else have the rest in another pocket in case of absolute emergency. Then I listen to the seller's patter: how superb this particular example is (once he has worked out what sort of thing I like) and how I am unlikely ever to find anything quite like it. The chances are, of course, that I will already have seen something at least as good next door.

I agree; which always seems to throw the seller a little. I tell him how much I like it, and ask him how much he wants for it. It is safe to assume that he will ask anything from a third to a half more than he is really prepared to accept, so a little calculation is necessary. Then I tell him how much I am prepared to pay, which will always be a little but not too much less than my maximum figure. The danger is that when the real negotiating starts one will be lured into moving upwards; it is absolutely necessary, I find, to be firm about it, even if it means I have to walk out without the carpet.

And yet this never happens. The desire to make a sale, whether of an azan alarm clock or a piece of jewellery or a carpet, usually transcends the need to make a set amount of money. But there is always a test. Sometimes at the end the seller will show a certain irritability, to the point where he won't offer you another cup of tea; that is an indication that you have driven a really hard bargain. At other times he will ask if you are married, or have daughters, and will give you bracelets or earrings for them. Once I even got a small additional carpet. Then you realize with embarrassment that you have paid too much. But it's a game, and a highly enjoyable one. All it requires is enough time; a buyer who has to get away quickly is a buyer at a real disadvantage. The other necessity is a strong bladder. Everything else is just a question of common sense.

The city of Lima, ugly, flat, featureless and dangerous, is a perpetual disappointment. Anyone whose mental image of it derives from, say, Thornton Wilder's *Bridge of San Luis Rey* is certain to be disappointed. In what is left of the old colonial centre, the *plazas* and *calles* are occupied by depressingly old-fashioned shops with empty shelves, and beggars, drug addicts and thieves stalk the streets. The expensive suburb of Miraflores is charming enough, but there are a dozen like it in Latin America. Elsewhere, the colonial cities of Peru are superb; Lima is not one of them.

It has, nevertheless, the most beautiful restaurant I have ever come across. The approach to it is scarcely inspiring. The road leads down through camps inhabited by down-and-outs and refugees from the poorest parts of the country, living in huts made of woven reed. At night, fires of rubbish burn beside them to give light and keep out animals. The stink of refuse and decay seeps into the car as you drive past, and hungry faces peer at you out of the darkness. It does not seem like a journey which is likely to end in enjoyment.

At the foot of the hillside lies the Pacific coast: as ugly, flat, featureless and dangerous as the city itself. The rollers come sullenly in from two thousand miles away, regular and menacing. The beach is littered with rusting, abandoned cars and heaps of rubbish. People live here, too, in their little square box-like huts of reed. This is not a beach to walk on, and certainly not one to swim from. Instead, people use it to live and defecate and discard and die. Peru is a wonderful country for tourism, but you have to be exceedingly selective.

And yet there, in the middle of all the decay and ugliness, is a small gothic gem, a structure so neat and attractive and well-maintained that it could come from the south coast of England: a white-painted pier of gothic curlicues and arches and pillars jutting out into the water, and ending in a delightful glass-roofed gazebo, octagonal in shape, which is brightly lit in the evening gloom and shines like a lighthouse in the surrounding dreariness. This is La Rosa Nautica; and I have never eaten anywhere more surprising or more attractive in my life.

In the car park half a dozen large thugs in suits hung around the entrance to the narrow boardwalk leading to the pier itself. They were the bodyguards of the politicians who favoured La Rosa Nautica with their custom. It was 1992, and the situation in Peru was extremely volatile. The lunatic Maoist terrorist group, the Shining Path, had been carrying out a savage campaign of murdering and bombing. The President, Alberto Fujimori, deeply suspect, had suspended the Constitution. Big drugs interests were said to be disturbingly close to the seat of power, and the armed forces were involved with them at a high level. There were death squads and grudge killings and disappearances. And La Rosa Nautica floated above all of this, a little haven of peace and tranquillity in the dark waters.

My friends and I walked along the pier in the dull evening light, with the Pacific breaking on the shoreline beneath our feet and the planks moving uneasily at our every step. A waiter in an impeccably starched white coat bowed us in, and asked – as waiters always seem to in empty restaurants – whether we had a reservation. As it happened, we had; and we sat down at a large round wrought-iron table with a cloth as white and starched as the waiters' uniforms, overlooking the sea. The only other occupants of the place were the employers of the thugs we had seen in the car park: a tableful of men in their fifties in well-cut double-breasted suits, their jackets over the backs of their chairs, heavily moustachioed, their fingers in their braces, roaring with laughter while the country rotted around them.

Grosz would have drawn them with scars and fangs and grotesque chins, with half-naked call-girls on their laps. But there were no call-girls, and they were mostly good-looking men who looked after themselves and did themselves well: politicos, members of a culture which is rarely useful or ornamental, yet which is as unavoidable as cockroaches in a restaurant kitchen.

We were starting out the following morning on a trip which would take us to meet Luis Zambrano, the mayor of Tocache in the Huallaga Valley, plus a cast of extremely unpleasant characters. We didn't know how dangerous it was going to be, but we had our suspicions. And so our dinner was a little subdued at first. We listened to the laughter of the politicos and the waves breaking against the cast-iron pillars below us, and watched the last of the daylight fade away on the muddy clouds. A line of pelicans, silhouetted against the sky, caught the light from the restaurant as they headed downwards and skidded into the luminescent water. Small points of light grew stronger along the coast: often, no doubt, the distant blaze of rubbish, yet loaned a kind of attraction by the growing dusk. The navigation lights of fishing boats moved up and down on the regular face of the sea. It was magical, and slowly the beauty of it began to affect us more strongly.

A round or two of pisco sours loosened our spirits, and soon we were laughing louder than the politicians ourselves. And because our group included two attractive women the waiters gathered round to listen and watch and share in the laughter from time to time. The politicians left, looking at us enviously as they went to rejoin their bodyguards and make the perilous home journey through the shanty towns. We were alone in the restaurant now, while the waves built up and the sky darkened: half a dozen people who had no idea how, or even whether, they would get through the journey which lay before them, and who nevertheless enjoyed each other's company and were glad to be there.

The ceviche, the steaks, the eggs, the plantains, the fried yucca were all excellent; so was the Chilean red. In other countries the waiters would have piled the chairs onto the tables and started sweeping the floors. Here they merely sat down close by, drinking a little and keeping a genial eye on us. The sea was getting up, and we had an early start the next morning. In the end, reluctantly, we paid the bill and tipped the waiters heavily for their good manners and their easy company, and filed out into the coolness of the night. The southern stars shone through the breaking cloud, and the sound of the night birds crying mingled with the crash of the waves under the unsteady planks of the boardwalk. The car park was empty of gunmen.

The wrecked cars and the heaps of rubbish looked no worse in the darkness than the bushes and boulders on the edge of the beach. Behind us, as we drove back up the hillside, lay La Rosa Nautica like a diamond bracelet on a black velvet glove. And as I looked the lights went off one by one, and the pier was no longer visible against the ocean.

The best meal I ever had was somewhere even more unlovely: Shen Zhen, just across the Chinese border from Hong Kong, a place so new that it was marked as a small town on my 1978 atlas, and as one of the largest cities in China in the 2000 version.

To call Shen Zhen a mushroom growth gives no real idea of the speed with which it has emerged, nor the tackiness with which it was built. Enormous, ludicrously designed buildings block out the light in the main streets, and are so shabbily constructed that you feel the need to look behind them to check that there is anything more than a façade of ground-down, reconstituted marble and the kind of blue-tinted glass that one always associates with the Asian economic miracle and its eventual collapse. The roads are blocked by cheap cars driven by people who have lived in the city for a while and made a bit of money, and the pavements are thronged with men and women from the poorer parts of China who have flocked to Shen Zhen in the hope of following their example.

Our hotel had the kind of empty name that characterizes the new China – something to do with emperors or gold or jade, though it was made from cinder-blocks like everything else. The lobby was enormous. The old waste of space that accompanied state-financed building under Maoism is echoed by the new capitalist structures. In Shen Zhen, floor-space is cheap, and it looks it.

A thin doorman greeted us as our absurdly large limousine drew up at the entrance to the Imperial Golden Palace. He was wearing an oversized buttoned-up maroon carriage-coat, like a coachman out of a television adaptation of Jane Austen, and a top hat that would have fitted someone with a very much larger head. Inside, the reception desk was at the far end of the enormous lobby, with a staircase fit for a Busby Berkeley musical erupting into the middle of it. I had the impression of being in one of those dreadful showcases the Victorians went in for, where stuffed mice or frogs are dressed in ball gowns or white tie and tails.

Yet by the evening it was clear that the Ming Emperor Hotel needed to be that size in order to accommodate all the people who wanted to crowd in there. Chief among them were the hookers: pairs and trios of young girls, holding hands and giggling or listening to Walkmen while they circled around looking for customers. They seemed to me to be about as charged with eroticism as a children's programme on television, but the Chinese, Japanese and Malaysian businessmen who were to be the hotel's mainstay would pounce on a two- or threesome with every sign of pleasurable anticipation.

Most hotel rooms are anonymous; at the Jade Dynasty anonymity had been turned into an art form. It had as much character as a Do Not Disturb sign. The furniture, the paintings, the bathroom, the bed were a study in averageness. A man threw my cases down beside the television set (CNN, the awful Star TV from Hong Kong and Chinese channels only) and hung around meaningfully until I had to give him some RMB – tourist currency – to make him go away. Did I need anything else? he asked. The list was so long I couldn't begin to answer, but up at the top of it somewhere would have been a heavy-duty injection of taste.

Once I had got rid of him I glanced at the room service menu, but I knew already what was going to be on it: burgers, hot dogs, club sandwiches and Caesar salad, spelt wrong. I could also have Coca-Cola, or Japanese whisky. Surrounded by the most exciting cuisine in the world, the Imperial Golden Ming Dynasty Jade Emperor Hotel was offering me a special cheeseburger with fries and my personal choice of ketchup.

My producer, Simon Smith, the cameraman, Fred Scott, and a Chinese fixer all agreed that we had to go out to eat. We pushed our way through the massed whores, the doorman tipped his loose top hat down over his eyes to us, and we were free of the place at last. Our fixer was from Beijing and had never been to Shen Zhen before, but he claimed to know where there were some good restaurants. He strode off into the darkness, and we followed him trustingly.

He didn't know. We wandered away from the smiling neon dragons and the twenty-foot tiny tots which advertised the shops and restaurants of the centre of town, and struck an older, less settled part of town. The pavement had given way to muddy strips along the sides of the road, with pieces of broken brick set in it. The lighting came mostly from little hovels where old men and women sat huddled over tasks we could only imagine. There were a couple of old-fashioned large co-operative shops, both closed, and some building-sites.

'I know Beijing, not Shen Zhen,' the fixer apologized.

He needn't have. We turned a corner and saw a row of three restaurants: old-fashioned ones, with little flags fluttering from them and small windows closed with shutters. They were, however, all open. You could tell, because round the doorway of each there were baskets of the kind fishermen keep lobsters in. I looked inside. Some had little birds like guinea-fowls in them; some had ducks; and some had snakes. It was death row for animals. The snakes made an impression on the rest of us, though not on the fixer.

'Good to eat,' was all he said.

We were greeted by a man who looked like a pirate from the South China Sea, with an expansive manner and a drooping Fu Manchu moustache. The rest of his clientele were all Chinese, naturally, and I had the impression they were the older kind of Shen Zhen resident: not the reconstituted marble and blue glass kind. They looked at us from behind their bowls of soup with a certain dislike. Fu Manchu, though, was politeness itself, bowing us upstairs to a private room and bringing in the tea himself before bowing himself out again. He was a big man, but he bent almost double.

We started to relax after our walk. The fixer called Fu Manchu back, and ordered *mao-tai*. It tasted, as it always does, fairly lavatorial at first sip, but it does something to the throat which connects with the brain and encourages you to take another sip, and then another, and then get another bottle. I got another bottle. By the time we had to order, I was beyond knowing what I wanted, except that I didn't want snake. Not even the *mao-tai* could make me forget that. So the fixer ordered for us.

When it came, it was in dozens of different forms: little baskets, dishes with concave and convex lids, sauces which could have been meant to accompany anything, pots of preserves and things in oil, or fried, or roasted, or raw. I detected octopus and duck, and suspected sea cucumber, and enjoyed the cold jellyfish enough to take everybody else's portion – with their agreement. After that came some strange little cakes which looked sweet and weren't, and strips of some meat with a fat kind of noodle I had never see before. I imagine we ate things we would never have thought of ordering for ourselves, but it was all excellent.

We ended up with a bowl of bird's nest soup: not, contrary to the usual assumption, made from swallows' nests, but from the nests of a type of swift which thrives in the Philippines. Or, rather, throve; as with so many other things, edible bird's nests are now becoming expensive rarities. Tasting the little bits of neutral-flavoured jelly it occurred to me to wonder how and why anyone might have thought that a boiled-up bird's nest might be something you would consider putting in a soup; but the same applies to sea cucumbers and jellyfish, and presumably to snakes.

Finally, tea. Not the jasmine of a hundred thousand restaurants, but something rich and strange; so rich and so strange that the important thing about it was less the drinking of it than appreciating the aroma. One of the charming young women who were waiting on us had to fill a special nose-sized vessel for each person, so that we could draw in the scent before pouring it out again into a more usual cup. In that scent was everything distant and rare and languorous, so that we were noticeably quiet, and the young women sometimes had to ask us twice if we wanted a refill.

The last cup was smelt and then drunk, and we sat back to talk about the meal and digest it. I had brought a brand-new box of Upmann No. 2's with me, and I opened it and handed them around; and soon the room was filled with pungent blue smoke. A sense of benevolence filled us all and we heaped praise on our fixer, who was not altogether certain about the cigars but having had so many new taste experiences decided to try one anyway.

When the last Upmann's had turned into ash, we paid the bill. As we left, I decided, I would offer the Fu Manchu character a cigar, as a gesture of gratitude. So they cost £12 each: the meal had been thoroughly worth it. We made our way down the rickety staircase, and found him bowing at the foot. I opened the cigar box: there were still eight on the top layer, and thirteen below.

'Have a cigar,' I said grandly, holding out the open box.

'Ah,' said Fu Manchu, and took it.

Should I wrestle it back from him? Should I try to explain? The fixer had wandered out by now, and the box had already been handed to one of the giggling young women. I made a sound or two, but gave it up: a meal like that outweighed any number of cigars.

'Don't make soup out of them,' I warned him.

He nodded and bowed again.

Outside in the warm darkness I found the others peering into the snake boxes.

'Just counting them,' explained Simon Smith.

'Too late now anyway,' I said.

12

MILESTONES

> I went but a little way, and sat down upon the ground,
> looking out upon the sea, which was just before me, and
> very calm and smooth. As I sat here, some such thoughts as
> these occurred to me: What is this earth and sea, of which I
> have seen so much? Whence is it produced, and what am
> I, and all the other creatures, wild and tame, human and
> brutal? Whence are we?
>
> Daniel Defoe, *Robinson Crusoe*

On 30 June 1997 a very long chapter of British history closed with the return of Hong Kong to Chinese rule. It was, as it happens, five hundred years almost to the day after this chapter had first been opened.

Nowadays it is fashionable to regard the British Empire with shame and embarrassment, as though it was nothing but a prolonged exhibition of race prejudice, greed and arrogance. All those things certainly entered into it, yet I am old enough to remember the people who administered this empire during its last century, and that was certainly not their approach to it. For them it was, quite unselfconsciously, a matter of trust: of administering vast territories in the interests of the inhabitants, largely without the need for any force, until such time as they governed themselves.

No doubt there was a great deal of self-delusion in all of this, and not a little hypocrisy. It wouldn't have been British unless that were the case. Yet for the most part the empire was well governed, and usually with the tacit consent of the governed. Probably there will never be another empire in human history again, and a good thing too. But we shouldn't allow ourselves to imagine that the British

Empire was simply a larger version of King Leopold's appalling Belgian Congo.

My generation, those who were born at the end of the war, are the last to have been taught that the empire was A Good Thing. I was brought up – by a father who at that stage was still a strong Labour supporter, and had voted enthusiastically for the Labour landslide of 1945 – with *Our Empire Story* and *Our Island Story* next to *The Coral Island* and the books of A.A. Milne on the shelf over my bed. My father thought this perfectly reasonable, and the vast majority of Labour supporters and Labour politicians at the time would have felt the same. When I opened *Our Empire Story* and read how, on 24 June 1497, John Cabot discovered his New Found Land, there would have been no irony, no mockery in it for me, and certainly no sense of shame:

> The flag of England fluttered out to the sound of an English cheer as the brave sailor claimed the land for Henry VII, King of England and France, and lord of Ireland.

And so when, five hundred years and six days later, the end of this empire effectively came with the handing over of the last important colonial possession, it was the end of the world as I had known it. Rather a good end, as it happened, and entirely inevitable; but an end, nevertheless.

In fact, as Churchill had understood decades before, the dissolution of the British Empire began with the end of British control over India. When that happened in 1947, the rest was only a matter of time. Yet it was another fifty years before the last jewel was handed back to its original owners. In 1997 Hong Kong reverted to China, after a rather shabby agreement negotiated by Margaret Thatcher and Deng Xiaoping.

By coincidence, the end of empire came, not just five centuries after its beginning, but a hundred years and eight days after its highest point: Queen Victoria's diamond jubilee, which brought representatives of a quarter of the world's population to celebrate the sixtieth year of its sovereign's reign.

On 22 June 1897 the biggest military assembly in London's history – 50,000 soldiers – marched to St Paul's Cathedral to celebrate the occasion. One column was led by the biggest man in the British army, Captain Ames, in the breastplate and helmet of the Horse Guards, all six-foot-eight of him, and the other was headed by the most popular of its commanders, Field Marshal Lord Roberts; 'Bobs'. Behind them rode or marched figures from every conceivable part of the empire: Red Indians from Canada, Dyak headhunters from Borneo, seventeen resplendent Indian princes, Zulu warriors, a detachment from New South Wales in wideawake hats, a particularly smart contingent from Jamaica and Antigua, South Sea Islanders. It was a day when size mattered: one of the Maori chiefs on parade weighed 28 stone, and needed help to finish the course.

The *Pall Mall Gazette*, which was by no means imperialist, revelled in it as much as the *Daily Mail* did. 'This shimmering array of colour', it called it. And indeed the colours were superb: the scarlets of the African regiments, the blues and emerald greens of the Indian ones, the gold and black of the Canadians. For the enormous crowds which had turned out, it was an education in the enormous extent of their empire: a quarter of the world's population, a quarter of its land-mass.

And yet not everyone gave themselves over to a frenzy of national self-congratulation. Rudyard Kipling, much more than the unthinking imperial flag-waver of popular assumption, wrote *Recessional* to mark the Diamond Jubilee. It clearly foreshadowed the empire's eventual decline:

> Far-called, our navies melt away;
> > On dune and headland sinks the fire:
> Lo, all our pomp of yesterday
> > Is one with Nineveh and Tyre!
> Judge of the Nations, spare us yet,
> > Lest we forget – lest we forget!

He understood, perhaps, the arrogance and self-regard of the British Empire's rulers in the 1920s and 30s, the hardening of its arteries, the lack of clarity about its eventual purpose. Was it, as most of the adventurers who won it would have assumed, the greatest booty in the world? Was it a sacred trust, whose inhabitants had to be educated and brought forward to the level where they could look after their own affairs? Or was it merely an historical accident, something that had to be managed as well as possible and dispersed when there was no real alternative to doing so?

It doesn't work in the long run for people of one country to govern another, and it shouldn't. Times changed, and the European empires disappeared. In the end, empires always do.

Hong Kong, though, was special. For a start, there had never been any question of its becoming independent. If it didn't belong to Britain it would belong to China, and a treaty to that effect had existed for a century. Secondly, it was a success story like no other. Hong Kong had a higher standard of living than fifteen countries in Europe, and a gross domestic product which put it among the international top ten. It was so well run that for three successive years before it became independent it was listed as the freest economy in the world. (China, because of the inefficiency and corruption of its Marxist economic system and its rejection of basic human rights, came 140th in this scale.)

And it was sensationally beautiful. To take the little green Star ferry from Central to Tsimshatsui and sit on the slatted seats looking out over the water was to observe one of the loveliest shorefronts anywhere, the clean tall buildings crowding in on one another higher and higher as the 1980s and 90s progressed. It was a highly nervous and volatile society: everything that happened in China, Europe or the United States seemed to evoke a response on the stockmarket and in the price of property. Its streets teemed with noisy life and the sound of people doing deals. The last jewel was in some ways the richest and best of all, and there must have been many British people who gravitated to Hong Kong at the time of the hand-over of power on 30 June who felt, as they looked at the crowded buildings and walked the crowded streets, *It's much too good to give up*.

At the top of a rickety staircase on Nathan Road in Kowloon, Dee and I sat opposite a slight, neatly dressed Chinese man in a grey suit who pressed our hands in turn and looked fixedly at different points on our faces. He spoke no English, and a pretty Chinese girl in a neat camel-coloured sweater translated.

'Says you have very competitive job and many people do not like you though you also have many friends. Says he cannot tell what you do but many people in different countries know you. Says you sometimes in much danger but will live long life.'

'How long is long?' I asked.

Even if you don't believe in palmistry, you might as well hear what it has to say.

She translated. The man spread his hands a foot or more apart.

'Says eighty, maybe ninety.'

'And he doesn't by any chance watch satellite television?'

'Sorry?'

I let it go.

The man turned to Dee, holding her hands with his thumb and forefinger and looking at her forehead and the way her face was configured around the eyes. His assessment of her character and her job seemed to me to be spot on, and he can't have seen that on BBC World.

'You quick temper and loving, travelled a long way.'

'I am a writer. Will I be successful?' Dee asked, giving away more of herself than she'd intended to.

'Not till you forty.'

'And what,' I put in, 'about the future of Hong Kong?'

The young woman coloured and laughed, and the man said something quite long and elaborate.

'Says doesn't know. Very difficult say.'

So that was that.

Chris Patten, the last governor, had done a good job under very difficult circumstances. Not only were the Chinese against him: they had the help of former British civil servants, some of whom went onto Beijing's payroll and advised the Chinese government how to deal with him. Others merely sniped from the safety of a civil service pension.

Before he took over in Hong Kong he came to lunch at the *Spectator*, when I was still on the editorial staff. He and I had had a certain falling out over John Major's election campaign, which he had run as Conservative Party chairman. (I had been tactless enough to suggest on air that the campaign was boring and unimaginative.) Although Major had won, Patten himself had lost his seat and had been rewarded with the last great imperial job: governing Hong Kong until the hand-over.

Spectator lunches were traditionally long and bibulous, and the bottles of red kept coming. It had gone four o'clock when, in the boozy certainty that I knew what I was talking about, I told Patten that he must remember one thing: how he governed Hong Kong would colour the entire way the British Empire would be viewed by future generations. I don't entirely think it was true, and I don't suppose Patten remembered it afterwards; but there was a strongly ethical dimension to his rule, and he did his best to protect and enhance the human rights of the people whose lives he controlled.

That was what upset the British mandarins, who felt it was much more important not to upset the Communist regime in Beijing. They had a certain amount in common, these mandarins and the Communist bureaucrats: both groups felt instinctively that if they wanted the opinion of the people of Hong Kong, they would give it to them.

'I'm hoping something will happen to stop it happening,' said a Chinese man I happened to meet at the airport a few months before the hand-over. 'You see, I escaped here from China; many of us did. We preferred British rule then, and we prefer it now. Prefer it to China rule, anyhow. Maybe the government in Beijing will collapse. You never know.'

It wasn't forelock-tugging colonial sentiment; it was merely that the choice before the people of Hong Kong wasn't a particularly appetizing one, and they preferred the distant, benevolent rule of a country on the other side of the world to being gathered up and taken over by a government which had shot down a thousand demonstrators in Tiananmen Square eight years before, and had shown itself to be completely ignorant of the way a free society should be run. Time and again Chinese people in Hong Kong hinted at the same feeling: maybe it won't happen after all, maybe something will come up.

Nothing came up. On the afternoon of 30 June 1997 we watched Chris Patten receiving the folded Union Jack which had flown outside his official residence. It marked the end of his tenure, and he was visibly moved. Of the vast territories and diverse populations over which the flag had once flown, this was the last remnant except for a few islands and promontories in distant parts of the world. For anyone with an ounce of patriotism and the glimmer of a sense of history, it was a moving moment.

And certainly not a bad one. For thirty years the sense of an imperial past had been a burden rather than a help to the British. They had consistently failed to adapt to their new position in the world, either dreaming guiltily of the past or trying to pretend it hadn't happened. The way Britain had cut itself off from the older countries of the Commonwealth betrayed an absence of vision on the part of the men and women who negotiated British entry into what was still, in the 1960s and 70s, the European Common Market.

There was no sense that the links of the past had a value which was worth capitalizing on and transforming into something new. At best British officialdom regarded the imperial past as an embarrassment; at worst it was seen as an outright threat, and millions of people who had always been brought up to think of themselves essentially as British were treated with a disgraceful shabbiness. Few of us behave particularly well when we have come down in the world, and countries are much like people in this respect.

Two examples. At airports, no serious effort was made when Britain entered the EEC in 1973 to ensure that Commonwealth citizens coming into Britain could have a separate immigration channel of their own. Overnight, they were relegated to alien status, while EEC citizens assumed the same rights as the British themselves. There was a lack of imagination about this which eventually overstrained the bonds of the Commonwealth.

In May 1995 the Ministry of Defence planned to celebrate VE Day, the anniversary of the defeat of Nazi Germany, with a march-past down Whitehall by citizens of every country which had taken part in the Second World War on the Allied side. There were to be Poles and Czechs and French and Danes and Norwegians and Australians and South Africans and New Zealanders and Canadians and Indians and people from dozens of other countries. But there would be no West Indian contingent, said the Ministry of Defence – not a very imaginative institution – because they had not had a separate regiment of their own fighting in the war, but had been absorbed by the various arms of the British services.

No matter that, proportionate to their numbers, more West Indians had joined the British forces at the start of the Second World War than people from any other part of the Empire, including Australia and Canada. There were no assisted passages as there were for volunteers from other imperial territories: each West Indian had to pay his or her own way to come to Britain. In the end there was such a campaign on their behalf and the case was such a clear one that the Ministry gave in, and a contingent from the West Indies marched down Whitehall with the rest; but it had been an unnecessarily graceless approach to repaying a debt of gratitude.

Still, this was all history now. After five hundred years the imperial party was over, and the moment needed to be marked. The Hong Kong treasury shelled out for the celebrations, but not too much: the careful housekeeping which had marked Britain's government of Hong Kong was not going to be eased simply because the British were leaving. There would be a moderate display of fireworks over Victoria Harbour, and a farewell ceremony at the naval base of HMS *Tamar*, where the royal yacht *Britannia* – on her last voyage herself – was moored.

There were in fact fireworks for two nights, and huge crowds gathered to watch them; more turned out for the rival ceremony the second night, which the Chinese government was financing and which cost many times more than the British version. 'Ah, well,' the British in Hong Kong told themselves, 'it's the way things are going. We're on the way out, and they're on the way in.' Only it wasn't quite like that. The Chinese display lasted a shorter time and turned out to be a good deal feebler than the British effort, and several of the barges moored in the harbour stayed silent and dark as the technicians on them struggled ineffectually to light the expensive array of fireworks. It also started to rain; only we didn't take too much notice of it at the time.

The morning of Monday 30 June had dawned heavy and overcast, and the grey cumuli hung low over the ambitious buildings of Central and Wanchai. 'Ah, well,' the British told themselves, 'if it rains tonight the Chinese will say we've lost the mandate of Heaven. And we probably have.' The mandate of Heaven is one of those notions like 'face' which the British have picked up and used to interpret the Chinese view of the world; not always very accurately.

It rained on and off during the day. Sometimes the organizers of the evening's celebrations would convince themselves that the sun was about to break through the clouds; but it never quite happened. I went to the tailor's shop in my hotel – the lovely Furama, quiet and discreetly opulent – and took possession of a double-breasted grey suit which I had had made for the occasion.

'You will look good for tonight, sir,' said the chief fitter, looking me up and down critically.

Earlier in the suit-making process he had made some remarks about my general size and shape and the slope of one of my shoulders which still rankled a little, but now he gave the impression that his firm's handiwork had compensated for my physical imperfections.

'And how will you be celebrating?' I asked.

'My family and I feel there is nothing to celebrate. Thank you, sir. Have a good evening.'

Dee and I were in Hong Kong for the BBC, but like other senior British editors and their wives we were also the guests of the Foreign Office at the evening's events. Or at least I was. Dee was invited to the open-air celebration in the early evening which marked the pulling down of the Union Jack, but only I was to go to the banquet which the British were giving for the Chinese, and to the final hand-over ceremony at HMS *Tamar*.

This did not go down well with Dee. I later found that in rooms paid for by the Foreign Office throughout the more expensive hotels of Hong Kong the wives of British editors were saying much the same thing, and accompanying it with something of the same critique of our characters as the tailor in the Furama had directed towards my figure.

It was drizzling by the time she and I left the Furama and struggled over the complex of over- and underpasses which the pedestrian in Hong Kong has to navigate. Dee looked quite superb in a lapis lazuli outfit she had bought just off the Place des Vosges, and blue satin high heels from Bloomingdales.

'I hope the rain keeps off,' she said as we hurried along, a little late, 'otherwise everything I'm wearing will melt.'

'Come on, rain,' I answered.

The show had started by the time we found the way to our seats. But we couldn't sit in them. The organizers had sensibly arranged for one of the largest consignments of umbrellas in history, and pleasant, eager young stewardesses handed us one each. The audience was hidden under an entire cloud of yellow and blue, and we had to stand on tiptoe to see over them. All round us were the families of civilians, some British or Indian but mostly Chinese, on whom the administration of the colony had depended. It was a difficult and moving moment for them all, the Chinese especially; not everyone cares to shift loyalties in an instant, and the future was still not certain.

Much of the celebration must have been pretty opaque for them. Aside from the schoolchildren parading and singing, and the dragons, there was a sound and light show narrated by an actor and an actress in terms that were dignified and pleasant, but distinctly reminiscent of a village pageant back home: 'And then Queen Elizabeth – Good Queen Bess, as she was soon known – came to the throne', that kind of thing.

And there were songs. Not, thank God, anything bombastic or national in tone: nothing about there always being an England, or ruling the waves, or honour and glory. The organizers had chosen wisely. Instead we had old, half-familiar songs of parting and hope, cheery, stiff upper-lip, keep-your-chin-up nostalgic songs, the kind of thing people sing when times are hard:

> We'll meet again, don't know where, don't know when,
> But I know we'll meet again some sunny day.
> Keep smiling through, just like you always do,
> 'Til the blue skies drive the dark clouds far away.
>
> So will you please say hello to the folks that I know,
> Tell them I won't be long.
> They'll be happy to know that as you saw me go,
> I was singing this song.
>
> After the rain comes the rainbow,
> You'll see the rain go, never fear,
> We two can wait for tomorrow,
> Goodbye to sorrow, my dear.

The audience was noticeably quiet when that finished, and you could see the handkerchiefs at work.

At the end we sang *Auld Lang Syne*. The Chinese people around us struggled to get through the impenetrable Lowland Scots, and the rest of us knew little except the basic words.

By this time it was raining as hard as anything I have encountered in the Amazon, chilly and insidious. It had begun while the Prince of Wales was making a speech, and grew worse and heavier until it seeped through the umbrellas and the soles of our shoes and ran down our arms and necks. 'The Chinese will make great play with this,' the British thought; 'they'll say it's proof that we're finished in more ways than one.' And they shrugged and grinned. 'So what's new?'

We stood as the sailors and airmen and the soldiers of the Black Watch, kilts flaring in the wind that blew the rain across the parade ground, presented arms. Slowly the Union Jack and the colonial flag of Hong Kong were lowered, and I was glad that even for a short while they wouldn't be raising the scarlet flag of China: the flag which had flown over the massacre in Tiananmen Square. *The Last Post*, the last national anthem: God save a Queen who would only reign over this place for another three hours. A single piper played *Auld Lang Syne* again, the shrill notes cutting through the chilly rain.

Beside me Dee, the descendant of voortrekkers whose wives and children were imprisoned and died in concentration camps while the British confiscated their Republics, wiped the tears away. Around us the Chinese civil servants and their families wept openly. And I? Well, I suppose I should have been reflecting on the imperial greatness that was passing. Instead my thoughts rested for some reason on my great-uncle Harold, a man of great ability and promise who was so badly injured at the Somme and Passchendaele that he ended his life a homeless outcast on Waterloo Station. An empire is never just about winning, whether it is being formed or is passing away.

The rain fell harder than ever: harder than the sound from the loudspeakers, harder than the brilliant spotlight on the piper. The Prince of Wales took Chris Patten on board *Britannia*, which had formed a backdrop to the ceremony. Dee and I fought our way against the wind and rain into the huge convention centre, where the final hand-over was to take place and which had been finished only a matter of days before. It wouldn't have been Hong Kong if there hadn't been a last-minute rush.

Everyone there was wet as well: Rupert Murdoch stood by a window, surrounded by nervous aides, blowing his nose on his fingers; Sir Geoffrey Howe padded along in squelching shoes; I caught a glimpse of a saturnine figure who might have been Stanley Ho.

Emily Lau, incorruptible and perpetually dissident, waved elegantly to us. I thought of encouraging Dee to come to the banquet, but chickened out at the thought of those frosty Foreign Office faces checking the invitations. Cross – though not with me – she went back to the Furama, and threw away her shoes from Bloomingdales.

Instead, I joined up with Dominic Lawson, heading up an escalator as the team surrounding Tony Blair swept past us.

'Shouldn't you be down here?' Blair asked; it was the first time I had seen him since his election a few months before.

'We seem to be going up,' I answered.

'As long as you're going somewhere.'

His voice trailed away behind us.

'Do you think he was being snide?' I asked Dominic.

'Safer to assume so,' he said.

There were no frosty Foreign Office faces checking the invitations. In fact, it was clear they would have preferred to see more people there. Some of the tables were almost empty; the Chinese government, with their exquisite manners and concern for the proprieties, didn't even bother to turn up. It was the final snub of a long series which they had paid to Chris Patten for daring to suggest that Hong Kong should be a democratic entity; this was the kind of rudeness which had so terrified the British mandarins who had taken the Beijing line against Patten.

Sitting between Dominic and Alan Rusbridger, the editor of the *Guardian* and a fellow pupil of my old teacher Arthur Sale at Cambridge, I listened to the left-right banter and looked round at the empty seats. The food was rotten, and the Chinese were not missed: all that phoney raising of glasses would have been too insincere for words.

The finale was even more depressing, as though we were back at school and the ceremony was being held in the gym because of rain. On the wooden stage of the great conference hall British soldiers stamped with ludicrous softness on their rubber soles, and doll-like soldiers in the uniform of the Tiananmen Square fusiliers presented arms and marched manically around the stage as though they were taking part in some strange pageant.

At midnight – probably on the dot, if any of us had been interested enough to check – the flags went up and down and the weirdly operatic national anthem of China followed *God Save The Queen*. Hong Kong was formally handed over; except that for us the real occasion had taken place hours before, in front of *Britannia*. Dominic and I were still in the building when, with the Prince of Wales and Chris Patten on board, she edged away from HMS *Tamar*, her Royal Marine band playing *Rule Britannia*, and headed out into Victoria Harbour. From on board, Chris Patten sent his final communiqué to London by radio:

> I have relinquished the administration of this government. God
> Save The Queen.

In the awkward, embarrassed, stilted style in which they had governed it since planting the flag at Possession Point on 26 January 1841, the British were leaving Hong Kong.

The Chinese government, meanwhile, was giving a reception in the building to mark the moment. Not being invited, we passed through it on our way out. Through the windows you could clearly see *Britannia*, superbly lit up and accompanied by a flotilla of small boats, making for the open sea. The new men and women, the Hong Kong Chinese who wanted to make their number with Beijing, were chewing their spring rolls and their fried prawns, standing with their backs to the magnificent sight as though it had no relevance to them. Perhaps it didn't. There was a new reality to take into account, and they were in there, paying court to it as hard as they could manage.

Elsewhere in the building, though, there were people who were standing at the windows watching *Britannia* sail away. Most of them were Chinese: waiters, security men, businessmen who hadn't been invited to the Beijing government reception. No one spoke. Each of them must have been wondering what the change would mean for them and their life.

The first morning after the end of the British Empire, it was still raining, harder than ever. It had rained so hard during the night that in some parts of Hong Kong there was serious flooding. Cliffs were washed away, houses destroyed, a few people lost their lives. Detachments from the People's Liberation Army drove into the various barracks around Hong Kong, liberating them on behalf of the People they represented. We were politely turned away from one where, under the British, there had never been any problem about filming for television. A new reality had come into being now.

Rain streamed down our faces and soaked the thin, poorly cut uniforms of the Chinese soldiers. It washed along the streets, leaking into the roofs of the expensive high-rise buildings and driving the poor out of their homes. The British, and not only the British, began to wonder about the symbolism of all this rain, which had begun with such ferocity during the hand-over speech by the Prince of Wales and was to continue on and off for months.

On the morning after the hand-over the *South China Morning Post* published the result of an opinion poll it had carried out in Hong Kong: 72 per cent of people believed that British rule had been beneficial to the colony.

Within days the Indonesian economy collapsed, and a depression spread throughout Asia. Property values dropped dramatically in Hong Kong. The Chinese managed to stave off financial disaster only by an enormous effort of will. No one would talk confidently about the Asian economies for years to come. Perhaps the British hadn't entirely lost the mandate of Heaven, after all.

Behind a crumbling red brick wall on the edge of Peshawar, in the north-west province of Pakistan, lies the British cemetery. These are not the beautifully manicured lawns of the Commonwealth War Graves Commission, superbly maintained gardens from Ypres to the jungles of Burma. This cemetery is cheerfully overgrown, with a couple of gardeners dozing under a tree and jumping up in confusion and simulated activity when you push open the squeaking wrought-iron gate. Mongooses and snakes hunt each other through the undergrowth, and birds of a particular sweetness of song hover in the branches of the trees and are mocked and imitated by the mynahs.

All around are the quiet graves of the sahibs and memsahibs and the inhabitants of the *babalog* who lived and died here; gothic lettering on gothic altars of crumbling stone, mostly from the lower end of the undertaker's price range. By the time these graves were laid down, from the 1840s onwards, the British had long since given up the thought that India was their personal goldmine, and they vied with each other to behave with honesty and moderation. And with affection for each other: *With Ever-Lasting Sorrow, To the Unforgettable Memory of A Loving Wife, To Our Beloved Daughter, In Affectionate Remembrance of a Dutiful Son . . .*

And so they pass before us, these Alfreds and Ethelreds and Emilys and Carolines, dying in droves when they reach their twenties and thirties, or even before they can leave childhood. Here in Peshawar, in the midst of life they were in death; duty kept them here, and duty killed them in a variety of ways, from a disease bravely borne to one contracted overnight or a bullet in the head from behind a rock. Their widows and widowers and orphans grieved, but life went on. Amelia Horsburgh lost three husbands before succumbing to the climate herself. William Edward Jenkins lost both his parents and was buried by his sorrowing aunt. Captain Athelstan Jones was killed by a bullet from just the kind of *jezail* that stands by my fireplace: he lingered for a month, then rendered his life to the Almighty in peace and the confidence of eternal life.

Their lives may have been short, but confidence was something these people had in abundance. It wasn't just the dubious assurance of belonging to a master-race; it was the knowledge that they were doing their duty. They were prepared to sacrifice their lives to it, and knew they would probably have to. It was a simple, uncomplicated faith which the locals often shared. Not far away, in the old city centre, Peter Jouvenal and I once spotted a railing composed of twelve portraits in iron-work of the young Queen Victoria around the house of a local merchant. The building was about to be pulled down, and Peter and I bought them: not cheaply.

From 1 July 1997 Britain was back where it started, before the first ships sailed for Newfoundland or Bermuda or Barbados. I seriously doubt whether the act of owning the territories of other people ever does much good to the countries which own them, and it certainly doesn't do much good to the people who are colonized; yet afterwards, if the colonizers and the colonized are wise about the experience, it can enrich them both. What is foolish is to try to pretend it hasn't happened.

For months, the newspapers, television stations and politicians of the world had been worrying about little else: the aircraft that were going to fall out of the sky, the pensions that would no longer be paid, the operations that would go wrong, the food that would go bad, and all because our computers would reach midnight on 31 December 1999 and think the next year would be 1900.

With only a few weeks to go before this catastrophe was due to happen, I found myself eating a dreary meal in the darkened dining room of the cold and almost entirely empty Inter-Continental Hotel in Kabul. A couple of ancient electric heaters kept us from freezing, and there was nothing to drink but Pepsi-Cola and fizzy orange and nothing to eat but rice and the meat of animals as old as the heaters. One of the other four guests there was in Afghanistan to oversee the installation of a new set of flight beacons across the country. I asked him whether we had anything to be afraid of at the turn of the year.

'Don't even think about it,' he said. 'Nothing's going to crash. I'm telling you: it's just a load of hype to get idiots to buy new software.'

He was right. No aircraft crashed, no one went hungry or unpaid, no computers seriously thought Queen Victoria was back. I should have guessed it would all end happily when the top management of China's national airline announced that they were going to be flying around on their aircraft on New Year's Day to prove their service was safe. Of course it was safe; the top managements of big undertakings, I've noticed, dislike taking risks with their own lives.

As for the New Year's celebrations themselves, we took to calling them 'the Millennium', shrinking a thousand years of the unknown into a single night: 'Where are you going to spend the Millennium?' Precision was out, hype was in. It wasn't really the start of the Millennium any way; it wasn't even the start of a new century. We were just too impatient to wait twelve months for accuracy. Thanks to a series of fairly elementary mistakes made around 527 AD by a Scythian monk called Dionysius Exiguus ('Little Denis') who, besides being short, was not particularly good at mathematics and knew as little as every other Westerner of his time about the concept of zero, it was merely the start of the final year of the twentieth century.

When Dionysius worked out a date for the birth of Jesus Christ he not only forgot one or two key pointers (the death of King Herod, for instance) but he also made the Christian era start on 1 January, 1 AD instead of the year 0, which he could not comprehend; as a result the third millennium would only start at midnight on 1 January 2001.

But as the irritable, pedantic letters which started appearing in British newspapers from at least the 1790s onwards show, most people wrongly assume that directly the second figure of the year's number changes, a new century begins. This may be technically wrong, but only the most blinkered of purists could go on insisting that nothing had happened when all around them people were trying to remember to put '2000' on their letters and cheques.

The fact is, our calendar is an arbitrary construct, and we are free to date the third millennium AD from any moment we choose. The Romans originally divided their year into ten months, and until 153 BC their year began on 1 March (hence 'December' for the last month of the year); January and February were added only as an afterthought. For centuries the Christian church regarded 25 March, nine months before Jesus' birthday on Christmas Day, as the start of the year, and the British, naturally, carried on the habit long after everyone else had given it up.

In the end almost everybody throughout the world decided to regard the new millennium as beginning on 1 January 2000, and the BBC prepared the biggest international television programme ever attempted, sending people to every corner of the globe to report for it. It was my task to travel to the first piece of land over which the sun would rise on 1 January.

This wasn't altogether straightforward either. The International Date Line, itself a completely imaginary divide, runs north and south down the globe at 180 degrees or thereabouts. But the Republic of Kiribati, which was previously part of the British-run Gilbert and Ellice Islands ('Kiribati', pronounced 'Kiribass', is the closest the locals could easily get to saying 'Gilbert'), is about three thousand miles from west to east and used to run right across the Date Line. Until the mid-1990s Christmas Island, in the east of the group, lay on one side of it, while the capital, Tarawa, and all the other inhabited islands lay on the other. As a result, when it was Monday in one half of the country, it was still only Sunday in the rest.

Then President Tito (pronounced, mysteriously, 'Sutto') was elected by his mild, gentle people with a mandate to change this. He did. The Date Line, with international agreement, was suddenly stretched out like a line of chewing gum thirty degrees – two thousand miles – to the east, in order to take in the farthest island in the group. This island was uninhabited, and had been called Caroline after the daughter of a nineteenth-century British official. It was only afterwards, as the fuss about the Millennium built up, that the I-Kiribati people realized the immense advantage Caroline Island had over everywhere else along the Date Line. It was rechristened Millennium Island.

The government of Kiribati had two aims in mind. Firstly, it wanted to bring the very existence of its country – low-lying coral islands which cover an area of ocean as wide as the continental United States, and yet which have a population of only 77,000 – to the world's attention. Secondly, it wanted to remind the world that coral islands right across the world were in serious danger. By the end of the twentieth century the rise in the ocean levels caused by global warming seemed likely to destroy the Kiribati group entirely within as little as thirty or forty years.

And so it was that soon after dawn on 30 December 1999 I made my way across the heaving deck of the MV *Matangare*, registered in Tarawa, and saw Millennium across the surf. It was everyone's dream of a desert island, precisely as I had imagined it when I had read R.M. Ballantyne's *The Coral Island* at the age of, I suppose, nine. It was all there: the dark olive green of densely packed palm trees, the achingly white sand, the milky emerald-green lagoon, purer and more startling than any water I had ever seen, the blue Pacific surf booming against the reef, birds of a bewildering number of species hovering in the still, hot, pure air.

For the first time, I understood what an atoll was. I had always assumed it was a small individual coral island; now I could see that Millennium wasn't one island but a circle, a necklace of islets, which had grown up all around the lip of an enormous submerged volcano. The lagoon lay in the middle, in all its clarity and indescribable loveliness. This was one of the world's great wonders: an uninhabited Pacific island so glorious that your heart leapt at the sight of it. All along the rail the I-Kiribati islanders who had travelled with us started to clap their hands and sing a hymn in its praise.

Our journey had not been easy, though Dee and I had a slightly better time than the others, since the Kiribati government had been warned to expect an elderly couple and had set aside a cabin for us; we seized it before there could be a recount. Everyone else, including a group of I-Kiribati dancers and singers who were going to take part in the celebrations on Millennium Island, had to sleep on the open deck.

There were four others in the BBC team: Mike Donkin, a quiet yet adventurous reporter who was going to cover the radio side of the occasion and had already spent some time in Kiribati, falling in love with it in the process; Simon Wilson, a high-flying news producer based in Brussels, which was about as different from the South Pacific as you could easily imagine; Nigel Bateson, a bearded giant of a cameraman originally from South Africa who had often worked with me before, scaring off violent Serbs at roadblocks in Bosnia and facing incoming shellfire with admirable good humour; and my wife Dee.

It was fortunate that the five of us got on extremely well; this was an important Christmas and New Year – particularly the New Year, above all – to spend in the company of people who liked each other. It isn't always like this.

The *Matangare* was due to sail, suitably enough, from Christmas Island on Christmas Day. We gathered all our gear together and drove to the capital of Christmas Island. Mockingly called London, it is not an attractive place with its few run-down stores, a dog or two, and several old Second World War landing craft rusting in the clear water. Mike Donkin, an instinctive pioneer, volunteered to go on board first and prepare the way for us all. He climbed onto the ancient tender which was to ferry passengers and luggage across to the *Matangare*, while the rest of us stayed behind and helped with the loading process. Or, in my case, rather stood around.

Fifty or so islanders, stout, good-natured, religious people with pleasant open faces, stout bodies and heavy arms and legs, were sailing with us: the singers and dancers who would celebrate the new year on Millennium island. They carried very little: just those red and blue striped bags, made in China from some thin plasticated material, which you see at every Third World airport. We, by contrast, were carrying more gear than I have ever seen five people take anywhere. It was inevitable, given that we were sailing to a desert island. Every piece of equipment, from camera to editing gear, had to be duplicated in case it broke down. There would be no chance of getting something repaired, more than a thousand miles from anywhere.

Even Dee and I, though we were mercifully free of television equipment, were carrying a lot of luggage. We would be heading on from the South Pacific to the frozen north-west of the United States, so we needed clothing to cope with both climates. And there were the books. Ten days on a boat, five days on a desert island, and a month altogether on the road: it was a long stretch.

Getting across the Pacific rollers to the *Matangare* took three quarters of an hour. The islanders sang hymns, as they were inclined to do for the next five days afloat. After the twelfth time of listening to *Abide With Me* in I-Kiribati you begin to get a little tired of the cadences of the language, but the choir was too pleasant and their faith too great for me to ask them to sing something else.

The *Matangare* was not a big ship – a hundred and fifty feet long, perhaps – but from a tender alongside she seemed as big as an office building. This was the difficult moment. Ever since my accident in Belgrade during the NATO bombing seven months before, I had gone everywhere with a walking-stick. It had proved its worth again and again; I prodded an interfering Chinese policeman in the stomach with it, tripped up a thug who seemed about to attack my camera-man, hailed innumerable taxis, and won the undeserved sympathy of a range of people in different countries. But it was a serious foretaste of my eighties, and reminded me of the title of a pamphlet which (according to legend) was once produced by HM Stationery Office: *The Population of Britain, Broken Down By Age And Sex*.

Now the side of the ship reached above me like a cliff – a *moving* cliff – and the ladder of wood and rope which I had to climb floated towards me and away from me as the tender rose and dropped on the waves. I could see the patches where the rust had been covered with white paint. This was the moment that my colleagues in London had had their doubts about. Was I really up to climbing on and off ships in difficult seas? Suppose my leg gave way? Wouldn't it be better to send someone younger, more active? Absolute nonsense, I had said. Now, as the tender shifted under my feet and the ladder swung towards me, I could see their point.

I reached up. The rope and the wooden slats which served as steps were wet and slippery, but it was done in a moment. The tender came sweetly up under me and lifted me. I hoisted myself higher and higher, grasped the metal poles at the top, and was on board. The islanders applauded.

Mike Donkin had arranged everything magnificently on the aft deck for us. There was a kind of raised hatch, the height and shape of a table, and he had covered this with a large white napkin which served perfectly as a tablecloth and set it with glasses and knives and forks. Five folding chairs were arranged round it. Ten or fifteen islanders immediately laid out their mats and began a prayer meeting nearby, while a Japanese photographer, already affected by the journey on the tender, lay down a couple of yards from us and stayed there with his eyes closed for the next five days.

As for us, we dug out the little luxuries we had brought with us. We were determined not to let Christmas Day go by without some kind of celebration. My daughter Julia had given us a couple of collapsible plastic glasses so that they could be the first vessels in the world to toast the new Millennium; I found them, and we opened a bottle of Nigel Bateson's champagne.

Later in the trip he taught me how to open a bottle of champagne with a sword or a large hunting knife; something I had seen done in Paris, but had never had the courage or sufficient bottles of disposable champagne to attempt myself. You strip off the foil, find the join in the glass of the bottle neck, run the blade experimentally up the join once or twice and then strike a purposeful but not violent tap with the blade at the point where the neck bulges out, just below the cork. Try it: it's a great feeling.

The pressure of gas inside the bottle, harnessed by the blow from your sword, will take off the bottle neck so neatly that when you retrieve it there will be a ring of glass neatly enclosing the unharmed cork. The champagne will gush out satisfyingly from the open neck of the bottle, there is no appreciable danger from slivers of glass falling into the wine, and your friends will applaud you as delightedly as we did Bateson; who stood, red-faced and beaming, his machete in one great hand and his headless bottle of champagne foaming and ready to pour, in the other. He looked like a Saxon warrior who had just decapitated a Celtic monk.

Apart from chocolates and preserves, the only seasonable element we had brought with us from England was a large Christmas pudding donated by Dee's sister, Gina. Dee now slipped away and found the ship's galley, where a pleasant but quite uncomprehending I-Kiribati cook who spoke no English thought she was asking him to take the china basin which contained the pudding and make coffee in it. The Gilbert Islands might have belonged to the British Empire for more than a century, but not all the key ingredients that made up the imperial cement seem to have made it to the South Pacific: Christmas pudding being one of them. Eventually, by a series of dumb-show gestures, she made the cook understand that this cannonball-like object was edible, and that he should boil it for a certain amount of time. She even managed to tell him how long.

An hour or so later, the grinning, sweating cook came along the deck with the pudding on a large plate, the steam rising from it in the heat of the tropical night and trailing behind him as he came. To the applause of everyone, including the islanders, he set it down on our makeshift table and we invited the other anglophones on board (an ecologist from New Zealand, a Canadian journalist, and a volunteer from the American Peace Corps who, we had convinced ourselves, was really training for the CIA) to join us.

The champagne and the pudding went round four times in all, while we took photographs of each other eating and drinking I strove to remember the words of *How'd You Like To Spend Christmas On Christmas Island?*, a song from the distant 1950s, and someone wound up a little clockwork Santa and set him running round between the paper plates and the plastic spoons. It was a weird way to celebrate Christmas, but then it was a weird sort of journey that we were beginning.

That night, things were not quite so entertaining. The sea got up and the little *Matangare* began to pitch and toss like an umbrella in a windy street. Dee went to our cabin and stayed there for the next three days, groaning, sleeping fitfully, and trying hard to keep the anti-seasickness pills down. The Japanese photographer lay in exactly the same position, as though he had died early on and not been touched; which is probably how he felt. The islanders lay on their mats, staring listlessly upwards as the green canvas awnings flapped and cracked around them in the powerful wind. They were too demoralized to sing, clap or even pray aloud.

The rest of us did reasonably well. We would fight our way along the deck, grabbing onto anything we could and trying not to tread on any islanders. It was good for me in particular, since I had to give up using my walking-stick. 'One hand for yourself and the other for the ship' is the old Royal Navy adage, and that didn't leave enough hands to carry a stick as well. The New Zealand ecologist, a delightfully crazy lady with red hair called Kay, went around handing out some specially powerful seasickness pills, made for the US Coastguard.

We jammed ourselves into the little mess room three times a day, eating the kind of greasy fry-ups which sailors of all nationalities delight in and trying to keep our plates, our cups and ourselves from spilling over onto our neighbours. The sun would go down like a celestial conflagration at six o'clock every night, and stars of an unexpected violence hung over the *Matangare* in patterns I longed to decipher.

At around eight each night the aft deck began to settle into sleep. The islanders closed their eyes at last. Bateson had abandoned his stylish waterproof hammock early on, and so did everyone else who tried it; the movement of the ship, simultaneously upwards and sideways or downwards and forwards and often the combination of any three, gave a hammock the quality of a bad fairground ride. Instead he, Simon Wilson and Mike Donkin slept on rickety fold-up beds, which slithered round the deck but were at least a little more stable.

Simon, tall, calm, and rather elegant, lay on his with his eyes closed, his hands folded across his chest and his feet pointing directly over the *Matangare's* stern in what he called 'the burial at sea' position, directly in front of a hawse-hole through which, if the pressure was right, he could probably have been shot into the ship's wake like a human cannonball in a circus. At night, no one would have noticed; and I doubt very much if the *Matangare's* captain, an approachable but dedicated young man, could have been persuaded to turn back to look for him.

There was a Japanese television crew on board, a pleasant group who ate the ship's food with a certain distaste and carried their own condiments with them. Being young themselves, they were discreetly surprised that someone of my age and seniority would get involved in a venture like this; in Japanese television, they assured me, I would be sitting in the studio in Tokyo, dispensing wisdom, and they found my aversion to that kind of thing hard to understand.

Their politeness belied the fact that on this trip they were essentially pirates. The London-based television agency APTN had done a deal with the Kiribati government to have exclusive rights to cover the dawn of 1 January on Millennium Island, and the BBC had bought the rights from APTN to be the sole broadcaster from the island for the occasion. You always get a certain amount of professional competition on these things, as well as the inevitable skulduggery; it's part of the traditional way of doing things. At least two American television networks, whose planning was not as advanced as the BBC's, had offered bigger money to take our place when they found out what was going on, but the Kiribati government and APTN stayed loyal to the agreement.

The Japanese were tougher. When they discovered that Millennium Island had been sewn up they demanded that the Kiribati government should give them a place on the island anyway. As politely as possible, the Kiribati government (which gets a good deal of financial support from Japan) explained that this could not happen. Very well, the Japanese television company said, we shall rent a ship, take it to Millennium Island, and broadcast from that. And we shall moor it between your island and the sunrise.

The Kiribati government and APTN could see no way round this, but the BBC was unworried. Its Millennium programme was intended to be seen around the globe; Japanese television would merely be seen in Japan. It might have been nicer to have been able to boast that I was the only television broadcaster on the island, but as long as there was no international competition it scarcely mattered. The Japanese television crew, travelling on the *Matangare*, were as pleasant and polite as Japanese people invariably are in the West, and in Japan itself. But when they operate in their backyard they behave as though they own the place.

On the third day, Dee rose from the dead. She and I would sit for hours on the slanting deck, gripping onto the rail and playing chess on a moving board, and on the occasions when I managed to win she would attribute it to the aftermath of the seasickness. The islanders, too, began to recover, and held prayer meetings and sing-songs, holding hands and clapping in an intricate, pleasing way. They were devoutly Christian, and although there is a good deal of rivalry on the islands between the Catholic and Protestant churches, they all sing the same hymns in the same I-Kiribati language. The hours passed pleasantly enough, with the *Matangare* digging her head into the big Pacific rollers, the occasional frigate bird floating overhead, and the wind shaking the tarpaulins that held off the sun's ferocity.

I had seen desert islands before, but never one as remote or as beautiful as this. The whole R.M. Ballantyne experience was there: palm trees, the reef, the lagoon, the booming surf. All it needed, it seemed to me, was a few outrigger canoes and a group of ferocious warriors with bones through their noses and an appetite for Long Pig. I glanced instinctively down the rail. Alongside me, the Kiribati choir in their large floral shirts and dresses smiled and greeted me cheerfully. They were anticipating a feast, true; but it wasn't human flesh.

Millennium Island was the last big undisturbed breeding-ground on earth for the coconut crab, a blue and red monster which can grow as large as three feet across and climbs trees to get to its favourite food. The coconut crab is not a particularly amiable character; it lurches around like an armoured personnel carrier, putting up its huge claws in heavyweight boxer-fashion if anything threatening comes near it, and when it catches a young bird it will haul it down into its underground hole and sit there in the dark eating it alive, bit by slow bit, for days on end. Nevertheless it is magnificent, and it is seriously endangered. Its big problem in life is that it is, by all accounts, absolutely delicious to eat. And the islanders lining up with me to gaze at the last undisturbed habitat of the coconut crab were thoroughly aware of it.

I had already seen my first coconut crab, in disturbing circumstances. When Dee finally got to sleep on our first night on board, I slipped out of the cabin to stand out on deck and look at the stars. But as I closed the cabin door behind me, I saw something shocking close by in the dim light: a huge creature with curled legs and waving antennae, tied up by thick string and clutching onto a wooden batten which had been fixed across the door to my left. At first I thought it was some monstrous spider; but then, as I went closer, I could see that it was a crab, about a yard across. It reared up as I approached, holding out its claws. There was no hint of blue or red in its colour; that disappears with the trauma of capture.

The *Matangare*'s crew must have caught it on their previous trip to Millennium Island a couple of weeks earlier, and had tied it up so

that it could just stand on the wooden batten but could not move
around. It was there for the next four nights, a reproach to all of us.
The Canadian journalist tried to give it water. We even thought of
releasing it overboard, until Kay, the ecologist from New Zealand,
explained that the coconut crab had developed lungs for living on
the land, and would drown directly it was submerged. Anyway, the
enormous depth of the Pacific Ocean would have crushed its heavy
shell within seconds.

There was nothing to be done. Maybe our horror was hypocrit-
ical, since the ship's crew were looking forward to eating the crab
with as much relish as we might have felt about a Christmas turkey.
And after all, why should we who enjoy the output of the abattoir
and the factory farm have any right to criticize the way the crew
treated a mere crustacean? On the fourth and last night of the voyage
it was taken away for the pot.

Now it was time to disembark. We handed down all our cumber-
some gear into the *Matangare*'s yellow lifeboats, and I successfully
negotiated the rope ladder again. There was a real excitement among
us all: we had been reading and talking about this island for so long,
and here we were speeding across the rollers to the small gap in the
coral reef which led into the extraordinarily beautiful waters of the
lagoon. Kay was the most excited of us all, because this atoll was her
great speciality and she had written the definitive study of its natural
history. But she was worried about two things: the coconut crabs,
and the giant clams which also breed undisturbed on the islands.

She glanced with a kind of vexed affection at the small group of
islanders who had come with us on the first boat ashore. 'I'm worried
that all they'll want is to get there and start eating everything.'

Her unruly red hair flew everywhere in the powerful headwind,
exceedingly hot even at eight in the morning.

'Look,' she said, forgetting the crabs and the clams for a moment
in her delight, 'that's a red-footed booby!'

Our desert island had been inhabited for a week or so by a small
group of television people from APTN, satellite engineers, cameramen, sound recordists, directors and others. As we staggered up the
beach in the hot sunshine, lugging our equipment and our suitcases
across the soft white coral sand, some of them came out and greeted
us; most were New Zealanders, though there was a variety of people

from other countries: Belgium, Russia, Britain itself. When an international outfit like APTN stages a big event like this, it can call on
people from around the world.

We felt like interlopers on Robinson Crusoe's island. Everything
had been set up, including a kitchen range with huge amounts of
food, shower stalls and a lavatory sheltered by woven coconut palms.
They had made themselves as comfortable as possible under the
circumstances, clearing the undergrowth under the coconut palms
with chainsaws and setting up tents that were generous in size. The
Japanese team's area had been christened 'Little Tokyo' and ours
'Mayfair', but most of the settlers were perfectly friendly towards us.
Nevertheless they must have felt their kingdom had been invaded.

The coconut palms were superb: curves of delicate fronds the
colour of the waters of the lagoon, perfectly formed and regular so
that they met overhead against the perfect sky like a living cathedral,
arched and groyned and buttressed in greenery. Between the fronds
swept perfect white birds, fairy terns, which fluttered like the doves
of God above the head of the Madonna in a *trecento* painting.
Fairy terns enjoy the challenge of hatching their eggs in the most
difficult places, like the curved centre of a palm frond or the little
projection from the trunk of a palm tree. One sat on her egg right
beside the place where we washed our dishes after a meal, and she
would look at us with calm, peaceful eyes, completely trustingly,
as we scrubbed the remains off our plates and washed our hands, as
though it were perfectly natural for humans to come and invade her
grove.

Yet, whatever impression I had received from Ballantyne, the
palm tree is not indigenous to Millennium Island, but was introduced
at the end of the nineteenth century by those inveterate transplanters
of trees, bushes and flowers, the British. The coconut crabs, which
presumably were called something else until then, must have been
delighted when they found the present they had been given. It was a
stroke of good luck to make up for the fact that they should have
such a good flavour; and the coconuts must have made the flavour
even better.

The islanders had scarcely put their red and blue plastic bags and
their mats down in the shelter of the trees before they headed out to
hunt down the crabs; and within a few days there were boxes of them

everywhere, little prisons with thirty or forty crammed in together, waiting to be taken back to the inhabited islands a couple of thousand miles away. The beach and the islanders' quarters were scattered with broken claws and empty shells. For the record, though we were offered crab once or twice, we refused it.

The broadcasting part of our trip to the island swiftly passed: twelve or thirteen minutes' airtime, for which we had spent thirteen days' travelling there and another fourteen home. Apparently the pictures which accompanied my voice were out of synch by more than two seconds, and the studio engineers in London managed to ensure that my voice came back to me around the world, so as I was speaking I was hearing what I had said four seconds earlier in my ear. It didn't matter: I wasn't saying anything of great interest anyway. What did matter was to be there, with the early morning sun warming the chill of the beach and painting the clouds extraordinary colours of scarlet and gold. We shared yet another bottle of champagne, and drank it from my daughter's patent glasses; which did indeed become the first to welcome the new year, and – if we so chose – the new millennium.

Nigel Bateson had brought a gadget of his own: a thing made of plastic and shaped like a tennis racket, with wires instead of strings. They were charged with electricity, and if you hit a mosquito with the racket the mosquito would explode with a most satisfying crackle. The mosquitoes on Millennium Island were small and persistent, and before we came they cannot have had a square meal in a very long time. But like the islanders with the crabs, the mosquitoes took full advantage of the event to feed on us. The television people who had been there for a few days were appallingly bitten, but we newcomers were careful to cover ourselves with various lotions.

Even so, sitting in Bateson's tent in the ferocious heat to edit a couple of news reports about the celebration of midnight and sunrise, we were natural victims. Nigel was too busy with the editing machines to be able to do much about the mosquitoes himself, but I laid about me with the tennis racket like André Agassi, and Nigel greeted each electrical crackle with a victorious guffaw.

That evening, with our live broadcasts finished, the President of Kiribati and his cabinet gave us all a dinner. The New Zealanders who were running the APTN operation told us quietly that we would be expected to sing our national song, and that I would have to make a speech.

But the English, as Flanders and Swann pointed out in the early 1960s, don't have a national song.

The Welsh have *Men of Harlech*, the Scots have *Scotland the Brave*. And the English? The English have *Jerusalem*.

'What about *Jerusalem*?' I ventured.

Dee was scathing. 'You'll bore everyone rigid,' she said; this from an Afrikaner whose national song is *Sarie Marais*, which is all about some inevitably unhappy love affair of the *veld*, and goes on a great deal about the Old Transvaal. 'Sing about something that really matters to the English. Sing *I Like A Nice Cuppa Tea*.'

As it happened, I knew the words to *I Like A Nice Cuppa Tea*. I wrote them out for everyone to practise. We might not have much of a national song, I told them, but we were going to belt it out better than anyone else. We were going to shine.

> I like a nice cuppa tea in the morning,
> Just to start the day, you see.
> Then at half past eleven
> My idea of heaven
> Is a nice cuppa tea.
>
> I like a nice cuppa tea with my dinner,
> And a nice cuppa tea with my tea.
> And when it's time for bed,
> There's a lot to be said
> For a nice cuppa tea.

As for the speech, I decided I couldn't entirely let the I-Kiribati off for what they had done to Millennium Island; but I would coat the pill as best I could. As I took the microphone and spoke into it as though I were doing a karaoke act, I looked round at them all.

There sat the President, a bright-looking, stocky figure in a traditional kilt and strong, thick bare legs, sporting, for some reason, a dark red tie. There sat his ministers, including the pleasant and rather apologetic minister for the environment; he had quite a lot to be apologetic about, given that he had laid into the crabs and the giant clams with as much enthusiasm as any of them.

There sat the dancers, the women wearing a kind of stiff brassiere that stayed still when they moved their bodies from side to side, and grass skirts which they could flick over their heads with a final and rather exciting swing of their heavy hips, and the men with their torsos naked and oiled. There sat the Japanese, looking nervous at the thought of having to sing a national song. ('Banzai to the Emperor', a New Zealander suggested, but they managed to get out of singing anything.) There sat the APTN people, and my own contingent, grinning encouragingly at the back. White fairy terns, caught in the brilliant light, fluttered overhead, and behind me the surf was booming against the coral reef in the hot night.

I started off by explaining how I had first heard about the Gilbert and Ellice Islands in the 1960s, when a colleague of mine had just returned from a year's leave of absence there, setting up a radio service for the islands. (They still only have radio, which may be one reason why they are so gentle and crime is almost non-existent among them. Television is an impossibility for a nation of 77,000 people, spread out across three thousand miles of empty ocean.) He had told me of their kindness and charm, I said; though I left out the details he had given me about the sexual enthusiasm of the women. And now, thirty-two years later, I found myself on the islands myself, appreciating their beauty. And in particular the beauty of this one, Millennium Island.

I paused: time for a sermon. I told them that they were the guardians of this place, and that the coconut crabs and the giant clams which were here were the envy of the entire world, and that these were things to be protected with the greatest care; not to be destroyed and eaten. I saw the President shift in his chair, and it seemed to me that the minister of the environment looked even more apologetic than ever. Nigel Bateson, by contrast, was beaming, and his rugged Falstaffian face with its red beard gleamed out at me through the darkness. An unlikely conservationist, he felt particularly strongly about the destruction of the crabs.

After that I felt I could relax a little.

'I'm told,' I said, 'that the dancers and musicians here took a magic potion before this morning's events, which makes them shake, so that they could play longer and better, and sing loudly and in tune. We in Britain have a magic potion of our own, which makes us shake and protects us against the cold and enables us, too, to sing very loudly indeed if we have to. It's called "whisky", and I've brought a bottle of the best to give to you, Mr President.'

I had bought this superb cask-strength Laphroaig at the Heathrow duty-free shop so that we could welcome in the New Year in proper style, but I had nothing else to give the President and I felt the occasion demanded something of the kind. It was a sacrifice, but sometimes the exigencies of the service cannot be ignored. At least when he took it from me he gripped my hand warmly and held it to himself as though he knew how good it was. I would have to make do with champagne instead, I thought, remembering W.C. Fields: 'It took us a week to cross the desert. Things got so bad we had to drink water.'

The next day we filmed an edition of *Simpson's World*. The interviewee was to be Kay, and Dee decided we should shoot it on the islet opposite our own. This meant wading about half a mile across the coral; no problem when the tide was out and the water was a few inches deep, but more difficult when it came in. There were black-tipped sharks the size of dogs in this part of the lagoon – they could slip in from the ocean through the same gap in the main reef that our boats had come through – and by all accounts they specialized in trying to bite out your calf muscles as you walked.

'It'll be fine as long as we go back at the right time,' Kay said.

Great.

We interviewed her when we reached the island, accompanied by Nigel burning a bright red in the ferocious mid-morning sun, and insisting on carrying all the equipment himself. It was an extraordinary business. Because there are no human beings on this island and (except for a brief period of a few years in the early 1990s, when a family settled on one of the other islets) never have been, there is no fear whatever among the birds and fish. Since it is a thousand miles from anywhere, Millennium Island is free of mammals of all kinds, and the only predators are themselves birds and fish. A strange biped, and especially a bearded one carrying a camera on his shoulder, arouses only a certain quizzical interest among the island's wild life.

And so Nigel was able to walk up close to boobies and to the wonderful, elegant frigate birds, whose entire bone structure only weighs as much as their feathers, and which can cruise for hundreds of miles across the sea without resting. He even got close to the much shyer non-natives such as the bristle-thighed curlews which migrate here from the cold lands far to the north.

Kay had an appointment to take a group of people on a tour around the lagoon so she waded across the reef in the direction of our camp on the other island, warning us not to be too long. But television takes time. Dee felt we needed more shots of the birds, and particularly of the curlews, and we had to film close-ups of the giant clams Kay had shown us, big shells with protruding lips of brilliant blue and turquoise green, which had so far survived the hunting trips of the I-Kiribati.

By the time we were finished the water was almost up to our knees, and rising. Then began one of the most magical experiences of my entire life. We waded back across the reef, with the dead coral crunching under foot. In the water were all sorts of reef creatures, which like the birds had no conception of danger from human beings. A black and white spotted trunk-fish, squarish in shape and one of the most charming and nervous inhabitants of the coral reef, was so interested in us that it stared up through the water, almost breaking the surface in its curiosity.

Octopuses, which never appear in the daytime in the places where I have dived, remained where they were, turning their heads from side to side in an attempt to work out what these extraordinary shapes were. The only thing that would make them move was if you actually reached out and touched them: then they would shoot away, putting out clouds of protective ink. Yet they would halt close by, in order to inspect us again. In the shallower water Dee noticed a moray eel, usually the most secluded and protective of creatures, swim about easily and stop to examine these curious monsters, standing half in and half out of the water. None of the animals here seemed to have the slightest anxiety about us; they had never encountered humans and their destructive ways before.

I could have stayed for hours in this new Eden, where man meant nothing and his shadow had scarcely reached. It was only when I looked out across the lagoon that I remembered ours was not the only shadow.

'Watch out – sharks!'

The triangular black tips circled a while, as though they were trying to get the range and decide on a strategy, and then they would turn and come fast towards us.

Kay had said: 'Don't worry – just throw something at them. That should probably keep them off.'

'Probably?'

'No, it will. It's just better not to wait until the water gets that high.'

We had. I bent down quickly.

'Grab any loose bits of coral and chuck them at them,' I called to Dee.

She kept remarkably calm: but of course this was someone who had filmed in the townships of South Africa at the worst times. Nigel needed no urging. I could hear his chuckling laugh: the laugh I remembered from Bosnia, when the phosphorous bombs were landing closer and closer to us on Mount Zuć.

I found a good-sized piece of dead coral lying by my feet on the surface of the reef, a foot or so below the surface, and lobbed it at the nearest black triangle in the water twenty yards away. This landed right in front of the shark's nose, and it turned in a panic and took two or three others away with it.

'On the right, there!' I called out.

Dee's rock made a splash, and again the sharks turned. They were all round us, but now they kept their distance. One darted in fast – faster than I had imagined they could swim – but I had another piece of rock in my hand by this time and I lobbed it directly in its path. The shark jumped half out of the water in its panic, and didn't come back.

At last we were in water which reached only above our ankles. The smallest black-tips were capable of reaching us even here, but the fight seemed to have gone out of them. They were the one form of life on Millennium Island which I felt no guilt about disturbing.

By the time the whole expedition, all eighty of us, television people and dancers and I-Kiribati politicians, packed up and left, the island had been occupied for eleven days. During that time our presence had had a lasting effect on its ecological balance. What had been almost unique about Millennium was the fact that giant clams and coconut crabs could breed there undisturbed. Now Kay estimated that the clam population had dropped by 40 per cent, and that it would require ten or fifteen years of complete peace and isolation to recover.

The outlook for the coconut crabs was worse: at least 70 per cent of them had been killed or captured. Given that it took fifty or sixty years for each crab to reach its full size, it would take almost a century for their population to reach the level it had been at on the day our brief occupation began.

Irony was wrapped in irony. We had violated Millennium Island's isolation in order to celebrate a new phase of human existence, and in doing so had stripped it of some of its chief characteristics. But if the estimates about the increasing speed of global warming are correct, then coral islands like Millennium will soon disappear beneath the encroaching sea, long before the population of coconut crabs will have recovered from our millennial celebrations. What the I-Kiribati did on Millennium is nothing to what the outside world will have done to Millennium itself, and to all the other coral islands where these gentle and innocent people live.

And even here, a thousand miles from the nearest human habitation, the effects of human activity were clear enough even before we arrived. On the day before we left I went diving on one of the reefs in the central lagoon. Vast quantities of the coral, instead of being a healthy brownish-red, were turning as white as bleached bones, and the reef fish no longer gathered here. The 1998 El Niño, that extraordinary weather system which we are only now starting to understand and which can affect the weather of the entire Pacific Ocean and far beyond, had raised the temperature of the sea by around one degree Celsius: enough to kill off large quantities of coral life.

El Niño is a natural effect, but in the past thirty years it has been recurring with an extraordinary frequency; and the strong suggestion is that the greenhouse effect which our cars and factories create has somehow allied itself to the phenomena that cause El Niño, and made it happen more often. The results are starting to devastate the most delicate and distant structures on our planet.

So who was more destructive? The islanders, who in their innocence came close to destroying a couple of species? Or we with our advanced cultures, which are trashing places we have never heard of and will never visit? The foremost authority on global warming in the United States whom I interviewed told me that if every American merely settled for a smaller car the increase in the process would be halted. But of course Americans will not settle for smaller cars unless they are forced to; and neither will the rest of us. The link between what we do as individuals and what happens to the coral islands or the rain forests or the polar ice-caps seems impossibly tenuous, and people who would never think of reaching down and pulling a three-foot coconut crab out of its hole to eat or rip a giant clam off a reef can have a far more savage effect on the wildlife of the earth simply by continuing with a way of life that has come to seem normal to them.

We carried all our equipment down to the beach in the blazing sun and waited for the *Matangare*'s bright yellow boats to come and pick it up.

'Looks like the retreat from Dunkirk,' Nigel Bateson grunted, and took a photograph of the hundreds of metal boxes and packing cases on the beach. He also took photographs of the wooden crates in which the islanders had stowed their coconut crabs.

It took most of an afternoon to load everything into the boats. By the time we climbed in ourselves it was past four o'clock, and the sun had reached that low, golden position that made the island seem like paradise again. Behind us we had left a few structures to help any passing ships which might be in trouble. The undergrowth would quickly re-establish itself where it had been cut down. The fairy terns, the boobies and the frigate birds could recolonize the place again as though nothing had happened. We were leaving the island to its millennial peace once more, and there were no voices ringing out on it any longer: just silence.

'It did occur to me to slip away from you all and stay there,' the Canadian journalist said to me quietly as we looked back at the island.

I think the idea had crossed the minds of most of us at some point.

Our boat's engine stalled briefly as we headed for the small gap in the surrounding reef which was the only exit from the lagoon. In the peace and silence as the sailors worked on it I glanced down into the crystalline water. There beneath us were hundreds of fish swimming to and fro: it was their entrance and exit too, and you could see great wrasses and rays and sharks moving restlessly backwards and forwards in the deep channel. *Natura naturans*, the scholars of the Middle Ages would have called it; nature doing its thing.

We made it through the gap eventually, and out into the ocean surf. The island with its trusting birds and sea-life began to slip away behind us as we headed for the *Matangare*. And then, suddenly, all around us, the sea boiled up and the islanders with us shouted out for joy: a school of dolphins had come curving out of the dark-blue waters and was escorting us on our way for the sheer pleasure of it. I looked around at the others, and saw that there were tears of happiness in their eyes as well as my own.

Afterword

> We carry within us the Wonders we seek without us; there
> is all Africa and her Prodigies in us.
>
> Sir Thomas Browne, *Religio Medici*

In 1919, at a special meeting of the Royal Geographical Society in
Kensington Gore, the soldier, explorer and mystic Sir Francis Younghusband stood up to propose the formation of an expedition to climb
Mount Everest. George Mallory, perhaps the best and bravest of all
twentieth-century mountaineers, was sitting in the hall and would
soon be chosen to take part in the expedition. It failed, and another
was formed two years afterwards, in 1924. Mallory was on that
expedition, too, and it is possible he reached the summit before falling
to his death. Mallory was a wonderful man: so absent-minded that
he forgot to take his compass with him when he made his last attempt
on the summit, and left his tent in a mess.

All sorts of motives we would now find questionable went into
the determination to climb Everest first: the need to demonstrate
British imperial power after the First World War, the basic idea that
man had to dominate his environment rather than be dominated by
it. Mallory was a socialist and an anti-imperialist, and disliked all
this kind of thing; so when someone asked why he wanted to climb
Everest, he reportedly answered, 'Because it's there.' It was a mini-
malist attitude, the reverse of imperialism and grandeur.

Younghusband was from a different generation, and had a different background. He commanded the dreadful expedition to Tibet in
1904, when so many Tibetans had been killed unnecessarily. Yet he
wasn't simply an identikit imperialist either; in his sixties, impelled
by his Eastern faith, he started living the life of a hippy.

His argument for an Everest expedition was simple.

'Whilst, however, climbing Mount Everest will not put a pound in anyone's pocket, it will take a good many pounds out, the accomplishment of such a feat will elevate the human spirit and will give man, especially us geographers, a feeling that we are really getting the upper hand on Earth, and that we are acquiring a true mastery of our surroundings.'

Eighty years later, at the start of a new century, it is absolutely clear that we haven't merely got the upper hand on Earth, we have a stranglehold on it. Those eighty years have seen the most remarkable progress in every way; but they have changed everything about the way we live, and about the way the Earth co-exists with its noisy, troublesome tenants.

The balance sheet is not good. The forests are disappearing, the seas are increasingly polluted, the ice-fields are melting at a frightening rate. At the end of 1999 I made a film which looked at the climatic changes which man had wrought, and the findings were gloomy.

As part of our film we went to the Maldives, a pattern of coral atolls which (like Millennium Island) may not even exist in a few decades' time. We visited a resort there, and I went diving to inspect the condition of the coral reef.

The gear I was wearing wasn't my own, and it felt unnatural and awkward. My knee, still recovering from the operation I had had on it in Belgrade a few months before, was weak. When I tried to stand up with the heavy air-tank on my back I felt like some antediluvian monster, heavy and outmoded. A local cameraman was going with me, and he slipped easily over the edge of the boat. It took me much longer to lurch after him. I put my hand over my mask, paused a moment, and took a giant stride into the water.

Instantly, the weight was taken off me and I was free: you don't limp or feel old in the water. I equalized, getting rid of the pressure of air inside my nasal passages, and kicked down towards the reef. It felt as good as flying. The silence, broken only by the sound of my breathing, took me and held me. Fish of a startling variety filled the water: wrasses, parrot-fish, blue tangs, the lovely emperor angel-fish, as big as a large dinner plate, blennies, blue and yellow chromis. I used to dive to see the fish, but nowadays it is the reef itself that interests me most: the extraordinary formations of brain coral, the delicate sea-fans, the brown elkhorns branching upwards, the sensational oranges and blues and pinks of a healthy reef.

Except that this reef wasn't healthy. I had never seen so many different kinds of fish in my life, but they were the wrong fish, attracted by the fact that the coral was dead and dying. There were no oranges and blues: just bone-like white. A blue parrot-fish cruised close to me, and jabbed its beak at a piece of coral. The whole thing came away, and the fish shook its head and let the coral fall. The water was filled with a kind of dust: the sweepings of the dead reef. Two years earlier, in 1997, El Niño had visited the Pacific, and here, just as with the more remote Millennium Island, had raised the temperature of the ocean by a degree. That was enough to kill the coral. There were occasional patches where it was trying to grow back, but essentially this reef was dead.

After an hour I broke surface, heavy again, and dragged myself over the side of the boat.

'You look pretty shocked,' someone said.

It was true. I had seen the future: a world without coral.

The experience turned me into a passionate conservationist. I had always been that way inclined, but preferred not to know the horrors which were being committed across the globe because I found them too depressing. Now, I decided, there was no room for defeatism.

It may be too late to save many things. I have watched the huge diggers moving into the Brazilian rain-forest and seen the red earth churned up and the giant trees falling. I have seen Ashaninca indians still wearing their coarse brown robes or *kushmas* as they are brought by the truckload and deposited in the small, dirty towns of the jungle, where the earlier arrivals sway around drunk or lie on doorways clutching empty bottles. I have seen the deserts where riders used to hunt deer across the savannah. I have seen buildings a thousand years old crushed into rubble in order to make way for government high-rises or the headquarters for banks which are already insolvent.

We are turning energies which Younghusband could never have imagined onto areas of the globe which are weaker and more delicate than he ever realized. The upper slopes of Everest itself are littered with empty cans, bits of unwanted equipment, and the unburied bodies of climbers who succumbed to the cold and the altitude. In the Mariana Trench, the deepest part of the ocean, unmanned probes have spotted plastic bags and the rings from Coca-Cola tins.

And yet not everything is wrecked. As you fly over the Amazonian rain forest it still shocks you with its vastness. There are few more wonderful sights on earth than watching the last Buddhist temple fade away behind you as you set your face towards the Himalayan peaks ahead. The empty surface of the Pacific Ocean gives you a faint sense even now of mankind's smallness. To watch a group of Turkomen riders racing across the steppe alongside the remains of 'Alexander's Wall', a huge and still partly undiscovered rampart built by the Sassanian Kings of Persia to keep out the Mongols, or to mount the sudden hills that erupt out of the surface of the plain and are the untouched remains of entire lost cities, is to experience a little of the life which has nothing to do with the cities and the commerce of the First World.

One of the happiest men I ever met in my life lived at the farthest end of the earth. We were in the depths of Amazonia, as far from a town as it was possible to be: seven days' journey, at least. It was a good place not to get appendicitis.

Our plan was to travel as far north along our river as we could get. The boat headed upstream, moving as cautiously through the creamy brown waters as though they were filled with mines instead of skeletal, submerged trees. The forest closed in on either side of us, so dense that the gentle greenery seemed to have turned to blackness. There was no animal life to be seen, beyond the birds and the occasional shrieking monkey. Everything else, hearing the noise of our motor, had slunk away long before.

Man too. Up here the forest still contains entire tribes of indians who have never been in contact with civilization. One is thought to be called the Jaminawa. They are hereditary enemies of the Ashaninca and occasionally shoot at them with bows and arrows, or even shotguns. Since the Jaminawa are consummate hunters (the best in the forest), they have tracked the Ashaninca many times, stealing their guns and, by meticulous observation, eventually learning how to fire them for themselves.

Ahead of us the river forked, passing out of sight to left and right. Between the two branches there are believed to be more than eighty tribes of 'uncontacted' indians.

'This is it,' said someone. 'The end of the known world.'

It felt like it. There was shouting from the cliff top, and a Robinson Crusoe-like figure waved his arms and pointed to the place where we could beach our dug-out. His name was Jose Carlos dos Reis Meirelles, and he was the representative of the Brazilian ministry for indian affairs. Close up, he seemed less of a castaway than a natural philosopher, and his eyes lit up with the pleasure of having someone to talk to.

It was a place to be proud of. The radio mast was in good repair, the grass was properly mown, there were potted plants on the wooden steps to his hut, and chickens were everywhere: under the hut, in the vegetable beds, and nestling beside the water filtration plant. If we had thought to find a Brazilian version of Joseph Conrad's Mr Kurtz, growing steadily crazier and more vicious in his heart of darkness, we were utterly wrong. Meirelles, with his luxuriant golden-brown beard, was more like a hospitable Afrikaans farmer from the Karoo desert. He spoke to his wife, who lived a thousand miles away in the provincial capital, twice every day by radio.

We sat in his clean, high, well-made house with its thatch and its springy floor of split cane and its cool corridors, and ate a lunch of wild deer, tapir meat, which tasted like boiled beef, and a bony river fish with something of the texture of cod though none of its flavour. There was also a great deal of manioc, a white vegetable which, crushed into a gritty flour, forms the basic diet in the Amazon. Here it was boiled whole, and provided a welcome contrast with the kind of thing we had been eating for days now in the indian villages lower down the river.

It was a pleasure to sit on chairs and rest our arms on a table. His cats, ginger and black, lay beside the water butt, relishing its coolness. Meirelles turned his Boer farmer's beard in my direction and answered the question I had asked a minute or two earlier.

'I'm here because of an accident. I was brought up in São Paulo, and was training to be an engineer. Then, completely by mistake, my brother pulled the trigger on a shotgun and hit me. I was pretty badly injured, and had to spend three months in hospital. During that time I had nothing else to do but look at the ceiling and think.

'It was providential in a way; you see, I had never had a chance to work out what I was going to do with my life. And the more I thought, the more I realized that what I really wanted to do was to work with the indians. I had liked the idea of them ever since I was a kid, and I loved the forest. And so in 1970 I went off and joined the government agency at Maranhao.'

The trouble was, the agency wasn't very good at looking after the indians' interests. Instead, it tended to look after the interests of the loggers and the rubber-tappers and the oil prospectors. Meirelles found himself in constant rebellion against his own bosses. Once he was sacked for defending the indians too strongly. He reminded me a little of a missionary complaining against his bishop, or perhaps a liberation theologist inveighing against the Pope: something religious, anyway.

Gradually, he said, the agency had become poorer and weaker, until it was scarcely able to function at all; which is what he maintained the Brazilian government really wanted. Now it had stopped paying him altogether.

'If it wasn't for my vegetable patch, I'd probably have starved to death by now.'

He grinned. This was a seriously happy man.

'You see, I like to live somewhere where I can get up in the morning and shout at the very top of my voice, and no one notices.'

His face took on a gentler expression: he was a Robinson Crusoe who gave thanks for being marooned.

As we sat talking, the ferocity passed slowly from the heat of the day. The cooler, more benign late afternoon lay ahead of us: the best part of the day. I looked down through the narrow gaps between the split canes and saw the pigs rooting contentedly under the house. Meirelles saw me looking.

'The cane we use for the floors comes from the *paxiuba* tree. The indians believe that the souls of people who have not been good migrate into the *paxiubas*.'

Merely talking about the indians made his face seemed calmer, and his eyes were focused on the distant trees.

'Sometimes I wake up in the morning and find an arrow sticking in the hut. They don't seem to want to kill me; maybe it's just that they're marking their territory. We've counted thirteen arrows from tribes we don't know.'

We went out to sit on the front steps. The Ashaninca girls were singing quietly to themselves. I thought of the great sixteenth-century French explorer Jean de Léry, a Calvinist who was at first horrified by the rituals and behaviour of the Brazilian indians and thought they were inspired by Satan, but who learned slowly to love them when he lived among the Tupinamba indians of the Bay of Rio in 1557.

He was Meirelles' spiritual predecessor. In his great work *The History of a Voyage in the Land of Brazil* (1578) he writes:

> Although I had been among the savages for more than half a year and was already fairly well used to their ways, nonetheless (to be frank) being somewhat frightened and not knowing how the game might turn out, I wished I were back at our fort. However . . . we heard them once again singing and making their voices resound in a harmony so marvellous that you would hardly have needed to ask whether, since I was now somewhat easier in my mind at hearing such sweet and graceful sounds, I wished to watch them from close by . . .
>
> [N]ow I received in recompense such joy, hearing the measured harmonies of such a multitude, and especially in the cadence and refrain of the song, when at every verse all of them would let their voices trail away, saying *Heu, heuaure, heura, heuraure, heura, heura, oueh* – that I stood there completely ravished with delight. Whenever I remember it, my heart trembles, and it seems their voices are still in my ears.

Above us, the enormous cumulus clouds built up into towering shapes, tinged by the afternoon gold of the sun. Little round-headed monkeys, their tails curled, sat and watched us from among the red blossoms of the *mulungu* trees.

The Ashanincas who looked after the house smiled their goodbyes to us. The river lay brown and smooth-running below, and for the first time I saw the forest through Meirelles' eyes rather than my own. It seemed protective now, rather than menacing.

I shook his hand. 'I envy you. You really are the man at the end of the world.'

He thought about it a little. 'No, not really. I think I'm the man at the world's beginning.'

The truth is, I suppose, that however much our world shrinks, it can still be as large as we wish it to be.

Index